PUBLIC SPEAKING

ABOUT THE AUTHORS

George W. Fluharty is Professor Emeritus of Speech Communication and former Director of the Program in Speech Communication at New York University. He received his B.S. degree from Boston University, his M.A. degree from Columbia University, and his Ph.D. degree from New York University. Dr. Fluharty is author of *Speechmaker*, an audio-cassette public speaking program. He is also a teacher and consultant for various business and professional groups.

Harold R. Ross was formerly on the speech faculty of New York University. He is co-author of *How To Write for Pleasure and Profit*, *Speaking in Public*, and a book in the Barnes & Noble Outline Series, *Outlines of Shakespeare's Plays*.

PUBLIC
SPEAKING
AND OTHER FORMS OF
SPEECH COMMUNICATION

Second Edition

George W. Fluharty
Harold R. Ross

BARNES & NOBLE BOOKS
A DIVISION OF HARPER & ROW, PUBLISHERS
New York, Cambridge, Hagerstown,
Philadelphia, San Francisco, London,
Mexico City, São Paulo, Sydney

PUBLIC SPEAKING (Second Edition). Copyright © 1966, 1981 by Harper & Row, Publishers, Inc. All rights reserved. Printed in the United States of America. No part of this book may be used or reproduced in any manner whatsoever without written permission except in the case of brief quotations embodied in critical articles and reviews. For information address Harper & Row, Publishers, Inc., 10 East 53rd Street, New York, N.Y. 10022. Published simultaneously in Canada by Fitzhenry & Whiteside Limited, Toronto.

Designer: Ruth Markiewicz

Library of Congress Cataloging in Publication Data

Fluharty, George W
  Public speaking and other forms of speech
communication.
  (Everyday handbook; 525)
  Edition of 1966 published under title: Public
speaking.
  Includes index.
  1. Public speaking. I. Ross, Harold Raymond,
joint author. II. Title.
PN4121.F527 1981   808.5'1   80–8389
ISBN 0–06–463525–2 (pbk.)

88 89 90   10 9 8 7

CONTENTS

ACKNOWLEDGMENTS

Grateful acknowledgment is made to the following publishers for permission to reprint:

Brandt & Brandt for an excerpt from *Hot Countries* by Alec Waugh.

The John Day Company, Inc., for an excerpt from *The Importance of Living* by Lin Yutang.

E. P. Dutton & Co., Inc., for excerpts from *The Anatomy of Dessert* by Edward A. Bunyard, and from *The Sea and the Jungle* by H. M. Tomlinson.

Alfred A. Knopf, Inc., for an excerpt from *The Plumed Serpent* by D. H. Lawrence.

Liveright Publishing Corporation for excerpts from *Moods of Earth and Sky* by E. L. Grant Watson.

Princeton University Press for an excerpt from *Fenelson's Dialogues on Eloquence,* translated by W. S. Howell, copyright 1951.

G. P. Putnam's Sons and Coward-McCann, Inc., for an excerpt from *Advertisements for Myself* by Norman Mailer, copyright 1959.

The authors are also grateful to the publishers for permission to reprint material acknowledged in the footnotes.

INTRODUCTION

The purpose of this book is to help individuals meet the speech demands made upon them in everyday life, when, for example, they go for a job interview, become a club parliamentarian, or take part in a debate or panel discussion. In such situations the individual needs to understand the nature of the task and to learn how to perform it well.

This book covers public speaking in a broad and inclusive manner so that it will be useful to persons of varying degrees of experience in speaking. It is suitable as a text for classroom use, as a student aid, or for self-study at home.

The basic principles and practices of speech communication are explained in order to give the student a suitable background of knowledge. We can profit best by what others have done if we understand *why* it has been done.

The book covers five major areas: basic principles of speech communication, speech preparation, speech presentation, adapting to the main purpose in speaking, and forms of oral communication other than public speaking. In order to avoid repetition, each major topic is treated in one place. However, some material is briefly restated when it seems necessary. The index should be consulted for complete references to a topic.

No book, either with or without the guidance of a teacher, can be a substitute for practice. Anyone desiring to improve his or her speaking ability must learn by speaking, both in rehearsals and in actual speech situations. Fortunately, the average individual has considerable speaking experience. Since childhood we have taken part in daily social situations requiring speech communication. Speaking in social life, in business, and in public have common elements. All situations with other people involve principles of suitable behavior.

The individual adapts to each occasion's requirements, which always includes restraint, self-control, the feeling of capability, and ease. The better we do this, the better we can learn to adapt to any new speaking situation, for public speaking is a form of social adjustment and group leadership.

1.
SPEECH COMMUNICATION

"Communication" is not only a much-used word but is also a basic concept in today's world. It is vital in human relations, decision-making, and in all matters where human beings express ideas to one another. In fact, we cannot *not* communicate.

Since this book is about speech communication, it is interesting to note how the field has adapted the word and idea. Many former speech departments in schools and colleges are now called departments of speech communication. These departments are often included in larger divisions of communication arts and sciences. The titles of national organizations and journals, such as the Speech Communication Association, the International Communication Association, and the Eastern Speech Communication Association, reflect the change in emphasis. Many titles of books on public speaking are being changed to something like *Public Communication*. This book seeks to make very clear that speechmaking, to be effective, must be successful communication.

In learning how to become good public speakers, let us use the best ways of transferring our ideas to our listeners and at the same time make sure that *we* are listening and responding to those with whom we speak. Speech communication always involves observing, listening, and speaking; it may also include reading and writing.

THE COMMUNICATION PROCESS

What is communication? There are many ways of defining the major concern of public speakers. Perhaps the best approach is to examine its elements.

The first inclusive and systematic model of the communicative process was introduced by the Greek philosopher Aristotle (384–322 B.C.) in his *Rhetoric*. Aristotle said that in order to produce an effect, four principal ingredients were necessary: a speaker, a speech, an audience, and an occasion. Modern communication theorists do not basically differ with Aristotle, but they point out several distinctions that are vital to our understanding of communication.

The core of all communication is the message, which is sent and received. The simple model is that of sender, message, and receiver. The model can also be stated in this way: the encoder, the code, the decoder. Even in this model, the situational context, or setting, will frequently determine the message that is both sent and received. The originator of the message is often called the source. A closer look at the elements of communication will reveal various ways in which the sender, or source, can send a message. We shall understand that a public speaker's words are only one possible way, or channel. Many types of symbols, verbal and nonverbal, can be used in the encoding of a message. However, these must be understood by the receiver if he is to decode it correctly.

Another view of communication states that something happens as a result of it. The message from the source may cause responses that were not intended. The message may be misinterpreted or completely rejected. It may be improperly encoded, or improperly transmitted. In all such cases we can say that the communication failed.

Other important concepts concerning communication should be considered. Communication is a *process*. A speaker does not just give a speech to an audience. As he prepares to speak and finally does speak, his message is continually changing and developing. Communication is not static: it is dynamic and ongoing. A continuous interaction takes place between sender and receiver. Both send and receive messages and try to adapt to the other's messages. Thus, communication can be viewed as *transaction*. Another important term to the speechmaker is *feedback*. Attention to listeners' reactions as the speech is being made, and adapting it to them, is vital to the speaker's success. Feedback is a two-way process: as the receivers respond, the sender in turn responds to them.

The first communication model to introduce the concept of *noise* was the Shannon-Weaver Mathematical Theory. In electronic communication static can distort the message so badly that it is not received as intended. This concept was quickly related to in-person human communication. It includes anything that interferes with the transmission, reception, and interpretation of a message. The noise may be external, or it may be internal within either sender or receiver. These unwanted and distracting stimuli are thus either physical or psychological.

Levels of Communication. Communication takes place in different situations and is of three levels, or types: intrapersonal, interpersonal, and person-to-persons.

It is commonly thought that communication involves at least two individuals, a source and a receiver. However, the communication that goes on within each one of us is vital. In this situation, the sender and receiver is one person who originates and receives his own messages. In other words, we talk to ourselves as part of our thinking. If, for instance, a public speaker tells himself that he is not a good speaker, is poorly prepared, or is not liked by his listeners, he may fail in his endeavor. Such messages to one's self are part of the internal noise mentioned previously. However, some intrapersonal messages can be positive and helpful.

Any communication between one individual and another is said to be interpersonal. It may take place in a one-to-one situation, as in an interview, or in a small group, as in a meeting. The question period which often follows the conclusion of a speech can also be considered interpersonal communication.

Public communication occurs when one person delivers a definite message in a specific situation in order to elicit particular responses from those listening. The context is usually public, formal, and structured. Other terms used are *person-to-persons* and *speaker-to-group* communication. Our description of communication emphasizes transaction, interaction, and identification of the listeners with the speaker and the speaker with them. The person-to-persons concept is probably the most suitable, because the speaker does not view his listeners as one big audience. He sees them as many individuals, each one with certain interests, needs, and feelings.

Message Stimuli. Messages are composed of many stimuli, or channels. Those we hear are auditory; those we see are visual.

Auditory stimuli include all sounds produced by the speaker, whether vocal or nonvocal. Snapping the fingers or striking a table are examples of nonvocal sounds. Vocal sounds are those produced

by the speaker's vocal mechanism. These sounds can be verbal or
nonverbal. Verbal sounds are words and other components of a given
language. Examples of nonverbal sounds are sighs, chuckles, or vocalized pauses (uh's).

Visual stimuli include all things an audience sees when it looks
at a speaker and the special space he occupies—the way he sits,
stands, moves, and gestures, his audiovisual aids, and his manner
of presenting them.

Meaning always depends upon the actual stimuli as sent, as received, and as interpreted. The interpretation involves not only auditory and visual sensations and perceptions but also tactile, olfactory,
gustatory, and kinesthetic reactions. The meaning as encoded may
differ more or less from the meaning as received and decoded. When
they approximately agree, the communication is successful.

Types of Nonverbal Messages.   Other types of nonverbal messages and message codes are important. The study of paralanguage,
or extraverbal communication, reveals that variations in the pitch,
rate, volume, and quality of the speaking voice can give messages
different from the meanings of the words they accompany. Vocal
tone and inflections, for example, may affirm or deny what is being
said.

When researcher John Starkweather filtered out the verbal components of speech to leave only a mumble, listeners could decode the
semantics of voice quality and other nonverbal signals of speech.
He also found that content-free speech provides some meanings more
clearly than full-content speech.[1]

Kinesics refers to communication through gestures and other body
movements, such as a raised eyebrow or a shift of posture. While
we hear the phonetic signals of speech, we see and feel the kinesic
signals. The different meaningful vocal phonemes and morphemes
are accompanied by different meaningful kinemes and kinemor-
phemes.

Listeners are attracted or repelled by what they see. A speaker
thus can encourage or discourage desirable emotional states. A fidgity
public speaker, for example, suggests escape from the speaking situation as soon as possible.

---

[1] Alfred G. Smith, *Communication and Culture* (New York: Holt, Rinehart and
Winston, 1966), pp. 168, 189–199.

Time and the use of it is another factor in communication. *Chronemics* considers the time elements of a speech: its length, its portion of the program, the hour of the day, the day of the week, the month or season of the year, and so forth.

A communication is transmitted from sender to receiver through more or less space. *Proxemics* is concerned with the use of personal and public space, including interpersonal distance, spacial arrangement, and size of the space used. The contextual field of speech exists psychologically in a space around each person. Edward T. Hall has shown that people often reduce the space between themselves and powerful members of a group, and increase their distance from less powerful members.[2]

Silence can communicate. We can be encouraged by it or rebuffed by it. A meaningful pause may reinforce an idea or challenge it. A silent response to a question can be the acceptance of an idea or the refusal of it. What is *not* said is a vital part of communication.

Perception. We receive sensations and then perceive them. Perception, or interpretation of what our senses tell us, is determined by what we already know. Our knowledge depends upon our experience, our past perceptions and feelings. People, therefore, perceive things in different ways. Our expectations, our emotions and attitudes, states of mind, and physical health at a given time also affect perception. The list of factors could be extended. The key point is that a listener reacts only to what he perceives among the many appeals to his senses. As he decodes the message, the meaning he reaches may not be the one intended by the speaker. Such unintentional communication on the speaker's part may result in a breakdown in communication, causing it to be unsuccessful.

Situational Context. Communication always takes place in a particular context. In public communication this is partly determined by the physical dimensions of the settings: size of the room, seating arrangements, presence or absence of a lectern, use of a public address system, and so forth.

It is also determined by the psychological dimensions: number of listeners, their feelings and emotional states, their backgrounds and interests, the time of day or year, and so forth. The physical

---

[2] Edward T. Hall, *The Hidden Dimension* (Garden City, N.Y.: Doubleday, 1966).

and emotional closeness of the listeners tend to influence their feelings, thinking, and reactions.

Summary. A brief summary of what has been discussed may give a manageable view of what communication is and does. An act of communication consists of basic elements: a sender (source) encodes a message which is then decoded by a receiver. These acts take place in a particular setting.

Communication is a process: all elements are constantly in motion with interaction and transaction occurring between the sender and receiver. Adaptation to feedback from each is vital. Possible noise (interference) must be considered in getting the intended message to its destination.

There are three levels of communication: intrapersonal, interpersonal, and person-to-persons. Communication is verbal or nonverbal, vocal or nonvocal. Messages are sent and received through many codes, including language, paralanguage, kinesics, chronemics, proxemics, and silence. Communication is intentional or unintentional. Perception depends a great deal upon past experiences of both the sender and the receiver of a message.

When the sender transmits a message, he desires to evoke the intended understanding and response from the listener. If the result is not as intended, the communication has not succeeded.

BARRIERS TO SPEECH COMMUNICATION

The process of speech communication is simple in pattern but complex in practice. Its social nature gives rise to many barriers, a few of which deserve mention.

Difference in Meaning. Word signs do not have the same reference for both speaker and hearer. Even though the meanings assigned to words are agreed upon, words still have connotations or shades of meaning that vary with the individual user. Each listener tends to interpret words in terms of his own life and limitations. The word "dog" refers to a domestic animal, but it has different actual meanings for an owner living on an isolated farm and for a city-dweller who is annoyed by the barking of a neighbor's pet.

Unintelligible Signs. A message may not be sufficiently intelligible. The voice may be too soft, the articulation too indistinct, or the grouping of words into phrases too indefinite. "Djeatchet," for instance, might not mean "Did you eat yet" to all listeners.

Irrelevant Action. A speaker's gestures and motions may be so constant, erratic, or spasmodic that the listener's attention is distracted from the message.

Obtrusive Appearance. An unfavorable style of grooming, such as an unshaved face, too much makeup, or noticeably unkempt clothing, may interfere with the speaker's intended meaning.

Offensive Smell. In face-to-face communicative situations the sense of smell comes into play. Malodorous breath, body, or clothing drives the hearer to make a quick escape from the speaker and his message.

Poor Health. The physical condition of the speaker and the listener affects communication. Illness, dullness, and lassitude act as a bar to attention and understanding.

Unpleasant Surroundings. The nature of the physical surroundings is also a factor. A hot, stuffy atmosphere, overly dim or overly glaring lighting, uncomfortable seats, and persistent noises interfere with the proper reception and interpretation of messages.

Difference in Status. The social and economic status of the speaker and the listener may be a barrier to communication. A listener tends to judge the speaker from the standpoint of his own inferior or superior position. Many tenants dislike landlords, workers hate the boss, law-abiding citizens distrust ex-convicts, and persons on salary cannot understand those permanently on welfare.

Personal Difficulties. Emotional maladjustments and tensions over personal problems may make it impossible for a listener to understand a speaker's ideas. Such individual barriers are usually unknown to the speaker and are almost impossible to offset.

Personal Concerns. Messages are often distorted by the personal prejudices and special interests of the listener. The appearance or voice of a speaker may remind the listener of someone he dislikes and he may decide that the speaker's ideas are the same as those of the remembered detested person. National, racial, and religious prejudices are usually borrowed from other persons and may be somewhat less personal than prejudices based on the individual's own experience.

Lack of Ideas. A frequent barrier to oral communication is lack of ideas, which means ideas of significance to listeners. Most of us have friends or relatives who repeat the same anecdotes, the same likes and dislikes, and the same wishes every time we see them without realizing that these things have no value for us. A public speaker may forget that people in different walks of life have different interests. To corporation stockholders personal income tax on dividends is punitive double taxation, because the owned corporation has already paid income taxes on those earnings. But the issue of double taxation would be unimportant to those without stock holdings. Many ideas must be related to the listener's point of view before they can be understood or shared.

Improper Sequence. To convey a message the signs must be organized in a proper sequence and emphasized according to the conventions of grammar and syntax. The following example, "What is uttered until it is worth anything," contains the word signs necessary for a message but lacks the other signs. With the right word order to indicate the grammatical construction, the message becomes intelligible: "What is anything worth until it is uttered?"

INTRODUCTION TO PUBLIC SPEAKING

Public speaking is speech communication before a listening audience. Some forms of discussion, performances by actors, and oral interpretations of literature by public readers are sometimes classified under public speaking. Specifically, public speaking is the presentation of a speech by an individual to an audience, or person-to-persons speaking.

Six factors are involved in public speaking: an occasion which makes speaking desirable; an audience to whom an important message is to be communicated; a speech, which consists of significant ideas arranged in a special order; a response by the audience; a symbolic medium, which is oral language in all its aspects, including gesture and facial expression; and a speaker, who conveys the speech in person to the audience.

Before these factors are discussed, a brief view of the history of public speaking, some current misconceptions of it, and the nature of good public speaking are offered as background to individual improvement in speaking.

History of Public Speaking. Public speaking has a long history and plays a vital role in various fields, such as religion, education, and public affairs. Two of the world's great religious teachers, Buddha and Jesus, did not communicate by writing. Instead, they spoke, and their ideas still influence the minds and conduct of millions of human beings. Many people have always gone to places of worship to hear sermons. Outstanding preachers like Savonarola, Wesley, Bossuet, Newman, and Phillips Brooks have spoken from the pulpit. Billy Graham is a contemporary religious speaker who commands vast audiences.

In Athens during the sixth century B.C. boys of sixteen attended public gymnasiums, listened to adult discussions, and imitated the speeches as part of their preparation for citizenship. The democratic institutions of Athens made public service a duty of all citizens. Skill in oratory was thus a necessity. Teachers of speech developed the study of rhetoric, which comprised the theory and practice of eloquence, or speech designed to influence the judgment and feelings of men.

During the Middle Ages, the rise and growth of universities established the custom of lectures. The backbone of education ever since has been a teacher speaking to an audience of pupils.

Public speaking is essential to government and affairs of state, as shown by the fact that some of the world's greatest speakers were active in public affairs: Demosthenes, Cicero, Edmund Burke, Daniel Webster, Abraham Lincoln, Franklin D. Roosevelt, Sir Winston Churchill, and John F. Kennedy.

The first handbook on the art of rhetoric was written by Corax of Syracuse, who flourished about 465 B.C. His interest was in arguments to be used in court and in evidence to establish probable truth where absolute truth could not be proved. Antiphon (480?–411 B.C.) was the first orator to combine the theory and practice of rhetoric. Isocrates (436–338 B.C.) broadened rhetoric into a cultural study or philosophy with a practical purpose. Plato (427–347 B.C.) stood against rhetoric that manipulated language and advocated rhetoric that conveyed truth and morality. He held that speech should be based upon logic and a thorough knowledge of the topic to be discussed. At the same time, the speech should be adjusted to the understanding of the audience.

The first inclusive and systematic treatise on rhetoric was produced by Aristotle (384–322 B.C.) He emphasized the persuasive uses of truth and considered the speaker and his education, the speech and its development, the audience, and methods of adapting the speech to it. Cicero (106–43 B.C.) was a great and influential Roman orator. His works, such as *The Orator* and *On Oratory,* emphasized broad education, style of composition, and skill in delivery. Quintilian was a Roman teacher of the first century A.D. His *Institutes of Oratory* is a thorough and practical treatment of rhetoric. A good speaker, he believed, must have knowledge, character, and skill in eloquence.

Speech assumed a crucial role in modern times. The last four hundred years witnessed the rise of freedom of speech, an essential part of the struggle for individual liberty and democratic government.

Freedom of expression was not recognized to any extent in the ancient and medieval world. The Renaissance, the Reformation, and the rapid growth of the middle class created a demand for such freedom. American liberty was bound up with free speech. In 1776 the Constitution of Virginia guaranteed freedom of speech and the other states followed suit. The Constitution of the United States, which became effective in 1789, guaranteed free speech. In the same year, the French Declaration of the Rights of Man and of the Citizen made freedom of speech an inalienable right.

Authorities on rhetoric have analyzed and amplified the principles of persuasion laid down by the classical writers. A few influential authorities were Thomas Wilson, Hugh Blair, George Campbell, Richard Whately, and, in our time, Kenneth Burke.

Although books on public speaking and on every aspect of speech have multiplied rapidly during the twentieth century, basic speech material is found in the Greek and Roman writers, an indication that there are permanent factors in the relationship between speaker and audience. Modern authorities, however, have enlarged upon the psychological, sociological, and scientific aspects of speech.

The rise of persuasion as a social process in advertising and political propaganda creates the necessity for critical listening as a daily habit. Along with international propaganda come new threats to freedom of speech.

The character and subject matter of public speeches have changed. Not only public affairs but all branches of life and experience offer material for speaking. Speeches are presented not only by ministers, educators, and political leaders, but also by individuals in all walks of life.

Speeches are usually shorter than formerly. It is true that both short and long speeches have been given from antiquity to the present, but the conditions and pressures of modern living tend to encourage brevity.

Speakers no longer try to put on a lively show, since motion pictures, radio, television, and night clubs offer a constant variety of entertainment. Furthermore, the practical values of public speaking in the business of living are stressed more than the arts of rhetoric, oratory, and declamation.

Current Misconceptions.   Preconceived ideas about public speaking prevent many individuals from learning to be good speakers. It is wise to avoid these popular misconceptions and to concentrate on essential problems of improving speaking ability.

Speakers Are Born Not Made.   The notion that public speaking is a natural gift ignores the fact that all speech is a learned activity. It is true that some children learn to speak their native language more easily and better than others; it is also true that some individuals learn to speak well in public without conscious effort. Training cannot give ability, it can only develop it. Fortunately, few people totally lack the ability to speak. Most of us can learn to speak convincingly in public if we have the desire and will to work at it. For nearly three thousand years men have been trained in public speaking. Courses given in today's schools and colleges, business and financial houses, and social organizations, such as athletic, advertising, and engineering clubs, establish the fact that public speakers are made *not* born.

Exhibition of Skill.   The idea that a speaker shows off his knowledge, his mastery of vocabulary, grammar, and syntax, the beauty and scope of his voice, and his personal charm together with his dramatic and artistic skill puts the wrong elements of public speaking first. The speaker is only the means of conveying a message to listeners. His attention should always be on the message and the response of his audience to it. Public speaking is not a dramatic performance or a form of self-advertisement. It is a direct and sincere attempt to arouse desirable responses in particular listeners at a given time.

No Special Skill Needed.   Some people believe that anybody can speak well in public because everyone talks to others daily. This misconception confuses the habit of speaking with the ability to communicate. Public speaking demands something worth saying arranged in proper order and said in a suitable way. The preparation and presentation of oral material require special skill. Good public speaking sounds natural, but some naturalness is the result of knowledge, practice, and judgment.

Delivery Is Everything.   A seductive theory states that what is important is not what is said but how it is said. William Jennings Bryan once told an audience of students that he would speak to them for ten minutes about nothing and make them like it. He did. Emptying the mind of content and basking in pure sensations can be a source of pleasure. There is a charm in listening to an unknown language, since the musical aspects of language have an aesthetic appeal of their own. The arts are based on the relationship of the sensuous elements of line, color, mass, and tone. This relationship has no meaning or mental content beyond itself, as can be most clearly seen in non-representational painting and sculpture. Public speaking is representational: it deals with mental content. It uses words, not for themselves but for their references to the external world of reality.

Skill Is a Menace.   Good public speaking is more than a marshaling of communication techniques; it is also a marshaling of truth. A common misapprehension is that a skilled speaker is not to be trusted because he can convince you and control you against your will. This opinion is part of the suspicion of anyone who seems to do anything too well. Some persons distrust all doctors, lawyers, politicians, employers, and labor leaders because of the questionable actions of a few; they forget that there are all kinds of persons possessing special abilities just as there are all kinds of individuals who do not possess them.

Speech Provides a New Personality.   The notion is sometimes advanced that studying speaking will miraculously change one's personality, just as a visit to a hairdresser and fashion boutique can instantly change a woman's appearance. Serious study and practice of public speaking definitely increases one's knowledge, one's ability to communicate with others, and one's self-confidence and poise. An individual's character and personality change as a result of daily effort and experience.

The Nature of Good Speaking.
A good speaker has a genuine urge to communicate ideas. He is convinced that his message will

be of value to others. He meets the expectations of his audience; they want to hear his ideas and the results of his experience. His message is in a form they can understand, including arrangement, language, and presentation. His message is the result of honest, serious thinking and contains ideas which he firmly believes. A speaker's integrity, character, and reputation have a definite effect upon listeners. A good speaker understands people and has insight into the thoughts, feelings, and needs of others. In approach and attitude, he is conversational rather than formal or dogmatic. He adapts or alters his speech in accordance with his audience's reactions. He knows that good public speaking is a two-way process: a conversation with listeners even though they do not respond in words.

The good speaker has a sense of social responsibility based on sympathy and respect for others and on a deep concern for their rights and welfare. He wants to help solve problems. He has moral judgment and courage. He says what he ought to say for the common good, even when circumstances are not favorable. Even if he fails in his purpose, he makes a good speech that ought to succeed.

Approaches to Speaking. To study public speaking for purposes of improvement four basic approaches are possible: rhetorical, psychological, semantic, and eclectic.

Rhetorical. Ancient authorities recommended the study of speech in five necessary parts. (1) Invention or investigation is the exploration, analysis, and selection of materials for the speech. (2) Arrangement is the organization of the selected material to fit the audience, the occasion, and the abilities of the speaker. (3) Style is the expression of ideas in language and concerns the way words, phrases, sentences, paragraphs, and divisions of the speech are handled. (4) Memory is the storehouse of learning which makes suitable invention, arrangement, and style possible. (5) Delivery is the speaker's contact with his audience and involves voice, posture, gesture, action, and manner. The rhetorical approach included learning by imitation of models. Great speeches were studied to show the learner how to use anecdotes and figures of speech, how to manage contrast and emphasis, and how to secure unity, coherence, and climax.

Psychological. Public speaking is a branch of applied psychology and deals with stimulus and response in one-to-one and group situations.

Psychologists have added to our knowledge of almost all phases of speech behavior, including sensation and perception, attention and interest, feeling and emotion, learning and habit, suggestion and belief, and the motives, attitudes, and responses of the audience.

The various factors of the public speaking situation have psychological aspects. The speaker may have problems of fear and self-confidence, of adequate thinking and speaking at an appointed time. The attitudes, values, and listening habits of audiences also vary. Differences in individual responses depend on age, sex, occupation, and social background. What an audience expects from a speaker is conditioned by the time, place, and reason for the speech. Thus the psychological approach emphasizes the human basis of public speaking.

Semantic. The semantic approach concentrates upon the use of language or a system of word signs to convey meaning. Words do not constitute mental processes of either speaker or hearer: words are symbols of thought processes or meanings.

Misunderstandings in speaking are due to inaccurate symbolization. If a man, when referring to another, calls him a dog and a jackal, it is obvious to both speaker and listener that he is expressing a personal opinion by means of epithets. However, if the speaker calls a man an atheist, degenerate, and psychopath, it is no longer obvious that he is using epithets to express his personal opinion. Both speaker and hearer may believe that the man actually is all of these things, when, in fact, he is not. Semantics analyzes the loopholes and fallacies in the use of language and attempts to correct them. Great stress is placed on the fact that good speech reports the real world correctly.

Eclectic. None of the above approaches includes the whole domain of public speaking. The modern study of speech is based on the eclectic approach and offers the broadest basis for individual improvement in public speaking. This approach adopts whatever is valuable and helpful in all other approaches, and does not hesitate to profit by contributions from linguistics and the science of communications, from sociology and history, from merchandising and business management, and from literature and other arts. As Robert Henri once told the students of the Art Students League: "All the past up to a moment ago is your legacy. You have a right to it."[3]

---

[3] Robert Henri, *The Art Spirit* (Philadelphia: J. B. Lippincott, 1923), p. 89.

The speaker's legacy includes the work of ancient orators, modern speeches, talks by fellow students and workers, yesterday's broadcast discussion, and the opinion voiced recently by a friend. The student of speech can claim the entire heritage of the past; he can study it, use it, and profit by it.

2.
IMPROVING SPEECH COMMUNICATION SKILLS

We live, it is said, in many ages: the space age, the atomic age, the electronic age, the chemical age, the technological age, and the age of computers. We also live in an age which does much to explain the others: the age of improvement. Improvement is part of the complex structure of modern life. The urge for improvement brings new advances in medicine, surgery, and dentistry. The adult education movement, the expansion of higher education, the phenomenal sale of paperbound books on all subjects reveal a widespread desire for self-improvement. In all other areas, such as sports, public utilities, manufacturing, and transportation, tremendous efforts are devoted to all kinds of improvement.

WHY IMPROVE SPEAKING?

Why should a person realize more clearly the importance of speech and strive to improve his own speech communication? The reasons are economic, social, and personal.

Economic Value of Speech. Most individuals earn their living by working for someone else. They must talk well enough to get a job and to fulfill many of the required duties. Speech is important not only for those who work in direct contact with the public but also for those who work only with others in the same firm. A business enterprise is a variety of teamwork and requires the ability to get along with all associates. This skill is based on the ability to speak well with others. Speaking well in this sense means talking cooperatively rather than antagonistically. In business it literally pays to be friendly and considerate.

Advancement in many occupations depends on speaking ability. A person's speech shows one's willingness to work, makes one's ideas and suggestions known, and helps reveal one's ability and judgment. In the daily conduct of every sizeable organization, supervisors, department heads, managers, coordinators, or directors speak to various groups of employees. When the speaking is well done, the speaker becomes more valuable to the organization.

Many professions demand good speaking skills not only in private but also in public. The ministry, law, diplomatic service, television, and the theater are well-known examples. Business, industrial, and labor leaders are also associated with public speaking. In fact, a person who accomplishes something of worth in any field is expected to be articulate before an audience.

To earn a living and to advance a career are not the only practical reasons for us to improve our speech. Another reason is to attain leadership. Our economic society cannot function without leaders. From ancient Athens to modern Washington, a leader is a person who can influence the minds, feelings, and actions of others.

Social Value of Speech. Speech is important to the individual in his immediate social surroundings and also in his relationship to the complete social structure of his time.

Immediate Social Sphere. The richest man in the world once said in a television interview that he wished he were a better conversationalist. A person does not have to be a billionaire to be lonely. One advantage of improving speech communication is being able to converse freely with all kinds of individuals. Being at ease with others makes social life more enjoyable. An agreeable and interesting conversationalist attracts friends and acquaintances. The ability to communicate is also the basis of the deep relations of love, marriage, and family life.

Speech not only communicates messages to others but also creates a sense of human solidarity. Our life includes a need for fellowship, for belonging with those who share our language. Within the framework of a common language are smaller linguistic groups composed of those who speak more nearly as we do. This special quality of speaking may be due to locality, vocation, avocation, or other important interest. A complete stranger sometimes seems like an old friend, and we explain it by saying, "He speaks my language."

Inconsequential small talk, as Sapir points out, establishes rapport between members of a casual group who have no previous basis for intimacy. "This caressing or reassuring quality of speech in general, even where no one has anything of moment to communicate, reminds us how much more language is than a mere technique of communication."[1]

Society at Large. Besides helping the individual to adapt himself to his own social sphere, speech enables him to adjust himself meaningfully to the society in which he lives. Good speech communication allows a person to become active in civic affairs and serve the community. By talking with others and speaking to groups he can champion causes, shape public opinion, and contribute to national welfare. Social control in a democracy is maintained by citizens exercising their right of free speech. If the individual does not fulfill his potential, or if he neglects to develop his ability to communicate, society is the loser. When public communication and social control are left to a few, democracy is in danger.

Speech has always been more powerful than blows because its effects are longer lasting. "Blowing off steam" often prevents actual conflict not only in a haranguer on a soapbox but also in a dictator before a microphone. Now that weapons have become instruments of total destruction, speech is of necessity a substitue for blows. Thus another important reason for improving speech communication is to be able to speak convincingly for peaceful dealings between nations so that humanity can survive.

Personal Value of Speech. In a society each member has a dual problem: to become one with the group and to remain one with himself. Group customs, traditions, and other cultural patterns exert powerful pressures for conformity. The physical and mental constitution of each person exerts strong pressures for nonconformity. Speech is the medium for the movement toward solidarity and the movement toward individuality. Speech communication in the first instance is interpersonal, in the second, intrapersonal.

Speech, which refers to reality by means of signs, represents peo-

---

[1] Edward Sapir, "Language," *The Encyclopedia of the Social Sciences* (New York: The Macmillan Co., 1933), Vol. 9, p. 160.

ple's tendency to express symbolically their reactions to the external world. Speech is not objective reality nor is it the meaning or relationship to reality in which it conveys. What meaning is or what the self is aware of seems impossible to explain except symbolically by speech.

Perception, awareness, thinking, realization probably depend on unuttered speech. Pleasures and pains, likes and dislikes, moral beliefs, aesthetic values, rational convictions, all that we know is known to us because we express it to ourselves in words. It is easy to see why self-realization is a never-ending process of communicating with others and with one's self.

GENERAL PURPOSES OF SPEECHMAKING

The preparation of a speech involves ideas and their organization and realization in words. The first step is to decide on the basic purpose or type of response desired from the audience, since the choice and treatment of the subject depend on why the speech is to be given. The general purpose will aid the speaker in deciding on a more specific purpose when he determines his subject. The general purposes of speaking are to inform, to entertain, and to persuade.

To Inform.   Much speaking is done to convey information, to satisfy curiosity, or to make things clear. Human beings have a strong desire for information: to know what is happening in the community, the country, the world; to understand the nature of things; to learn about the activities and achievements of persons living and dead. The typical informative speech describes, explains, defines, or demonstrates something—such as How a satellite remains in orbit; How to budget; How Social Security affects you; Mouth-to-mouth resuscitation.

To Entertain.   Some speeches are designed to amuse or divert listeners by putting them in a pleasant frame of mind and are suitable on such occasions as dinners, club meetings, and informal affairs. Personal experiences, human foibles, absurd proposals, and pretensions in marriage, politics, or other institutions furnish a wide variety of topics, such as: Win friends with teleportation; My impressions of Paris; To heaven on a credit card; The crabgrass roots of America.

Most speeches to entertain do not depend on humor but present novel, dramatic, or suspenseful topics, such as new scientific discoveries, creative concepts of city planning, or recent achievements in sports. Illustrated talks on arts and crafts are colorful examples of speeches to entertain, as are exhibits of swords, music boxes, or other objects collected as a hobby.

The traditional speech to entertain is the story or narrative. Adventure stories, love stories, success stories, and ghost stories have never lost their appeal to listeners. Accounts of mishaps, lucky breaks, premonitions, and discoveries offer the pleasure of escape from the daily pressures of living.

To Persuade.   A basic reason for many speeches is to influence the belief, feelings, or conduct of others by getting them to change or intensify their inclinations and points of view. Persuasion, in turn, can have three different aims.

To Convince.   The aim of a speech to convince is to alter or strengthen the opinions of the listeners. The speaker appeals to the listener's minds and induces belief in an idea by offering proof. Proof consists of facts, judgments of experts, logical arguments, and a judicious manner of presentation. The following are representative topics for a speech to convince: Our town needs a sewerage disposal plant, The state minimum retail price of milk is unfair to consumers, Overpopulation is one of the basic causes of world poverty.

To Actuate.   A speech to actuate influences listeners to perform a definite deed. The act may have political, social, economic, or personal value: vote for a candidate, contribute to a charity, buy an article, perform daily exercises.

A speaker has no authority to command an audience, and a mere request by even an influential person would probably be ignored. Listeners perform an action when they believe it is to their own satisfaction or advantage to do so. The speaker must give convincing reasons for the action in order to stimulate the listener's desire to perform it. The following are examples of specific actions sought in speeches of this nature: Give up smoking while you are able; Collect clothing for refugees; Write to the city authorities to place a traffic light at a dangerous crossing; Sign a petition against constructing a factory in a residential area.

To Stimulate.   This kind of speech stimulates the feelings and emotions of listeners, reinforces their appreciation of moral, aesthetic, or social values, or inspires them with great ideas and experiences. Certain themes—such as The Constitution protects our freedoms; All men are brothers; and Plan your future—need to be reaffirmed and reappreciated at frequent intervals. Listeners can be inspired to greater efforts of their own and to deeper appreciation of life by the example of men and women devoted to ideals of service to humanity, and by the achievements of authors, composers, and other creators in the face of illness and other obstacles. Speeches to stimulate have been given on topics like the following: What makes a champion; Our Constitution—the bulwark of our freedom; Breeding new varieties of plants; The work of a parole officer.

On some formal and solemn occasions a public prayer is offered as part of the ceremonies. Although addressed to the Deity, the prayer is designed to be heard by an audience. In that sense, the purpose of a prayer uttered in public is to impress, stimulate, and inspire the listeners.

THE SPEAKER'S PERSONALITY

Personality cannot be defined simply because it is not a simple entity. The word "person" comes from the Latin word *persona,* which was a mask worn by an actor to indicate the character he was assuming or portraying. In a sense, an individual's personality is assumed from his social surroundings. He adapts himself to others and assumes roles in ways that are expected of him by his mother, his father, his playmates, his teachers, and his fellow workers. A person is one type of personality to his brother, a different type to his friend. The individual has different vocabularies and frequently different types of grammar and syntax for various kinds of associations. Personality is probably the more or less organized total of a person's experience. From the standpoint of speech communication, personality is the effect the speaker's total behavior has upon the listener.

An audience expects a speaker to be honest, sincere, and truly himself. At the same time it expects him to look at his listeners, to speak so he can be heard, and to be suitably dressed. If a person feels natural in sloppy clothes, while gazing at the floor, or when mumbling without moving his jaw, the expectations of the audience will seem highly contradictory to him. The wise conclusion is that an audience expects a speaker to be his best self, and his best self includes necessary social adaptability.

The self or personality of the speaker includes the way he affects himself, the way others affect him, and the way he affects others. It is difficult for a person to understand and control the way he affects others, but this aspect of personality is most important in public speaking. The speaker's behavior while talking is largely determined by the attitudes he has during the speech. Attitude or outlook is part of any skilled activity. The training of a boxer includes the development of the "champion viewpoint"; a coloratura soprano cultivates the "coloratura consciousness" as part of her vocal technique. A speaker needs to cultivate the following attitudes toward himself, his message, and his listeners.

- *Modesty.* The speaker should expect to do his best, but he should not be thinking about himself while he speaks. A person who obviously thinks well of himself may appear unpleasantly conceited. The effective speaker overlooks himself, concentrates on what he has to say, and tries to get the audience to understand the message.
- *Equality.* Respect for his listeners enables a speaker to establish rapport with them. Patronizing or talking down to an audience should be avoided, but at the same time the speaker should not feel inferior to his listeners. A good speaker has a strong sense of communication, which is based on the sharing of ideas among equals.
- *Sincerity.* A convincing speaker knows what he is talking about and believes what he says. Because earnestness and the courage of one's convictions are highly persuasive attitudes, a speaker should show his honest feelings and reactions to his subject. If, on the other hand, he offers mere lip service to an idea or pretends to be deeply concerned only to gain something for himself, he does a disservice to his audience.
- *Broadmindedness.* A well-balanced, judicious, and good-tempered point of view helps the speaker establish an idea in the minds of his listeners. His fervor should grow out of the perspective derived from a thorough knowledge of all the issues involved in a question. By contrast, a dogmatic, intolerant, and fanatical attitude may repel the audience. Breadth of view is increasingly important, for as the world grows in complexity, many problems become more difficult to solve.
- *Tact.* Tact is closely related to breadth of outlook. Tact is a genuine consideration for the feelings and viewpoints of others. It

requires emotional stability and control, because the speaker must be objective enough to realize how others react to what he says. Tact is also part of common sense. A person speaks because he wants others to understand and accept his point of view. Offending them and arousing hostile reactions defeats his purpose. The speaker's attitude and speech should always be adjusted to the outlook and feelings of his audience. Knowing just what should be said at a given time demands imagination, insight, and experience in dealing with people.

• *Good Taste.* Likes and dislikes are part of the reactions to everything experienced by human beings. Judgments are formed from which taste is acquired. A person's taste is shown in his habits, clothes, companions, home, possessions, and speech.

A speaker's taste, revealed in his choice of speech subjects, illustrations, and use of language, will attract or repel his listeners.

• *Cheerfulness.* A cheerful attitude puts listeners at ease and creates in them a receptive frame of mind. On the other hand, a mournful, unhappy, and woebegone attitude tends to erect a barrier between speaker and listener. In public speaking present or future happiness is an element to be remembered and considered. Cheerfulness has great practical value, for unhappiness, like anger, is not conducive to sound judgment.

• *Hope.* Hope might be considered the opportunity for future happiness, or in the words of the Declaration of Independence, the pursuit of happiness. Criticism or condemnation offered by a speaker should be followed by positive suggestion and improvement. A speaker should not leave his listeners in undesirable straits; he should bring them hope.

• *Enthusiasm.* Enthusiasm means eager interest, zeal, or fervor. Sometimes speakers have a good topic, excellent organization, and suitable language but their speech produces no response. The presentation is routine and wooden. The speaker should use energy, vitality, and animation to put life into his words.

Enthusiasm provides spontaneity—the quick responsiveness of the speaker to his audience and subject. Liveliness, color, spiritedness, variety, and a warm emphatic manner attract listeners to the speaker and to his message. An ordinary speech enthusiastically presented is often more successful than an outstanding speech delivered in a tired, dull, and pedantic way.

STAGE FRIGHT

The condition troubling most speakers is fear, ranging from slight timidity to severe dread of addressing an audience. In daily life people usually talk freely without self-consciousness, but an individual getting up and facing a group is apt to suffer the upsetting apprehension known as stage fright. Sometimes the disturbance is temporary and disappears when the person begins to talk. At other times, the qualms are persistent and painful.

Symptoms.   Stage fright has mental, emotional, and physical manifestations. The speaker's mind tends to focus upon the fact that he is going to give a speech. He interprets this fact as a necessity: he *has* to give a speech. He becomes more conscious of himself than usual, and pictures himself as being the object of close scrutiny. Even in an everyday situation, a person may be disconcerted if he discovers that all eyes are turned upon him. All performers—actors, athletes, speakers—at times get nervous.

The anticipation of speaking before people becomes a source of excitement and tension. Stage fright creates a pattern of withdrawal. The speaker becomes hesitant, apologetic, or embarrassed, and avoids talking directly to his listeners. In some cases withdrawal produces a flight from the platform; in certain others, a refusal to get up to speak under any circumstances.

The physiological symptoms of stage fright are rapid, tremulous breathing, or gasping for breath. The mouth becomes dry and the heart beats rapidly; sometimes the individual can feel the pulsations in his chest and blood vessels. Tension of the skeletal muscles either produces a rigid posture or uncontrollable fidgeting. The vocal musculature is constricted; the voice becomes weak, breathy, or harsh, and its pitch becomes high and often monotonous. The rate of utterance is either extremely rapid or else slow and broken with "uh's" and other vocalized pauses.

Causes.   Various theories have been advanced to explain the nature and causes of stage fright and an understanding of these often helps the individual to gain self-control.

Any unfamiliar activity or situation may create a feeling of inadequacy, inspire fear, and cause flight reactions. A neurotic condition is sometimes set up in which the individual wants to speak because he should and wants to avoid speaking because he fears the results. Everybody has a deep sense of belonging to a group. When a person gets up to speak, he detaches himself and no longer feels the group security. The new relationship is uncomfortable and creates a feeling of vulnerability. In some cases the fear of speaking is a learned reaction based on previous unpleasant experiences in speaking to others.

Stage fright may seem to the speaker to come from any of various causes, such as fear of criticism, of failure, of looking bad, of social inadequacy, or the often-expressed fear of "making a fool of oneself." Frequently there is a fear of stage fright itself. These fears seem to be different manifestations of the fear of what others will think. It is quite natural to feel apprehension over the criticisms of others, for everyone is used to adapting himself to the requirements of society. Direct, personal social pressures are more constant and usually more effective than laws in enforcing good conduct and conformity to group customs.

Control. Fear is a normal human reaction because it is part of the equipment for self-protection. No speaker can hope to be entirely free of stage fright, but he can learn to control it as he has learned to master other unfounded fears. People who perform in public have faced the problem of stage fright and have learned to control it by various methods of adjustment.

One method of controlling stage fright is to face the challenge and speak. The situation should not be avoided but should be met with determination. The speaker continues his talk even if his hands tremble or his knees knock together. He remembers that few persons are free from fear, and that courage means going ahead in spite of it. As he becomes accustomed to speaking, he will be less afraid and will realize that nervousness and fear are actually beneficial; they equip him to meet a challenge and release the extra energy needed to adjust himself to it. Speaking to a group is not a crisis and is similar in many ways to talking with friends. The speaker should try to feel that his listeners are friends, or at least kindly disposed toward him. Actually, listeners want a speaker to succeed and will appreciate the fact that he is doing his best. Memorizing the opening may help. Once underway, the speech is easier.

Many speakers are helped by assuming a confident body set even though they do not feel confident. They walk to the platform in an assured manner, stand erect before the audience, and use strong, definite gestures and motions as they speak. Confident actions tend to arouse confident feelings. All movements and positions that make the speaker look timid should be avoided. Visual aids can help speakers who feel unable to make gestures. Purposeful activity is usually vigorous activity and thus helps the speaker to concentrate on his message and forget his fear. The speaker may feel less nervous if he becomes familiar with the room where he is to speak. When he later gives his talk he will feel more at home if the room and its equipment have no surprises.

The speaker should prepare thoroughly and should remember that the message is the important thing. Ask how the listeners can best be served. Put them before yourself. Concentrate on their needs and interests. Knowing exactly what is to be said provides self-confidence. When giving the speech, the speaker resolutely turns his mind away from himself. And if possible, the speech should be practiced before several friends and acquaintances. The more often a person presents talks to others, the sooner he will be able to speak easily in public. Many speakers replace fear with other emotions, such as enthusiasm for a subject, or ardor for a cause. A good plan is to select topics of absorbing interest or those that arouse the speaker's zeal for reform. Being in earnest about the problems and sufferings of others leaves the speaker no time for self-consciousness and fear.

Deep breathing is a traditional release for nervous fear. A full breath should be taken and exhaled slowly and completely. Experienced performers do this several times prior to their appearance before an audience. Once in position, they acknowledge their audience with a friendly look, and breathe slowly. When a speaker pauses for breath during his speech, he should inhale comfortably to avoid gasping and the nervousness it tends to promote.

DEVELOPMENT OF SELF-CONFIDENCE

The preceding suggestions for the control of stage fright are ways of developing confidence for the speaking situation. Most individuals probably need to develop more self-confidence, not only for speaking but for living. The strengthening of the self to meet the requirements of existence with any degree of liberty and happiness is a continuous process. There are many programs an individual can follow to help him solve his problems of communication and adjustment to others.

The Pleasure of Talking. The individual should remember that talking is not only a necessity but also a pleasure. Conversations with friends and interesting discussions with associates have created a storehouse of agreeable memories. The person who concentrates on the pleasant experiences of speech communication will find his part in interviews, conferences, and public speeches more attractive and absorbing.

The Urge to Communicate. The individual should encourage and develop a stronger urge to communicate. Speaking is not only pleasant but purposeful. Some ideas are too important not to be communicated. The speaker should discover these and realize that he has an important message to prepare and deliver. He may be dissatisfied with the initial results, but he can determine that he will do better next time.

Constructive View of the Self. Everyone benefits by looking at himself positively and expectantly. Each person has unrealized abilities to meet challenges. The refusal to dwell on weaknesses and past failures should be definite. Nobody can always succeed, but one can learn from one's failures and the gain in understanding should be realized and appreciated. What can be changed should be changed; what cannot be changed must be accepted. It is better mental hygiene to remember healthy experiences than details of illness. If "nothing succeeds like success," it is also wise to remember successes. Instead of building up a history of troubles and disappointments, the individual should prepare the more stimulating history of successes and good experiences.

Knowledge of Public Speaking. The speaker adds to his confidence by learning all he can about public speaking. Adequate knowledge will enable him to formulate a guiding philosophy or effective viewpoint for speaking. He learns specifically what is justifiably expected of a speaker by his audience and also what he can reasonably expect from himself.

The Memory of Ideas. For every speech, the sequence of ideas should be firmly fixed in memory. The organization and outlining of the speech is an essential part of both preparation and delivery. Notes of the sequence of points should be prepared for the presentation of the speech. Such a safeguard against a lapse of memory gives the speaker the confidence that comes from complete preparation.

Nevertheless, it is wise to plan what to do in case memory should fail. Many speakers, when they simply cannot think of what to say next, briefly summarize what they have just presented. Running through the first part of the thought sequence usually recalls the remainder. If, however, the speaker's memory still balks, the simplest thing for him to do is to tell the audience he has forgotten what he wanted to say. If he smiles and treats his confession lightly, he can probably continue his speech or at least say something more about his subject. If this too is impossible, he must go immediately to his prepared conclusion or else improvise one on the spot.

Habits of Relaxation. The conditions of modern living tend to create undue tensions. The secret of relaxation is change. The customs of the coffee break, recess, a full hour for lunch, a holiday, the weekend, and a vacation are all methods of securing the benefits of relaxation. The student and other performers of concentrated mental work can relieve nervous tension by switching the mind to an entirely different matter, or by doing a physical task.

One method of relaxation is based on the alternation of tension and relaxation. Yawning and stretching are familiar examples of tightening muscles to relax them. Activity is usually the quickest way to relax. Finding something to do relieves jumpiness, irritability, resentment, and other emotional tensions. A speaker who moves about on the platform and gestures with energy loses much of his self-consciousness, tension, and inhibitions.

LISTENING

Listening is the primary source of human learning. From birth to death the individual acquires habits, language, knowledge, and social relationships by listening to directions and information uttered directly by persons or transmitted by mechanical devices. The modern dissemination and prestige of printed matter brought new and heavy demands on the eyes. However, most people, because they learn to speak before they learn to read, are still ear-minded rather than print-minded. It is a conservative estimate that adults get more than half of their current ideas from listening to television and radio broadcasts. Most persons listen more than they talk, talk much more than they read, and write comparatively little.

Definition of Listening.   Listening is not the same as hearing. Listening is active, concentrated, and directed, while hearing is passive and unpremeditated. Hearing is the act or process of receiving and perceiving sounds. Perception in this sense means the awareness or consciousness of sounds. Listening is hearing with a purpose. It is attending closely, or making a conscious effort to hear and perceive. Perception in this sense means understanding or grasping the meaning of sounds. The sensation of hearing, like seeing, undergoes a process of symbolization, which in turn affects the act of sensation. In other words, what we hear or see is determined by the way we look at it. Specifically, in speech communication listening is the act or process of receiving and perceiving messages. Listening therefore includes the perception of the visual components of spoken messages.

The Listening Process.   The receiving and perceiving of a message can be described in six steps.

• *Hearing.* Sound waves are received by the ear and arouse sensations of sound in the brain.
• *Concentration.* Attention is closely focused upon these sounds as hearing continues.
• *Comprehension.* The meanings associated with the sounds by past experience are recalled and perceived in their pattern. Naturally the sounds must be in a familiar language.
• *Interpretation.* The pattern of meaning symbolized by the sounds is interpreted. An effort is made to determine the true meaning, including any hidden meanings.
• *Understanding.* After consideration a decision is made that the message is understood.
• *Reaction.* A response is made to the message, such as smiling, frowning, nodding or shaking the head, applauding, setting the jaw, or leaning forward.

Factors of Good Listening.   Effective listening, whether for information, enjoyment, or critical judgment, depends on the factors of readiness, receptivity, retention, and revaluation.

Readiness.   The good listener prepares to listen by choosing a seat where he can clearly hear and see the speaker. He lays aside emotions and favorite trains of thought and ignores noises and other distractions. Being mentally and physically prepared to listen, his entire attention is then concentrated upon the speaker.

Receptivity.   The listener wants to hear what the speaker has to say. This interest makes him open-minded and willing to suspend judgment until the message is completed. A good listener is patient and considerate and avoids interrupting the speaker or disturbing him with unnecessary sounds and motions. Each point the speaker makes is noted as he says it, and the mind anticipates the next point. The good listener actively receives and absorbs ideas and assumes full responsibility for getting the most value from the speaker's message.

Retention.   The listener must remember the sequence of the speaker's ideas and relate each new point to it. The complete pattern of ideas should be grasped or guessed as soon as possible so that the full meaning can be verified by the speaker's conclusion. Many listeners at the end of a speech remember only half of the ideas presented, but a good listener retains the organization of ideas as a whole.

Revaluation.   The good listener does not accept the speaker's evaluation of his subject, but revaluates it for himself. He understands what the speaker means but must determine what it means to himself. Because appraisal is the foundation of real knowledge, revaluation is the most important factor of listening skill. Ideas, their support, and their application are weighed and considered. Ideas are measured for clarity, accuracy, logic, and relevance to the subject. The whole thought structure is finally judged. To exercise good judgment the listener must recognize logical fallacies and propaganda techniques.

Barriers to Listening.   Some of the barriers to speech communication described in Chapter 1 are barriers to listening. Barriers of other kinds prevent the perception of the speaker's message.

Passivity.   A poor listener does not exert himself to listen but expects the speaker to do all the work of communication. This passivity may be due to laziness, fatigue, indifference to the subject, dislike of being required to listen, or the habitual tendency to believe whatever is said. True belief is the result of active comparison, estimation, and choice. The poor listener does not care to become involved in such mental activities.

Concern with Nonessentials.   If attention is occupied with distractions, good listening is impossible. Some listeners forget the speaker because they are fascinated by the woman across the aisle, amused at the long-haired man in front, or incensed at a couple of gum-chewing juveniles in the offing. Other individuals criticize the speaker instead of listening to what he says. Still others notice every cough, sneeze, or scraping of shoes in the audience, every automobile, every whistle, or airplane outside, and many other noises which they try to identify.

Self-Preoccupation. A listener cannot concentrate on a speaker's ideas if his mind is absorbed with his own thoughts, feelings, wishes, and problems. The listener may hear only those parts of the speaker's message that happen to be associated with his own difficulties. Or, something said by the speaker reminds him of a favorite interest and his mind goes off on a trail of its own. Daydreaming is sometimes inspired by the person or personality of the speaker, and the apparent listener enlarges his ego in a chain of victorious fantasies.

Resistance. Some individuals cannot listen to presented ideas because they habitually disagree with whatever anyone says. This aggressive attitude is usually a defense against inner vulnerability. No matter whether the speaker makes a statement for an idea or against it, the declaration sets the listener off on his own system of arguments.

Moral Inflexibility. Certain individuals are incapable of listening to anything that contradicts what they believe. They have decided absolutely what is good, right, and true, and refuse to perceive messages that in any way disagree with their faith. There is one right way to pronounce a word, to brew coffee, to judge a criminal, to deal with foreign nations. Experience has not yet shown the narrowly righteous that conditions change the application of ideas and that morality requires judicious choices.

Lack of Training. Individuals who have not trained themselves to listen may lack the ability to analyze spoken messages. They take an idea at its separate or face value without relating it to the main concept under discussion. Many persons have not been taught to analyze subjects into component parts, to seek causes for conditions, to find evidence for and against the truth of an idea. They may suspect that phenomena are not spontaneous and unrelated but lack sufficient intellectual development to see connections between ideas and events.

Improvement of Listening. Listening can be trained like all other communicative skills. Good listening is not predominantly a matter of intelligence, for some highly gifted persons are poor listeners, while other individuals of average intelligence have formed the habit of excellent listening. Efficient listening is learned by those who have the desire and determination to practice until they master it. Directed practice in listening broadens a person's knowledge, enlarges his sympathies, and improves his language facility. We can learn something from anyone we listen to, and we may also enable the other person to make a better adjustment to life. The therapeutic value of listening is well known in the confessional and in psychotherapy.

PROGRAM FOR IMPROVEMENT IN SPEECH COMMUNICATION

To solve the problems of speech communication that present themselves, the student should plan a definite program of improvement, based on considerations such as the following.

Self-Analysis. Personal communicative habits and abilities should be analyzed. Among these are past experiences in speaking and attitudes toward addressing an audience. Can these attitudes be explained by personal, moral, social, or intellectual viewpoints? The subjects of speeches previously given should be jotted down. Were they political, sociological, or personal? An attempt should be made to decide what personality traits were a help or hindrance in preparing and presenting the speeches. A frank appraisal of relations with family members, friends, and other persons will also shed light on one's speaking and listening habits.

Criticism. Speaking without critical evaluation cannot establish good habits. Improvement depends on dispassionate self-judgment, which is acquired from outside criticism and from self-criticism.

Outside Criticism. All criticism by listeners deserves careful consideration. If it turns out to be unfounded or unhelpful, it is discarded. The same criticism offered by a number of listeners probably indicates a specific need for improvement. Criticism of worth deals with both good and bad aspects of the speech. It considers what the speaker aimed to do and how well he accomplished it, and also judges the value of his aim and accomplishment. Criticism by experienced or expert observers is to be prized.

To profit by outside judgments, the speaker must understand criticism exactly. Criticism should be received without resentment, and the speaker must learn, if necessary, to desire it. A worthy criticism should not be explained away. An alibi for a fault does not enable the speaker to correct it. Since criticism is offered for the improvement of speaking, the speaker must resist feelings of futility or despair. It takes courage and persistence to improve.

Self-Criticism. A speaker cannot rely entirely upon others but must develop the capacity for self-criticism. Self-criticism should be as objective as possible, rather than emotional and destructive. The speaker must remember that the purpose of criticism is to encourage good points and correct weak points. To be valuable self-criticism must rest on a thorough grasp of the principles of public speaking and on good sense in applying them to a speech. The study of this book will help develop a basis for criticism as will reading and listening to the speeches of other persons.

LEARNING FROM THE PAST. Printed speeches are an excellent source of technical knowledge. The arrangement of ideas, their development, and their methods of support can be studied at leisure. Differences in style offer the speaker a broad background for the development of his own direct and expressive use of language. In addition to Demosthenes, the speeches of many Greek orators, such as Aeschines, Isaeus, Isocrates, and Lysias, survive and are available in translation. Among the Romans the orations of Cicero are extant. The historians Thucydides, Sallust, Livy, Tacitus, Plutarch, and Dio Cassius report speeches by many other famous men.

The speeches of great English, Irish, and American statesmen are also available. The following are a few not already mentioned in this book: William Pitt the Elder, Charles James Fox, William Ewart Gladstone, John Philpot Curran, Henry Grattan, John C. Calhoun, and Henry Clay.

Many twentieth-century speakers, such as William Jennings Bryan, Franklin D. Roosevelt, Sir Winston Churchill, Martin Luther King, Jr., and John F. Kennedy, can be heard and studied in recordings.

Certain plays that contain public speeches are available on disks— for example, Shakespeare's *Julius Caesar* and T. S. Eliot's *Murder in the Cathedral.*

LEARNING FROM THE PRESENT. Significant recent speeches are reprinted in *The Reference Shelf* series, the periodical *Vital Speeches of the Day* (from which many quotations in this book are excerpted), and in many leading newspapers. The student owes it to his development to go hear speakers in person whenever possible and also to take advantage of hearing and evaluating broadcast speeches. Listening is one half of speaking.

Practice. Studying the principles and techniques of speaking and reading and hearing speeches will not by themselves improve an individual's speaking ability. One must prepare and give speeches to apply and realize the value of what has been studied. Knowledge cannot be a substitute for practice. In the absence of an audience, a speaker must practice aloud to imaginary listeners in his own quarters, as a singer and actor must do, or he may use a tape recorder. A speech class or other public speaking group offers the advantage of a live audience. The best experience is speaking in real communicative situations. Opportunities to speak should be sought. Joining a civic, campus, or business club, for instance, offers a chance to take part in discussions or to prepare and make oral reports on aspects of the club program. A teacher, minister, or social worker may know of groups that would welcome short speeches on suitable topics.

All practice should be done with confidence in the capacity to improve. Improvement comes from the speaker doing his very best each time he speaks. Projects should be within the speaker's present abilities so that he can handle them successfully. On the other hand, practicing only what can be done easily dulls initiative; therefore new challenges should be introduced as the individual improves. Each practice period should have a definite, well-chosen objective. It is impractical to try to improve all aspects of speech at the same time.

3.
UNDERSTANDING THE
SPEECH SITUATION

A public speech, since it is heard but once by the listeners, must succeed when it is presented. To achieve acceptance the speech should be suited to the audience in choice of subject, treatment, and delivery. The more the speaker knows about his listeners, the better he can adapt his speech to them. Early teachers of speaking recommended an analysis of the audience; Aristotle, for example, gave a thorough analysis of the popular audience of Athens. Most modern authorities also stress the necessity of audience analysis.

An analysis approaching accuracy is admittedly difficult. Nevertheless, the speaker should attempt the task, for presenting a speech without analysis is like giving medicine without diagnosis. What would be the success of a doctor who prescribed aspirin for every patient? The speaker who prepares a speech without knowledge of his audience can succeed only by chance.

The essential purpose of audience analysis is to find what the speaker and his listeners have in common according to background, experience, ideals, hopes, and loyalties. In this soil the speaker plants and cultivates new ideas and realizations. Certain things are true of any audience. It is made up of individual hearers who usually have a reason for listening to the speaker. Each individual tends to react both mentally and emotionally to what he hears, and each listener affects the response of others. The listening situation may thus create a group response. Unless the tendency is disturbed, listeners tend to think along with the speaker.

American audiences generally have many ideas in common. They believe in democracy, individualism, success, education, and justice. These common ideas are not, however, as simple as they seem. For example, Americans believe in free enterprise, but tend to favor government regulation; they believe in earning money, but lavishly give money away to those who are unable to earn it. The speaker should not depend on the general characteristics of audiences but should seek as much information as possible about the specific audience he is planning to address. Even if he is unable to learn more significant facts in advance, his efforts to do so will help him concentrate on his listeners and thus make his speech more genuinely communicative.

SOURCES OF INFORMATION

The person extending the invitation to speak can probably furnish information about the listeners, including other speakers and subjects heard and enjoyed by them. If the speech is one of a series, the speaker might possibly attend another meeting and make his own observations of the audience. When invited to address a special group, the speaker can usually confer with a member of the group or with someone who has had dealings with it. Publications or trade journals read by members of the organization can also be consulted. If the listeners are citizens in one area, local viewpoints and attitudes are sometimes obtained from key residents. A few issues of local newspapers will furnish an idea of current problems, cultural events, and matters of public interest. The editorial pages should be checked for evidence of the policy and political bias of the papers.

The public library is an important source of information. Books and articles on the states and various communities are available. These deal with such matters as economic conditions, population trends, political beliefs, and other group attitudes. Published public-opinion polls may yield clues to local concepts; census reports will furnish data on sex, age, occupation, education, and other population characteristics.

AUDIENCE CHARACTERISTICS

The speaker needs information about his listeners in order to prepare a speech that will arouse predictable reactions. Such advance information comprises physical and psychological characteristics of the audience.

Physical Characteristics. The physical composition of the audience can only be estimated, since the size and nature of the audience will not be actual facts until the time of the speech. Nevertheless, this information is an important factor in speech planning. The speaker must be prepared and willing to make necessary changes in his speech when he actually faces his audience.

Age. Human needs, interests, problems, and attitudes vary with age. Young people are relatively easy to impress because their minds are not already made up about the world and their relationship to it. Many subjects are novel and absorbing in themselves and can be presented directly and seriously without the necessity of constant variety. A speech on securities, including what they are, how they differ from bank savings, and how they are bought and sold would be informative. The information could be enlivened by examples of stocks that produced fortunes for their owners, proxy fights, and stocks based on the exploration of space.

Mature people are concerned with present needs and future security, including better homes, social status, and the education of their children. Mature minds are more certain of what they believe and do not respond quickly to suggestion. They think things over, see discrepancies, and demand proof for assertions. Adults are seriously involved in economic and social responsibilities and enjoy the compensations of variety, humor, and human interest stories. To this audience, securities offer methods of building future capital and income. Effective illustrations would be specific companies in growth industries whose management is far-seeing and aggressive.

Older persons have solidified their habits, interests, and points of view and are not easily swayed. Being comparatively disillusioned, they enjoy humor and appreciate the ironic view of things, but are highly critical and do not expect or accept radical and sudden changes. Older people, however, value and appreciate good feelings, good deeds, and good motives. Older listeners would be interested in securities as a source of steady income. High class bonds, preferred stocks, and guaranteed stocks are appealing because they offer safety of principal. The best illustrations for this audience would be high-grade securities offering reasonable income.

Sex. Although research has shown that women are more easily persuaded than men, this does not help much in aiming a subject to them. Men and women are alike in so many ways that probably the best way to approach the sex factor is to look at the particular interests and backgrounds of both women and men. Their family, business, and professional career orientations need to be considered.

Size of the Audience. The approximate size of the audience is important information for the speaker. A large group is usually easier to motivate than a small one; each member becomes part of the group and tends to forget his personal feelings. This group awareness makes the individual a better listener and makes him respond more freely to the speaker's ideas. A small audience, on the other hand, is less subject to group feeling. Each listener tends to respond personally to the speaker. The speaker can more easily establish rapport with an audience sitting close together rather than widely dispersed. If a small number of listeners are scattered about the room, the speaker should ask them to move together and sit directly in front of him. A small space well-filled is better than a large one half-filled.

Bodily Condition of Listeners. Listeners who are rested and alert respond differently from those who are fatigued or well fed. The occupations of the listeners and the hour of the speech may affect the speaker's treatment of his material. Strong emphasis and marked contrast in the development of ideas and in the delivery of the speech are needed to arouse tired listeners to a complete response.

Psychological Characteristics. The mental abilities and attitudes of an audience should be estimated beyond the clues offered by age and sex.

Intelligence. The ability of listeners to learn and the capacity to profit by what is learned vary from high to low. Communities can often provide indications of the intelligence level of its citizens. A progressive well-managed town, industries requiring highly skilled personnel, large museums, concert halls, and fine homes are signs of above average intelligence. Intelligent individuals think clearly and are receptive to new ideas and solutions to problems. A static or unchanging town, having buildings and homes in poor repair, lacking cultural facilities, and offering low-skilled jobs, indicates a population of lower intelligence. A speech, to be successful with such an audience, must appeal to their wants and emotions and make ample use of suggestion.

Education. The amount of formal education is an indication of audience receptivity. Highly educated listeners, for example, appreciate intellectual and moral values and are slow to respond to obvious emotional aspects. Less educated listeners value common sense and are moved by emphatic statement, practical illustrations, and familiar feelings.

Background of Experience.   Besides their formal education individuals acquire knowledge and skill in their occupations. Doctors, lawyers, and teachers are always learning by experience. The same thing is true of salespeople, executives, designers, and builders. The nature of a person's vocation often has a limiting effect on his range of interests and ideas.

Avocations are also a significant part of experience. Many executive careers, it is said, are charted on the golf course. Some hobbies like chess, music, foreign-language study, and book-collecting are predominantly mental, while others, such as swimming, tennis, skating, and bowling, are predominantly physical.

Cultural Status.   An audience may be composed of moderately or highly cultured persons. Do they or their communities support artistic and other cultural interests? Do they read books and magazines or just newspapers? Do they travel? The answers to such questions will affect the planning of the speech.

Marital Status.   Married listeners will probably be strongly concerned with family and community affairs. Unmarried listeners, students, and professional people will probably be interested in business and professional opportunities, hobbies, personal improvement, and social contacts.

Affiliations.   The interests and attitudes of the audience are also shown by their membership in church groups, political parties, social clubs, business associations, and professional organizations. The speaker should know and respect the fundamental beliefs of such groups in order to avoid antagonizing group loyalties.

Knowledge of the Subject.   The speaker should estimate from available sources how much the audience already knows about his subject. Has there been evidence of public opinion in recent local events or in newspaper editorials? If the subject is unfamiliar, the speaker must develop it carefully with definition, explanation, and familiar illustrations and analogies. If the subject is familiar, the audience will be bored unless the speech is developed in a fresh and colorful manner.

Familiarity of the Speaker.   A local speaker will be well known to his listeners. A famous person will also be known. Even if the speaker is unknown the audience will have some information about him gained from advance publicity or from the reputation of the sponsors of the talk. The speaker also may be considered favorably or unfavorably according to the audience attitude toward his subject.

TYPES OF AUDIENCES

An analysis of all the information about the audience that can be acquired will probably show that it is one of five types: friendly, indifferent, uninitiated, neutral, or hostile. The speech is then planned for the expected type of audience.

Friendly Audiences. In a friendly audience the listeners will be favorable to the subject and will probably agree with the speaker. They will not be difficult to convince. The speaker can be one with his listeners and identify himself closely with them; he uses "we" throughout his speech. If he is presenting ideas that they already know and believe, he develops them with gusto, using illustrations which his listeners can identify with themselves. However, if his topic is unfamiliar to his audience, the speaker uses their approving attitude to make commanding statements as an authority on his subject. Then he proceeds to his main task, perhaps stirring them to action by picturing it as more desirable than lethargy.

Indifferent Audiences. If an audience is indifferent, the speaker stimulates his listeners to awaken their interest in the topic. Why the topic is important is shown and how it involves their wants, needs, hopes, and ideals. The speaker suggests common ground by using the "we" and "you" approach. He uses vivid illustrations and enthusiastic delivery to keep the speech forceful, fast-moving, and alive. An indifferent audience cannot be easily persuaded. Although shock treatment may be successful, the appeal to listeners should not be overemotional. The speaker tries to get the audience to react in some favorable way, because any suitable reaction will open the door to further receptivity.

Uninitiated Audiences. Uninitiated listeners know nothing about the subject but are willing to listen and acquire information. The speaker instructs them by presenting information in a clear, accurate, and interesting way. Commanding statements will have little effect and emotional appeals will be futile until the groundwork for them is laid. The purpose should be clearly stated and all important terms carefully explained. Frequent summaries and transitions are needed. Stories, examples, and testimonials are better than mere statements. Specific facts, lively descriptions, and imaginative language will help make the topic part of the listeners' actual experience.

Neutral Audiences.   Listeners are neutral because they are open-minded; they have not made up their minds about the topic. They want information and illumination; they expect the speaker to give them facts and carefully reasoned opinions. To have an open mind means to be interested and capable of change without emotional hostility to the speaker's case. The speaker's purpose is to explain his viewpoint and to persuade his audience to accept it. Proof should make the idea more appealing than indecision, doubt, or neutrality. Neutral auditors are less likely to respond to "togetherness" or emotional stimulation than to suitable data. They want the truth, and truth rests on evidence. When listeners do not all have the same viewpoint or when the speaker does not know their viewpoint, it is probably best to treat the audience as neutral.

Hostile Audiences.   The hearers in a hostile audience are critical of the speaker and opposed to his beliefs and conclusions; therefore, the speaker should have dependable data and as many unassailable facts as possible. The talk should begin with material that cannot be challenged. The strongest argument is offered first to establish a common ground of agreement. Tact should be used as well as fact: the speaker presents this strongest argument as belonging to the listeners' point of view with which he agrees. From this favorable foothold he goes on to ideas that his listeners might accept if shown that they vitally affect their interests. In 1863 Henry Ward Beecher faced an extremely hostile audience in Liverpool, England. British sentiment was running strong against the North in the Civil War. Beecher's problem was to gain support for the Union by turning his audience against slavery. He did so by pointing out to his listeners, who were dependent upon commerce, that slavery was a detriment to international trade.

Argument is reduced by using concession to a hostile audience. The good qualities of competing plans and products are admitted. The speaker makes his own claims conservative, but qualifies them carefully and states them exactly. The subject is developed so that

listeners will forget their objections. The speaker refuses to feel hostile
and does not try too strenuously to convince. Listeners are allowed
to explore the idea with him and thus to persuade themselves in
the process. A hostile audience will be more likely to be convinced
if presented with two sides of a question. By being fair the speaker
will go a long way in removing hostility. He must make the audience
want to believe differently or must try to establish some motivating
factor. These motivations can later be reinforced and developed until
the audience has a new set of attitudes toward the proposition.

NATURE OF THE SITUATION

A speech must be suited to the occasion, or rather to the audience
assembled upon that occasion. Analyzing the situation is in a sense
an extension of audience analysis. The situation is important to the
speaker because it affects the expectations and reactions of the listeners.

Purpose of the Meeting.   The occasion may be a regular meeting of a group or one of a series of special meetings. Or it may be
a specially called or single public meeting. Members of a group who
meet regularly are probably well-informed about the purpose and
advisability of the meeting. Listeners at a single public meeting will
presumably know about its purpose from advance publicity. Audience
expectations will be homogeneous if the whole group has formulated
the purpose of the meeting, and fairly homogeneous if the planning
was done by a program committee. If the purpose was decided by
an extraneous agency or by the speaker himself, audience expectations
will be more difficult to gauge.

It should be ascertained whether the occasion commemorates an
event in national, state, or local history or celebrates an achievement
of the community or special group. The speaker then estimates audience interest and concern in the event so as to adapt his speech in
a suitable manner. The speaker also seeks to discover whether the
audience expects to be predominantly instructed, entertained, or persuaded so that he can formulate the purpose of his speech.

The Program.   The speaker needs to know whether or not he
will be the only speaker and what is scheduled to precede and follow
his address. Music, cocktails, a banquet, or other features may influence the mood of the audience. If there are to be other speakers,

the subjects and purposes of their talks should be learned. A speech that is to be the main feature of the program requires a fuller treatment than a speech that is one of several. In all cases the speaker should find out the time allowed for his speech as well as the probable length of the whole program. When taking part in a long program, the wise speaker stays strictly within his time limit. If the audience is to participate, the speaker must be prepared to answer questions and offset arguments after his speech.

The Setting. The place of the speech will have an effect upon the listeners, and so will the time of day, the location of the hall, and means of transportation. The size, shape, and appearance of the room should be suited to the expected audience. A huge hall with a lofty ceiling may create a forbidding atmosphere that dwarfs the speaker and the listeners. A smaller room suggests a more intimate and cheerful atmosphere. The room should be properly heated and ventilated so that listeners will be comfortable and ready to listen.

The room's acoustics should be investigated, and the speaker should make sure that he can be heard clearly. If the room sounds dead or has unwelcome reverberations, the speaker is less likely to be disturbed by the fact if he knows it in advance. The use of the microphone for a public address system or broadcasting equipment is discussed in Chapter 16.

The lighting should enable the audience to see the speaker clearly and also allow the speaker to observe facial expressions and other physical reactions of his listeners. If footlights or spotlights are used, the speaker will not see his listeners and cannot adjust his presentation to their reactions. The speaker should find out whether he will speak from a platform or from floor level, and also whether a lectern is available. Knowing the seating arrangement and the distance between the audience and himself enables the speaker to prepare and rehearse his speech more adequately.

Prevailing Customs. The community, the sponsoring organization, or the nature of the occasion may indicate certain things that a speaker should or should not do. The speaker should inquire what is expected from him in matters of dress, manner of delivery, and use of language and diction. He should also know whether he will receive a fee and whether the audience will pay admission. Important also is the degree of formality of the occasion. Will the meeting be regulated by parliamentary procedure, individual bylaws, informal rules, or no rules at all? In addition, is the speaker to walk out and greet his audience or is he to be presented by a chairperson? In the latter case the speaker must decide what information to furnish the chairperson for his introduction.

4.
SELECTING AND EXPLORING THE SUBJECT

The worth of a speech depends upon the choice of subject and its treatment. A speaker's task is not to originate or create ideas but to make existing information and ideas understandable and valuable to his listeners. The speaker's originality is revealed in the way he selects and treats his subject. His treatment involves analysis and synthesis; the latter includes limiting the subject, determining the specific goal, choosing a title, gathering materials to support the specific purpose, and arranging materials under main and subordinate ideas.

SELECTING THE SUBJECT

Since the speech must arouse a desirable response in the audience, a good subject is highly important. A well-chosen subject fulfills several requirements; it is suited to the speaker, to the audience, to the occasion, and to the time limit.

Suited to the Speaker. The subject should be of vital interest to the speaker. If he is not enthusiastic about it, how can he hope to spark a reaction in his listeners? The subject should be part of the speaker's previous knowledge and also be one about which he can find additional information. Every individual is surrounded by materials that can be used for speeches; their familiarity should not cause them to be overlooked. The speaker's storehouse of knowledge, observation, and experience, his work, hobbies, and studies should be considered along with special accomplishments and any previous jobs he has had. Subjects can also be found in the speaker's own thoughts and impressions, his own reactions to books, persons, and events. A subject should have special significance for him; no one else should speak about it as he does.

Suited to the Audience.   Audience analysis, as explained in the preceding chapter, helps the speaker estimate the interest and receptivity of a given group of listeners. All adults would probably be interested in new income tax regulations, while only owners of foreign stocks would be concerned with new amendments to the Securities and Exchange Act approved by the House Interstate and Foreign Commerce Committee. Lawyers would readily hear a talk on "Is the Supreme Court Going Too Far?" and P.T.A. members are a likely audience for raising funds for a school library. Young working women would be interested in the subject "Dressing Well on a Limited Budget," but who would think that male college students would enjoy a talk on "How to Make a Dress?" One young woman, whose hobby was dressmaking, thought so and gave an illustrated talk on this subject to an audience composed largely of men. The talk was very well done and very well received.

Suited to the Occasion.   In cases where a subject has not been assigned to the speaker, an analysis of the occasion helps him to choose a suitable topic. The occasion also guides him in treating both assigned and unassigned subjects. The locale of the speech is an important source of ideas: Texas and Vermont, Chicago and St. Petersburg, Atlantic City and Palm Beach suggest different points of view and contrasting topics.

The date of the speech, such as a national holiday, may put the audience into a certain mood, into a special state of expectation. Halloween and Ash Wednesday suggest different types of subjects. As commencement time approaches, graduating seniors are more interested in "How to Pass Examinations" than ever before. Before Election Day union workers wish to find out which candidate their leaders recommend. Obviously, a speech does not have to be based on special-day traditions. Other interests also exist; other events have transpired on those dates. Isaac Newton (1642), for instance, was born on Christmas Day, Nathaniel Hawthorne (1804) and Calvin Coolidge (1872) on the Fourth of July. A dictionary of dates, almanacs, yearbooks, and calendars of special events list events and anniversaries of all kinds. These can suggest political, business, social, scientific, religious, or other subjects. Every day of the year can have significance for the inquiring speaker.

Suited to the Time Limit. A scheduled speech is for a definite number of minutes. It should be treated competently in the allotted time. Broad or complicated topics, such as "The Vietnam War" or "The Causes of Business Cycles," cannot be discussed in a few minutes. A speaker who doubts this should prepare adequate notes for such a speech or make an outline of his main and supporting ideas. He will find that it takes several minutes to read his notes or outline aloud. The mere citation of a list of points is not a speech. Ideas must be explained and illustrated so that they are vivid and meaningful. For example, "Mexico: Its Economic Growth in the Last Ten Years" would require at least a half-hour to do it justice. In twenty minutes, several tax regulations might be explained; in five minutes, one regulation is all that could be discussed. In three minutes a safety expert can give sufficient information on "The First Minute After You Discover a Fire." An interesting incident might be told in two minutes, a joke in one minute.

ANALYZING THE SUBJECT

Analysis is the process of dividing a subject into its parts. Such division enables the relative importance of the parts to be seen and makes possible a judicious limitation of the subject. Some subjects fall easily into natural or logical divisions, but all divisions are the result of some basis of analysis. Human beings are divided by sex into men and women, by age into children, adolescents, and adults. For speech subjects, the main bases of division are time, space, function, cause, and physical characteristics.

Division by Time. Some subjects can be analyzed into a sequence or series of parts. A story consists of events or episodes that happen one after the other. A mechanical or creative process, such as the Carbon 14 process in dating archaeological objects, or the growing of miniature trees, is composed of activities performed in succession. As a rule historical and biographical subjects are also divided into periods of time.

Division by Space. Certain topics can be divided into areas or locations. Ocean currents are separated into surface and undersea currents, surface currents into Atlantic, Pacific, and Indian ocean currents. Subjects concerning geography, geology, anthropology, and descriptions of various kinds are often divided according to space.

Division by Function. Use or activity furnishes a basis for analysis of certain subjects. The human body is divided into functional systems, such as circulatory, digestive, and reproductive. A retail organization is separated into purchasing, sales, accounting, and other departments. Human activities as a whole are divided by function into types or fields of action, such as social, scientific, and artistic.

Division by Cause. Division by cause is analysis by cause, effect, or both and is used for many informative and persuasive subjects. For example, in a speech to inform, the division is into causes of the event or condition. In a speech to persuade, the results predicted are separated into types or areas of application.

Division by Physical Characteristics. Physical attributes or qualities form a practical basis for division. Matter is thus divided into animate and inanimate. According to more specific physical qualities matter is also divided into the elements. Physical characteristics include less tangible qualities like beauty, strength, and skill.

LIMITING THE SUBJECT

The process of division, which reveals the main aspects or principles of a subject, provides the speaker with his main ideas and assertions. Every speech should be complete in itself and satisfying to the listeners' understanding. Some completed subjects contain a confusing or burdensome number of main ideas or divisions. Such a topic should be limited so that it can be discussed more precisely. The speaker, instead of saying a little about a lot of the subject, says a lot about a little of the subject.

Limiting is done by reducing the number of main concepts. These main ideas should be written down and carefully considered. The most important ideas are then selected and the rest rejected. For example, sound recording is divided into four types or procedures:

sound waves actuate a cutting device to press mechanically into a plastic record; sound waves are transformed into electrical impulses which are amplified and used to actuate a mechanical cutting device; sound waves are amplified electrically and made to vary the size or intensity of a light beam which is photographed on film; sound waves are amplified and made to magnetize a magnetic substance according to variations in the structure of the sound. The last method is highly important from the standpoint of the widespread use of recording tapes, but the first method has the more important advantage of being more readily understood by the average audience. Consequently, the first method is chosen as the limited subject of the speech, and is divided, in turn, into its components or main ideas.

DETERMINING THE SPECIFIC PURPOSE

The subject of the speech should not be handled in a general, roundabout, or indefinite manner, but should be made specific. A good speech has not only a subject and a general purpose but also an object or specific purpose. The specific purpose must be carefully chosen in order to keep both speaker and audience from wandering off the main road into vague byways. The exercise of critical judgment in choosing and stating the specific purpose of the speech is thus an additional way of limiting the subject. The specific purpose should be based on the speaker's nature and experience as indicated by his answers to the following questions: Are you inclined to explain things to other persons? To get people to share your ideas? To urge others to do things? The specific purpose is also adjusted to the audience, place, and time limit.

The specific purpose is what the speaker wants his audience to know, feel, believe, or do. It should be precise and limited to what the speaker can reasonably hope to accomplish. It can be worded in two ways, as a statement of the speaker's intention or as the central idea or essence of the subject.

The statement of the speaker's intention is expressed in terms of desired audience reaction and is labeled *Specific Purpose*. It does not merely say, for example, that listeners are to contribute to the Community Chest, but tells them exactly how to contribute: sign up at work; give to volunteer canvassers who will call at their homes; or send contributions to a specified address. The following are examples of Specific Purposes: To give a clear explanation of the sense of equilibrium; To stimulate interest and support for educational television; To describe the extraordinary experience of reading *The Brothers Karamazov;* To point out that bicycling is a healthful recreation.

The statement of the central idea of the subject is expressed in terms of the stimulus for audience reaction and is labeled *Subject Sentence, Topic Sentence,* or *Purpose Sentence.* It may be worded as a definition, proposition, question, or in any form that expresses the central idea. The following are Subject Sentences: The sense of equilibrium is an ingenious process; To enjoy cultural television without commercials, send your contribution to Channel 13, WNET, Newark, N.J.; When you finish reading *The Brothers Karamazov* you will not be the same person as when you began it.

SELECTING A TITLE

The speech should be given an appropriate title, since speeches are often announced in advance. The title should make prospective listeners want to hear the speech. It should be interesting, reasonably short, and consistent with the specific purpose of the speech. Many effective titles are epigrammatic, provocative, or paradoxical. A single word title, such as "Reincarnation" or "Existentialism," is too brief and general to arouse interest. Long titles, on the other hand, whether pedantic or original, are usually ineffective or misleading: "Conditions and Events That Contributed to the Crisis in Panama," "Shall We Shift the Blame for Juvenile Delinquency Clear Back to Adam and Eve?" The following recent speeches have effective titles: "Have It Your Way," by Elizabeth B. Bolton; "What We Don't Know Can Hurt Us," by John W. Hanley; "Pardon Me . . . Your Knee Is on My Chest!" by J. W. Marriott, Jr.

GATHERING MATERIALS

The speaker gathers materials by searching for ideas, illustrations, or arguments with which to build the speech. Suitable and pertinent speech material is anything which will develop or establish the specific purpose of the speech. It is important to keep in mind the main points to which the subject has been limited, for it is to support these that materials must be gathered.

Kinds of Material. Two important types of material are facts and testimony. Facts in speaking are acts, events, and things known to have existence. They include examples, illustrations, figures, and statistics. Testimony includes declarations of facts by witnesses and interpretations of facts by recognized experts. Using different kinds of supporting materials creates greater interest.

Sources of Material. The speaker himself is the first source of material. He should take stock of what he knows about the topic and what experiences he has had which relate to it or illustrate it. A search of his own experience will reveal gaps in his knowledge and stimulate him to investigate his subject further.

People can often supply material. It is helpful to introduce the topic into conversations and discussions and listen to what others say about it, to ask questions and get reactions from those who are well informed or specially interested in the topic. This can be done by letter if a personal interview is not possible. Radio and television programs, motion pictures, lectures, and public meetings are other sources of material. Unless the subject is one in which the speaker is an expert, he will need to gather information about it from printed sources. Reading is the practical way to find speech materials. No speaker should be satisfied with one magazine article, but should continue reading widely until he has a thorough and comprehensive grasp of his topic.

Using the Library. The quickest and most convenient access to printed matter is the library. Its wealth of material can be frustrating unless the speaker knows how to locate information pertinent to his purpose. Should there be any problem in finding pertinent material, consult the librarians; they are willing to assist. Also, an excellent source is Constance M. Winchell's *Guide to Reference Books.*

The Card Catalogue. All books in a library and many pamphlets and bulletins are listed in the card catalogue. A book usually has a card in three places: under the author's name, under the title, and under the subject. Each publication has a call number which is indicated on a call slip in order to get the book from the librarian, or which will direct the reader to a particular section if the library has open stacks.

Books are valuable sources for all but the most recent information and they are more thorough and authoritative than magazine articles. The publication data of a book indicates whether its contents are up to date. Except for certain authoritative works, the latest books are probably of the most value. The table of contents and index of a book are checked for the specific topic. If the book includes a bibliography, it may list additional sources of information. The annual *Subject Guide to Books in Print* is invaluable for locating books on particular topics.

Encyclopedias. The following encyclopedias are listed in the card file of most libraries and are located on specific reference shelves or in a reference room: *Encyclopaedia Britannica, Encyclopedia Americana, The New Encyclopaedia Britannica,* and the one-volume *Columbia Encyclopedia.* Other excellent works include the *Encyclopedia of the Social Sciences, An Encyclopedia of World History,* and the McGraw-Hill *Encyclopedia of Science and Technology.*

Magazines. For a brief treatment of a topic and for current points of view, periodicals are generally more useful than books. To locate material in leading magazines the following reference works, which list by subject and author, are consulted: *Poole's Guide to Periodical Literature* (before 1902) and *Reader's Guide to Periodical Literature.* For articles in more specialized journals these guides are used: the *International Index to Periodicals,* the *Educational Index,* the *Agricultural Index,* the *Art Index,* and the *Industrial Arts Index.* Similar guides are available for other specialized fields. The *Annual Magazine Subject Index* catalogues many periodicals not listed in other indexes. Material on current events can be found in leading magazines, such as *The Altantic, Harper's Magazine, New Republic, The Nation, Reader's Digest, Saturday Review, The Yale Review, Time, Fortune, Newsweek,* and *U.S. News and World Report.* Material on both sides of controversial issues can be obtained in the *Congressional Digest,* which is in magazine form, and the *Reference Shelf,* which is in book form. *The Congressional Record* is the official government publication of debates in Congress, speeches and remarks of members, and annual messages of the president of the United States.

Book Reviews. The *Book Review Digest,* issued bimonthly, offers brief evaluations of books published and reviewed since 1905. The desired material is found in the volume for the year in which the book was published.

Pamphlets and Bulletins. The *Public Affairs Information Service Bulletin* lists special studies published as pamphlets and bulletins. Many of these are also listed in the card catalogue of the library.

Quotations. A speaker may need to find the author or the exact wording of a quotation. The standard works are Bartlett's *Familiar Quotations* and Stevenson's *Home Book of Quotations, Classical and Modern.* Other good references include Benham's *Book of Quotations, Proverbs and Household Words,* Evans' *Dictionary of Quotations,* and the *Oxford Dictionary of Quotations.* Concordances are available for the works of many authors, such as Bartlett's for Shakespeare, in which the principal words used are listed with their contexts.

Statistics. Statistical information and specific facts can often be found in the *Statistical Abstract of the United States,* the *Statesman's Year Book, The New International Year Book, The World Almanac,* and the *Information Please Almanac.*

Biographies. Information about living persons is found in the following: *Who's Who* (England), *Who's Who in America,* and the regional volumes *Who's Who in the East, Who's Who in the Midwest, Who's Who in the South and Southwest,* and *Who's Who in the West.* Also to be consulted are *Who's Who in Education,* the *Directory of American Scholars, Current Biography,* and *Twentieth Century Authors.* Authoritative and detailed information about prominent deceased persons can be found in the *Dictionary of National Biography* (British) and the *Dictionary of American Biography.*

Recent News. A speaker should know how to find current local, national, and international news. Although newspapers take sides politically, there are some that have achieved a reputation for objectivity, such as *The New York Times, The Christian Science Monitor,* and the *London Times.* Newspaper articles on various subjects can be located by means of the annual indexes of *The New York Times* and the *London Times.*

Efficient Research. The speaker might begin his reading with an encyclopedia article; many such articles end with a bibliography listing important references which can be checked in the card catalogue in the library. Each book selected is looked over quickly to see whether it contains usable material. Skimming through the sections dealing with the topic will reveal passages worth careful reading; these are read closely and critically.

The following suggestions for careful reading should be helpful to the speaker. (1) Actual words should be read and their meaning understood. Unfamiliar terms should be looked up in a dictionary. The true gist of the passage is essential. It should be carefully noted whether the true meaning depends on qualifying words and expressions, such as *not, never, seldom, most, frequently, probably,* and *on the whole.* (2) Definite facts should be sifted out and checked with other authorities. Facts are also tested by judging the author's data, the soundness of his reasoning, and the setting or context of his statement. (3) Vague expressions and emotional convictions should not be accepted as actual facts. (4) Reading should be done with an open mind. All the facts and opinions of the subject should be gathered, not just those that agree with the speaker's own ideas. The opposite point of view should be carefully analyzed. This may or may not cause the speaker to change his mind, but close thinking will give him a better understanding of his subject. (5) Appropriate and accurate notes taken during reading and research will supply adequate material to support the specific purpose of the speech. Furthermore, an audience has more confidence in a speaker who presents material from definite sources.

Taking Notes. Taking notes as material is found has several advantages over depending on memory. Information is available in tangible form so that the speaker will not forget to use it. Time and effort will be saved as he will be able to recall information without going back to the source. Details, such as figures and quotations, will be accurate. Finally, new aspects and ways of handling the subject are often suggested by jotting down notes.

Good note-taking follows a consistent and accurate plan. Notes should be recorded on cards or slips of paper of uniform size. Cards are better, for they are more durable than slips and allow the notes to be more easily classified and arranged in order. A single item or fact is noted on each card. The topic and the main division or subdivision under which the item belongs is indicated at the top of the card. The complete source of the entry is given at the bottom of the card.

D'Annunzio as Political
Speaker

Candidate for
Ortona in 1898

Expressed capitalist beliefs late in campaign; speech later known as "Hedge Speech" because hedge used as symbol for property protection: "Few things in the world seem so full of meaning, so eternal, so inviolable, as the hedge. And by that, I do not mean the rural one, with flowers and berries in it, and nests built into it, pearly with dew—but the circular thing which surrounds a man's property, which protects all that he has justly earned . . ." p. 82.

Anthony Rhodes, *D'Annunzio: The Poet as Superman* (New York: McDowell and Obolensky, 1959)[1]

Figure 1. Sample card.

Citing Sources. The various types of sources are cited in the following manner so that they can be quickly found and checked in the future.

Book. Author's name as it appears on the title page, complete title of the book, volume number (if more than one), edition (unless it is the first one), place of publication, publisher, and date of copyright: Joseph A. DeVito, *Communicology: An Introduction to the Study of Communication* (New York: Harper & Row, 1978).

Magazine Article. Author's full name, complete title of the article, name of the magazine, month and year of publication, volume number, and inclusive pages of the article: William R. Brown, "Ideology as Communication Process," *Quarterly Journal of Speech,* April 1978, 64:123–140.

Encyclopedia Article. Author's full name (if listed), complete title of article, date of edition, volume, and inclusive pages of the article. Some encyclopedias have unsigned articles. Others give the author's initials at the end of the article, and his full name can be found in the list of contributors in the front matter of the first

---

[1] Copyright © 1959 by Anthony Rhodes. Reprinted here by permission of Ivan Obolensky.

volume: S. I. Hayakawa, "Semantics," *Encyclopaedia Britannica,*
1955, 313–313D.

Works by Several Authors. Full names of all authors, followed by
the information listed for a book or article: Jerry W. Koehler,
Karl W. E. Anatol, and Ronald L. Applbaum, *Organizational
Communication: Behavioral Perspectives* (New York: Holt, Rinehart & Winston, 1976).

Anthology. If the book is a collection or anthology, the editor's name
is listed in place of an author: William Clarke, ed., *Political Orations
From Wentworth to Macaulay* (London: Walter Scott, no date).

Pamphlet. Author or name of group gathering and writing the information, title, name of the organization that published it, date,
and inclusive pages if the pamphlet includes more than one article
or subject: Bloomfield, Lincoln Palmer, *The Peaceful Uses of Space*
(New York: Public Affairs Committee, 1962), Public Affairs Pamphlet No. 331.

Newspaper. Author's name (if given), type of story (feature, column,
editorial, etc.), name of paper, date, and page number: Jane E.
Brody, "Latest Data Suggest Exercise Helps Curb Heart Attacks,"
The New York Times, March 27, 1979, pp. C1–2.

Radio or Television Broadcast. Speaker's name, title of program, date,
broadcasting company, and sponsor of the program: Leslie Nielsen,
narrator, "Thor Heyerdahl and the Tigris," *National Geographic,*
April 1, 1979, 8:00 P.M., Channel 13, WNET.

Interview. Name of the person interviewed, name of the interviewer,
and date: Joseph Stalin, interviewed by H. G. Wells, July 23,
1934.

Letter. Name of the writer, name of the addressee, and date: Aaron
Burr to Alexander Hamilton, New York, June 22, 1804.

Basic Methods of Note-Taking. There are two basic methods
of taking notes. The first is to make an abstract of the whole article
or book. Such an abstract suggests the continuity of the author's
thought, but it may record a great deal of unwanted material. The
second is to make notes of the pertinent and important points in
the work consulted. These notes will give usable material for the
speech, but may ignore the relation of a point to the author's basic
concepts. Each method has its advantages, but the pitfalls just mentioned should be kept in mind.

Types of Notes.   A note is either a direct quotation of an author's words or a paraphrase or summary. Striking statements of an idea may be worth quoting directly in the speech. Each word-for-word excerpt is enclosed in quotation marks. Any omitted words in a quotation are shown by points of ellipsis (. . .). If the quotation contains a seemingly incorrect word, this is shown by inserting the word *sic* in brackets after the error:

> *Hood cannot stand even a drawn battle, so far from his supplies of ordnance stores. If he retreats and you follow him he must loose* [sic] *his material and much of his Army . . . Delay no longer for weather, or reinforcements.*—From a letter by LT. GEN. ULYSSES S. GRANT to MAJ. GEN. GEORGE H. THOMAS, City Point, Va., Dec. 11, 1864.

If a quoted passage contains explanatory words by an editor or someone else, these words are enclosed in brackets:

> *It would then be necessary either not to make tnem* [i.e., gestures] *at all under similar circumstances in a public speech, or to make very few of them; for everything the speaker does ought to follow nature.*— *Fenelon's Dialogues on Eloquence,* translation and introduction by WILBER SAMUEL HOWELL.

When paraphrasing or summarizing, the speaker must be sure that he does not change the author's meaning. The condensation should be checked for faithfulness to the thought and point of view of the source.

When a lengthy work is consulted, each chapter is sampled by reading headings and topic sentences. If it contains usable material, it is then read from the beginning. Several pages are read before notes are made. Every sentence or paragraph is not worth a note. Only the important thoughts or points should be transcribed. Jotting down the bare topic is insufficient; what is said in support of the topic is also noted. The essential points that show the development of the thought are picked out and abridged as much as possible. Details are omitted except important names, dates, and examples. To save time, short phrases are used instead of full sentences. Abbreviations and shortcuts help, provided the speaker can understand them later.

Arranging Notes.   As the research progresses, the subject is divided into subheadings. Further reading and note-taking may require additional main headings and subheadings. Finally, the cards are sorted and grouped into the main headings, and the subheadings are arranged in logical order under the proper main headings. The notes are then studied and the ideas that will accomplish the specific purpose of the speech are selected.

5.
ORGANIZING THE SPEECH

A good speech is not a mass of ideas and details but an organized whole. Coherence is an absolute necessity: the speaker cannot remember disorganized ideas well enough to present them, nor can listeners remember helter-skelter ideas well enough to classify them into an understandable system. On the other hand, a unified structure of ideas repays the listener for his attention by keeping him from being distracted by unrelated details and by helping him to distinguish important ideas.

A good speech should have divisions and at the same time it should have unity. The division of a speech into introduction, body, and conclusion implies unity. This basic form has endured through the centuries because it is simple, adaptable to all purposes, and workable.

THE INTRODUCTION

The speaker must secure goodwill and audience respect the moment the speech begins. The introduction should be carefully planned with this aim in mind. The speaker's paramount concern is the individuals who are listening.

The introduction has two basic functions: to arouse the listeners' interest and to lead into the discussion or body of the speech. These two functions can be achieved by a single device or by a combination of devices. Most speeches include a method of creating interest and also a method of leading into the subject. Many speeches have a third function: to relate to the listeners' needs.

Methods of Creating Interest.   The first part of the introduction aims to command the immediate attention of the audience, establish a common ground between the speaker and his listeners, and prepare the audience for what is to follow. Interest-creating devices are of two sorts: preliminary remarks, which relate to the subject indirectly, and material which is directly related to the subject of the speech.

Preliminary Remarks. Initial remarks can take various forms. The speaker can acknowledge the chairperson's introduction; refer to something the preceding speaker said; say something relevant to the time, occasion, place, or audience; or refer to local persons or events. An interesting reference to place was offered by Dr. Heinz Nordhoff, President of the Volkswagenwerke, Wolfsburg, Germany, when he spoke at Boston University:

> *Coming to Boston has special meaning for me. To us Europeans, Boston means tradition, culture and education—concepts, I am afraid, that most of the world does not think of when America is mentioned.*
>
> *I am told that within an hour's drive of here there are more than 25 colleges. Such concentrated scholarship must create a highly refined atmosphere, proving the correctness of the European conception of Boston.*[1]

Lewis W. Foy referred to the date when speaking in Chicago one April 1:

> *It's traditional to kid around on April Fool's Day, but I'm not in the mood. It's hard to make jokes when your desk is piled high, not with problems, but* dilemmas. *A "dilemma" is a problem that* can't *be solved. The best you can do is decide on the lesser of two evils.*
>
> *I'm thinking about one of those dilemmas right now. I'm talking about trade—international trade—and more specifically* foreign steel imports.[2]

Introduction Related to the Subject. Some types of introductions not only arouse interest but can also suggest the subject.

QUESTION. Asking a question or questions is a good way to begin a speech provided the questions are unusual, stimulating, or challenging and are related in some manner to the subject. Since the interrogative introduction has been overworked in radio and television commercials, its use in public speaking demands originality and dis-

---

[1] *Vital Speeches,* XXIX, 4 (Dec. 1, 1962), p. 114.
[2] *Vital Speeches,* XLIII, 14 (May 1, 1977), p. 435.

crimination. Lewis H. Young, editor-in-chief of *Business Week*, used a question to open a speech on "Business and the Media":

> *If the Constitutional Convention were to be held in September 1978, instead of in 1787, would the people embrace such a broad First Amendment guaranteeing freedom of the press? My guess is they would not. Because in 1978, many segments of the American population are down on the press, criticize it, and sometimes are openly hostile.*[3]

STATEMENT. A series of strong, startling, or stimulating statements is a frequently used introduction. A speech by Cornell C. Maier on free enterprise began with an unusual announcement:

> *The free enterprise system is dying. We are gathered here around its deathbed. The initiative, the innovation, the hope and freedom that have given this country's people more of the fruits of life and liberty than mankind has ever enjoyed, are dying with it.*
>
> *In our deathwatch, as we sit meekly letting it happen, we should know that when it dies here, a long night of mediocrity will descend on us and our children.*[4]

QUOTATION. A quotation in itself may not interest the audience. The quotation used in an introduction must be related to the subject or to the audience's attitude toward the subject. Fred D. Silverman used a direct quotation to open a speech on "Censorship" delivered before the American Association of Advertising Agencies:

> *A few weeks ago I was on a panel with a disgruntled writer who apparently had scripts turned down by those impudent networks too nearsighted to spot his obvious genius. At one point in our discussion, he turned to me and with great affectation said, "Silverman, if Shakespeare brought you* Hamlet *you'd probably want to put a dog in the first act."*
>
> *Well, it was not a bad idea. Shakespeare was quite a showman. If he thought a dog would have improved the first act, he might have written one in himself.*
>
> *But the funny part of this story is that the writer who made that remark had sent me a script that I remembered rejecting myself. It was a story about a talking monkey.*
>
> *That is an example of the crazy contradiction running through much of the criticism of television today.*[5]

---

[3] *Vital Speeches*, XLV, 3 (Nov. 15, 1978), p. 73.

[4] *Vital Speeches*, XLIV, 6 (Jan. 1, 1978), p. 181.

[5] *Ibid.*, p. 175.

INCIDENT. An incident or a narrative can be used as an introduction. A famous and effective example is President Franklin D. Roosevelt's address to Congress on December 8, 1941, asking for a declaration of war against Japan. In a speech titled "The Little Platoon We Belong To in Society," Russell Kird used an incident as part of his introduction:

> On the cover of a textbook used last year by my little daughters in their parish school, there was printed the legend, "The family does things together." Over this line appeared a picture of a family doing things together. What were they doing together? Why, they were sitting in a semicircle, watching the television set.[6]

HUMOR. Wit and humor can help establish rapport between audience and speaker or it can serve as a bridge to the subject. Humor was used by President John F. Kennedy in the introduction of his speech on "Government and Business," delivered to the United States Chamber of Commerce at Washington on April 30, 1962.

> I want to congratulate you on your new president, President Plumley—and it's nice to have a president from Massachusetts, and we're glad to have him here.[7]

Leading into the Subject. The second phase of the introduction serves as a transition from the audience's first attention and interest to the body of the speech and presents the subject of the speech and the speaker's basic approach. Every introduction should make the subject of the speech definitely known. If the audience is kept too long in suspense over what is going to be discussed, the speech may seem rambling, confused, or lacking in purpose.

In many informative speeches the speaker can utter his purpose sentence or declare the central theme of his talk. For example, Antonio Segni, speaking before Congress, used a subject sentence: "The Atlantic alliance, which firmly binds our two countries, was born of a common determination to defend, not only a territory, but our liberty and our way of life."[8] Maj. Gen. Kenneth P. Bergquist led into his subject of a military career as follows: "I speak frankly in saying that even though the citizenry is supporting the largest peace-

---

[6] *Vital Speeches,* XLIV, 7 (Jan. 15, 1978), p. 200.

[7] *Vital Speeches,* XXVIII, 16 (June 1, 1962), p. 482.

[8] *Vital Speeches,* XXX, 9 (Feb. 15, 1964), p. 259.

time budget for defense in history, they do not know enough about our Armed Forces generally; and they do not know enough, specifically, about what a career in the military forces really means in today's world."[9]

In persuasive speeches other forms of transitional material are often desirable: the background of the topic, such as its importance or history, can be presented; terms essential to the subject can be explained; or the main ideas of the speech can be stated. To lead into a highly controversial subject, Joseph McDowell Mitchell, in his speech "The Revolt in Newburgh," asked a series of fourteen questions and gave a series of nineteen answers. This excerpt contains the last four questions and the first four answers:

> *What caused the special investigation by the State Board of Social Welfare of the State of New York into the operation of welfare in the City of Newburgh? What caused the New York State Attorney General to seek an injunction against us? What caused a New York State Supreme Court Judge to grant this injunction? What could a little City by the Hudson have done to have caused such a furor?*
>
> *We challenged the welfare state and everything it stood for.*
>
> *We challenged the minority voting bloc racket. We challenged the right of the state to interfere in local affairs. We seized the reins of home rule.*[10]

Relating to the Listeners' Needs.   This phase of the introduction points out how the subject concerns the listeners, how their needs and desires will be affected by it. In speeches where approval or action is desired, it is especially important to show the listeners that they have specific needs that will be met. Allen H. Neuharth's speech on "Future Directions in American Newspapers" delivered to a convention of journalists did this.

> *I assure you—despite what some doomsayers were saying a few years ago—newspapers do have a future, and it's a bright one. Decades from now, the presses will be roaring right on. . . .*
>
> *Some of our readers will be informed, some will be inspired, and some will even be satisfied by what they find in our newspapers. . . .*
>
> *The future of our newspapers depends on us, and it will be as strong, and as secure, as our professionalism can make it. . . .*

---

[9] *Vital Speeches*, XXX, 18 (July 1, 1964), p. 562.
[10] *Vital Speeches*, XXVIII, 7 (Jan. 15, 1962), p. 214.

So my message to you tonight is a challenge, a call to arms, a summons for strong defense.[11]

Common Weaknesses to Avoid. Several types of errors, which are made by many speakers, weaken the introduction and are best avoided. The speaker should not waste time saying he is here to talk; that is quite obvious. He should not open his speech with an apology, because the audience might question his ability to speak. The speaker should also shun irrelevant material or a "false" introduction that might mislead his listeners. He should not merely announce his topic, unless he wishes to make it provocative by its wording; otherwise, the audience might be immediately disinterested.

THE BODY

Most modern teachers agree that the speaker should prepare the body of the speech before deciding on the introduction, because he must know what he is talking about before he can introduce it. The body is the core of the speech, the substance of the discussion, in which the speaker accomplishes his specific purpose. The body of the speech has two major functions: to explain the subject, topic, or theme and to establish the subject in the minds of the listeners.

The main, secondary, and supporting ideas must be organized in an appropriate pattern if the speech is to be effective. A pattern of organization is a method of controlling attention, a plan for moving the awareness of the audience in the desired direction. In addition to the divisions noted under "Analyzing the Subject" in Chapter 4, several other patterns of organization are widely used.

Definitional Pattern. An informative talk or a persuasive talk using indirect suggestion may consist of an elaborated or extended definition. The following subjects phrased as questions can be organized in a definitional pattern: What is the electoral college? What is a profit? What is air pollution? What is psychodrama? What is the value-added tax?

A definitional pattern may explain likenesses and differences from other things; it may describe other examples; it may explain causes, activities, or results. Since the purpose of the definitional order is to make the subject clear and satisfying to the listeners, the speaker

---

[11] *Vital Speeches,* XLV, 8 (Feb. 1, 1979), p. 253.

must establish an appropriate point of view, frame of reference, or specific context for his explanation.

Topical Pattern.   The organization called topical or classificational is based on some method of grouping parts into suitable categories. The main ideas may be assembled to explain functions, viewpoints, groups of people involved, fields of application, physical attributes, or qualities like ability, cost, and importance.

Many topical arrangements are familiar: civil, military; creative, critical; practical, theoretical; legal, moral; legislative, executive, judicial. Other categories for subjects include economic, emotional, political, logical, aesthetic, philosophical, literary, historical, linguistic, scientific, educational, and so forth. A topical arrangement is arbitrary rather than causal or logical in that the main ideas of the speech are organized for emphasis. The subject of recording by writing could be discussed as systems of indicating words, syllables, and sounds; this pattern would feature the advantages of alphabetical writing. The reverse order, however, would be suitable if the purpose was to explain the nature and value of Chinese script.

Causal Pattern.   An organization by cause proceeds either from cause to effect or from effect to cause. When necessary, the causal factors or results may be classified into social, economic, political, or other categories. The organization of material into a causal pattern is highly exacting, and forms the basis for all speeches of argument and persuasion. Causal reasoning is discussed in Chapter 14.

Causal order is used here in outlining the reasons for the decline in net operating profit of a chain of major hotels in major cities:

  I. Motels have reduced the big city hotel occupancy rate.
 II. Air travel affords one-day excursion business trips.
III. Growing competition for convention business affects hotel earnings.

Logical Pattern.   As used in persuasion speeches, the logical pattern is deductive, proceeding from certain premises or ideas to a conclusion by carefully reasoned steps. All points are established by acceptable evidence.

Psychological Pattern.   A psychological pattern is based on certain audience reactions. While all speeches are planned for the reactions of listeners, the psychological pattern is specifically based on what the audience will find interesting, important, complex, or acceptable.

Degrees of Interest.   The main points are arranged in terms of more or less audience interest. The progression is from most interesting to less interesting or vice versa. In a discussion of Chopin, devotees of the piano would find point I below most interesting. For other listeners, who might be more interested in his personal life than in his compositions, the following arrangement is more suitable:

I. Chopin is the greatest composer of music for the piano.
II. Chopin was successful in obtaining good prices for his compositions.
III. Chopin had an ill-fated love affair with George Sand.

Degrees of Importance.   The main points of the speech are arranged according to their impressiveness to the audience. The most important point can be first or last. For example, the social advantages of a college education might be important to some students, the economic advantages to others. For teachers, the advantages of a college education might follow this order:

I. College graduates have greater earning power than noncollege graduates.
II. College graduates have more knowledge to help them function intelligently as leading citizens.
III. College graduates have more insight to help them fulfill themselves as human beings.

Degrees of Complexity.   If the subject of the speech is technical, difficult, or complicated, it is wise to proceed from the simplest point to the most complex one, or from what is probably known to the audience to what is unknown. For instance, the dictionary method of marking pronunciation could precede a discussion of phonetic symbols; basic principles of musical chords in thirds might come before an explanation of chords in fourths.

The order of known to unknown is sometimes shifted when the speaker is addressing specialists in his own field; in that case, another arrangement would probably be more suitable. To an audience grounded in biology the results of an experiment in gene mutation would be discussed before its relationship to previous findings.

Degrees of Acceptability.   Some ideas may be more controversial or less acceptable than others; for that reason, progression is from what is agreed upon to what is subject to argument. For example, the necessity of expert medical testimony in legal proceedings involving insanity would precede a discussion of contradictory expert testimonies and a recommendation for a group of official medical experts whose decisions would be final. This recommendation is highly controversial because it conflicts with established common law principles, such as the jury deciding upon the facts and the defendant presenting evidence for his own case. If no area of agreement exists, the less controversial leads to the more controversial. To a hostile or resistant audience, it is often valuable to present the strongest point first, the next strongest last, and any other needed points in the middle. In this way some listeners may be favorably impressed in the beginning, and still others, who are slow to change their opinions, may be convinced at the end.

A psychological pattern is sometimes difficult to achieve, for the categories are not always separate and distinct. What is most interesting may be the most complex or the most controversial. What is most simple may be the least interesting or important. The advantages and disadvantages must be carefully weighed. In general, the main ideas presented first and last make strong impressions on the listeners. Authorities differ as to whether the first or last position creates the strongest effect. The speaker should choose the psychological arrangement that best suits the content of the speech, the character of the audience, and his own manner of presentation.

Problem-Solution Pattern. An arrangement based on inquiry or more or less inductive investigation of a situation is called the problem-solution pattern. It is based on scientific method, or rather on John Dewey's formulation of reflective thinking in *How We Think*.[12] This book was a summary for teachers of his ideas of logical theory, first presented in *Studies in Logical Theory* and later expanded in *Essays in Experimental Logic*. Dewey's steps in problem-solving are approximately as follows: (1) An awareness of a perplexing situation, of something wrong, or a problem requiring an answer. (2) An analysis of the specific nature and causes of the situation through observation of the facts. (3) A suggestion of possible solutions of the problem gained from these and other remembered facts and situations. (4) An examination of each proposed solution to predict its

---

[12] John Dewey, *How We Think* (Boston: D. C. Heath and Co., 1933), p. 15.

probable results. (5) A determination of the best possible solution by further observation and a trial of this solution in actual practice, and later modification if necessary.

A solution reached by this five-step process has the advantage of being the product of a systematic study of the facts and factors of the entire situation. A speaker uses reflective thinking to make sure that he and his audience have a sound product. For example, in discussing financial security, the speaker would consider the problem and the advantages and disadvantages of the various proposed solutions, such as savings plans (in a regular bank, savings and loan, or certificates of deposit), stocks, bonds (corporate, municipal, or federal), real estate, and commodities (gold, silver, antiques, or other collectibles). The speaker would then point out and recommend the solution best suited to present conditions.

The problem-solution pattern is adaptable to long speeches and to nonpartisan audiences. In other situations, a given speech may not include all five steps of the pattern. The order will be varied to suit the speaker's specific purpose, and considerable deduction may be used to determine the best solution. In a speech to actuate, the speaker may go from the nature of the problem directly to the best solution; other possible solutions are merely mentioned and dismissed. The one solution is presented with strong support and recommended for action.

Monroe's Motivated Sequence Pattern.   Another popular plan, especially for decision-making and problem-solving, is the one developed by Professor Alan H. Monroe of Purdue University. Like Dewey's sequence, it usually consists of five steps to secure an answer to a problem or question. The speaker: (1) Gets attention. (2) Shows the need; points out how it affects the listeners to believe, to know, and to act. (3) Satisfies the need; offers the best solution or answer. (4) Visualizes the results; points out why carrying out the decision is to the listeners' advantage. (5) Requests action or approval; asks for action or agreement.

For informative speeches, Monroe recommends using only the first three steps; for entertainment speeches only the first step may be needed.

Number of Main Points.   Only those main points which are essential to the specific purpose of the speech should be used, for too many main points overburden and fatigue the listener. If the body of the speech as planned has a great many divisions, the speaker should reanalyze his material. It can perhaps be reorganized so that some of the present main points will become subpoints under new and fewer headings. If this is not possible, the speaker should re-examine his specific purpose and restrict it to a more limited aspect of the subject. Significant coverage of a topic is more valuable than wide coverage.

THE CONCLUSION

A definite ending to the speech is necessary, first, to let listeners know that the message is rounded out and complete and, second, to gain final acceptance of the theme. Viewed in its broadest aspect, the proper conclusion should enable the speaker to stop in the most appropriate manner; leave the audience in an appropriate mood; help the audience remember the gist of the speech; and make the listeners want to respond to the speaker's suggestions.

The basic elements of a conclusion include repetition, application, and reinforcement of the subject. The conclusion of a given speech may consist of one or more of these elements in suitable form. Some speakers also use additional personal remarks not directly related to the subject of the speech.

Forms of Repetition. The element providing a conclusion most directly related to the subject is repetition. The most frequently used forms of repetition are summary, abridgment, and restatement.

Summary. A summary or recapitulation is important for clarity if the body of the speech has been lengthy or complicated. The main points of the speech are often briefly and separately stated. Such an itemized repetition gives the audience a better grasp and retention of the subject as a whole. A summary concluded Peter J. Brennan's speech on "Jobs and Energy":

> *1. We must use more of our home-grown energy resources—that means coal, nuclear power and domestic oil.*
>
> *2. We must develop new energy sources to help shoulder more of the burden in future years, but we cannot allow ourselves to substitute these promises for today's real choices.*
>
> *3. We must conserve energy resources. At the same time we should recognize that saving energy does not really create energy. . . .*

4. Reasonable growth is essential to America's future; those who want to halt growth want to change our democratic form of government, and its most basic elements—freedom of choice and opportunity. . . .
5. We no longer have the luxury of time to solve these problems. We are well down the road toward energy default and disaster. . . .[13]

Abridgment. A concise abridgment or précis of the content of the speech in paragraph style is often more effective than a point by point summary. The ideas and supporting material are woven together and stated in an interesting and significant way. Such a running digest should be brief, for undue wordiness would dull audience interest and defeat the purpose. The following is an example of a concise abridgment:

In all this discussion, I have said:
    —We need nuclear energy
    —There is no viable alternative in sight at this moment
    —Nuclear energy is economical
    —It is the safest environmentally of the currently available sources of energy.
So I say to you: be thoughtful—not emotional—about nuclear energy. For the well-being of our species, we will need to apply the utmost reaches of wisdom when considering our energy future.[14]—B. F. SHAW, "Why Nuclear Energy!"

Restatement. In most conclusions a part of the subject is repeated for emphasis, such as the central idea, the thesis or proposal, or the most important idea for that particular audience. The restatement can be an exact repetition or an illuminating paraphrase. The speaker restates whatever idea will help him achieve his specific purpose:

I see a constant that defines the best. It says that there can be no effective corporate strategy that is not marketing oriented, that does not in the end follow this unyielding prescript: The purpose of a business is to create and keep a customer. To do that, you have to do those things that will make people want *to do business with you. All other truths on this subject are merely derivative.*[15]—THEODORE LEVITT, "Marketing and the Corporate Purpose."

---

[13] *Vital Speeches,* XLIV, 18 (July 1, 1978), p. 571.
[14] *Vital Speeches,* XLIII, 21 (Aug. 15, 1977), p. 651.
[15] *Vital Speeches,* XLIII, 14 (May 1, 1977), p. 443.

Forms of Application. The speaker may desire to apply the subject in some way to a specified need, desire, or problem. Such application is important for persuasion when the body of the speech has been devoted to impressing, motivating, or arousing an audience. The conclusion can take the form of an appeal for immediate action, for future action, for emotional response, or for dedication to policy.

Immediate Action. On some occasions the speaker may want his listeners to perform a definite act before leaving the hall, as signing a petition or giving money. Benjamin Franklin made such an appeal before the Constitutional Convention of 1787: "On the whole, sir, I can not help expressing a wish that every member of the convention who may still have objections to it, would, with me, on this occasion, doubt a little of his own infallibility, and, to make manifest our unanimity, put his name to this instrument."

Future Action. Most actions desired by a speaker cannot be performed at once but must be carried out at a later date; these would include voting for a political candidate, visiting a foreign city, or taking up a new hobby. Other future action is requested in the following example:

> There is still time. We can carve the moral decay from America. You have the weapon—your type, printer, and your Linotype. For God's and America's sake, let us have the courage to speak up.[16]
> —ALAN C. MCINTOSH, "A Challenge to Our American Press."

Emotional Response. An audience may recognize the need for action and yet, when the time comes, not perform it. It is usually necessary to arouse emotions that will cause the listeners to act. Emotional appeals in conclusions are as old as oral communication and are based on the fact that man does not live by logic alone. William Pitt the Elder ended a speech on taxing America in 1766 with an appeal to emotion:

> My lords, I am old and weak, and at present unable to say more; but my feelings and indignation were too strong to have said less. I could not have slept this night in my bed, nor reposed my head on my pillow, without giving this vent to my eternal abhorrence of such preposterous and enormous principles.

---

[16] *Vital Speeches*, XXVIII, 16 (June 1, 1962), p. 508.

In a speech titled "Learning a Lesson from David," Robert W. Bunke sought to evoke emotion in his conclusion:

> *In conclusion, I urge you to get going now despite the risks. What better epitaph can we hope for than these words on the tombstone of an Alpine guide who lost his life carrying out his duty. His tombstone says simply: "He died climbing."*[17]

Dedication to Policy.   A specific act or emotional response may be less important to the speaker's purpose than a consistent and more permanent attitude or viewpoint. Many attitudes, such as faith, cooperation, and resistance, are based on a blend of rational and emotional experience and are therefore more persistent than direct actions or strong feelings. Charles S. Rhyne, speaking to the Conference on World Peace Through the Rule of Law of the Lawyers of Europe, at Rome, April 2, 1962, concluded with such an appeal:

> *Rome was not built in a day. But when it was built it became the "Eternal City." Nor will the international rule of law be achieved within a year. But if we persevere we will leave mankind with an equally durable—and noble—monument: Peace with Justice under Law.*[18]

Forms of Reinforcement.   The theme or central idea of the speech can be reinforced by concluding material that epitomizes or represents the subject. Forms frequently used are the statement, question, quotation, example, incident, prediction, and offer of service.

Striking Statement.   The last sentence or sentences of a speech have great strategic value, and many speakers take advantage of this opportunity for a final reinforcement of their purpose. The following endings exemplify the variety of epigrammatic, memorable, and startling statements that have been used for striking effect.

> *And therefore I do declare unto you, that I do dissolve this Parliament* —CROMWELL, Jan. 22, 1655.

> *And now, Mr. Speaker, I announce to you and to this House, that I am no longer a member of the Thirty-fourth Congress.*—PRESTON S. BROOKS, in the House of Representatives, July 14, 1856.

> *We have only to make the choice: Will we use the energy and revitalize the heart, or will we abandon both for false securities?*

---

[17] *Vital Speeches,* XLIII, 12 (April 1, 1977), p. 379.
[18] *Vital Speeches,* XXVIII, 15 (May 15, 1962), p. 466.

In this choice we will either build tomorrow or write our epitaph.[19]
—BARRY GOLDWATER, Jan. 15, 1964.

Challenging Question. To focus audience attention upon the theme, problem, or proposal, the speaker can use a question. A question conclusion succeeds best when it is direct, challenging, and effectively worded. For example:

> *For what will it profit a nation to become the greatest economic power in history, if its people lose the qualities of their greatness— self-discipline, self-reliance, industry, thrift, courage, character, faith?" This is not a crisis of economic power. We have the potential power. This is not even a crisis of defense. We have the potential strength. This is a crisis of the inward spirit of man. The question is "Have we as a people the spirit of greatness?"*[20]—HERBERT V. PROCHNOW, "Major Challenges to American Foreign Policy."

Significant Quotation. A conclusion often consists of or includes a quotation. The type of quotation depends upon the subject and audience. For speeches on practical problems a pertinent prose quotation is indicated. In his speech "The Need for Politically Sophisticated Managers," presented at a management conference, Henry R. Hall ended with a quotation: "Remember Plato's sage observation: 'The punishment wise men suffer for indifference to public affairs is to be ruled by unwise men.' "[21]

In discussing social, ethical, and cultural subjects, some speakers use a poetical conclusion for emotional effect. His Royal Highness Prince Bernhard of the Netherlands did so when he spoke at West Point:

> *One always hears the following quotation of Kipling: "Oh, East is East and West is West, and never the twain shall meet," but one should not forget that the same ballad goes on, saying:*
> *"But there is neither East nor West, Border nor Breed, nor Birth, when two strong men stand face to face, though they come from the ends of the earth."*[22]

Concrete Example. The theme of the speech is sometimes reinforced by concluding with a concrete example, such as: "As you

---

[19] *Vital Speeches,* XXX, 8 (Feb. 1, 1964), p. 237.
[20] *Vital Speeches,* XXVIII, 14 (May 1, 1962), p. 425.
[21] *Vital Speeches,* XXVIII, 2 (Nov. 1, 1961), p. 54.
[22] *Vital Speeches,* XXX, 8 (Feb. 1, 1964), p. 233.

remember, George Williams sat down, figured out what his family would need in case of his death, and bought insurance to cover such an emergency. Can you think of a better way?" In his speech on the Foote Resolution in 1830, Robert Hayne included an example in his conclusion:

> *These, sir, are the principles which induced the immortal Hampden to resist the payment of a tax of twenty shillings. Would twenty shillings have ruined his fortune? No! but the payment of half twenty shillings, on the principle on which it was demanded, would have made him a slave . . .*

Narrative Incident.   A real or imaginary incident or anecdote often makes a strong conclusion. An example is Mirabeau's speech on Necker's Financial Plan delivered in the National Assembly on September 26, 1789.

> *Why, gentlemen, it was but the other day, that, in reference to a ridiculous commotion at the Palais-Royal—a quixotic insurrection, which never had any importance save in the feeble imaginations or perverse designs of certain faithless men—you heard these wild words: "Catiline is at the gates of Rome, and yet you deliberate!" And verily there was neither a Catiline nor a Rome, neither perils nor factions around you. But, today, bankruptcy, hideous bankruptcy, is there before you, and threatens to consume you, yourselves, your property, your honor—and yet you deliberate!*

Prediction.   The speaker may wish to reinforce his ideas by stating their future results or by expressing his own faith and hope.

> *Markets will grow. Populations will prosper. The economic network of affluence will spread. I am convinced it will happen.*
>
> *The challenge will persist because, like the mountain, it is there. It is there like the earth itself is there, like Mankind is there. And the common bonds of humanity will be our lifeline in the long ascent to the summit.*[23]—LEE A. IACOCCA, "Multinational Investment and Global Purpose."

Offer of Service.   An offer of future service or cooperation is used in the conclusion of some business and political speeches. The following conclusion is from a speech given at a dealers' conference:

---

[23] *Vital Speeches*, XLIII, 23 (Sept. 15, 1977), p. 724.

"Our Special Sales Service is always available. Drop us a line or give us a call, and one of our men will be assigned to you at once."

British Ambassador Sir David Ormsby Gore concluded his speech in Denver in this manner:

> All around the world we are willing to make our full contribution and it gives us comfort that in this task we are working alongside our good friends and war-tried comrades, the United States of America. Indeed, I do not believe that ever before in peacetime have two independent sovereign states cooperated so intimately. Long may it be so.[24]

Additional Remarks. Most speakers end their speeches with material directly related to the subject. Some speakers, however, wish to conclude by relating themselves to the audience. Personal conclusions include leave-taking and expression of gratitude.

Leave-Taking. Certain speech situations seem to call for some form of farewell. In his speech before Congress, for example, Gen. Douglas MacArthur said "Goodbye." In his speech on withdrawing from the Union in the United States Senate on January 21, 1861, Jefferson Davis uttered a farewell:

> Mr. President and senators, having made the announcement which the occasion seemed to me to require, it only remains for me to bid you a final adieu.

Expression of Gratitude. Some speakers desire to show their appreciation or thankfulness toward their listeners. Addressing the International Association of Machinists, George Meany concluded as follows:

> The IAM has, I am sure, made a major contribution to a better understanding of trade problems through this pace-setting conference, and as it concludes, I want to extend to your officers my hearty congratulations for their foresight in arranging it.[25]

Common Weaknesses of Conclusions. The device of referring back to the introduction, although used by some speakers, usually has the disadvantage of distracting attention away from the body of the speech. As a result, the listener may remember the introduction and conclusion but forget the substance of the speech. A

---

[24] *Vital Speeches,* XXX, 9 (Feb. 15, 1964), p. 288.

[25] *Vital Speeches,* XXVIII, 6 (Jan. 1, 1962), p. 173.

safe practice is to relate both the introduction and conclusion to the body of the speech.

Some speakers seem unable to conclude, but offer double or triple conclusions that tire or exasperate the audience. The conclusion should be what the name implies, a definite ending. Other speakers end abruptly without an apparent reason. Sudden stoppage leaves the audience wondering whether the speaker's message is complete or whether he had a lapse of memory. The conclusion should be clear and should follow naturally what has gone before.

Another weakness is introducing new or irrelevant material. A good conclusion is intimately related to the theme of the speech. A weak conclusion may be better than none, but a good speech deserves a strong conclusion. One of the weakest conclusions is an apology for one's ideas or manner of speaking. If the speaker does his best in the introduction, body, and conclusion of his speech, he has no need to apologize.

OUTLINING THE SPEECH

An outline is the visual record of a systematically organized thought structure. When the speaker has selected, divided, and limited his subject, determined its specific purpose, gathered and arranged supporting materials, he has already done much of the mental work of outlining. The main ideas of the subject become the main headings of the outline and the subordinate ideas become the subheadings. The remaining supporting materials are recorded in their proper places. Making an outline puts the results of the speaker's analysis and synthesis on paper.

Importance of an Outline.   A good outline often results in a good speech. An outline provides a systematic arrangement of material and helps the speaker to understand his subject more thoroughly. It enables him to check the relationship of subordinate ideas to main ideas and to check the clarity of his thinking. He can also make sure that each main point is treated according to its importance. Hidden weaknesses and digressions can be detected. The material already gathered should finally be arranged in the form that makes the best speech possible. This perfected outline ensures unity, coherence, and progress of thought from the beginning to the end of the speech. It also provides a gauge for the length of the speech. Furthermore, it offers a plan to follow for the development, wording, and rehearsal of the speech and helps impress its content more firmly in the speaker's memory.

The outline is strictly a preliminary plan for the speech. In extemporaneous speeches, the speaker does not refer to it or follow its plan exactly during delivery, since he must adapt parts of his material to suit audience reactions. If the speaker needs written support, he prepares simple notes based on the outline; their number, type, and wording depend on individual needs. The outline is closely followed when the speech is written out to be read from manuscript.

Types of Outlines. The three types of outlines are the topical, the complete sentence, and the logical brief. The logical brief is searchingly exhaustive and rigorously logical. Since the main and subordinate ideas of a speech must be appropriately limited and supporting materials judiciously selected, the logical brief is often unwieldy and impractical.

Topical Outline. A topical, or key-phrase, outline lists all ideas as words or phrases. This structure is easy to grasp and remember, but the weakness of the outline is that the speaker might forget the complete thought represented by the word or phrase. However, some experienced speakers prefer a topical outline and many speakers use it for short, informal speeches.

Complete Sentence Outline. The complete sentence outline states ideas fully and exactly and is the best type for most speakers. It is inclusive, specific, and detailed and briefly expresses the content of the speech. Supporting materials are also clearly stated, thus assuring a complete speech. Sections of the two types of outlines are offered for comparison.

II. Be buoyant	II. Become more buoyant.
A. Get rid of weight	A. Get rid of extra weight.
B. Become horizontal	B. Assume a horizontal position.
1. Flat on back	1. Throw yourself flat on your back.
2. Keep arms flat	2. Keep your arms outstretched on the surface of the quicksand for extra buoyancy.
3. Call for help	3. Float and call for help if you are not alone.

Constructing the Outline.   As a preparatory statement, an outline contains the title of the speech, the general purpose, and either the specific purpose or the subject sentence.

What Is Freedom?

General Purpose:	To inform.
Specific Purpose:	To make the audience realize that our society places necessary legal restrictions upon our constitutional freedoms.

The remainder of the standard outline, the outline proper, includes the three main divisions of a speech: the introduction, the body, and the conclusion.

In making an outline, certain rules and suggestions evolved from the experience of others are helpful. A simple, standard set of symbols and indentations should be used. Care should be taken that the contents of coordinate points or headings do not overlap. Subordinate points must actually and logically reinforce, develop, or clarify the headings they are meant to support. Double or compound headings, which are the result of confused thinking, should be avoided. Parallel phrasing is used for coordinate headings. A coordinate point has two or more subheadings. Unnecessary headings should be eliminated. Supporting material should be included in the outline. The outline should be worded as clearly, concretely, and concisely as possible.

A good test for valid organization is to insert coordinating words—such as *and, or,* and *but*—between headings of equal value, and to insert subordinating words—such as *for, since,* and *for example*—before subordinate headings. If these connective words make sense, the chances are that the outline has a clear and logical structure.

6.
DEVELOPING IDEAS

The outline of a speech may be satisfying to the speaker, but it would be a dissatisfying and unconvincing skeleton to an audience. The speaker organizes his ideas out of a knowledge of the topic built up by his study and evaluation of essential facts, reasons, and opinions. An audience cannot understand or be convinced unless it too is offered the essential material which enabled the speaker to understand and reach his conclusions.

The outline of the speech is a blueprint for further work by the speaker: it must be filled in, or elaborated into a complete speech. Each of its assertions must be justified by supporting material. To awaken the desired response in the audience, the speech must be developed until it is clear, believable, and interesting.

MAKING IDEAS CLEAR

A good speech must be immediately understood. If listeners have to disentangle the meaning of what a speaker has just said, they miss what he is saying now and soon lose interest in what they cannot understand. Clarity is thus a strong method of holding interest, satisfying as it does the human desire to know the *what, where,* and *when* of an unfolding situation. The pattern of thought can be made more understandable by the use of explanation, reinforcement, and transition.

Explanation. Explanation in its broad sense means to make clear to the understanding. But explanation has certain specific aspects of concern to the speaker: it may be of words (definition), of appearance or other qualities (description), or of facts, ideas, and relationships (exposition).

Definition. A definition is a statement revealing the meaning of a term. The statement is to be understood when the term is subsequently used. The meaning of a word can sometimes be shown by another word, or synonym. A synonym replaces the original term in a given context without loss of meaning. At times the use of several synonyms will give a more complete understanding of the point being discussed, but often the synonym needs to be defined to be useful. A speaker defines a word to establish exactly what he means by it and to avoid ambiguous, confusing, or irrelevant interpretations by listeners. Because a definition shows how the word will be used in that speech, the speaker must be careful to use it only in that sense.

TERMS REQUIRING DEFINITION. What kind of terms should be defined? The answer depends upon the nature of the audience. Individuals with special interest in and knowledge of a subject, such as economics, will have little difficulty in understanding its important terms. A more heterogeneous and non-specialist audience will undoubtedly require definitions of certain terms, for example, words that refer to concepts not commonly known, words that refer to complex ideas, words of more than one meaning, words embodying technical or scientific knowledge, and words that signify values of other times or places.

METHODS OF DEFINITION. The process of definition usually involves classification of similarities and analysis of differences. For instance, the palm falls into the classification of perennial plants in contrast to annuals and biennials that live only one or two seasons. Among perennials the palm is classified as a woody plant, as opposed to herbaceous plants which die down to the ground each season. The palm is further classified as a tree, or single-stemmed woody plant in contrast to many-stemmed shrubs. Continuing analysis shows that the palm, unlike most trees, has a branchless stem, or trunk, with a bunch of enormous leaves growing at the top. The most important methods of definition are by descriptive qualities, causation, function, origin, and combination of methods.

• *Descriptive Qualities.* The physical attributes of an object, such as size, shape, weight, color, surface, warmth, or movement, form the basis for definition. Satin, for instance, is a soft cloth of smooth finish, glossy on the face and dull on the back; velvet is soft, but has a rich thick pile texture.

• *Causation.* The definition of some terms requires a description of causes, effects, or both. The word embarrassment is made clear largely by a description of effects: a state of feeling self-conscious, confused, ill at ease, flustered, and disconcerted. The definition of inflation includes such causes as an increased amount of paper money issued, and such effects as the marked fall in the value of money and rising prices.

• *Function.* A definition may state what an item is used for, how it works, or what end it serves. An object like an antenna is described by its function: a wire or set of wires used in sending and receiving electromagnetic waves. A hospital is defined by its purposes and services: giving medical, surgical, and psychiatric treatment to the ill or injured and offering food, shelter, and nursing during the treatment.

• *Origin.* The beginning or source of something may be a partial basis of definition. The definition of starlight and autograph, for instance, are by origin, the latter being a piece of writing done by an individual. The statement that a plant is Alpine or South American is definition by origin.

• *Combination of Methods.* A great many definitions make use of more than one method. Classification and analysis state that a sheep is a cud-chewing mammal; its medium size and heavy wool are descriptive qualities; its edible flesh and skin used for making leather and parchment indicate its function or use.

Abstract terms, being less specific than objects, require a combination of methods for their definition. Some are so difficult to define that considerable explanation is required for accuracy. Mayo J. Thompson, in a speech on "Morality and Free Enterprise," explained what he meant by the adjective "good."

> *Tell them something else for a change. Tell them that men can be both good and free at the same time. Tell them that a man doesn't have to be a slave in order to be a good man. Tell them that a "morality" that can only be produced and maintained by tyranny is a contradiction in terms—that a coerced morality is no morality at all—that a people that can only be kept moral by the coercion of the state still has immorality in its heart—and that when the coercion is removed, as it will be some day in China as elsewhere, the problem of greed and avarice in the human heart will still be very much with them and us.*[1]

---

[1] *Vital Speeches*, XL, 7 (Jan. 15, 1974), p. 204.

FAULTS OF DEFINITION. Frequent faults are failure to define unfamiliar words, using words with multiple meanings, and offering routine definitions. A less common fault is overdefinition.

• *Unfamiliar Words.* The public at large does not know the specialized vocabularies, or jargon, of the arts, services, professions, businesses, and industries. In discussing any subject the wise procedure is to use words generally known as far as possible. When unfamiliar words must be used, they should be defined; otherwise many listeners will form a vague or incorrect impression of the subject. Terms like residuals, cyclical, dollar averaging, and contractual plans are clear to buyers and sellers of securities but may be obscure to other listeners. Since these terms are useful in discussing investments, they should be defined for the layperson.

• *Multiple Meanings.* Many words in common use have more than one meaning. Stout, for instance, can signify brave, sturdy, or fat. Story has a different sense in architecture than it has in fiction. The subject matter or context may indicate in which sense the word is being used, but if there is any doubt about audience interpretation, the speaker should define the word.

• *Routine Definition.* A dictionary will supply a definition, but it may sound dry and commonplace when spoken. The meaning may need to be specially adapted to the subject or worded to appeal to the listeners' knowledge of the world around them. William F. McKee made a technical term immediately understandable: " 'Overkill,' as you know, is the often advanced argument that our nuclear weapons stockpile is excessive."[2]

• *Overdefinition.* Too many definitions in one speech are annoying or boring. The person who meticulously defines terms both familiar and unfamiliar quickly loses audience participation. Such a speaker never seems to get under way or to come to grips with his subject. Even if he does finally offer significant ideas, they are lost upon his listeners, since their minds are elsewhere.

Also, in public speaking as in private conversation, a person who defines familiar words makes his listeners feel that he considers them ignorant. Resentment at being talked down to causes a repudiation of the speaker and his message.

---

[2] *Vital Speeches,* XXX, 1 (Oct. 15, 1963), p. 23.

Description.   Description tells how things appeal to the senses. Its purpose is to evoke persons, objects, and places in the listeners' awareness. The method of description is to present the telling detail, one that makes a definite impression upon the senses. Description is the basis of verbal illustration; carefully chosen concrete details build up an image more effectively than a general statement. "One day the newspaper copy, prepared according to the strict rules of scientific management, did not reach the presses" is a general statement. Specific details were used to express this idea by Louis B. Lundborg in his speech "Rx for Profits":

> Then one day a strange thing happened. The delivery boys noticed it first because they didn't get their papers to deliver. When the authorities entered the paper's offices they found a disturbing sight. The lights were on and the presses rolling, but no paper was streaming out. And everyone, the pressmen, the reporters, the copy boys—everyone was frozen into rigidity. And on all their faces was the same look of expectancy— all waiting for more information, waiting for a committee decision, waiting for more market research, for as they said, you can't make a decision, or write a story without all the facts.[3]

A description should usually be brief and should aim at a single, definite effect. A good practice is to set up and establish one point of view. It is often best to follow a systematic order: background to foreground, top to bottom, right to left, outside to inside. In describing a person the order might be from the whole to a part: his overall appearance, or size; build and clothing, his head, or face, hair, eyes. The description gains interest if the details are arranged for a cumulative effect. To show the mood or character of a man, for example, the description might lead up to the determined set of his jaw.

The speaker's aim may not be achieved by a single point of view. If the viewpoint needs to be shifted, the audience should grasp the shift and the purpose of it. The description of a man might turn from his appearance to his voice and speech, in which case the audience must realize that the speaker is painting the man's true character.

Description, as can be realized, often arouses more than images. Sometimes a certain emotional reaction is necessary to create the desired effect within the listeners. A political figure can be described

---

[3] *Vital Speeches,* XXX, 5 (Dec. 15, 1963), p. 147.

so as to arouse sympathy or antipathy. Picturing the feelings of underprivileged children is one way to stir the listeners' desire to help.

Description should be used with judgment and skill and not overused. The progress of the speech toward its goal should not be hampered by endless details, even though they may be interesting in themselves. Too much description fatigues and bores the audience. Skill in handling vivid, effective, and dynamic description requires much practice.

Exposition.   Exposition is the detailed explanation of facts and ideas. It is a continuation of analysis and synthesis, making use of definition, description, and illustration to achieve clarity. Exposition is virtually an extension of definition and uses the same basic methods: an object, event, or idea is elaborated, illustrated, and interpreted. In a speech "The Communist Apparatus in Canada Today," Marjorie Lamb explained "national front" by an amplification of function:

> The "national front" is the updated model of the "united front" tactic. It is now the preferred tactic for most Communist Parties. The "national front" technique is an attempt to cooperate with political parties of the center or even with a central non-Communist government in order to destroy from within. True motives are concealed while the Communists claim to be anxious to cooperate for the good of the country. An important feature of this tactic is that there is often no active political campaign against the government. Behind a facade of cooperation they work to secure the appointment of Communists or crypto Communists to key positions so that in time they can gain control of most of the main organizations of state. When this has been achieved the Communists then throw off the protective shield of the parties and groups they are working with and bring about the revolutionary coup which motivated their action from the start.[4]

Since definition is only the compact seed of explanation, the task of exposition is to create the full-grown plant. Some basic methods of exposition are by analysis, comparison, contrast, and illustration.

ANALYSIS.   Analysis is the breaking of an object, activity, or idea into its component parts. Analysis proceeds by asking questions, such as what is it, what does it do, how is it made, where did it come from, what is its value, why did it happen, who uses it?

---

[4] *Vital Speeches,* XXX, 5 (Dec. 15, 1963), p. 142.

Most topics when analyzed will be found to contain "multiplicity in unity and unity in multiplicity." In discussing collecting old stock certificates the topic can be analyzed into the following parts: the types of certificates in demand (those of early railroad, streetcar, maritime, automobile, and mining companies); the range of prices of the certificates; (largely through autograph, rare book, and antique dealers); the reasons for collecting certificates (special interest in the lore of mining and transportation companies, the desire for autographs of famous entrepreneurs, interest in engraving and illustration, and the fascination of the chase and thrill of discovery). These conditions all depend upon the fact that there are relatively few collectors of extinct securities. The purpose of making each part clear is to make the whole topic clear. Analysis is thus not an end in itself but instead is a step toward synthesis, or putting the parts together in a more meaningful unity.

Clarity frequently demands that a part be analyzed further into its elements. In discussing a hobby such as antiquing furniture, the whole process could be analyzed into preparing the wood, painting, and finishing. The last part would be subdivided into wiping the final raw umber coat with a dry cloth, washing the surface with a cloth moistened in turpentine, and rubbing raised surfaces for highlights.

A part should not be analyzed down into over-minute elements. Too many ramifications confuse the mind and make it impossible for listeners to grasp the pattern of meaning. The mechanism of the piano would seem overly complicated if the exposition were loaded with facts, such as the sizes of the keys and the lengths and diameters of the strings.

COMPARISON AND CONTRAST. Exposition like definition uses comparison of an item with others, in order to classify it into a group, and contrast, in order to analyze its differences from the group. Comparisons and contrasts can be found by asking the following questions: What is the relation of this with something already known? How does it differ from something already known? Could something already known be used to illustrate it?

A classification to illuminate something new and little understood can sometimes be built up by comparison with old, familiar things. Nonobjective painting is a difficult subject for many individuals. It might be explained by comparing it to various forms of abstract

design found in moldings, grilles, rugs, mosaics, etc. Since the beauty
and charm of such geometric patterns does not depend on likeness
to natural objects but on interrelationship of forms, the speaker may
succeed in establishing a "new" category of nonrepresentational
painting in the minds of his listeners.

ILLUSTRATION. The processes of comparison and contrast are
themselves illustrative in function. The purpose of illustration is to
make clear by stimulating the senses and imagination. Achieving
this purpose requires description, because the task of description is
to make listeners see, hear, and feel. The mere mention of an example
or illustrative object is not enough to accomplish this purpose. The
illustration must be made concrete; that is, become part of the physical experience and awareness of the hearers.

Reinforcement.   Reinforcement is a method of strengthening
or emphasizing an idea. The amount of time given to more important
ideas, the effectiveness of supporting materials, and the dynamics
of delivery are methods of making strong impressions upon the audience. Reinforcement specifically concerns the frequency with which
an idea is presented. A single statement may not allow enough time
for listeners to perceive an idea's true significance; listeners' attention
almost immediately goes on to another statement. Reinforcement
provides the time needed for comprehension by presenting the idea
again. Reinforcement includes repetition, restatement, and summary.

Repetition.   Important ideas in a speech must often be repeated,
because listeners, unlike readers of printed matter, cannot go over
spoken material again. Repetition means saying the same thing more
than once in the same words. An idea is then more firmly pressed
into listeners' minds. The following example of spaced repetition is
from a speech, "Supermarket for Subsidies," by Edwin P. Neilan:
"A major portion of the Federal urban renewal and public housing
dollars are being spent in areas where housing is relatively good
and incomes are relatively high. Poorer areas get the leftovers." After
listing four more points, the speaker repeats the first point with a
slight change in the second sentence as he begins his discussion:
"Let me repeat: a major portion . . . are relatively high. Poorer
areas get little or nothing."[5]

---

[5] *Vital Speeches,* XXX, 8 (Feb. 1, 1964), p. 238.

Maximum reinforcement may possibly be achieved by three or four repetitions, depending on the effectiveness of the wording. Continued repetitions grow monotonous and rapidly lose their value. But repetition, instead of reinforcing a concept, may also be used as a refrain to inspire and sustain emotion. In November 1963, the declaration that "she took a ring from her finger and placed it in his hand" became a refrain in Senator Mike Mansfield's televised speech delivered in the rotunda of the Capitol where President Kennedy's body lay in state.

Restatement. A variation of repetition is restatement, saying the same thing over in different words or from a somewhat different point of view. Restatement thus offers variety; it seems to be a new statement rather than a repetition of the old. Since an idea is expressed in more than one context, listeners find it of more interest and value. Repetitions immediately following one another sometimes create a strong impression upon auditors, but restatements are usually most effective if they are spaced at intervals in the discussion. Walter B. Wriston, speaking on "Let's Create Wealth, Not Allocate Shortages," skillfully wove restatements into the development of a major idea:

> There is no mystery about the definition of capital. Every economist from Adam Smith to Karl Marx has agreed that capital is nothing but stored-up labor, either your own or someone else's. Somebody has to work hard enough to earn a wage and then exhibit enough self-denial to save some of what he earned. There is no other way to create it. To use Marx's phrase, "As values, all commodities are only definite masses of congealed-labor time." Whether the commodity is money or goods, whether it belongs to a capitalist or a communist makes no difference. It's valuable because somebody's labor is stored up in it, and that is what you are paying for—or what you are borrowing. . .
>
> The reality of the need to work to produce capital is true under any economic system.[6]

Summary. A summary is a repetition or restatement of points that have been presented. A pattern of meaning cannot be clear until its elements are properly put together in the minds of listeners. Summary is essentially a method of synthesis; it ties what has been analyzed into parts back into a whole. Many speakers briefly summarize one section of a speech before going on to the next one. This

---

[6] *Vital Speeches*, XLIII, 21 (Aug. 15, 1977), pp. 654–5.

form of summary clarifies that part of the thought structure and
makes listeners ready to comprehend the next part.

Transition. Transitions are words, sentences, and paragraphs
that help reveal the coherent pattern of thought. Transitions show
the relationship of sentence to sentence, paragraph to paragraph,
supporting idea to main idea, illustration to the point being discussed,
or main idea to main idea. Transitions can recall what has just
been said or indicate what is about to be stated.

Transitions—often called connectives, guideposts, or links—can
be a single word: secondly, however, nevertheless, furthermore, more-
over, although, next, finally. Transitions can be phrases: for instance,
on the other hand, in spite of this, as a result, but still more important,
in addition, to get back to, from this point of view. Transitions
can be sentences: How can we reach this goal? The opposite is true.
What economies are possible? We can agree on one point. Let us
consider somewhat more fully how other nations see us.

A longer transitional sentence occurs in a speech by Royce Diener
on the business approach to health care:

> I would like to mention a few things relative to our position on the
> other side of the fence, as payers for the health care of our employees.[7]

Transitions can also be paragraphs. The following example is from
a speech by W. E. Callahan:

> We need, then, to take every possible step within the boundaries of
> good judgment to encourage not merely conservation but to provide
> increasing supplies of either present fuels or substitute fuels. I am sure
> you will all recall from your history books the wringing of hands that
> occurred in the nineteenth century when it appeared that the supply
> of whale oil was going to run out. Kerosene was substituted; and in
> light of what has happened since, it is hard to realize that there could
> have been a concern.[8]

A lack of proper transitions may make the sequence of thought
difficult to follow. The speaker can check upon the need for linking
expressions by asking himself the following questions: Is this statement definitely connected to the preceding one? Is the relationship
between the ideas clearly revealed?

Too many transitions, on the other hand, may reveal structure

---

[7] *Vital Speeches,* XLIV, 12 (April 1, 1978), p. 374.

[8] *Vital Speeches,* XLIII, 21 (Aug. 15, 1977), p. 657.

at the expense of interest. The purpose of clarity is to enhance meaning, to make it more important, to bring its structure to life. Thought should have a dynamic quality: its progress toward valid conclusions should be a continuous fresh approach.

MAKING IDEAS BELIEVABLE

The essentials of a thought may be stated as an assertion. If the listeners agree with it, no supporting material is necessary. An audience of dentists, no doubt, would immediately accept the statement that everyone should have a dental examination twice a year.

Necessity for Proof. Most audiences will not agree with an assertion just because the speaker makes it, but demand sufficient reasons for believing it. The speaker must present evidence to support his statements if he is to prove their validity. In a speech concerning the right to strike, the cost to American businesses in working days might be accepted if backed up by a report issued by the U.S. Labor Department on February 28, 1980. It pointed out that work stoppages cost businesses about 5.1 million working days in January 1978 as compared to 3.7 million days in January 1970.

Evidence, of course, cannot be complete: no conclusion can be based on *all* the facts, for new facts are constantly arising. The complexities of life make it impossible to wait until all the evidence is gathered. Conclusions must be drawn from the best evidence available, problems met with solutions that are as true as possible under the circumstances. A point when proved is not finally true but only probably true.

Even reasonable proof of an assertion may not be enough. Listeners, or many of them, may still refuse to accept the speaker's assertion. One cause of such repudiation may be a distrust of knowledge and reason themselves. Henry T. Heald mentions the concern of universities and foundations "for finding the facts, following them to logical conclusions, and making them available for use and action by the rest of society." The conclusions reached by science and logic often challenge deeply cherished beliefs and arouse waves of what is called anti-intellectualism. As Plato expressed the problem 2500 years ago, "Seven years of silent inquiry are needful for a man to learn the truth, but fourteen in order to learn how to make it known to his fellows."

In a world of varied and changing social, economic, and political institutions it is not surprising that different minds observe and interpret events in different ways and follow different lines of reasoning. "Honest differences of views and honest debate are not disunity," states Herbert Hoover, "they are the vital process of policy-making among free men."

Many differences of viewpoint have their roots in different emotional attitudes, a fact as important to the speaker as to the psychologist. A concept must appeal to more than the mind. A believable point of view is a convincing emotional point of view. The speaker cannot offer supported statements as such. He must find and use evidence that will satisfy not only reason and common sense but also the ingrained emotional and cultural attitudes of his audience.

Kinds of Evidence. Evidence is any material that makes ideas believable and acceptable. Many speakers follow a human tendency to shirk evidence: it is easier to take things at their face value and make whatever statements sound well at the moment. But a speaker who wants to convince his listeners will seek and use suitable evidence. Evidence consists of two main categories: facts and testimony.

Facts. Facts are items of observation and experience. A fact is something known to be true, something that exists or has happened. Facts are basic to thinking itself. The consideration of a group of facts may reveal relationships and lead to a principle or conclusion. Conversely, a general principle can be illustrated or established by pertinent facts. Facts or pertinent examples include specific instances, personal experiences, illustrations, statistics, and laws and principles.

SPECIFIC INSTANCES. Specific instances refer to an individual person, place, or event without details. Because they give substance and background to an assertion, specific instances are simple and valuable means of support. Note how Ellsworth Bunker backed up his statement with known instances:

> Third, we must overcome the belief that the Canal Zone is part of the United States or a United States territory.
>
> In the 1903 Treaty, Panama granted us "rights, powers and authority within the Zone . . . which the United States would possess . . . if it were the sovereign of the territory."
>
> We were not granted "sovereignty" as such.
>
> The United States for many years has considered the Canal Zone as Panamanian territory, albeit under the United States jurisdiction.[9]

---

[9] *Vital Speeches*, XLI, 18 (July 1, 1975), p. 549.

A specific instance may be hypothetical, telling what might have been or what could be, although these are less convincing than real cases. The Earl of Home, speaking on the crisis of confidence in the United Nations, used an instance on record in the first sentence, a hypothetical one in the second sentence:

> *Four countries which were members of the Security Council supported a resolution condoning the use of force by India against Goa. Had the debate been in the Assembly, many more countries—perhaps even a majority—would have voted the same way.*[10]

PERSONAL EXPERIENCES. Personal experiences are firsthand examples, if they are accurately remembered and told; otherwise they become hypothetical illustrations. Harvey C. Jacobs reported a personal experience to support his statement, "Our material progress is gaining in popularity, but very few are willing to pay the price of political and economic and spiritual freedom to get it":

> *An American hunting party, on safari in Africa, was being led by native guides and hunters. Suddenly, as the hunt was reaching a climax, the Africans sat down to rest. "Why," asked the impatient Americans. "Why stop now, when we are so near to our prey?"*
>
> *The Africans replied, "We have been running so fast our bodies have run away from our souls. Now we want to rest so that our souls can catch up."*[11]

ILLUSTRATIONS. Illustrations are extended examples of relations of events treated in enough detail to support the assertion being made or to enable it to be seen in proper perspective. This example is from a speech by William S. Royce on "Industrial Restructuring in the Pacific Basin":

> *Of first importance is the restructuring of several industries, world-wide, which is already having impacts on the countries and the businesses in the Pacific Basin. Much of it started with oil, the first cartel effectively organized by governments of developing countries, though certainly not the first cartel based on resources coming from such countries. The OPEC action to increase crude oil prices not only affected everyone who used oil; it upset the economic balances on which many other industries had long been planned, including chemicals, textiles, steel,*

---

[10] *Vital Speeches,* XXVIII, 8 (Feb. 1, 1962), p. 237.
[11] *Vital Speeches,* XLI, 7 (Jan. 15, 1975), p. 204.

shipbuilding, aluminum, and forest products, to name a few. Suddenly, a number of energy-based industries for which economies of scale had dictated locating production close to the markets were shifted into position where the location of an energy source became more important. In some cases, the energy source was closer to the supply of other raw materials, so transportation on both materials and energy could be saved. And reduced transportation, in turn, reduced the need for oil.[12]

STATISTICS. Statistics are facts or data collected, classified, and tabulated in order to give information about a complex subject. Since statistics provide a short method of dealing with large numbers of examples, they are a valuable form of evidence. "To meet competition and rising costs supermarkets must turn to automation" is a conclusion with suggested reasons, but it needs specific data to help make it believable. For example:

During the past six years an average of 2000 new supermarkets have been opened each year. During the same period the ratio of profits to sales has fallen from 1.4% to 1.2%. The price of food is only 6.5% higher than it was ten years ago, but supermarket wage rates have gone up on an average of 5.8% each year.[13]

In using statistics the speaker should make clear to the audience exactly what is being measured by the data and how it applies to the topic. Ambiguous terms are therefore to be avoided. "Only one person in five in the U.S. is physically fit" is vague. The standards of measuring physical fitness need to be stated if the figures are to have any meaning.

Statistics are effective when presented in a simply arranged form, as in this example from a speech, "Why Nuclear Energy!" by R. F. Shaw:

Don't buy the claim that hydroelectric developments are the safest energy producers. Since 1928, 2980 persons have been killed by dam failures. Although there have so far been no radiation deaths in the United States from reactor accidents, nevertheless the U.S. reactor safety report worked out the following probabilities of accidents per year to 15 million people living within 25 miles of 100 nuclear energy plants.

---

[12] *Vital Speeches,* XLIV, 7 (Jan. 15, 1978), pp. 197–8.
[13] Data from *Forbes* (Feb. 15, 1964), pp. 20–24.

Accident	Fatalities
Automobile	*4,200*
Accidental falls	*1,500*
Fires	*560*
Electrocution	*90*
Lightning	*8*
Reactor accidents	*2*

In simpler terms—your chances of being killed by a reactor accident are about the same as your chances of being struck by a meteor.[14]

In most cases round numbers should be used whenever the facts will not be distorted. For example, 300,000 and 25,000 are easier to grasp and retain than 300,192 and 24,975. Statistical citations should be as short as possible and also fairly infrequent. Long tabulations and constant lists of figures become burdensome and meaningless to many listeners. Statistics also prepared and presented in visual form make it easier for listeners to digest them.

LAWS AND PRINCIPLES. A physical law or scientific principle is a statement of the nature or relationship of a certain class of facts. The law is inferred from statistical information gathered by a great number of observers and may be verified by other observers. Its truth is so widely accepted that the opinion of an individual does not alter it. A natural law or principle is a short method of handling statistics, since only the inference needs to be presented.

The law of causation underlies all human reasoning. It is assumed that every change in nature is produced by some cause, that every fact or event has a reason for being as it is rather than otherwise. This assumption makes thoughtful listeners demand support for all assertions. Various special fields of knowledge have laws, such as the laws of motion in physics, the laws of superposition in geology, and the laws of association in psychology. The causes of inflation and corporate strategies against it were discussed by Geoffrey R. Simonds in a speech of which the following is an excerpt:

In preparing for this presentation, one of the things that struck me was that most of the organized power groups continuously generate inflation, while the private sector struggles to offset those inflationary pressures by continuously increasing efficiency and productivity.

---

[14] *Vital Speeches*, XLIII, 21 (Aug. 15, 1977), p. 650.

Look at the costly legislation we are being bombarded with, such as OSHA, ERISA, welfare reform, increased Social Security, higher minimum wage, plus continued deficit-financing, etc. Is it any wonder that inflation is here to stay? Some of our larger industries, such as chemicals and paper, have been required to spend enormous sums of money to clean up the environment. Most of this, desirable as it may be, has contributed absolutely nothing to productive efficiency. Every U.S. automobile manufactured today has included in its price about $700 of costs mandated by Washington. No wonder at times the business community feels its only friend in Washington is Mr. Burns, with his continuous prodding of the Government to stop manufacturing inflation.[15]

Testimony. A testimony is an interpretation of facts or a judgment of value based upon them. Testimony, or opinion, differs from fact in an important way: it is what someone thinks, not what has been objectively verified. Opinions are less conclusive than facts because they are more subject to errors of perception, interpretation, and evaluation. A speaker may give his own opinion. This is what he believes or thinks about a subject. It may or may not be founded upon observation, knowledge, and experience. A speaker's own opinion usually convinces nobody else, unless, of course, the speaker is a recognized authority.

An opinion may also be an assumption, a statement of widely accepted truth that does not claim to rest on proof. Some examples are: "Love is better than hate," "Peace is better than war," "Life has a purpose." An opinion is authoritative when its author has the prestige based on study, knowledge, experience, and good judgment in a given subject. Only an expert can evaluate the facts and state an opinion that we can respect. His judgment seems to us impersonal; he is probably not using his opinions to manipulate us. The testimony of an authority has the strength of being carefully formed; it can stand up under analysis and criticism. The value of such an opinion depends chiefly on the authority involved. Obviously, he must not be prejudiced in his judgments.

Testimony can be used by a speaker in various ways. He can quote the exact words of an authority as Bryce Mackasy did in his speech "The Labor Management Struggle":

---

[15] *Vital Speeches,* XLIV, 8 (Feb. 1, 1978), p. 246.

> *Managers today are well aware of the changing climate. As Sir Freder-*
> *ick Hooper, Managing Director of the Schweppes Group, puts it, "Suc-*
> *cessful management now has no place for the despot—not even the*
> *benevolent despot." Managers practice "management by objective," del-*
> *egating decisions down the line.*[16]

The opinion of an authority can be indirectly stated as J. E. Olson
did:

> *Still, I think [Peter] Drucker does have a point. The enormous invest-*
> *ment that employees' pension funds have in our industries and businesses*
> *certainly gives them a stake in the success or failure of our enterprise.*
> *And their stake in a business' ultimate success ought to make them*
> *thoughtful about the need for productivity and a good bottom line.*[17]

The authority may be handled in an original style for persuasive
effect. James V. Schall referred to authorities in this manner:

> *Animals are good in themselves, fascinating in their variety, breeds,*
> *and habits. But in a crunch, anyone who sacrifices man to animals,*
> *however this is done, is idolatrous. Thus, I am spiritually far closer*
> *to the Hindu respect for all life than I am to the Christian or liberal*
> *who approves, say, abortion or compulsory euthanasia, while joining*
> *the Sierra Club to preserve mountain goats, condors, and redwoods. I*
> *am in this also much closer to classical Marxism which was very dog-*
> *matic about what this planet was for, namely, men.*[18]

Testimony, in addition to offering support, can also arouse interest
and bring richer associations to an idea, thereby impressing it more
tellingly upon the audience. An unusually well-worded thought has
a special appeal. In addition, the testimony of authorities who enjoy
prestige helps an idea to be viewed in a favorable light.

Using Facts and Testimony. The speaker needs to find all
the facts, statistics, and testimony he can on his subject, especially
the most recent ones. Their meaning and value should be analyzed
and irrelevant facts discarded. To establish an idea, the speaker selects
the evidence that best supports his concept. The omission of less
important facts is a practical necessity, since a speech has a time
limit. All facts and figures used in a speech should come from sources
that the audience will accept as reliable. Facts taken from "extreme

---

[16] *Vital Speeches,* XLI, 17 (June 15, 1975), p. 522.

[17] *Vital Speeches,* XLII, 3 (Nov. 15, 1976), p. 90.

[18] *Ibid.,* p. 83.

right" or "extreme left" publications would be convincing only to those who shared those views.

The facts should be fairly chosen; that is, they should represent what is actually known about the subject. Unusual or exceptional cases do not prove a point and are best avoided. Important facts that contradict the speaker's assertion should not be unfairly suppressed. If such facts are already known to the audience, the speaker will appear biased and therefore unconvincing. The speaker should study contradictory facts and seek ways to answer them; for example, they may be exceptional cases or they may be conditioned by extraneous factors. If opposed facts cannot be offset, the speaker should either modify his concept or present it as the best conclusion that can be formed upon the controversial evidence.

To be sure that statistics prove what he intends, the speaker must consider who prepared them, how accurately they were compiled, and precisely what they were designed to prove. A given set of statistics can often be interpreted in more than one way. As a result, listeners feel that the speaker can prove anything by statistics.

The speaker cannot risk using a quotation from an authority merely because it is catchy and pleasing: the statement may be vague or irrelevant. Memorable phrases should express a significant truth. Authorities should not be used only for their prestige value but primarily for their value as evidence supporting the speaker's assertion. Unscrupulous propagandists, long on self-interest but short on proof, invoke famous names to gain acceptance of their ideas among the unthinking.

Too much reliance should not be placed on one authority. One person's judgment is often not enough to support an important argument. It is necessary to quote several authorities, since an audience may be convinced if it is shown that a consensus of opinion supports the speaker's statement. All authorities to be used should be carefully evaluated for reliability, thoroughness, and impartiality by comparing them with other sources. Their worth can be tested by the following questions: Is the authority qualified by training and experience to give information on this specific topic? Has he a reputation for good judgment? Would he benefit by concealing the truth or part of it? Does he belong to a partisan group? Is his statement specific and definite? Is he known and respected by this audience? Can he be made acceptable because of his achievement and position?

MAKING IDEAS INTERESTING

The speaker's most important task is to arouse and hold the listeners' interest. All the laws and principles of speech composition and delivery are concerned with the constant need to interest the audience. Making ideas clear and believable are basic steps toward making them interesting, because people quickly become disinterested in what they cannot understand or believe in. An author, even if he does not interest his contemporaries, can at least hope for future readers. William Blake and Emily Dickinson found recognition many years after their death. John Milton said: "Let me have fit audience though few." But a speaker cannot ignore the interest of the audience before him and assume a take-my-speech-or-leave-it attitude. If he does, the audience will leave it and all his efforts are wasted.

Interest is a feeling of curiosity, attentiveness, or concern about something. Attention is observing or giving heed to something that arouses interest. Attention and interest are so closely related that the terms are often used interchangeably. It is relatively easy to get a person to attend. To keep him intent is difficult: attention must be restimulated until interest is aroused to the point of deep concern. An understanding of the nature, conditions, and factors of attention should make the techniques of holding interest possible.

Nature of Attention.   Three facts about attention are outstanding: it is highly selective, it constantly shifts, and it can be directed toward a given goal.

Human beings are surrounded by a complex and changing environment. Vast numbers of stimuli crowd in on us at all times. We cannot attend or respond to all of them. We attend to one stimulus and select one response. As we focus on this one thing, we ignore the rest of the forces surrounding us. Then we shift our attention to another nearby object and still another as we investigate their significance. We finally return to the original object and respond by approaching or accepting it, or else by withdrawing or rejecting it.

The process of attention may be as short as this schematized one or it may be extended to complex explorations of great intentness and duration. A speech, like a motion picture, novel, or other time sequence pattern, must be built on the fact that to pay attention is to react to a single element of experience at least for a moment.

All elements of the speech, therefore, are arranged to keep attention focused on the unfolding of the speaker's ideas.

Stimulating Attention.   Certain conditions in the environment stimulate attention.

• *Strong Stimulus.* A strong stimulus, such as a large object, a sudden movement, a bright light, or a loud sound commands attention. For this reason a speaker can stimulate attention by using more volume, by making a gesture, or by changing position.

• *Repeated Stimulus.* A stimulus when repeated keeps getting attention until the responding individual gets used to it or fatigued by it. Repeating a phrase or idea in a speech impresses it upon the listeners. However if it is repeated too often, it becomes monotonous and causes a loss of attention.

• *Change of Stimulus.* Any definite change of stimulus attracts attention. A continuous noise is soon ignored, but if the sound suddenly stops, it will again capture attention. Similarly, a pause for effect in speaking challenges attention.

Since attention cannot be continuous or unbroken, it must be renewed at frequent intervals to keep listeners interested in the speech. The speaker must offer variety or successive changes in stimulation not only in the composition of the speech but also in its delivery. Different gestures and platform actions and changes in emphasis, rate, pitch inflection, and emotion can be used to stimulate interest.

Factors of Attention and Interest.   To hold attention beyond a short interval, a speech must appeal to basic factors, or underlying desires and attitudes of listeners. These interests or needs may be biological, psychological, or sociological; usually they are complex combinations of all three. We human beings are interested in ourselves, in others, in our surroundings, and in activities. A few of these fundamental factors are self-concern, struggle, proximity, human interest, and novelty.

Self-Concern.   Everyone's major interest is himself. Nothing is quite as real to a person as his own likes and dislikes, his own tastes and pleasures, his own thoughts and feelings, and his own works and responsibilities. He is the important island in an unimportant sea. To build a bridge to his listeners, a speaker must understand their needs, feelings, and problems and adapt his ideas to their concerns. What deeply interests most people are their own problems and how to solve them. The more a speaker understands the difficulties and hopes of other persons, the more he can speak directly to them and seem to express their own thoughts, convictions, and aspirations. He grasps their problems and offers a solution or at least a hope for favorable results.

Struggle. All living creatures share the struggle for existence and must constantly resist conflicting or dangerous elements in the environment. Life is an all important struggle against the forces of death. To some philosophers the basic conflict is between good and evil. Any newspaper or newscast captures interest with reports of conflict in all departments of life, whether social, economic, legislative, or judicial. Areas of conflict abound throughout the globe.

Many speech subjects can be made more interesting by building them on a pattern of struggle—not only sports, elections, and murder trials, but less obviously dramatic topics, such as fresh water from the sea. A phase of the struggle between Cuba and the United States over Guantanamo made the distillation of sea water a vitally interesting topic.

Proximity. What is close to a person is of deep concern to him. Food, drink, sex, physical comfort, and well-being are underlying wants that many advertisements use for their appeal. Family, friends, and the community are more meaningful to him than people of other places or those who do not speak his language. Here and today is much more important than there and yesterday. Local newspapers for this reason feature local news; speakers mention local leaders, landmarks, and progress. In a speech called "Do What You Can With What You've Got," Arch N. Booth related his subject to local listeners:

> —Last week I read some statistics which show that the best time to buy anything is about 40 years ago.
> —Some friends of ours were planning a trip to London this summer to see the sights—to see the Changing of the Guard.
> They decided it would be more exciting to stay home and watch the changing of the prices at the supermarket.[19]

Seeing that each listener is interested in his own life, situation, community, country, and ideas, a speech presenting new or different ideas must offer strong and moving evidence to win acceptance.

---

[19] *Vital Speeches,* XL, 23 (Sept. 15, 1974), p. 719.

Human Interest.   People are more interested in human beings than in most things. Pet owners are even prone to read human ideas and reactions into their dogs, cats, lovebirds, ocelots, or tropical fish. Fiction, drama, and biography appeal to human interest. News, whether spoken or written, is about persons much of the time. Human beings are in accidents, commit crimes, save lives, run for office; they marry, divorce, and denounce other individuals. Persons famous for their skill, power, possessions, or love affairs are of immediate interest. Therefore anecdotes, examples, and other illustrations based on individuals make a speech more interesting.

Novelty.   We may be deeply rooted in familiar things and our daily habits tend to make us resist change; but, on the other hand, the items in our lives are so familiar that they become humdrum and stifling. Then we seek change, such as an argument, a buying spree, a weekend trip, or a new romance. An audience responds to novelty, to recent developments, strange customs, or new dangers. Every topic for a speech should contain a new ingredient of some kind. What, for example, can be said of coffee drinking that has not been uttered before? A new twist might be the fact that coffee has been found to contain B vitamins.

Novelty is anything different, remarkable, unlooked for, or disturbing. The unusual element can be humorous, as one woman who explained her marriage by stating that her new husband had a better heating system in his house than she had in hers. Max D. Isaacson brought in a less common view of human relations:

> This uneducated black cleaning woman confided that she had faced a great deal of fear and tragedy and poverty all her life, and told of the time she had her three-year-old son in a public health clinic, waiting for treatment for pneumonia. But while waiting for that treatment, the little boy . . . died . . . in her arms. And then she added: "You see, doctor, the dying patients are just like old acquaintances to me, and I'm not afraid to touch them, to talk with them, or to offer them hope."
>
> As a result of her tremendous rapport with these patients, this woman subsequently was promoted to a job of "special counselor to the dying" and works in that capacity to this day. She was too noble for anger, too strong for fear, and too happy to permit the presense of trouble.[20]

---

[20] *Vital Speeches,* XLIV, 7 (Jan. 15, 1978), p. 205.

Techniques of Interest. Visual illustrations create interest as well as clarity if they are attractive, colorful, or are capable of movement. An alert, animated, and varied delivery of the speech is another method of holding interest. Human and verbal imagery are other attractors of interest. Narration is a highly important interest device and should be used without hesitation.

Narration. Narration offers action, a sense of something happening in a progressive sequence. Activity, as mentioned before, is a primary cause of attention. Passers-by, for instance, will stop to watch an excavator at work. Exciting action is part of the appeal of spectator sports, the ballet, or western movies.

In its simplest form, a narrative is a connected series of events leading to some sort of culmination. More typically, a narrative is a conflict between opposing desires, endeavors, or ideas. The opposition may be an individual, a group, nature itself, or fate. The progress of the struggle is absorbing because its outcome remains uncertain until the climax. The explanation of some subjects can be organized on the narrative pattern of struggle. As an example, the conflict inherent in rent strikes by tenants against slumlords can be given immediacy by quoting conversations of some of the individuals involved.

The most valuable use of narration is for illustration. The elements of conflict, suspense, and human sympathies make a narrative illustration more compelling than most factual examples. Narrative illustrations include the incident, the anecdote, the story, and the parable.

INCIDENT. An incident or episode is a minor event, often occurring as part of a more important happening. T. Earle Johnson quoted a contemporary incident to illustrate the growing cult of mediocrity:

> *A worried mother recently called me by telephone to ask me to intervene for her son who had failed to win a scholarship at a well known private school. "How did he do in his tests?" I asked. "I don't know," she confessed plaintively. "But what difference does that make? He is a lot better than most boys who get scholarships."*[21]

ANECDOTE. An anecdote is a brief entertaining account of a personal happening. Douglass C. Harvey, in a speech given at Purdue University, offered an anecdote to establish rapport with his listeners:

---

[21] *Vital Speeches,* XXVIII, 6 (Jan. 1, 1962), p. 184.

One young man came up to Senator Keating one evening as he was busy studying a Senate committee report and said, "Senator, I wish you would help me with my homework."

Being a little busy that evening, the Senator replied, "Why don't you ask your teacher?"

The young man replied, "I don't want to go that high."

If that's how teachers and politicians rank, I'm not going to ask about businessmen.[22]

An anecdote that gives pleasure is not only an interest device within itself but also enables the speaker to gain renewed attention after the audience has been refreshed with a minute or two of relaxation. All anecdotes are not necessarily humorous. Some are enjoyable because they illustrate a point aptly and succinctly.

STORY. A story is a connected series of events leading to a climax. A story has characters experiencing the happenings and a setting where the events occur. The more definite and specific are the *who, what,* and *when,* the stronger the effect on the audience. In addition, a story creates a mood, atmosphere, or emotional reaction. Since a story consists of a series of happenings it is longer than an incident or anecdote; in fact, a story includes incidents and anecdotes. Its length is a practical limitation. A story can be used for illustration only in longer speeches where there is time for such amplification of supporting material.

PARABLE. A parable is a brief, simple story illustrating a moral. When the characters, things, and events have another meaning, the parable, like the fable, is an allegory. *Gulliver's Travels* is a famous allegory, and *Aesop's Fables* are well known. The most familiar parables are probably those of Jesus.

Moral and ethical ideas such as duty or justice are abstractions difficult to explain. Analyzing an idea in component parts yields other abstract concepts that also require explanation. Since most listeners cannot follow philosophical discussions, many moral and spiritual teachers have used parables to bring principles of conduct home to their hearers. The following short fable, which the speaker heard in the Middle East, is from a speech by Chauncey E. Schmidt:

The scorpion came out of the desert to the banks of the Nile, whereupon he accosted a crocodile. He said to the crocodile, "My dear chap,

---

[22] *Vital Speeches,* XLI, 24 (Oct. 1, 1975), p. 761.

could we form an alliance to get to the other side of the Nile?"

The crocodile retorted, "Do you think I am stupid? I would be at your complete mercy. You could sting me and kill me at any time during the crossing."

"Of course not," said the scorpion. "I promise not to sting you, but more important is that even if I did sting you, I then would drown."

The crocodile thought for a second and agreed that that made sense and took the scorpion on his back. About midstream the scorpion became agitated and stung the crocodile.

As the two were about to go under, the crocodile turned to the scorpion and said, "Now we both will die. What possible explanation or logic is there for such an act?"

"There is none," said the scorpion, "this is the Middle East."[23]

---

[23] *Vital Speeches,* XLIV, 8 (Feb. 1, 1978), p. 241.

7.
LANGUAGE FOR SPEAKING

The speaker's meaning will not be complete until it is expressed in the actual words of the speech. In a written speech the language is selected, evaluated, and improved in advance. In an impromptu speech the language is composed and expressed as it is delivered to the audience. Extemporaneous speaking is a combination of preliminary composition and improvised performance. The speaker thoroughly prepares the content of his speech but expresses it in words during his presentation.

Extemporaneous and impromptu speaking presuppose a mastery of language, which includes a sufficient store of words to express ideas and an adequate facility in arranging words in sentences to convey the entire meaning. The speaker's language habits should be suitable for the immediate conveying of meaning; if they are not, he should set about improving them.

THE PROBLEM OF MEANING

Language presents difficult and unexpected problems to the speaker because its meanings depend on others. The study of meaning, or semantics, deals with the relations between words, things, and human responses. These relations have been studied from various points of view and for various purposes. The knowledge of even a few semantic principles should help the speaker to communicate more effectively.

According to some writers, meaningful communication has three elements: the word, which is merely a symbol composed of speech sounds; the referent, or the concrete thing the word indicates; and the reference, or the individual's total experience, real or imaginary, with the referent. For example, the word "aspirin" is a specific grouping of English speech sounds and refers to a specific chemical compound. The word evokes whatever the individual has heard, read, experienced, thought, or imagined about the chemical substance. Obviously, the referents of all words cannot be defined as accurately as $C_9H_8O_4$. Even in the case of aspirin, when a speaker talks about its uses, such as reducing fever or relieving headache, the meaning or reference becomes less definite, because all persons do not react to aspirin in the same way. Since the experience of individuals with a given object is never identical, the word will have different meanings for each person. It is quite impossible to know everything that individuals have experienced in connection with a given object; therefore, the meaning of a word is uncertain and variable. Fortunately, individuals are both speakers and listeners, and most of them have had similar experiences with many objects. Common meanings are currently attached to words referring to these objects, the meaning of a word being the context in which the speaker uses it and the response it elicits in the listener.

It is difficult to realize consistently that words are not the things they symbolize. "A rose is a rose" is not a meaningful answer to the question "What is a rose?" Words are abstract and arbitrary symbols; things are concrete and definite items in the world of reality. The word "water," for instance, will not help a man dying of thirst in a desert. Only the actual liquid can save his life.

It is sometimes difficult to realize that the word is not the meaning it evokes in the listener. The reference is an internal reaction, while the word is an external stimulus. A speaker, for example, might use the term "rose of Sharon" referring to the familiar shrub *Hibiscus syriacus,* but the listener may associate the term with the herbaceous perennial *Hypericum calycinum,* which is called "rose of Sharon" in some localities. A meaning can be successfully conveyed only when the speaker's word and the listener's reference are both associated with the same referent. Evidently a verbal communication should be preceded not only by a knowledge of the facts but also by a consideration of the listener's knowledge of the same or similar facts.

Kinds of Meaning. Many writers on semantics who are predominantly interested in judging the accuracy of statements distinguish two kinds of meaning. The referent is called *denotative meaning* and the reference, *connotative meaning*. A denotative meaning is objective or extensional: it is a definite area in the external world which can be located, observed, or verified by others. If someone says, "There's a bottle of port in the cupboard," the hearer can determine the truth of the statement by checking the designated cupboard. A connotative meaning is subjective or intensional: it is an unmeasurable region in the internal world of an individual which can only be imagined by others. The statement, "This port is the best in the world," obviously cannot be verified. The listener can only wonder at the speaker's opinion or perhaps share it along with the wine.

Since statements with denotative meanings are based on a core of common experience, they offer a basis for agreement in handling many practical problems. Statements with connotative meanings may interfere with the solution of problems because they are based on variations of experience which may be incompatible.

Utterances often have both denotative and connotative meanings. A statement may contain attitude as well as fact: "The bottle of port you gave me had a superb flavor." The listener knows that he made the gift but has no way of verifying the vanished wine's flavor or of measuring the speaker's taste. The two kinds of meaning may be so intermingled in a statement that they are difficult to distinguish. Any serious consideration of meaning reveals the need for a constant revaluation of individual meanings.

Meanings Are Dated.   The world is dynamic and different conditions and new experiences lead to changes in vocabulary. Some words are abandoned and new ones acquired. Many words, however, take on new meanings, the inevitable result of using a limited number of words to describe an unlimited number of things. The constant changes of word meanings make frequent definitions and explanations necessary in speaking. Many terms should be dated in some manner so that their meaning is made clearer by their context. The "national debt" of 1939, for instance, has a different meaning from the "national debt" of 1980.

Meanings Are Selected.   It is impossible to give every detail of an object referred to in a definition or description. For one reason, an existing thing cannot be fully known until it has been observed at all times and in all situations. Therefore, certain essential or characteristic features are selected or abstracted to represent the whole phenomenon. The fact that the utterance does not "tell all," that it omits other aspects of the item under consideration, should be indicated by "and so forth," "such as," "some of," or other qualifying expressions.

Meanings Are Graduated. The phenomena of the universe are classified into groups for treatment, discussion, and understanding. Most traits, conditions, or values are part of a spectrum or series of transitions and cannot be classified into only two groups, such as young and old, wise and foolish, freedom and bondage, and beauty and ugliness. The "either-or" classification should be avoided, since it does not fit the complexity of most things and situations. Honesty in evaluating the external world and in choosing words to discuss an item leads to a clearer understanding.

Limitations of Accuracy.

Accuracy, like all other aspects of meaning, poses practical problems. A lawyer's language may be highly accurate, but it is unintelligible to most audiences. A demagogue's language may be readily understood, but it has no relationship to the truth. There are drawbacks to both high and low degrees of accuracy in language use. An analogous situation exists in the manufacture of tools and machines. Certain parts must be accurate within one thousandth of an inch. All parts could be given the same accuracy, but the costs would be staggering. Speech at times must have high accuracy, but at other times it cannot bear the burden. Accuracy in language, for one thing, requires definition of terms. The terms used in defining terms require definitions. The terms used in defining definitions require definitions, and so on in never-ending ramifications.

At some point, for practical reasons, it must be agreed that certain words mean the "same" thing to a group of people. The speaker's task is to find these words, avoiding both highly specialized language and highly vague language. He must state some aspect of justifiable truth, but must remember than a justifiable truth is not stated until it is understood. Theoretically, it might be better for communication if human beings did not have bodies with fallible sensations, emotions, and thoughts. However, human beings have their present physiological equipment and communication must present symbolizations that are real to the senses and emotions as well as the intellect.

SPOKEN STYLE

Style, or the manner of using language, is the way of putting thoughts into words. The Platonic school regards style as a perfect or completely appropriate expression of the thought. A piece either has perfection of expression or else it lacks style. Jonathan Swift defined style as "Proper words in proper places." The Aristotelian school regards style as individual manners of expression. Every piece has some manner of style, which is neither good nor bad, but simply characteristic of its author. The Comte de Buffon said that "style is the man himself."

Modern conceptions of style incorporate elements of both viewpoints. The speaker not only puts his thoughts into his own expression but adapts his expression to the audience. When a speaker strives to improve his style, striving for qualities like clarity, vividness, and appropriateness, he is subscribing to the idea that style is more than personal expression.

SPOKEN AND WRITTEN STYLES

A spoken style is different in many ways from a written style. Spoken style is more direct and personal. The speaker conveys his ideas to a given group of listeners at a specific time and place. He is communicating orally and visually to his listeners. Oral style includes the vocal features of stress, pitch inflection, and tone quality. The audible features, together with gesture, posture, facial expression, and other visual features, help to convey the speaker's ideas, feelings, attitudes, and other personal qualities. The immediacy of the situation is enhanced by the fact that the speaker receives and reacts stylistically to the listeners' responses. Even when a speech is broadcast the speaker's style is adapted to listeners at a given time and to the current public situation. The writer, however, has no direct contact with his readers, but addresses himself to widely scattered and successive individual readers. He offers them an abstract record of his thoughts and cannot alter his style to suit the responses of his audience.

The attitude of a writer tends to be more aloof and impersonal than that of a speaker. Montaigne said, "To go preach to the first passer-by, to become tutor to the ignorance of the first I meet, is a thing I abhor." Yet the speaker is willing to speak to passers-by, to people he does not know. The fact that some listeners are ignorant does not deter him, but challenges him to present his ideas simply, clearly, and understandably.

Writers like Sir Winston Churchill bring some of the direct qualities of their spoken style into their writing. The following passage from Churchill's *The Gathering Storm* nevertheless is recognizably different from his speaking. The sentence structures are complex and the words *infringed, signatories, demilitarized,* and *perpetrated* are technical.

> *Should, however, Articles 42 or 43 of the Treaty of Versailles be infringed, such a violation would constitute "an unprovoked act of aggression," and immediate action would be required from the offended signatories because of the assembling of armed forces in the demilitarized zone. Such a violation should be brought at once before the League of Nations, and the League, having established the fact of violation, must then advise the signatory Powers that they were bound to give their military aid to the Power against whom the offence had been perpetrated.*[1]

In the following excerpt from Churchill's address to the House of Commons on May 13, 1940, all the words are familiar and none have more than three syllables. Four of the sentences are short and simple.

> *You ask, What is our aim? I can answer in one word. It is victory. Victory at all costs—victory in spite of terrors—victory, however long and hard the road may be, for without victory there is no survival. Let that be realized. No survival for the British Empire, no survival for all that the British Empire has stood for, no survival for the urge, the impulse of the ages, that mankind shall move forward toward his goal.*

QUALITIES OF SPOKEN STYLE

Among the most important qualities of spoken style is the use of direct and personal expressions, as well as clear words and understandable sentences.

Direct and Personal Expression. A speaker brings some of the frankness, simplicity, and freedom of daily speech into his public

---

[1] Winston S. Churchill, *The Second World War,* Vol. I: *The Gathering Storm* (Boston: Houghton Mifflin Co., 1948), p. 192.

addresses. He talks directly to his listeners as he does in conversation. This conversational quality is the outstanding feature of spoken style. The speaker's personal relationship to his audience is shown by his free use of the pronouns *you, we, us, I,* and *me.* These pronouns are as natural in formal addresses as in informal. Their use has long been standard practice as shown by these representative examples: "We have men ready to interpose their veto, ready to defend the republic with the sanctions of religion. We ought to be strangers to fear," Cicero; "If England is a tyrant, it is you have made her so: it is the slave that makes the tyrant, and then murmurs at the master whom he himself has constituted," Henry Grattan; "We can no more live without an attempt at international order than we can run New York's traffic without rules of the road," Adlai Stevenson.

Some beginning speakers hesitate to use "I" because they are afraid of appearing egotistical. It depends, of course, on why and how the pronoun is used. If a speaker is not conceited, he probably will not appear so. The danger of seeming to be self-centered is avoided by speakers who are idea-centered and have worthy reasons for stating their honest convictions. "We have those among us who think a speaker fully refuted by asking, 'What then is to be done?' To whom I answer, with the utmost truth and justice, 'Not what we are doing now,' " Demosthenes; "I say I am yet too young to understand that God is any respecter of persons. I believe that to have intervened as I have done—as I have always freely admitted I have done—was not wrong, but right," John Brown.

Clear Word Usage.   Spoken language must be instantly intelligible. A speech, unlike a written message, cannot be heard over and over again, nor can it be laid aside until later. The speaker cannot expect listeners to decipher obscure meanings. The audience has no dictionaries, maps, reference books, or explanatory notes. A speaker cannot wait to be understood and appreciated later. His speech succeeds or fails when it is delivered. Each word the speaker uses must express his meaning exactly and also be easy to comprehend. These conditions are best met by choosing short, familiar, and concrete words.

Short Words.   Some speakers pass over short words in favor of long ones, believing that terms of impressive size have more meaning. A large glass holds more water than a small one; therefore it is logical that a big word contains more meaning than a little one. In language, however, as in paper money, mere size is irrelevant. A twenty dollar bill is no larger than a one dollar bill. Small words express most of the essential things in daily life and therefore the most frequently talked about things. The following are sample words from a few aspects of experience:

Persons: father, mother, boy, girl, man, woman, friend.
Actions: eat, drink, sleep, wash, walk, run, work.
Places: home, school, church, store, street, town.
Feelings: pain, joy, grief, love, hate, hope.
Judgments: yes, no, good, bad, fair.
Concepts: life, death, God, duty, truth, justice, beauty.

Short words are economical and convenient. They require less time and effort to utter and understand. If a speaker, by the word *consideration,* means *fee, bribe,* or *payment,* he should use the shorter term. The following example shows how long words can obscure the meaning: "The President is asking for executive authority to negotiate these inequitable impediments to a more even basis by reciprocal adjustments." Since the context is a discussion of tariff barriers, this sentence may mean, "The President is asking for power to make fair tariff agreements with other countries."

A longer word should not be used if a shorter one expresses the meaning. *Incurable* is simpler than *irremediable.* If no adequate short word can be found, a group of words is clearer: *keen judgment* is easier to understand than *perspicacity.*

Familiar Words. It is more important for a word to be clear than to be short. Clear words are familiar words. The longer words in the following pairs would be understood more quickly by the majority of listeners: projection, jutty; widespread, rife; accustomed, inured; meadow, lea. Long words like *indispensable, formidable,* and *disadvantageous* may be familiar to most listeners, but too many words of several syllables make a message less direct and less personal. A clear, expressive spoken style has variety of word length, but short, simple words are its foundation.

Foreign Words. Highly educated people and those who have lived in foreign countries are apt to use foreign words and expressions. Since these terms are rarely understood by American audiences, familiar English words should be substituted for them. English, of course, has borrowed freely from other languages; many foreign words have become part of the language. Even so, many listeners do not understand these terms. For this reason it is better in a speech to use *sponsorship* rather than *aegis, newspaper stand* rather than *kiosk*. On the other hand, countless foreign words are in daily use, such as *studio, patio, rodeo, camouflage, salon, garage*. The speaker does not judge words by their origin but by their significance to his listeners.

Technical Words. A growing barrier to communication is jargon or the specialized vocabularies and methods of expression of the various fields of activity. Each science, technology, and vocation has developed a separate use of language to achieve an exactness of expression that cannot be misunderstood. The result is a jargon that cannot be understood by anyone except specialists in that activity. The worst feature of jargon is that it seems to travel all around an idea rather than to get to the gist of it. Most people reject jargon. They are not interested in carrying a ton of equipment around the block in order to go next door. A speaker, of course, is on the side of his listeners. He translates scientific terms like *abscissa, graminivorous, morphology, pyromagnetic,* and *subliminal* into simple, clear language. If he cannot find a familiar word to convey the meaning of a term, the speaker defines and explains it in words that everyone can understand.

Concrete Words. Language involves generalization, which is singling out traits that certain things have in common and then giving these common traits a group name. In this manner *John, George, Paul, Henry,* and so forth become the abstract or nonspecific concept *man*. The concept *man* can be divided into somewhat more specific groups as indicated by such terms as *fellow, youth, hero, villain, worker, husband, hoodlum, soldier, farmer, master, father,* or *astronaut*. Before using an abstract term the speaker should try to narrow down the concept and find a more concrete term. Abstract concepts can often be made concrete by putting them in terms of persons: not robbery, but a thief; not love, but a lover; not unemployment, but a laid-off worker.

Particulars are what a speaker should give rather than generalities tiring to his listeners and to himself. In a recent speech on our aging population Daniel Rose did not hesitate to use concrete language:

Since even young and healthy bachelors sometimes have trouble with shopping, meal preparation, house-cleaning, laundry, clothes-mending and so forth, it is not surprising that the elderly sometimes do (and are grateful if they get it).

The other side of the coin, however (and we can't forget this), is that regular building staff need real protection from "the clinger," who can't do anything unless you help him; or "the big boss," who must have the last word at all times on all subjects; or "the loner," who withdraws and can't be reached; or "the sitter," who just won't budge; or "the manipulator," who always has an angle, a counter-proposal, or what he is sure is a "special situation"; "the Lothario" or "Great Lover," who needs to demonstrate audibly and sometimes visibly that he is still interested in sex; and, finally from "the trouble-maker," who undoubtedly was a first class pain in the neck when young and has now become even worse.

But when all is said and done, everyone at all involved with the elderly in any capacity will have to be reminded from time to time of the requirements that all human beings share throughout the life-cycle: the need to love and be loved, the need for a sense of identity and belonging.[2]

Overworked Words. Certain words have been used and abused so constantly that they have lost much of their force. For example, *swell, hilarious, fabulous, colossal, terrific, marvelous.* An individual speaker more or less unconsciously may use a favorite word or phrase over and over, such as *actually, frankly, you know, okay, now, right-thinking, it seems to me.* The repetition of such words becomes annoying to listeners, and the speaker's meaning is lost or rejected. Overworked words can be avoided if the speaker first determines his exact meaning and then finds a word to express it.

Understandable Sentences. Most ideas are not communicated by individual words but by a group of words or a sentence. Each word in a phrase or sentence stands in a relation with other words and has a different value than it has by itself. Every language has its own methods of grammar and syntax, or methods of using words in combination. English, like many languages, tends to put the most important part of a sentence last; that is, the subject is followed by the predicate. The subject is introduced to say something about it, and usually what is said about it is more important than the

---

[2] *Vital Speeches,* XLIV, 20 (Aug. 1, 1978), p. 622.

mere mention of the subject. This fact of predicate emphasis means that the listener cannot be sure of the meaning of a sentence until he hears the end of it. Since the listener must remember the words of a sentence until the last word is pronounced, spoken sentences should not be too long or complex for the listener's memory span.

Forms of Sentence Structure.   A simple sentence or a clear sequence of subject and predicate is easy for the listener to grasp: "Every form of government has its happy accidents," Macaulay. The subject and predicate may contain various modifying groups of words without altering the basic pattern: "Character is that which reveals moral purpose, exposing the class of things a man chooses or avoids," Aristotle.

A single subject followed by a succession of predicates or objects is not difficult to follow: "Poverty blights whole cities; spreads horrible pestilence; strikes at the soul of all those who come within sight, sound or smell of it," G. B. Shaw. A succession of subjects before one predicate is less often used, but it can make an impression upon the listener: "Homes, factories, schools, hospitals, railways, communications, public utilities, government offices, and the like have been rebuilt," Harold Walter Sundstrom.

A compound sentence or a series of two or more independent clauses is also easy to follow: "Baloney is flattery so thick it cannot be true, and blarney is flattery so thin we like it," Bishop Fulton J. Sheen.

Complex sentences are more difficult to understand because they contain one or more subordinate clauses. A complex sentence is easier for the listener to interpret if the subordinate clause follows the main clause. The opposite arrangement offers an impediment to understanding, because the reason for a statement cannot be grasped until the statement is presented: "Because we will not solve the problems of tomorrow with yesterday's tools, new problems will require new ideas, new approaches, and new concepts." The meaning is much clearer the way Walter P. Reuther said it: "New problems will require new ideas, new approaches, and new concepts, because we will not solve the problems of tomorrow with yesterday's tools."

Any sentence is difficult to grasp if it contains too many long modifying phrases, extended parentheses, and other inserted material. Too many points have to be connected by special stress, pause, and pitch inflection. "Human beings, who come in various sizes, shapes, and colors, are thrown together on this earth, and, in spite of an equal diversity in religious beliefs and political ideologies, have to live together." The meaning of such a sentence becomes clearer when the parts are offered in several sentences: "Human beings come in various sizes, shapes, and colors. This variety is equaled by a diversity in religious beliefs and political ideologies. We are thrown together on this earth and must live together."

Connectives. A continuous series of short, simple sentences gives an effect of bareness, overconciseness, and lack of full development of the thought. Variety alone demands the use of sentences of varying lengths. The connection between parts of longer sentences is shown by connective words. The continuity of thought running through several sentences may be obvious; if not, it is shown by connective words or phrases.

The simplest connectives are effective in speaking. The commonest ones are *and, because, but, for,* and *so.* Simple connectives like these give a clear style without calling attention to themselves. Some connectives suggest a formal or technical written style and should be avoided. A few examples are: *at the same time, for this reason, hence, hereupon, notwithstanding, nonetheless, whereas, whereupon, that is to say,* and *thereby.*

It is not advisable to use a large number of different connectives in one speech for they create an effect of artificiality. A speaker can have a clear but natural spoken style by using the connective words which are part of his daily conversation. However, some speakers repeatedly begin sentences with *and* or *now;* this habit soon becomes distractive.

FORCEFUL LANGUAGE

Spoken style must be more than accurate and clear. It must also be vigorous, idiomatic, and emphatic to make a forceful impression upon the listener. Forcefulness implies movement, change, progression, and climax.

Verbs for Action. Verbs express activity, and well-chosen verbs intensify the force of what is happening. Nouns can also denote action but their effect is usually less emphatic. "After considerable thought, his decision for confession was made" is unidiomatic and weak compared to "He thought it over and decided to confess."

Active verbs convey a more definite sense of movement than passive verbs. "My opinion is rested on no general theory of government. All general theories of government are distrusted by me." Fortunately for his listeners, Macaulay used active verbs: "I rest my opinion on no general theory of government. I distrust all general theories of government."

Spoken Usage.   Spoken usage is more forceful and informal than written. Good spoken grammar is the usage acceptable in good conversation. For example, in colloquial speech *like* is often used as a conjunction; an adjective may be a "flat" or invariable adverb. An example of the latter is Lincoln's use of *easier,* although he used the adverbial form of *faithful* in the next sentence. "Can aliens make treaties easier than friends can make laws? Can treaties be more faithfully enforced between aliens than laws can among friends?"

Speakers do not avoid ending sentences with prepositions and adverbs whenever the effect is natural. "At what are you looking?" and "I want to think through the matter" are stilted. "What are you looking at?" and "I want to think the matter through" are more emphatic.

Spoken usage, however, allows only certain kinds of flexibilities. The speaker should know what grammatical errors are not acceptable. Double negatives, for example, and incorrect verb forms should be avoided: "You won't find none of those things in the contract." "I seen everything that happens."

Variety in Sentence Types.   Statements can be varied in length, structure, and other ways, but speakers have always valued the immediacy, intensity, and personal quality of commands, exclamations, and questions. Not only does variety in types of sentences reawaken interest but it directs and challenges the thinking of the audience.

Direct commands are used less often than questions but are often effective. The wording usually suggests favorable attitudes or emotions in the audience. The following are examples from speeches: "Question history, and learn how all the defenders of liberty, in all times, have been overwhelmed by calumny," Robespierre; "Never, never underestimate the power of the smalltown newspapers," Alan C. McIntosh.

Exclamations appeal to the emotions and emphasize the urgency of an idea, problem, or situation. Exclamations should be appropriate to the context; their overuse may suggest overemotionalism or melo-dramatics. Exclamations can be either serious or sarcastic: "Heroic knight! Exalted senator! A second Moses come for a second exodus!" Sumner; "Simpleton! he prefers his conscience to a place, and the love of his country to a participation in her plunder!" Charles Phillips.

Questions have been used by speakers to sharpen interest, focus attention, create suspense, and evoke convictions. Direct questions are those which the speaker proceeds to answer himself: "How difficult is it for just one man to control a precinct? Let's take a close-up look," Arnold Maremont.

Rhetorical questions are those which the speaker leaves unan-swered, because he has worded them so that the audience can answer them in only one way. Rhetorical questions depend for their effect on common beliefs, common attitudes, and common emotions: "Is peace a rash system? Is it dangerous for nations to live in unity with each other?" Fox.

Partial Sentences. A sentence fragment or partial sentence pre-sents a meaning without the wording being complete in the strict grammatical sense. The subject, verb, or object may be lacking. The sentence is still complete and the meaning is completely understood by the listeners. Alan Gardiner observed that "No amount of words will ever 'complete the meaning' of an utterance, if by 'meaning' is intended the thing-meant. The thing-meant is always outside the words, not within them. It is in the situation, but not within the utterance. Thus in the sense that the exclamation Fire! is elliptic, every sentence whatsoever is elliptic."[3] "Dear money. Lower credit. Less enterprise in business and manufacture. A reduced home de-mand. Therefore, reduced output to meet it. Therefore, reduction in wages, increase of pauperism, nonemployment," Henry Campbell-Bannerman.

Climax in Sentences. Climax is the cumulative effect of details in a sentence, and might be called suspense in miniature. The details challenge interest by becoming increasingly important or significant. The rising sequence "good-better" makes a definite impression in the sentence, "His arguments are as good as yours, or better." By

---

[3] Sir Alan Gardiner, *The Theory of Speech and Language,* 2nd ed. (Oxford: Claren-don Press, 1951), p. 50.

contrast, the falling sequence "better-good" is vaguer and less conclusive: "His arguments are better, or as good as, yours."

The sequence of terms "winter and summer homes, three cars, and six television sets" diminishes interest. The number of items is less significant in indicating financial status than their cost. The sentence should be arranged to lead on to a climax: "Each family in this group owns six television sets, three cars, and both summer and winter homes."

Mark Antony in his speech as reported by Dio Cassius used climactic epithets for Julius Caesar: "Yet this father, this high priest, this inviolable being, hero, god, is dead." The effectiveness of the climactic order of arrangement is illustrated also by this sentence of Daniel O'Connell: "Thus are we treated by our friends, and our enemies, and our seceders; the first abandon, the second oppress, the third betray us, and they all join in calumniating us; in the last they are all combined."

Transitional Sentences. Spoken style reinforces the connection between major and subordinate ideas by use of repetition, restatement, or internal summaries of what has just been said. Transitions, as shown in the use of questions, also suggest suspense and climax by centering attention on what is to follow. Transitions have a stronger effect if they also indicate a progression toward establishing the theme of the speech: "Let's take a hard look at two show-window items in the subsidy supermarket: urban renewal and public housing," Edwin P. Neilan.

Contracted Forms. Spoken style uses the contractions of conversation rather than the full forms of written style. "I do not know the reason" and "Did you not foresee the results?" are stilted and weak. The natural rhythm is stronger: "I don't know the reason." "Didn't you foresee the results?" Natural rhythms are those familiar to everyone. The absence of familiar rhythm gives an air of impersonality or pomposity to utterances.

Use of Dialogue. The words of individuals growing out of actual experiences can be used to good effect. Dialogue may be more forceful than the speaker's summary of what others have said. Dialogue is not only suitable to humorous speeches and narrative illustrations but also helps explain the importance, use, or results of an idea or process. Plato used dialogue dramatically to present opposed moral, political, and social ideas, but such complete use of conversation is not suited to public speaking. Dialogue is most effective when used occasionally to reinforce a point.

> *There is a story about an Englishwoman living in India who needed extensive repairs to her house, so she contracted with a young engineer to do the work.*
>
> *But much to her exasperation the engineer kept coming back to her with questions concerning every detail of the job. Finally losing her patience, she said, "Young man, why don't you just use your common sense?"*
>
> *"Madam," the engineer replied, "Common sense is a gift of God, and I have only a technical education."*[4]—JOHN T. GURASH

Original Expression. The speaker should give his ideas as fresh and personal expression as possible. To do so means avoiding routine thinking, commonplace analogies, and stereotyped illustrations. Ideas should be studied for their hidden implications, for their relationships and applications to different areas of experience. These wider associations may yield elements that suggest new and striking phraseology. Even familiar expressions can sometimes be given a new twist, as in the following examples. "We have reached the stomach-turning point," Jenkin Lloyd Jones. "Humor is emotional chaos remembered in tranquility," James Thurber.

Terse Expression. Spoken sentences should be simple enough to be clear; the phrasing should seem natural to the direct communication of thought. Sometimes, though not always, simplicity means conciseness or saying much in little. Two methods of explaining the same idea are shown in the following sentences: "From infancy we gradually grow older; the aging process continues until it finally overtakes and conquers us" versus "We begin to die as soon as we are born," German Proverb. Terse expressiveness is found in countless speakers and writers: "In war there is no substitute for victory," Douglas MacArthur; "A thick skin is a gift from God," Konrad Adenauer; "What is history but a fable agreed upon?" Napoleon; "To be great is to be misunderstood," Emerson.

A series of terse expressions alone will not make a subject forceful

---

[4] *Vital Speeches,* XXXIX, 19 (July 15, 1973), p. 589.

and clear. A terse expression is a highlight of style or a climax of thought resulting from a more supple, relaxed, and leisurely explanation. Too little said can be as dissatisfying as too much. All truth and knowledge, of course, cannot be reduced to catch phrases or slogans. Truth and knowledge are not easy to come by and a phrase is not a substitute for reality.

On the other hand, there is often no reality without the proper phrase. Unless a person can express truth in terms of human experience, in apt, living phrases, he lacks something as a speaker. A good speaker must indeed be able when necessary to express reality in a phrase, to catch truth in a saying. Catch phrases and slogans are part of living speech. Some have mobilized people and changed history: God is love; Not one cent for tribute; Liberty, equality, fraternity.

VIVID LANGUAGE

The full effect of a speech depends on its power to rouse the whole man. Spoken style not only satisfies the mind but also stirs the emotions and appeals to the imagination. Speech itself is based on the symbolizing nature of thought. "The symbol-making function is one of man's primary activities, like eating, looking, or moving about. It is the fundamental process of his mind and goes on all the time."[5]

Meaning is created by thought. All kinds of things might exist without thinking beings, but thinking beings try to find the meaning of things by reading in one thing the reference to another. William Blake called this activity imagination. "Nature has no Outline, But Imagination has. Nature has no Time, but Imagination has."

Human beings cannot be convinced or moved to action until previous causes, present conditions, and subsequent results are real to the imagination. Vivid language persuades the imagination by being attractive, absorbing, and alive, using words to evoke images based on all the bodily senses. The words are chosen to add meaning to an item, for specific sensory words create a richer and fuller image. This image is a sensitized or intensified complex of denotations and connotations.

---

[5] Susanne Langer, *Philosophy in a New Key* (Cambridge, Mass.: Harvard University Press, 1942), p. 32.

Visual Imagery. The sense of sight and the memory of visual experience is highly developed in most people. Visual language presents essential details and describes size, shape, structure, color, movement, and other pictorial qualities so that the listener can "see" and feel the effect of the person, object, or event.

> *"The right ankle of one, indeed, is connected with the left ankle of another by a small iron fetter, and if they are turbulent, by another on their wrists. They have several meals a day—some of their own country provisions . . . another meal of pulse, etc., according to European taste. After breakfast they have water to wash themselves, while their apartments are perfumed with frankincense and lime juice . . ."* The pulse which Mr. Norris talks of are horse beans . . . Mr. Norris talks of frankincense and lime juice: when the surgeons tell you the slaves are stored so close that there is not room to tread among them.—
> WILLIAM WILBERFORCE

Auditory Imagery. A simple description of sounds may or may not evoke vivid hearing experience. The context helps give more reality. Edward R. Murrow described his airplane being swept down by a hurricane: "We then hit something with a bang that was audible above the roar of the motors, and more than one man flinched."

Sound images are usually evoked by the power of suggestion and by indicating their psychological effects:

> *The horns hooted, the bells rang and the earth vibrated under the wheels of the traffic. At intervals along the side of the road, in amongst the smartly dressed crowd, disabled soldiers were singing. They stood each one separate in the midst of that turmoil, and lifted up their voices. The sound, raucous and harsh, was borne upward. They sang, surely, not to give pleasure, but their singing seemed rather like some fierce protest against the people for whom they had been compelled to fight. They sang to remind these jostling crowds of women and men of their maimed bodies, and to ask for charity. No one seemed to notice; every one hurried by.*[6]

Olfactory Imagery. The sense of smell is a relatively unexplored source of images. A familiar odor may be called up by mentioning or describing the object, such as frying bacon, freshly mown grass, and burning leaves in autumn. Odors are difficult to classify, and

---

[6] E. L. Grant Watson, *Moods of Earth and Sky* (New York: Boni and Liveright, no date), pp. 58–59.

most descriptive adjectives are based on data of the other senses: sweet, heavy, sharp, nauseous, and so forth. Images of the sense of smell usually need to be suggested by analogies or other connotations.

> *In Tlalpam there was a heavy scent of nightflowers, a feeling of ponderous darkness, with a few sparks of intermittent fireflies. And always the heavy calling of nightflower scents. To Kate, there seemed a faint whiff of blood in all tropical-scented flowers: of blood or sweat.*
> —D. H. LAWRENCE

Gustatory Imagery.
Taste sensations are classified into sweet, sour, salt, and bitter. An image of taste may be built up by the use of these terms, but a more stimulating image can be obtained by resemblances to familiar foods and drinks, to sensations of color and consistency, and to other associations.

> *Its white tuberous root is crisp and tender, and leaves in the mouth distinctly a taste of cucumber.*—JOHN BURROUGHS

> *Yes, Bellegarde [peach], with its wide gamut of flavours and richnesses, and its not too solid flesh, stands unapproachable. What better end to a golden September day could be desired, as we toy with our dessert and see through the open windows a great tawny moon sailing bravely over the sleeping elms?*—EDWARD A. BUNYARD

Tactual Imagery.
Skin sensations are usually classified into pressure, temperature, and pain. Pressure includes images of contour and texture. Temperature is divided into sensations of heat and cold.

> *Heat and glare quivered from the stone pavements and the yellow buildings. I had not walked ten yards before I had begun to feel my shoulders damp against my shirt.*—ALEC WAUGH

> *As the hand is one of the finest and most responsive organs in the body, every possible variety of pressure is possible. First you may have the Y.M.C.A. type of handshaking; the man pats you on the shoulder with one hand and gives you a violent shake with the other until all your joints are ready to burst within you.*—LIN YUTANG

Kinaesthetic Imagery.
The sensation of bodily movement and muscular effort are the basis for images of physical activity. Since movement is a basic activity, the mere sight or sound of a thing in motion also arouses sympathetic kinaesthetic images.

> *He waited there, wondering if he should make a sudden tackle. Could he get the guy before he yelled? But he couldn't do it, the legs gave*

out first, every good athlete got it in the legs first. Slowly, holding his body an inch from the ground, he began to edge away on hands and toes, one foot back, one hand back, the other foot back. When he was thirty yards away, he stood up in a crouch, and backed into the shadow of a tree.—NORMAN MAILER

Organic Imagery.   Among internal or overall body sensations are fatigue, sleepiness, hunger, thirst, dizziness, faintness, and nausea. Images of inward sensations are effective if the theme of the speech demands it. The details should be chosen with discretion so that the image will not be overcandid or repulsive.

We came upon it late, and my bones, through a longer ride than usual in the wooden saddle, had grown into an unjointed frame. This was the real meaning of fatigue. My body was a comprehensive ache.—
H. M. TOMLINSON

Vividness Through Slang.   A popular type of vivid expression is slang. Slang is an inventive use of language, an attempt at fresh, personal expression, but it is often an exuberant playing or showing-off with words rather than an effort at enhanced communication. Besides being verbal entertainment, slang is frequently a revolt against communication, a desire to baffle listeners who do not share a given defiance of convention. A systematic secret slang of a special group is called cant and bears resemblances to jargon.

Slang uses sound effects, novel comparisons, and violent metaphors or transfers of meaning. The aim may be either conciseness or lavish expansiveness of expression. The meaning is usually intense but often indefinite at the same time. The fact that slang fulfills a human need is shown by its universality. It abounds in all widely spoken languages and in all classes of society. Slang tends to enrich language with new words and new meanings for old words, for some slang terms persist and become part of the standard language. For example, the words *dumbfound, flippant, graft, humbug, mob, sham,* and *sky-scraper* were once condemned as slang. Most slang terms are vivacious but transitory. Their intensity is lost through frequent and indiscriminate repetition and the expressions die out.

Slang often favors short forms of words, such as the following, some of which have gained acceptability: *bus, cab* or *taxi, exam, phone, piano, rum, zoo* instead of *omnibus, taxicab, examination, telephone, pianoforte, rumbullion,* and *zoological garden.*

Slang has several disadvantages. It often suggests cheapness and vulgarity. Its playfulness and its very cleverness make it unsuitable for many serious subjects. Most listeners on most occasions do not expect a speaker to use slang; they take it for granted that he will have good pronunciation, use accepted grammar, and show better than average taste in his choice of words. Slang in its vivacity and intimacy has an impudent lack of courtesy and respect for others. One of the worst features of slang is its deteriorating effect upon linguistic ability, for many terms become less and less specific as they express a generalized judgment. The habitual user of slang loses his verbal discrimination and his ability to express himself in the standard or accepted language.

Slang therefore should be used by the speaker only when it fits appropriately into a speech. A touch of slang at the right time in the right way can give humor, emphasis, or vividness to the point being made. An example is from a speech by Paul H. Nitze: "We are all for the 'slugfest.' It is late in time for private enterprise and the American taxpayer to do a little slugging on their own behalf."

FIGURATIVE LANGUAGE

Another means of vivid expression is figurative language in which the speaker means more than he says. These rhetorical devices are so common in everyday speech that they are often not recognized as such. The user of figurative language often does not realize that he is making special demands upon the listener, who must interpret a meaning different from the literal meaning of the words. The imagination is called upon to make comparisons, transfers, contradictions, and amplifications of ideas. Figurative expressions, for convenience of discussion, are divided into figures of speech and figures of arrangement.

Figures of Speech. A figure of speech is an expression using words in a non-literal sense to give vividness or attractiveness to ideas. Many of them are used by good speakers, the most common being simile, metaphor, metonymy, and irony.

Simile. A stated comparison of one thing to another is called a simile. Since the purpose of a simile is to enrich the meaning of a term, the comparison is between things that are different. To liken a sugar maple tree to a sweet gum tree would not give a more vivid concept of the maple because the trees are too much alike. But to liken a sugar maple tree to a syrup factory would be a simile, since the two things are different in most respects. For a simile to be effective the resemblance pointed out must be to a thing known to the listener.

A simile is often, but not necessarily, introduced by the word *like* or *as.* For example: "Listening to her views was like looking at the world through a pair of cracked binoculars" and "Loaning money to you is safer than putting it in the bank." A simile may be incompletely stated, the thing compared being omitted: "Every tub should stand upon its own bottom." The context shows that every man should stand upon his own feet and that the whole simile is a symbol of self-reliance. An extended simile, using a sequence of details to show that one thing resembles another, is called an analogy. It is systematic and establishes a point-by-point similarity. A totalitarian state, for instance, might be pictured in terms of an ant colony.

Metaphor.   A metaphor is a comparison made between two things by stating that one thing is the other thing. "This checkerboard of nights and days," Omar Khayyám; "A daily [newspaper] column is a grave two inches wide and twenty inches deep," Don Marquis. A variety of metaphor is personification, which attributes human traits to inanimate things or mental concepts. It is a vital part of speech because it gives closeness and reality to ideas and things. For example: "True devotion never counts the cost"; "America will always fight for freedom"; "Hatred carefully seeks out weakness."

Metonymy.   A figure of speech which substitutes the name of something associated with an item for the item itself is called metonymy. For example: *"City Hall* exerted its influence" for *"the mayor* exerted his influence." Hollywood and Madison Avenue are often used to signify the motion picture and the advertising industries.

ANTONOMASIA. A variety of metonymy is antonomasia which uses a proper noun instead of a common noun: *an Einstein* is used for *an intellectual genius; a Benedict Arnold* for *a traitor.*

SYNECDOCHE. Synecdoche is a kind of metonymy and has several aspects. A part of a thing may be used for the whole: "He won the record-breaking wheel race," where *wheel* is used for *automobile.* The whole may be used for a part: "The navy moved in slugging," where *navy* means *sailor.* The more general may be used for the less general: "The club's profits depend on liquids." *Liquids* is used for the less broad term *alcoholic drinks.* The material of which a thing is made may be used for the thing itself: "He decided to buy the pale blue seersucker," where *seersucker* means *summer suit.*

Irony. A figure of irony says one thing and means another. In the broad sense, irony is a contrast between appearance and reality, between expectation and fulfillment. The meaning of an ironical expression is usually opposite to the literal meaning of the words. "To prove his spirit of helpfulness he told her all her faults." "Legislators raise taxes so that people won't squander their own money." "The higher standard of living will soon reach the five-cent-toothpick level."

HYPERBOLE. A variation of irony is hyperbole in which the thing said is more than expected or warranted by the thing meant. Exaggeration is used for emphasis, vivacity, or dramatic effect. "May God strike me dead if I'm not telling the truth!" "Twenty-five bulldozers couldn't get me to move out of this house." "And fired the shot heard round the world," Emerson.

UNDERSTATEMENT. Another variation of irony is understatement, where what is said is less strong than expected under the circumstances. The contrast heightens the true importance of the idea. Famous examples are Julius Caesar's "I came, I saw, I conquered," and the New Testament verse "Jesus wept." Common examples are "I told him a thing or two" and "All I want is everything."

INNUENDO. A form of irony which implies something of a more or less derogatory nature is called innuendo. "The speaker had nothing to say and said it exhaustively." "Liszt was a master in handling the themes of other composers." "He was tired from clipping coupons and endorsing dividend checks."

Figures of Arrangement. A figure of arrangement is a device used to combine sounds or words into an expression which does not change the literal meaning but adds to it. Figures of arrangement are concerned with the musical aspects of language, what in literature is often called verbal music. Word music is the combination of sound and rhythm most appropriate to the meaning being expressed. The figures of arrangement include imitation of sound, repetition, and balance.

Imitation of Sound. Many words originated as imitation of natural sounds; for example, bobolink, bumblebee, hush, rustle, slap. The formation and use of words that suggest meanings by sounds is called onomatopoeia. In speaking, onomatopoeia involves choosing and using words so that their sounds suggest the meaning: "If I speak in the tongues of men and angels, but have not love, I am a noisy gong or a clanging cymbal," New Testament; "Like the faint ripple of the summer sea sounding in the hollow of the ear, so the sweet air ripples in the grass," Richard Jefferies.

In a speech, an obvious use of sound imitation detracts from the meaning. The subtle relationship between sound and sense is important. The speaker's ear rejects pleasing, harmonious language when the passage expresses strong indignation. The just relation between sound and meaning does not follow rules but must be felt and experienced by the discriminating user.

Repetition. Because speech is a time sequence, the planned repeating of sounds, words, or phrases is often advantageous. However, too much repetition of a single kind defeats the purpose of vivid expression.

ALLITERATION. The repetition of the same initial consonant in words or syllables for noticeable effect is called alliteration. For example, "The more, the merrier." "It has ever been my experience that folks who have no vices have very few virtues," Lincoln. Alliteration is successful when it emphasizes the meaning without seeming to be a striving for effect.

ASSONANCE. The repetition of a vowel sounded before different consonants, as in *time, tide,* is called assonance. A familiar example is "All roads lead to Rome." The words *kindness* and *violence,* which contain the same stressed diphthong, were used as an approximate rhyme by Edmund Burke: "Power and authority are sometimes bought by kindness; but they can never be begged as alms by an impoverished and defeated violence." Burke ends clauses in other sentences with *liberty, principle,* and with *evidence, mend it, penitence.* The assonance helps create vivid expression without its presence being noted. Assonance is generally used to create harmonious expression without any effect of rhyme.

RHYME. A rhyme is the repetition of the same sounds in the ends of words: the same vowel or vowel plus consonant follows after different consonants, as in lash, mash; funny, money. Rhyme is attractive to the ear and makes statements easy to remember: "Birds of a feather flock together."

However, rhyme should be avoided in public speaking except for a rare effect of humor or sarcasm. Rhyme diverts the listener's mind from the subject and arouses a distrust of the speaker's sincerity. Internal rhymes or a rhyming word within the sentence should be omitted even if they seem spontaneous. "He did not agree that admission should be free" should be changed to "He did not agree that admission should be without charge" or "He was not convinced that admission should be free."

WORD REPETITION. A word is often repeated for vividness of thought. The words *road* and *generation* are repeated in the following passage for harmonious integration of thought: "There is an old Chinese saying that each generation builds a road for the next. The road has been well built for us, and I believe it incumbent upon us, in our generation, to build our road for the next one," John F. Kennedy. A word can be repeated in another form: "The proper study of mankind is man," Alexander Pope; "I never found a companion who was as companionable as solitude," Henry David Thoreau.

Anaphora is the repetition of a word or phrase at the beginning of successive sections in a sentence. "The dream of conquering the vastness of space—the dream of partnership across the Atlantic and across the Pacific as well . . . and, above all, the dream of equal rights for all Americans whatever their race or color,"[7] Lyndon B. Johnson.

A repeated word or group of words sometimes introduces a series of sentences. "It is the American people themselves who are in the driver's seat. It is the American people themselves who want the furrows plowed. It is the American people themselves who expect the third horse to pull in unison with the other two," Franklin D. Roosevelt.

Balance. The arrangement of words, phrases, clauses, and sentences for proportion, symmetry, and harmony of structure is called balance. Many speakers depend on their inner feeling for balance; others find it helpful to understand devices like antithesis and parallelism.

ANTITHESIS. When sentences or parts of sentences are arranged for contrast the figure is called antithesis. The opposition can be direct or implied: "We see things not as they are, but as we are,"

---

[7] *Vital Speeches,* XXX, 5 (Dec. 15, 1963), p. 130.

H. M. Tomlinson; "True scholarship consists in knowing not what things exist, but what they mean; it is not memory but judgment," James Russell Lowell. When antithesis is implied without the contrast being expressed, it is called *balanced antithesis.* For example, "Love bears all things, believes all things, hopes all things, endures all things," New Testament.

Chiasmus is a special type of antithesis which reverses the grammatical order in the second clause of a statement. "She was much too proud to accept, but to refuse she was far too humble." *Antimetabole* is a similar balancing of words in reverse order. "A brave man among cowards, a coward among brave men."

Oxymoron, also a type of antithesis, combines two contradictory terms for the expression of an idea: silent clamor, rough gentleness, rational emotion, practical idealism. This minor figure of speech has more than passing importance. Springing from the balance or intermingling of opposites, it suggests that human analyses and classifications are not always conclusive, that there are unknown areas in human awareness of the universe.

PARALLELISM. In parallelism balance is achieved between statements by using phrases and clauses of similar length and grammatical structure. At its best and used occasionally parallel arrangement is vivid and effective; at its worst and used frequently it is artifical and tedious: "As long as war is regarded as wicked it will always have a fascination. When it is looked upon as vulgar, it will cease to be popular," Oscar Wilde; "Bigotry has no head and cannot think; no heart and cannot feel. When she moves it is in wrath; when she pauses it is amid ruin," Daniel O'Connell; "You can fool all the people some of the time, and some of the people all the time, but you can't fool all the people all the time," Abraham Lincoln.

SPOKEN RHYTHM

An important part of the conversational quality in public speaking is conversational rhythm. The preceding methods of securing clear, forceful, and vivid language are also methods of achieving rhythm.

Rhythm is a more or less periodic flow, a recurrence of certain elements or features in alternation. In speech the elements are stress, pitch, and length in alternations of strong-high-long and weak-low-short. The recurrences of speech are not as basically regular as those of most music and poetry. The rhythms of speech are obviously

unsuited for marching, dancing, or singing. In poetry, stressed syllables tend to occur at equal intervals. In prose, there may be fewer
or more unstressed or partially stressed syllables between main
stresses. Poetry and prose, however, are not in direct opposition
but shade gradually into each other. This fact is shown by the use
of such terms as *prose poem* and *poetic prose*. Poetry spoken in strict
rhythm is doggerel; prose spoken without marked stress is mumble.

The occurrence of main-stressed syllables and other factors of
rhythm in an utterance depend on the speaker's meaning. For example, spoken rhythm is varied to suggest different attitudes and moods
from impetuous to deliberate. A fine line separates spoken rhythms
from those that are too restrained and literary, or too rhetorical
and artificial. A keen ear and feeling for the rhythms and melodies
of daily speech keep a speaker from sing-song recitation, raised-voice
chanting, overtheatrical contrasts, and other meaningless rhythmic
effects.

PLAN FOR IMPROVEMENT

A speaker is a worker in words, and a good speaker is a master
craftsman. To achieve an effective spoken style requires systematic
and consistent steps toward improvement.

Suitable Vocabulary.   Good speaking demands an adequate supply of words. What amount is that? The speaker has an adequate
vocabulary when he can say what he really means and say it in
the best possible way. The actual number of words is not as important
as their suitability for conveying meaning to listeners. The right
choice presupposes a large store of usable words from which to
choose. A conscious interest in words and a curiosity about their
use make their study rewarding. A least ten words a week should
be added to the speaker's vocabulary, used in practice sentences,
and tried out in conversation.

Reading.   The number of words a person recognizes when he
sees or hears them is much larger than the number he uses when
speaking. The meaning of words can often be guessed from the context. Less familiar words should not be passed by, but should be
jotted down. Unfamiliar words encountered more than once should
also be added to the list. If the word is long, technical, or high-
sounding, it may not be usable enough to master.

Using the Dictionary.   Words that appeal to the speaker and seem valuable for oral communication should be entered in a notebook and looked up in the dictionary. If necessary, the pronounciation and the meaning are written down. Sentences should be written to illustrate the meaning of the words in speech.

Synonyms and Antonyms.   A dictionary entry gives words of similar meaning and sometimes of opposite meaning. Each of these should be looked up and studied. A book of synonyms, such as *Roget's Thesaurus,* lists synonyms and antonyms systematically. A book of synonyms is a convenient help for enlarging the vocabulary provided that the exact meanings of words are carefully checked in the dictionary.

Families of Words.   Since English has borrowed heavily from other languages, a knowledge of Greek, Latin, French, and other languages can help a speaker enlarge his vocabulary. The meaning of an unfamiliar English word can often be understood by its root. For example, the word emancipate comes from the Latin *emancipatus,* which is made up of *e,* "out," and *manus,* "hand," and *capere,* "to take." "To take out by hand" means to set free or release from bondage. The Latin root *manu* is found in English words like manual, manufacture, manuscript, manacle, manicure, maneuver, mandate, manage, and manure ("to work by hand"). The root *cape* is used in English words like capable, capacious, captive, capture, caption, and captivate. Many roots and English derivatives are given in Myers' *The Foundations of English,* and Mawson's *The Dictionary Companion.*

Suitable Usage.   A speaker is expected to use good grammar and usage. "Good" in this sense means acceptable to listeners of education and culture. Reviewing a good English grammar will enable the speaker to avoid gross errors. Further insight into suitable usage can be obtained from interesting and informative books like Fowler's *Dictionary of Modern English Usage,* Horwill's *Dictionary of Modern American Usage,* Evans and Evans' *Dictionary of Contemporary American Usage,* and Edwin Newman's *Strictly Speaking.*

Hearing and Reading Speeches.   The way various speakers use language should be carefully studied. Listening to speakers reveals the full effect of spoken styles, and studying recorded speeches is extremely valuable. Reading printed speeches reveals how the effects were obtained in language. In reading speeches it must be borne in mind that the printed version may not be exact: the speaker may have used contractions and omitted words like *that* and *which*. Most libraries have collections of speeches and also subscribe to the semi-monthly periodical *Vital Speeches of the Day*.

Writing.   Writing a speech or part of a speech enables the speaker to test his own results. He can see whether he is conveying ideas or getting tangled up in verbiage, whether he is being convincing or showing off an imposing vocabulary and style, whether his message is interesting and alive or dull and mechanical. He can rewrite and improve his manuscript until it has the ring of truth and reality.

Rephrasing the thoughts of others is another valuable practice. A passage from an essay, textbook, or editorial can be rewritten in spoken style. By doing this the speaker will gain practical knowledge of the differences between the written and spoken word.

Speaking.   Every occasion to speak affords the speaker an opportunity to improve his style. He should express himself as clearly and interestingly as he can in each daily conversation. Every speech to a group should be a forward step in the mastery of language expression. Over four thousand years ago an Egyptian King gave the following advice to his son. Since we live in a world war of words, the advice to Merikere is for us too: "Be a craftsman in speech that thou mayest be strong, for the strength of one is the tongue, and speech is mightier than all fighting."[8]

---

[8] James Henry Breasted, *The Dawn of Conscience* (New York: Charles Scribner's Sons, 1933), p. 131.

8.
DELIVERING THE SPEECH

Which is more essential in public speaking, content or delivery? When students beginning the study of speech communication are asked this question, most of them cast their vote for delivery. It is true that during the term of the course the content of a student's speech is often better than his presentation. However, adequate content and adequate delivery are both essential: a good speaker has an important message and presents it effectively.

PHASES OF DELIVERY

Speech presentation is concerned with two major factors: what listeners see, or the visual aspect, and what listeners hear, or the auditory aspect.

Visual. The speaker conveys and heightens his message by how he looks. This includes the way he is dressed, his posture, his walk, his gestures, and his facial expressions.

Auditory. The speaker conveys and enhances his message by how he sounds. It is through the voice that he reveals his emotions, whether intended or unintended. His pitch level, inflections, and variety of volume play important parts in the total effect. The way the speaker says his words—his articulation and pronunciation—gives a definite picture to his audience. This includes the way he forms sounds, stresses his syllables and words, and varies his rate.

DETERMINANTS OF THE DELIVERY

The delivery of a speech is mainly determined by the situation, which includes the audience, and the speaker himself.   ·

The Situation.   At the inaugural address of President Lyndon B. Johnson on January 20, 1965, reporters called attention to the fact that he did not use his customary gestures. This restriction was probably caused by the formality of the situation. The President's manner in his press conferences was more casual. The formality or informality of the situation greatly affects the delivery. The more formal it is, the fewer gestures and movements the speaker makes. He limits himself more to his position behind the lectern and uses a more emphatic speaking style. In a very informal situation, the speaker is free to move away from the speaker's stand; he may even sit on the edge of a table.

The equipment available for the speaker's use will also determine his delivery. He cannot move away from a microphone which is carrying the speech over a public address system. He may have to adapt himself to a table or a speaker's stand which holds needed data or other forms of support. Also, the handling of visual aids may create special delivery problems.

The larger the audience, the greater must be the volume of the speaker's voice, the more expansive his gestures, and the slower his rate of speaking. The smaller the group, the more informally conversational the delivery can be.

The Speaker.   The amount of preparation made by a speaker influences his delivery. Being well prepared with something valuable to communicate makes one freer physically and vocally. If he is so unsure of himself and his material that he has to read it word for word, his manner may be routine and uncommunicative. Self-consciousness, nervousness, and other emotional states will cause physical and vocal qualities and mannerisms that detract from the message. Too much concern with the ideas and too little with the audience will also hinder one's delivery.

The limitations of a speaker, such as an inadequate speaking voice, inarticulate speech, and poor physical expression, are other determinants of delivery. It should be the speaker's responsibility either to correct these faults, or to compensate for them in some way, such as by an outstanding arrangement or illustration of ideas.

ESSENTIALS OF DELIVERY

Delivery is not something outside the speech to be added or plastered on, but is part of the meaning of the speech or a further expression of the meaning. Good speech presentation requires the consideration and application of a number of important ingredients.

Keeping Attention on the Specific Purpose. A successful speaker knows the responses he wants to obtain from his listeners and avoids any factor that distracts attention away from the specific purpose of the speech. Visual distractions, such as fiddling with a pencil, scratching the nose, continual grinning or frowning, are to be avoided. Auditory distractions are also to be avoided, such as a noisy shifting of the heels or the jingling of coins and keys. Distractions cause the listener to begin thinking more about the speaker's mannerisms than about his message.

Being Heard and Understood. Ideas cannot be imparted by merely talking, for everyone must hear all that is said. Therefore, the speaker's voice must be loud enough to be heard in the very last row. Because he must also be understood, the speaker's pronunciation and phrasing must be distinct.

Sharing Ideas with Listeners. The speaker does not face a group to think out loud. He conveys his thoughts and feelings to others so that there is a give-and-take or constant circular response. Ideas may best be shared by manifesting interest in what is said, maintaining eye contact, speaking in a conversational manner, and maintaining direct communication.

Desire to Share Ideas. The subject should interest the speaker and he should have an urge to talk to his listeners about it. Enthusiasm is contagious, and listeners are quick to note it and respond to it. Thus, the speaker should be alert to his listeners' responses, and manifest enough warmth and vitality to interest them.

Eye Contact. Each listener should feel that the speaker is imparting his ideas to him as one of the group. Consequently, it is necessary that the speaker make eye contact. The speaker should not gaze at the floor, out of the window, or at the ceiling. Also, he should not constantly look at one side of the audience and ignore the other parts. Instead, the speaker should look at all listeners, talking to each one from time to time but to no particular person or segment of the audience for a prolonged time.

Conversational Manner. In group conversation, the voice, although loud enough to be heard by all, is held to a volume that does not give the impression of loud talk. At the same time, the voice does not give the impression of sharing a secret by being too quiet. People in conversation vary their voices and use gestures. It is true that when talking to a large audience, the speaker's voice and physical expression will be somewhat stronger than in social conversation. However, both should still be varied.

Directness.   It is not enough to look in the direction of the audience. The speaker must actually be talking with his listeners. He should not be involved with himself or seem to be talking to himself. He should not appear to be reciting from memory, for directness requires that the speaker think the thought and express it at the same time. Too much dependence on notes or a manuscript also makes delivery less direct.

Keeping Ideas Moving Ahead.

The attention of listeners can be held for a longer time if they are aware of a forward movement of ideas. The rate of speaking cannot be so labored, choppy, or interrupted, that the ideas do not seem connected. Nor can the rate be so fast that the audience is unable to grasp the idea and relate it to those following it. The mind can best understand a subject when it is presented in an organized, progressive pattern, without undue pauses to grope for ideas. The opposite of forward movement can be seen in many popular television games, where viewers are treated to "uh," "er," and other vocalized pauses in place of logical, organic progression of thought.

Making Ideas Stand Out.

One or more points in a speech are more important than others and should dominate. Main ideas should stand out more than the ideas supporting them. If all ideas are spoken in exactly the same way, true emphasis is impossible. A slower rate, a pause before and after the idea, a shift in body position, an increase or decrease in volume, are only a few of the possible ways to emphasize points through delivery.

Coloring Ideas.

An essential part of delivery is to keep listeners listening. One way of maintaining attention is to vary the delivery. A hypnotist often uses a falling pitch pattern over and over in order to put his subject to sleep. However, a speaker cannot get his desired responses from an audience that is headed toward sleep.

The speaker's voice, movements, and gestures should constantly change. When reaching an important point, the speaker's voice should sound as if he has something vital to say. When he describes an unfavorable situation, his voice and gestures show its undesirability. His voice and manner also reflect desirable objects, persons, and ideas.

Being Effective as a Personality. Judgments of personality are based on how a person looks and behaves. Aristotle, among other authorities on speechmaking, has said that a speaker's personality is his most powerful means of persuasion. A speaker's personality is judged by all the aspects of delivery—the way he walks to the platform, the way he looks when the listeners first see him, the impact of his voice on them. An awkward stride, a hasty adjustment of clothing as he takes his place before them, an embarrassed look at them, all contribute to the audience's first estimation. A fidgety body, rapid speech, and other forms of nervous behavior may be the result of stage fright, which the speaker should seek to understand and overcome by applying the methods discussed in Chapter 2.

The speaker should also cultivate favorable attitudes while speaking, for they condition his entire delivery and the audience's judgment of his personality. While a person in every communicative situation must adjust his attitudes to the interests and needs of his listeners, the speaker does not completely give up his own individuality. All speakers should not look, act, and sound alike. Each speaker has his own personality and should not attempt to become a carbon copy of someone he admires. A good speaker remains an individual and tries to improve those aspects of his personality that foster effective speech communication.

METHODS OF DELIVERY

There are three methods of giving a prepared speech: extemporaneous, manuscript, and memorized. The impromptu speech is delivered without previous preparation. The speaker chooses the method best suited to himself and the situation.

Extemporaneous Speaking. The extemporaneous speaker selects and prepares his material in advance and then, as he speaks, expresses it in the language of the moment. Preliminary thinking and preparation indicate *what* he is going to say; the *how* is created at the time of the speech. The organization of the speech, the order of ideas, the illustrations and other forms of support may be decided in advance and fixed in the speaker's mind, but there is no precise or predetermined wording. As in conversation, the speaker may increase, change, or abandon any part of his material to suit the confronting situation. Extemporaneous speeches may be given with or without notes, but require thorough preparation, for the speaker's feelings during delivery may spell success or failure. Also, he may deviate from the point of the speech, or be carried away with enthusiasm and talk too long.

However, the speaker can adapt an extemporaneous speech to a particular situation and achieve the most intimate communication between himself and his audience, thereby revealing the directness and spontaneity of his thinking. Simultaneously he learns to organize his ideas "on the firing line" and to think on his feet. Because extemporaneous speaking is the most adaptable and most communicative method, it is widely used by effective public speakers.

Notes are usually necessary for quotations and statistics or when accuracy of detail is demanded. Even if notes are not absolutely necessary, they may have certain advantages. They tend to give the speaker a sense of security; he does not feel at the mercy of his memory. He can feel confident that he will not omit any important points and will say what he means to say. The audience may be more impressed if certain ideas are quoted or stated accurately.

Whenever possible, however, it is best to speak without notes, for an audience prefers listening to a speaker who has a lively and direct sense of communication. A speaker who depends on his notes loses eye contact with his audience; the speech may lose fluency and expressiveness. A nervous and self-conscious speaker who looks at his notes may call attention to his lack of confidence. The excessive use of notes often diverts the minds of the listeners from the message, while speaking without notes gives the impression that the speaker knows his subject thoroughly and makes the audience want to listen.

Preparing Notes.   The speaker's notes are not a duplicate of the outline he has prepared, but usually consist of a list of points in sequence. Often a word or two is all that is required to remind the speaker of the idea. The notes should be prepared carefully on cards that can be handled quickly and silently. Only one side of the card should be written on and the cards should be numbered. Except for quotations, a card should contain only enough words to recall the thought to be conveyed and a suggestion of the next thought. Notes should be kept to a minimum. Too many notes may encourage superficial preparation and hinder rather than help the speaker.

Speaking with Notes. When the speaker steps forward to talk, he should put his notes on a table or lectern, if one is available, or hold the cards inconspicuously in his hand. If he makes a gesture with one hand, the cards should be held in the other hand, so the listeners will not be distracted by the cards being waved before them.

When he refers to a note, the speaker raises the card to the proper reading distance. He should not bend over a table or bow his head over a lectern to read his notes. Notes held in the hand should not be kept at hip level when the speaker reads them, as if he were trying to conceal the fact that he is using notes. Each card should be read as easily as possible. After a card has been used, it should be put to one side of the table or lectern or on the bottom of the cards held in the hand.

When the speaker is not consulting his notes, he should leave them alone. Fiddling with them or realigning them on the table or lectern is distracting. When the speaker moves about the platform, he must be sure to take his notes with him, thus avoiding an awkward dash to his notes in case he forgets what comes next.

When he gives a speech, the speaker must be sure that he knows what comes next. Thus, even though he uses notes, he should memorize thoroughly the sequence of ideas. He is prepared only when he completely masters his material.

Manuscript Speaking. In manuscript speaking the speech is written, revised, rehearsed, and then read word for word to the audience. It is actually a public reading. While offering certain advantages to the skilled speaker, its disadvantages make reading from manuscript a hazard to be avoided by the inexperienced. Manuscript speaking may lack lively, direct communication. It may not sound like talk. It is not easy to write in spoken style. Manuscript speaking induces monotonous delivery, because many speakers are poor readers and fail to color ideas. Furthermore, many listeners dislike being confronted with a manuscript; they think that the speaker is not sufficiently acquainted with his topic. Frequently, the speaker's personality is not freely revealed because he hides behind his manuscript.

Other disadvantages include the inability to adjust the speech to audience reaction, and, except for skilled readers, the loss of eye contact, and the excessive time required for writing and rehearsing.

Perhaps the main advantage of the manuscript speech is that the speaker can say exactly what he wants, thereby avoiding incorrect interpretations by the listeners. This factor is important to a political or business leader, whose every word will be closely analyzed. The language of a written speech can be more concise, more precise, more expressive, and more polished. Each word and phrase can be weighed, every aspect of the meaning can be considered judiciously in advance. The manuscript speech also gives the speaker a sense of security, especially if he is not experienced in public speaking. Furthermore, the speech is ready for publication, or nearly so, and the speaker's influence may be increased by releasing a copy of the address to the press. Finally, it can be edited to meet the requirements of the exact time limit and censorship in radio and television broadcasting.

Writing the Manuscript. Guided by his outline, the speaker should write the speech in his own words, just as he might say them to a friend. The result is not the speech to be given; it is just the first draft. If the speech has been prepared by a staff writer, it should definitely be considered as only a first draft. No one should ever read the first draft of a speech to an audience. The speaker should go over the manuscript carefully, improving it each time, until he is certain that it represents exactly what he wants to say in the way that he wants to say it. He should not be satisfied with any sentence until it seems easy and natural when spoken aloud.

A point will eventually be reached when what has been put on paper seems to create the desired effect. It should then be tried out with a listener, who may be asked to time it. It is wise to read it to someone who enjoys good speaking. Of course, if no listener is available, the speaker must read the manuscript aloud in privacy. This experiment will show what further improvements can be made. If the speaker mispronounces or stumbles over any words, he should learn to say them correctly and clearly. If he gets tangled up or cannot clearly bring out the meaning of any sentence, he should simplify it. If any words are not concrete and specific, he should change them. He should also check the progression of thought and supply needed transitions and illustrations.

Preparing the Final Manuscript. The speech should be typed on fairly heavy paper; thin paper makes the text harder to see and is risky to handle, because pages may stick together. The copy should be easy to read—free of erasures, crossed-out words, transposed words, or added words. Any messy and difficult-to-read page should be retyped after final revisions.

Although full-size sheets are harder to hold, they offer the advantage of not having to turn the page so often. If the speaker is not using a lectern, half-size sheets or cards are easy to hold and turn. They are also desirable because the eye sees less material in a glance, thus lessening the possibility of losing the place. The manuscript should be typed, double or triple spaced, on one side of the paper. Some speakers find a manuscript easier to read typed all in capital letters.

Material should be arranged in short paragraphs, but a sentence should not be continued from one to the next page. A two-inch margin on the left side of each page allows for notations about delivery. The pages should be numbered in the upper right-hand corner where they are easily visible, and anything avoided that will make the pages awkward to manage, such as pinning, clipping, or stapling them together.

Reading the Manuscript. Good reading sounds like good talking. Just because the speaker has written his speech in his own words is no assurance that his reading will sound like conversation. As the speaker reads aloud, he should try to react to what he means, and show in his face, voice, and gestures how he feels about each thing he is saying. This reaction to the material gives a natural conversational quality to the speech.

The speaker does not read to himself, but speaks to his audience. He should hold the manuscript high enough to see the text by merely dropping his gaze, instead of holding it so low that he must keep bowing his head. He should know his opening sentence and his concluding sentence thoroughly so that he can deliver them with direct eye contact. During the speech, the reader should see the words on the page in a quick glance and then express them to the audience face-to-face.

The manuscript speaker who finds it difficult to maintain eye contact can practice the following techniques. As the reader inhales,
he looks down to see what he is going to say and immediately raises
his eyes to his audience and says it. Since he takes breath at logical
pauses in the thought, the reader thus has direct eye contact while
he is actually speaking.

The beginner may have trouble seeing an entire breath group at
a glance and often has trouble remembering all that he has just
seen. In that case, he drops his gaze to see what comes next and
quickly looks at the audience again. The speaker should resist the
tendency to keep his eyes down until the end of the sentence, for
eye contact is important for the effective completion of a thought.
Practice will enable the manuscript speaker to take in more material
at a glance and to express it directly and convincingly to his listeners.
The mastery of the technique is expedited by rehearsing before a
mirror so that the reader can make sure he is looking at his own
image when speaking.

Many beginners hesitate to look up from their manuscript because
they lose their place. The remedy for this difficulty is fairly simple.
The reader rests his hand upon the lectern with his thumb and one
or two fingers on the margin of the page. He moves a finger down
as each line of the text is spoken so that he always knows his place.
If he holds the manuscript in his hands, he indicates the reading
line by moving his thumb down. The action of the hand, fingers,
and thumb should be so unobtrusive that the audience is not aware
of it. The speaker who needs glasses should wear them when he
makes his first appearance before the audience. To reach for his
glasses after making a few opening remarks may imply that speaking
is now over and reading is about to begin.

Memorized Speaking.   A memorized speech is written, revised,
rehearsed, committed to memory, and given word for word to the
audience. It is actually a public recitation. A consideration of the
advantages and disadvantages of this method shows why it is seldom
used.

A memorized speech puts a strain on the memory and causes
worry; the speaker cannot be sure his memory will not fail him at
a crucial point. He also becomes conscious of words, rather than

of his listeners' reactions, thus making it difficult to change or adjust the speech to an unexpected reaction. Furthermore, the speech is apt to sound memorized and to lack spontaneity. The memorized speech also demands much time and pains in its preparation.

Memorized speaking does enable the speaker to maintain eye communication with his listeners, to use gestures, and to be animated and expressive. His organization and wording can be exactly as he wishes them to be, and he can accurately gauge the length of his speech.

Impromptu Speaking.   Although one of the most frequently used methods of speaking, impromptu speaking is often one of the least effective. Many speakers are unable to make a point and stop without unnecessary rambling.

The impromptu speech is given without previous preparation. A person is asked to talk, perhaps to his surprise, and he must get up immediately and address the group. However, it is often possible to anticipate the request to give an impromptu speech. A person invited to a meeting should determine its purpose or subject to be considered. Then, by deciding how he might contribute to the meeting, and what he might be asked to say, the speaker can do some advance planning.

An individual will usually be asked to talk about a subject in which he is known to be an authority. If he should be called upon to talk about something he knows nothing about, he should honestly state that he cannot say anything meaningful. There are several ways, however, that one can prepare for successful impromptu speaking.

Preparation.   A well-informed person has much to talk about. He can usually back up his statements with needed examples and other supporting material. It is helpful for a prospective impromptu speaker to read widely, to be a good observer and listener, and to develop a rich background of experience.

At the actual meeting, careful listening to all speakers is essential. A person who notes where he agrees or disagrees with a speaker and which points were inadequately or incorrectly supported has a springboard for a talk. He may be able to think of a different angle or even of a new but related topic.

If a person already knows a great deal about public speaking, if he has had experience in analyzing, outlining, and developing subjects, and if he is used to addressing audiences, he can prepare a more effective speech at a moment's notice. The impromptu speaker should see his topic in outline form, grasp the specific purpose, and think of a pertinent example or quotation for an introduction; then assemble reasons and illustrations and decide upon an application of the idea for a conclusion. He prepares himself physically by relaxing and taking several slow breaths. When he begins to speak, he concentrates on what he is going to say. Such concentration takes attention away from himself and helps to control nervousness.

Organization. A definite form—a beginning, middle, and an end—helps a person deliver an impromptu speech. Simplicity is the keynote: a single point of view, one or two examples or illustrations, and a brief, clear conclusion. The simplest structures are therefore the best for the purpose: (1) State an idea and give reasons for it. (2) State an idea and illustrate it. (3) State a principle, illustrate it, relate it to the present situation, advocate action to be taken. (4) State a question and answer it. (5) Offer an illustration and state the point it suggests. (6) State a problem and give the solution. Such statements offer a quick introduction. One or two clearly reported reasons or illustrations make up the body of the speech. Restating the introduction gives a practical and definite conclusion.

Suggestions. The impromptu speaker should seize the first thought that comes into his mind without trying to find something of greater importance, for he may lose the initial thought and have nothing at all. He should develop his thought simply, graphically, and briefly, and then conclude without going on to another thought or viewpoint. Knowing when to stop is as important as knowing how to start.

REHEARSING THE SPEECH

A speech given with or without notes should be rehearsed. Some speakers believe that a speech is ready for presentation when they have prepared and gone over it silently until it is clear to the mind. Delivery, however, cannot be improved in silence; it demands the sensory and muscular experience of spoken rehearsal. A speech should be practiced aloud at least twice. A beginner would benefit by several repetitions. Oral rehearsal develops a mastery of the material and facilitates its presentation. As a result, the speaker will have more ease, confidence, and authority when he finally delivers his speech to an audience.

Methods of Rehearsal. There are two principal ways of rehearsing: auditory and visual.

Auditory. During an auditory rehearsal the speaker is conscious of the way he sounds. He notices his voice, pronunciation, grammar, and phrasing. How do they sound to him? One of the best ways for him to answer this question is to tape record his speech. A few playbacks will suggest improvements. After he has practiced and improved his speech, he should record it again. By comparing the recordings, he will quickly learn to hear better qualities and correct poorer ones.

Visual. Rehearsal includes paying attention to the communicative value of appearance. The speaker checks his posture, bearing, gestures, movements, and poise. Practice in front of a full-length mirror enables him to study what the audience will see. He does this only long enough to make necessary improvements. If possible, the speaker should practice before a friend, and ask him to comment on his visual communication.

Practicing the Extemporaneous Speech. Preliminary practice has two main objectives: to make the speaker familiar with the ideas and supporting material and to improve his delivery.

Becoming Familiar with the Outline. It is important to remember exactly how the specific purpose is to be achieved, the main ideas, the subordinate points used in their support, and the sequence of ideas that moves the speech forward from beginning to end. To help the speaker fix the pattern of the speech in his memory, the following instructions are often given:

1. Read the final revised outline silently. Read it slowly and carefully, grasping each point and its relationship to the following points. Do not reread or go back to an idea; keep moving ahead from start to finish.
2. Now stand as if facing an audience, and read the outline aloud, making each point clear. Again, do not go back or repeat anything.
3. For this rehearsal, attempt to speak the sequence of materials without the outline. Although details may be confusing or an important point is forgotten, do not look at the outline or try to correct yourself. Keep moving ahead and express the structure of ideas as well as possible.

4. Study the outline again to see what parts have been missed or where the planned development was not followed.

5. Stand up and read the outline aloud once again. Read slowly, thinking each thought as it is spoken, moving steadily forward without repeating anything.

6. Finally, deliver the speech to an imaginary audience without reference to the outline or going back to points out of sequence.

Improving the Delivery. When the pattern of ideas is thoroughly memorized, the speaker can be more alert and skillful in adapting his presentation to his listeners. He should practice expressing each idea in a forceful and varied manner. Mere repetition is not valuable; it must be repetition for a purpose. He should seek to vary his gestures, platform movements, and vocal expression, and then practice delivering his speech as he will deliver it when facing his audience.

Practicing with Notes. Using notes effectively also demands rehearsal. The speaker should practice giving his talk, referring to his notes only when necessary. He then discards any notes he did not need. If he follows this weeding-out procedure in subsequent rehearsals, he will be able to reduce his notes to one card containing only clues to main and subordinate ideas, or he may even be able to dispense with notes entirely.

Practicing the Manuscript Speech.

Not only is it necessary to go over the manuscript speech a number of times in order to improve the way ideas are expressed, but it is also necessary to develop confidence and skill in reading it aloud. Especially important is variety. Every word in a sentence must not be emphasized as if it were a pearl on a string. The meaning of the key words that convey the thought should be brought out by stressing important words in contrast to less important ones. The key word bearing the new idea is emphasized, or the new element in the unfolding of an idea. There is no need to reemphasize words whose meaning and impact are already understood. Only the new phrase needs to be brought out prominently.

The manuscript should be gone over carefully and the reader should note how one thought contrasts with another, how a series of thoughts leads to a concept, and which concepts are more important. Marginal notes are beneficial in showing various relationships. For instance, such words as *slow, faster, build to climax* may be jotted down as signposts. Marks can also be made on the speech itself, such as underlining stressed words and placing vertical bars between words to indicate pauses.

Principles of Rehearsal. To be of most use to a speaker, rehearsal should follow definite principles, some of which are listed here.

When to Rehearse. The first rehearsal should take place at least a few days before the speech is to be given. The speaker needs time to note the weak spots and correct them. It is unwise to have a last-minute rehearsal, because this often increases tension and makes the speaker more nervous. It is usually best to rehearse the speech for the last time the day before the scheduled date and then to forget it until it is delivered to the audience.

What to Rehearse. The speaker should give the complete speech first, and then practice those sections that give him trouble. The introduction, for example, may need extra work. He should practice transitions in order to lead from point to point smoothly and to make important evidence and quotations from authorities stand out. Special attention should be given to timing. The pacing should neither be like a pendulum with evenly spaced pauses nor like a racing motor that never stops. Rate and pauses should be varied to suit what is said. Important pauses should be practiced with special care.

The speaker should practice taking his place before his audience, using the lectern, handling notes, and leaving the platform. If he is using visual aids, or mechanical aids like a microphone, he should practice with them. It is highly important to practice with vitality, animation, and enthusiasm. The speaker has to make these qualities part of his delivery during rehearsal. He cannot successfully assume them for the first time when he presents the speech to an audience.

Where to Rehearse. The first rehearsal should be in a place where the speaker will not be interrupted. Since he needs to concentrate just on his material, the size or type of room is not important. However, the final rehearsal should be in a room similar in size to the one where the speaker will give his speech. If possible, it is best to rehearse the speech in the designated room in order to become familiar with the platform, lectern, and other facilities. The speaker should also know the acoustics and how to adjust his voice and speech to the room.

How Much to Rehearse. The speech should be practiced orally until the speaker is sure of the sequence of ideas and until words which convey his ideas come quickly and easily. One or two long periods of rehearsal are not as fruitful as several twenty minute sessions. The length, number, and spacing of oral rehearsals will vary with each individual. Trial and error should help a person to decide what procedures are best for him.

With Whom to Rehearse. At first, the speaker practices alone, but imagines there are people in front of him. He talks to an imaginary audience, and maintains eye contact with all sections of it. Later, it may help to rehearse the speech before friends or relatives. It is best to ask individuals who will be neither too kind nor too critical, but who will try to make helpful suggestions.

Final Suggestion. The speaker should not expect to deliver his speech exactly as he did in his practice sessions. Even though he knows his material thoroughly, he should watch his listeners' reactions and vary his presentation to suit the situation.

9.
THE SPEAKING VOICE

Speaking differs from writing in the completeness of communication. While both present the meaning of words in context, a spoken message includes the meaning added by the voice; thus the full meaning of the message in the immediate situation is conveyed to the receiver. What is said is conditioned by how it is said. For example, "Would you mind opening the door?" uttered in one manner is a courteous request. Spoken in another tone of voice, it means "You're too dumb to do anything but get in my way." A speaker's voice definitely should reinforce his meaning rather than weaken or contradict it. The best worded speech can leave listeners unmoved if it is delivered in a raspy, muffled, or seemingly bored voice.

The voice is part of the speaker's self: it not only identifies a person to others but also reveals some of his attitudes, emotions, and characteristics. Rightly or wrongly, people judge others by their voices, for various kinds of voices suggest different types of disposition, personality, or character. The sound of a person's voice may determine whether or not listeners want to listen to him. A good speaking voice is therefore a valuable asset. A sensible speaker with an unsatisfactory voice does not try to get by in spite of it, but learns how to use it in a better and more effective manner.

VOICE PRODUCTION

The voice is a complex series of sound waves produced by breath pressure setting the vocal folds into vibration, reinforced and modified by the resonators, and further conditioned by the movements of the articulators. These sound waves are received by the ear and perceived or interpreted by the brain. Voice production thus involves an actuator, a vibrator, a resonator, and an articulator. The many organs of the body included in these mechanisms are not concerned with speech alone; voice is produced by a highly specialized use of organs that have other biological functions.

The Actuator.   The actuator is breath pressure, which is built up and released under the control of the breathing muscles. The breathing mechanism resembles a bellows, the air space in the lungs being increased and decreased by the muscles of inhalation and exhalation.

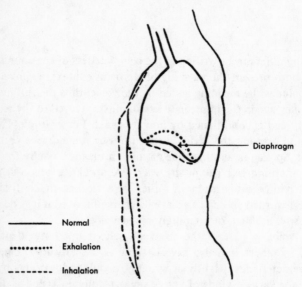

Figure 2. Diagram of breathing action.

The main muscles of inhalation are the diaphragm and the external intercostal muscles. The diaphragm is a dome-shaped muscular partition between the chest and abdominal cavities. As the diaphragm contracts and moves down, the abdominal viscera are displaced and the abdominal walls expand. The intercostal muscles lie between the ribs, and the expansion of the external set expands the chest.

The chest cavity contains the lungs and the heart. The lungs are two spongelike masses of elastic tissue that fill all the space not occupied by the heart. When the chest cavity enlarges during inhalation, the lungs expand, and air pressure within the lungs becomes less than atmospheric pressure, and outside air rushes in through the nose or mouth.

The main muscles of exhalation are the internal intercostal, the abdominal, and lower back muscles. As they contract the diaphragm relaxes and rises, aided by the upward pressure of the viscera. When the chest cavity decreases during exhalation, the lungs are compressed, the air pressure within them becomes greater than atmospheric pressure, and the air rushes out through the nose or mouth. During speech, however, exhalation is modified to a certain extent: the air pressure is controlled and the pressurized air released so as to produce the sounds of an utterance.

The lungs are never entirely emptied of air, nor are they usually completely filled. In ordinary quiet breathing the amount of air entering and leaving the lungs is comparatively small compared to the vital capacity that can be used for physical exertion. Since good voice production does not require strenuous physical effort, the exact control of the breath is more important than a large amount of breath. Control of the breath means supplying enough air under the proper pressure to activate the larynx and the articulators during the various sequences of speech. In quiet biological breathing, inhalation and exhalation are of approximately the same length. For speech, however, inhalation is comparatively short or rapid, while exhalation is longer or slower.

The Vibrator.   The vibrator, less accurately called the vocal cords, consists of the vocal folds. These are small ledges or lips of muscular tissue set into the walls of the larynx, or voice box. The larynx is a framework of cartilages located in the front part of the neck. The action of the jaw, neck, and other muscles during speech causes the larynx to undergo motions such as raising, lowering, and tilting. Within the larynx, by means of complex muscular adjustments, the vocal folds are drawn together and made to vibrate by breath pressure from the lungs. These muscular adjustments cause constant variations in the tension, thickness, and length of the vocal folds. Breath pressure increases through the range of soft to loud tones and also through the range of low-to high-pitched tones. The resulting vibrations of the vocal folds produce sound waves which pass through the mouth or nose into the outer air.

The larynx and vocal folds of different individuals vary in size, those of men being in general larger than those of women. The physical structure of the larynx and resonators impose certain limits upon the pitch range, volume, and quality of the individual voice, although many common vocal limitations are the result of physical, mental, and emotional habits.

The Resonators.   Resonance is the forced vibration of a body acted upon by another vibrating body of about the same frequency. In the voice, the vibrations of the vocal folds set the air within the resonators into vibration. The main cavity resonators are the throat, mouth, and nasal cavities. These modify and amplify the sound waves produced by the vocal folds. Although every speech sound has some form of resonance, most discussions of vocal resonance are concerned with vowel sounds. The relative size, shape, and opening of the throat and mouth cavities are altered by the actions of the tongue and lips to form and amplify the quality or timbre of the various vowels. In nasal resonance the soft palate is lowered, allowing air to pass up behind it into the nasal passages. A slight amount of nasal resonance may add mellowness and an appealing quality to the vowel tones; a large amount creates nasality, which is undesirable in vowel sounds, although it is an essential feature of the nasal consonants.

The Articulators.   The articulators are the lips, teeth, upper gum ridge, hard palate, soft palate, tongue, and related musculatures. By means of muscular adjustments the articulators form speech sounds and thus turn voice and breath into distinct and understandable words and sentences. The action of the lips, tongue, and soft palate shape the resonators for the articulation of the vowels and diphthongs. The articulators, however, are usually considered in connection with the production of consonant sounds, because the articulation of the vowel sounds is less clearly perceived by most persons than that of the consonant sounds.

The articulators approach or contact each other in paired action: lower lip to upper lip, lower lip to upper teeth, and so forth. The movements of the articulators create conditions that vary from a complete stoppage of the breath to a subtle shaping of its passageway. The stops, or plosives, are produced when the stream of breath is completely stopped and released; for example, a "p" sound is produced when the lips close and suddenly part to release the pressurized breath. The other speech sounds are made by obstructions, narrowings, and shapings at various points from the glottis to the lips, either with or without vibration of the vocal folds.

CHARACTERISTICS OF AN EFFECTIVE VOICE

A good voice is flexible and responsive, having enough variety of pitch, duration (rate), and volume to express not only the speaker's thoughts but also his moods, feelings, and emotions. The voice should thus be appropriate to the age, sex, and experience of the speaker. The voice must be strong enough or of sufficient volume to be audible to the listeners without being too loud or overpowering. It should be clear and pleasing, free from harshness, breathiness, nasality, or other distracting qualities. Listeners like voices that have a warm, sympathetic quality, that are adequately rich and full, and that are vibrant and alive.

Most persons have no idea what their voices sound like to others. The speaker should therefore have his voice recorded, preferably including examples of conversation, oral reading, and public speaking. Listening to the playback of his own voice several times and analyzing it in terms of the above characteristics will give him a better understanding of his good qualities and those in need of improvement.

VOICE IMPROVEMENT

The voice is a set of habits, the result of the speaker's customary way of using his speech mechanism. A speaker with a poor, weak, or unsatisfactory voice can improve it by becoming conscious of his vocal activity and by carefully building better voice habits. Like the player of a musical instrument, he can learn to master its potentialities. The speaker should train his ear to distinguish differences in tone quality as well as those in pitch, time, and loudness. A good practice is to listen to the voices of others and react to them. Deciding what he likes and dislikes in them develops an appreciation of good voice qualities and gives the speaker a basis for judging himself. When practicing voice exercises he should listen carefully to his own voice and cultivate what he considers to be better and more agreeable tones. Frequent practice with a tape recorder is especially valuable. Some individuals can make their voices clearer, more flexible, and more responsive by themselves. Others make better progress with a teacher. A good voice is based on good posture, proper relaxation, good breath control, and effective use of the attributes of the voice.

Posture.   To be suitable for efficient voice production, posture should include these features: (1) The weight should rest on the balls of the feet rather than on the heels. (2) The back should be erect. The chest should not sag, nor should it be thrown forward or held upward in an expanded condition. (3) The head should be comfortably poised, with the chin neither too high nor too low. The over-high or over-low chin creates overtension in the neck, jaw, and throat.

Posture Exercises

1. Assume a well-balanced posture before a full-length mirror; then look up at the top of the mirror for a half minute. Note the muscular sensations in the front and back of the tilted neck. Now look at your chin in the mirror. Notice the different feeling of the neck muscles.
2. Start as in Exercise 1; then look at the floor immediately in front of you. Note the sensations in your neck and throat. Now look at your chin in the mirror. Notice the feeling of relaxation in your neck area.
3. Start as in Exercise 1; then throw your chest out and your shoulders back. Hold this position while you clench your fists and make your arms rigid. Grit your teeth and push against the floor with your toes. Hold your breath as long as you can. Now relax and resume the well-balanced posture. The sensations of tension and relaxation should give you an awareness of proper tonicity.

Relaxation.   For the efficient and unhampered use of the voice, the body should be in a condition of alert relaxation, or proper muscular tonicity. Tonicity is the healthy tension or partial contraction of muscles during rest. Complete muscular relaxation is impossible; however, to most speakers, proper muscular tonicity seems like a complete relaxation from their customary overtension.

Relaxation Exercises

1. Stand comfortably erect without strain. Let your head loll forward. Now move your head slowly from side to side, as if describing the lower half of a circle, stretching the muscles in the back of the neck.
2. Stand erect. Move your shoulders forward and backward in a circle a few times. Reverse the direction of the rotation.
3. Move the jaw down slowly in a yawn position. Feel the stretch of the

muscles and then relax. Then drop the jaw down freely and loosely a few times.

Breath Control. Good voice production requires the intake of the needed amount of air and the accurate control of exhalation to regulate breath pressure. Breath pressure must be strong enough to create sounds that are audible to everyone in the audience. Pressure must be steady enough for the smoothness and emphasis of connected speech. Breath pressure must be lasting enough to sustain sentence endings, to prevent them from dwindling away into inaudibility. George Eliot admired the ability of John Duke Coleridge to make himself heard as he addressed the jury in the Tichborne trial in 1872: "He is a marvelous speaker among Englishmen; has an exquisitely melodious voice, perfect gesture, and a power of keeping the thread of his syntax to the end of his sentence, which makes him delightful to follow."

For speech, inhalation should be silent and quick and exhalation slow and controlled. Since voice is produced during exhalation and since many individuals ignore breathing when they speak, much voice training consists of controlling and coordinating exhalation.

Breath Control Exercises

1. Lie on your back on a flat surface with a book resting on your abdomen. Relax and feel at ease for a minute. You will then notice that your abdomen (and the book) rises when you inhale and falls when you exhale.
2. Stand comfortably erect and place your hands on your abdomen just below the ribs. Slow down your breathing and inhale to a mental count of three and exhale to a mental count of five. Repeat until you can control your breath smoothly.
3. Purse your lips and hold the tip of your finger one inch in front of them. Inhale silently and quickly and blow a fine, steady stream of air against your fingertip. Do this several times. Repeat the exercise daily until you can continue the stream of air smoothly for thirty seconds.

VOICE ATTRIBUTES

The voice can be described, studied, and improved in terms of time, loudness, pitch, and quality.

Time. The factor of timing is part of the expression of meaning and consists of the duration of the individual sounds comprising words and phrases and the duration of the pauses between words or phrases. The rate of change from one speech sound to the next varies according to the length of the sound. The duration of the phrase depends on the number and length of the words or syllables. The rate of change from one phrase to another varies with the length of the intervening pause. The sum of these variable durations and pauses compose the general rate of speaking.

Duration. Spoken English sounds have varying durations or lengths, depending on their position in the utterance. In general, stressed syllables or words are longer than unstressed. For example, in the following command, the second "go" is stressed and is therefore longer than the first: "Go and tell them we're ready to go." A word is sometimes prolonged to intensify the speaker's attitude or emotion, as in "That's a lo-o-ong way off." The lengthening may sometimes be a matter of dialect. Some Southern speakers, for instance, lengthen the first syllable of "suga(r)" to "su-uga(r)."

Many persons do not realize that stress includes length of the vowel or syllable as well as loudness and change of pitch. Hammering out stresses without lengthening the syllable reduces the clarity of the words which are most important to the meaning. In addition, and of great importance to voice, the sudden staccato attack on syllables creates a clang effect which makes the sounds less agreeable to the ear.

The duration of stressed syllables depends on the nature of the ideas and feelings being expressed. For example, the key words of meanings involving haste, urgency, and excitement, such as "Don't touch it!" are less noticeably prolonged than those involving doubt, deliberation, or deep emotion, such as "We need a thorough weighing of evidence." In the sentences "It was a week ago" and "It was a thousand years ago," the stressed syllables of "thousand years ago" are elongated more than those of "week ago," because of the idea of a great extent of time. The unaccented syllables, however, are not given extra duration even when an utterance is impressive and emphatic. To do so would weaken and obscure the rhythm and meaning of the sentence.

Duration Exercises
1. Inhale as if yawning, and slowly whisper the word "ah." Repeat several times until the "ah" can be prolonged for five seconds.
2. Speak the numbers one to five very slowly, prolonging the vowels for three seconds: o-o-one, two-o-o, three-e-e, fo-o-our, fi-i-ive.

3. Pronounce the following words, prolonging the vowel of each succeeding word longer than the one before it: quick, hurt, sun, moon, dull, slow, long.

4. Practice the following phrases, elongating the sounds as shown by the repeated letters. Use sufficient breath to make the sounds smooth, clear, and full.

> I said I-I kn-n-o-o-o-ow.
> O-Over he-e-er-re.
> Who-o-ose ho-o-o-o-om-me?
> A drea-ea-m-m of a kiss-s-s.

5. Observe which words or syllables are longest as you read the following sentences aloud.

> Who will be the unemployed of the future?
> The older the bird, the gayer the feathers.
> The answer is an emphatic yes.
> Where will these tax revenues come from?
> This is the most serious problem of all.

6. Read the sentences a second time with more interest, expression, and conviction. What changes occur in the length of words and syllables?

Pause. A stretch of communicative speech does not continue too long without a pause. A pause is an effective means of emphasis. An important word or idea can be featured by a marked delay just before or after it is uttered. This type of pause occurs within the breath group, which is a meaningful group of words uttered in one breath. The differentiation of meaning is shown in the following sentences spoken without and with a pause for emphasis.

> She said she was his wife.
> She said she was his—wife.
> Do you think you belong in this company?
> Do you think you—belong in this company?

Pauses, for the most part, are used between words grouped into meaningful grammatical and syntactical units (phrases, clauses, and sentences). Pauses thus mark divisions in the thought, and can be viewed as a form of oral punctuation, breaking speech into units that are easy to understand.

A pause between thoughts is a purposeful interval of silence, giving the audience time to digest the idea it has just heard and allowing the speaker to think about what he is going to say next. If the pauses are too long or too frequent, they may impress listeners as blank spaces or lapses of thinking. Distracting and undesirable vocalized pauses, such as "uh" and "er," should be avoided, because they only intensify the lag in communication. However, each pause, whether short, long, or very long, should be definite enough to accomplish the purpose. Considerable practice is necessary for expressive use of pausing. Many speakers pause too seldom, forgetting that listeners cannot grasp the meaning of continuous utterances that are not broken up into clearly related thought groups. The following sentence, for instance, needs spoken pauses to make the meaning immediately clear to the listener.

> *Toward the preservation of your government | and the permanency of your present happy state ‖ it is requisite | not only that you steadily discountenance irregular oppositions to the acknowledged authority, ‖ but also that you resist with care | the spirit of innovation upon its principles, ‖ however specious the pretexts.*—GEORGE WASHINGTON

Overlong phrases also are avoided because sufficient breath is needed for the word group. Running short of breath near the end of a sentence reduces audibility and audience comprehension. On the other hand, a constant succession of pauses creating short phrases may sound like tedious dictation and lose audience interest. In a well-communicated spoken message the phrases and pauses vary in length according to the meaning.

Pause Exercises.
1. Read the following sentences aloud, increasing the length of the pause at each successive comma.

> Down, down, down it sank, and disappeared.
> The light faded, faded, faded, and was suddenly a bright flash.

2. Read the sentences again, decreasing the length of each successive pause. Note the differences in effect. What changes in situation are suggested by your two readings of each sentence?
3. Read the following sentences with a pause of one second in the first, two seconds in the second, and three seconds in the third.

> But I thought you___knew.
> I hoped you would____care.
> I can't believe you were only_____lying.

4. Practice the following sentences to achieve an impressive, emphatic, and convincing expression of the ideas. How many pauses are necessary for each sentence? Do they agree with the punctuation?

> "Young men are fitter to invent than to judge, fitter for execution than for counsel, and fitter for new projects than for settled business."—FRANCIS BACON
>
> "Government is a trust, and the officers of the government are trustees; and both the trust and the trustee are created for the benefit of the people."—HENRY CLAY

General Rate of Speaking. The general or overall rate of speaking depends on the temperament, personality, and communicative habits of the speaker and the content of his messages. The conversation of most individuals, since it is often casual in nature, is more rapid than their more serious public speaking. In general, important subject matter slows down speech; however, urgent emotions tend to make the rate more rapid.

The general rate of many good speakers is from about 115 to 175 words a minute. A rate of less than 100 words a minute is too slow to hold the interest of most listeners; over 200 words a minute makes it difficult for many listeners to grasp the entire meaning. A general rate, such as 120 words a minute, does not mean that the speaker utters two words each second. A uniform rate would be monotonous and unreal. A varied rate is needed to convey thought and feeling. The pace changes continually to suit changes in meaning. For example, the speaker may dwell on an important word, state an idea more slowly, or pick up the tempo in less important material.

The general rate can be tested by reading the preceding paragraph aloud. Sixty seconds indicates a medium rate, forty seconds is too rapid, and ninety seconds is too slow.

The speaker with too fast a rate can modify it by carefully thinking and reacting to his ideas as he says them. He can prolong key words, dwell on important points, and pause for effect before proceeding to the next point. The speaker with too slow a rate should thoroughly master his ideas in advance. He can feature lively elements in his material, such as excitement, suspense, and humor, all of which encourage faster pacing. He should avoid complicated, dangling sentences in favor of those of simpler construction, and should concentrate on the forward movement of his ideas.

Rate Exercises

1. Time yourself by the second hand of a watch. (a) Count from one to ten in five seconds. (b) Count from one to ten slowly in ten seconds. (c) Prolong the vowels and count from one to ten in fifteen seconds.
2. Practice the following sentence so that you can read it in fifteen, twenty, twenty-five, and thirty seconds.

> "All, too, will bear in mind this sacred principle, that though the will of the majority is in all cases to prevail, that will, to be rightful, must be reasonable; that the minority possess their equal rights, which equal law must protect, and to violate would be oppression."—THOMAS JEFFERSON

3. Practice the following sentences aloud. Read the first one at a slow rate and each of the others at a faster rate than the one which precedes it. Read the last one as fast as possible within the limits of intelligibility.

> "Look, O Lord, and behold, for I am despised."—LAMENTATIONS OF JEREMIAS
> "To some generations much is given; from others, much is demanded."—FRANKLIN D. ROOSEVELT
> "We would all be idle if we could."—SAMUEL JOHNSON
> "Only dull people are brilliant at breakfast."—OSCAR WILDE
> "If you don't get everything you want, think of the things you get that you don't want."

Loudness. The voice when heard has some degree of loudness. The amplitude or extent of vibration in its relation to frequency is called intensity, and is interpreted by the hearer as loudness. Loudness also depends on the amplifying action of the resonators. How loud should the speaker speak? Loud enough to be easily heard, yet not so loud as to irritate listeners. Some of the factors that determine suitable loudness are the size and acoustics of the room and the size of the audience. Other factors are the varying aspects of the meaning being expressed.

Loudness is controlled by breath pressure. Louder phrases require more pressure. Inhalation should be adjusted to the word group about to be spoken, and the breath pressure suitably regulated by the exhalation muscles. Gasping for breath, taking in too much or too little air makes control of the utterance difficult. Breathing should be consciously trained until all necessary degrees of volume from loud to soft can be produced at will.

Loudness should not be monotonously strong or weak, but should change to bring out differences in meaning. The same pattern of force, such as the strong beginning of sentences, should not be repeated. The last words of a sentence are often the clue to the meaning and should be made prominent by a proper degree of loudness. Variation of loudness is a requirement for emphasis. One of the most difficult things for a beginning speaker to learn is to make important ideas stand out. This may best be done by uttering important words, phrases, and ideas with additional force.

Stress is loudness or force applied to a word or syllable. Stress also includes features of pitch and length. An English word of more than one syllable has stress on at least one syllable as part of the pronunciation of the word: vólume, attráctive, fórmidable, incōmprehénsible. A group of words or breath group has a peak of loudness on a given word according to the speaker's meaning: It was lást night, That's what yóu think. This stress is called sentence stress, whether the word group is a phrase, clause, or sentence. The word receiving sentence stress is the important clue to the speaker's meaning and usually reveals some degree of his feeling or attitude.

Loudness Exercises

1. Count slowly from one to five, making each number louder than the preceding one.
2. Count slowly from one to nine, increasing the loudness to five and decreasing it from five to nine.
3. Count slowly as follows, stressing the capitalized words.
   a. ONE, two, three, ONE, two, three, ONE, two, three.
   b. One, TWO, three, one, TWO, three, one, TWO, three.
   c. One, two, THREE, one, two, THREE, one, two, THREE.
4. Inhale for each repetition of the greeting "Hello!" Start softly and increase the volume gradually, stopping before you begin to shout.
5. Repeat Exercise 4, reversing the volume from loud to soft.
6. Loudness is also used for special contrast. Each one of the following quotations requires special stresses to reveal a contrast in the thought.

   "We have just enough religion to make us hate, but not enough to make us love one another."—JONATHAN SWIFT
   "When a man assumes a public trust, he should consider himself as public property."—THOMAS JEFFERSON
   "Our country, right or wrong. When right, to be kept right; when wrong, to be put right."—CARL SCHURZ

Pitch.   A spoken sentence has a pitch or melodic feature. Pitch is the perception, on a scale from low to high, of the frequency or speed of vibration. The perception in pitch is also influenced by the resonators, because they weaken some component frequencies of a sound and reinforce others. Pitch inflections or contours, along with stress and pause, are part of spoken syntax. Pitch features not only indicate intellectual meanings but also tend to express emotional meanings.

Key. Each utterance is spoken within a given pitch range of the musical scale. Key is the median note of the utterance, the pitch level above and below which the voice fluctuates in a spoken melody.

The speaking pitch range often averages about one octave, although it may include more or less, depending on the meaning intended by the speaker. A narrow range, for example, may result from thoughtfulness, calmness, indifference, repressed emotion, or matter-of-fact material. A wide range may reflect cheerfulness, excitement, impatience, anger, or unusually interesting material. The range may be transposed higher, such as from c—c′ to g—g′ (c′ = middle c). The upward shift can express mockery, nervous embarrassment, and youthful gaiety.

You didn't *lose* it? Oh,

Lost it?   no.

The range may be shifted downward, perhaps to a′-a to indicate boredom, pompous dignity, hopelessness, or other attitudes.

Here she comes now—

get a load of that hat.

Optimum Pitch. Each person's voice has an optimum pitch or key. The optimum pitch depends on the structure of the individual speech mechanism. Women's voices have a higher optimum pitch than men's, although there is considerable variation among members of both sexes. Soprano and tenor voices, for example, have higher optimum pitches than contralto and bass voices. The best speaking range of the voice has the optimum pitch as its center. Some individuals, however, do not speak in their best vocal range, but have a habitual pitch level that lies above or below their optimum pitch. As a result, their voices do not function at their best.

The optimum pitch can be located by following these directions: (1) Close your ears with your fingers and hum up and down the scale until you find the pitch where the hum sounds loudest or most vibrant to you. This pitch will be near your optimum pitch. (2) Sing down the scale as far as you can go without forcing. Call this note *do* and sing up the scale to *sol*. This note will be near your optimum pitch. (3) If you have a piano, locate the lowest note you can produce and also your highest falsetto note. Your optimum pitch will be approximately one fourth of the distance from your lowest note.

Pitch Flexibility. A good voice has the flexibility of conversation. In conversation we use pitch changes between words and on individual words: pitch can change either by a step or a slide.

STEP. The step is an abrupt change or marked skip in pitch from one syllable to another and often indicates a distinct shift in meaning. An upward step may express emotions like surprise or may emphasize the importance of a thought or feeling.

cares?   great!

Who   That's

A downward step may express an emotion like exasperation or disgust or reduce the importance of a thought or feeling.

Who   That's

cares?   great!

An up and down combination of steps may have a special emotional implication, such as challenge, doubt, or polite concern.

not   I

Why   so.

go?   think

SLIDE. The slide is a constant feature of the English language and is part of the smoothness and flow of connected speech. The slide is also part of spoken syntax as mentioned above under pitch inflection. The slide also frequently communicates subtle aspects of meaning. The role of pitch inflection in English is complex, but a few basic principles are helpful for most speakers.

A rising inflection suggests curiosity, uncertainty, or incompleteness of thought. The rise in pitch is found in most questions not containing an interrogative word, in suspended or broken off sentences, and in attitudes of hesitation or confusion.

```
        ly?              ble.                    it—
    real-               si-               mean
 Are you         It's pos-        I didn't
```

A falling inflection suggests knowledge, conviction, determination, or completeness of thought. The falling pitch is found in most statements, commands, and questions containing an interrogative word.

```
              we-                          mo-
     rived last  e-                   the    on-
 He ar-          ek.    Give me            ney.
```

```
              i-
         ti-  me
     What          is
                      it?
```

Compound inflections—rising-falling and falling-rising—indicate emphasis, emotion, double meanings, or subtlety of thought. Compound inflections are used in strong statements, exclamations, polite questions, and requests.

Faults of Pitch. Certain faults in using pitch limit the voices of many speakers. Their correction is an important step in voice improvement.

HIGH KEY. The voice cannot function efficiently if the speaker's habitual key is above his optimum pitch. The tones are nasal, shrill, lacking in fullness and body, or resemble the falsetto. In extreme cases the voice is aspirate and hoarse. The speaker labors under muscular strain, because a higher range requires more breath pressure and effort than the best range. The speaker should realize that the control of breath and resonance is easier when the voice is in its proper range.

LOW KEY. A pitch level that is too far below the optimum pitch also hampers or cramps the voice, making it sound hollow, muffled, gravelly, or hoarse. To get his voice to function within its proper range the speaker may have to challenge his laziness, shyness, defensiveness, or disinclination to communicate.

The optimum pitch should be located, recognized, and practiced until the speaker can remember how it feels and sounds. Words and phrases should be practiced with inflections that undulate around the optimum pitch. The best octave of the voice should be exercised and used often and persistently enough until it becomes the habitual basis of speech.

Exercises for Optimum Pitch

1. Hum slowly up the scale for an octave and back. Detach each note and make it vibrate freely, inhaling whenever necessary. Select the two notes that have the fullest sound or vibration. Hum these notes slowly in alternation several times. Repeat the octave scale and end on your optimum pitch.

2. Chant each of the following phrases on your approximate optimum pitch, then on a note a tone higher, and then on a note a tone lower than the optimum. Decide which level enables you to produce tones of the same volume with the least effort. Your voice on this level will probably sound clearer, richer, and more vibrant. Once you find your best pitch level, repeat the phrases in a conversational manner, letting the voice rise and fall below this central pitch.

> Let's go! That's much too far. Whom did you see? He made a definite appointment. Can't you decide which one?

3. Pronounce each of these words with a rising inflection in a range that seems high, in a range that seems low, and in a range midway between the two.

> Who? There? Home?

NARROW RANGE. Probably nothing is more detrimental to effective use of the voice in speech than the absence of expressive pitch changes. A near monotone suggests indifference, insecurity, or depression and dulls the interest of listeners, causing their minds to wander. Spoken melodies are likely to be interesting if they have an average range of at least an octave. Expressive variety is obtained by using narrower and wider pitch changes only for special emphasis.

REPEATED PATTERN. The same melody or pitch pattern continually repeated soon becomes monotonous. Sentences, for example, should not end exactly on the same note. Sentence endings should also have a variety of inflections. The pitch changes should vary in height, extent, and type. Falling inflections should be varied by being higher or lower, by falling to a greater or lesser extent, or by being interspersed with rising-falling or rising patterns according to facets of the meaning. Some speakers may need to free themselves from a melody limited by self-consciousness, overtension, or inadequate discrimination of meaning.

Exercises for Pitch Variety

1. Speak "Hello" to indicate the following persons you meet on the street: Your boy friend. Your girl friend. Someone you would like to know better. An acquaintance you would like to avoid. A neighbor who bores you. A teacher whom you like.
2. Ask the question "Why do you ask?" to indicate these various meanings: I'm surprised you want to know. What are you up to? I shouldn't really tell you. You'd better mind your own business.
3. See how many ways you can vary "I don't know what to say." Make sure that each way fits an imagined communicative situation.

Quality.   The structure of sound waves, or the relation between the complexity of the vibration and the action of the resonators, is perceived as tone quality. The resonators can modify their size and shape, can be coupled together or uncoupled, can alter the size of their openings, and can tense or relax some of their surfaces. As a result, an almost endless variety of vocal qualities is possible.

Undesirable Vocal Qualities.   A poor voice often seems to be produced with effort against some form of interference. The voice may sound small, wispy, and weak; it may be breathy, raspy, husky, or hoarse; it may seem hollow, muffled, throaty, or swallowed; it may be harsh, strident, or piercing. Poor vocal qualities often express attitudes not intended by the speaker, such as whining, boredom, annoyance, or belligerence.

Good Voice Quality.   In general, to produce good voice quality the speech mechanism must be free to function efficiently. Poor posture, stiffness, or overtension of the neck and jaw hamper the muscles of breathing, phonation, and resonation. The muscles of the jaw, neck, shoulders, and upper chest should be consciously relaxed until they feel comfortably at ease. The lips should be actively used as part of vowel quality. Most English consonants require the actions of articulators located in the front of the mouth. Careful attention to those articulators often allows the vocal folds and resonators to function readily and effectively.

When practicing for good vocal quality, try to feel the tone as well as hear it. Look for the differences in the way it feels and the way it sounds in successive repetitions. Train both your auditory awareness and your muscular coordination.

Quality Exercises

1. Lie on a flat surface with a book on your abdomen. Inhale and say the word "four." As you repeat the word, try to let the weight of the book

produce the sounds without any effort on your part. Also say the words "who," "sure," "wall," and "way." Which word seems clearest in quality? If you can do one word or vowel better than another, use it as a model, and try to make the others match it.

2. Stand erect with your hands on your abdomen just below the lower ribs. Inhale and slowly say the word "do." Repeat a few times. Then say, "What did you do?" stressing the word "do" in an interested conversational manner. Then alternate the word and the sentence and make the word "do" sound equally clear and full both times.

3. Hold your fingertip in front of your lips. Practice the following words and phrases and note the action of the lips and the warmth from the mouth against your fingertip: Go. Let's go. Far. It's too far. See. Whom did you see?

4. Place your hands on the upper part of your abdomen. Count "one" on the first breath, "one, two" on the second, "one, two, three" on the third, etc. Stress the last number of each breath group and note the muscular activity of the abdomen. Go only as far on one breath as you can without strain. Always end with breath in reserve.

CONTINUED PRACTICE

The suggestions in this chapter are offered only as a beginning for voice improvement. Intelligent practice and discriminating use of the voice are necessary over a long period of time. Further information and practice materials for analyzing and conveying meaning can be found in Chapter 21. Fifteen minutes of daily exercises, plus fifteen minutes of reading aloud will help train and develop the voice. All types of material should be practiced.

Voice should never be consciously practiced during the delivery of a speech. To do so robs the message of its spontaneity and reality. Instead, the speaker should concentrate on his material and his audience, and take for granted that his voice is equal to its task. A good speaking voice is not an end in itself; it is a valuable part of good communication.

10.
ARTICULATION AND PRONUNCIATION

Speech must not only be audible but also intelligible. A speaker's voice may carry and be easily heard, but his speech sounds may be so indistinctly articulated or his words so poorly pronounced that he cannot be readily understood.

ARTICULATION

Articulation is the systematic modification of the pressurized breath stream by means of the movements and adjustments of the speech organs in order to produce the sounds of speech joined in syllables, words, and phrases. Clear articulation is necessary for successful communication. Poor articulation leads to errors and delays in messages and actions that result from communication. Since both correct and incorrect pronunciations of words can be enunciated distinctly or indistinctly, articulation is distinguished from pronunciation, which is the use of socially acceptable patterns of speech sounds.

Importance of Consonants. The vowels and diphthongs are the basis of the sonority and carrying power of the voice, while the consonants are the basis of the intelligibility of speech. Some early forms of writing recorded only the consonants of utterances, leaving the vowels to be supplied by the reader. In English, for example, the sequence of written vowels "-a- -o- -ou- -i-" yields no meaning. However, the consonants of the same sentence, "wh-t d-y-- th-nk," enable the reader to interpret the meaning as "What do you think?" Likewise, from the standpoint of clear, intelligible speech, articulation is primarily concerned with distinct consonant sounds. The articulation of vowels, of course, is of great importance in acceptable pronunciation.

Causes of Poor Articulation. Some persons are unaware that their speech cannot be readily understood. When asked "What did you say?" they presume that the listener does not hear well. Some speakers are too lazy and careless to exert themselves to speak clearly; others are indifferent to speech and the need for communication. Many other causes can be mentioned, such as inert lips, habitual tight jaw, sluggish tongue action, imitation of indistinct speech, or the influence of a foreign language. Good articulation is based on the knowledge of how sounds are made, the ability to form them precisely, and the habit of uttering them distinctly in daily life.

Indicating Speech Sounds. The spoken language has no way of indicating sounds except by articulating them. For recording speech sounds in writing some system of representing individual sounds is required.

The Alphabet. Our alphabet of twenty-six letters is used to represent some forty-four English sounds. The alphabet is particularly inadequate to indicate vowel sounds, for five letters must represent about twenty vowels and diphthongs. For example, the letter "e" is pronounced in many different ways, or is silent: me, deer, eight, height, let, new, sew, sergeant, serpent, George, crate, crater, crated. The vowel sound in "me" is represented by various spellings: aegis, be, bee, beat, receive, people, key, machine, believe, amoeba, quay. Dictionaries are therefore obliged to modify the alphabetical letters by diacritical signs in order to indicate pronunciation.

International Phonetic Alphabet. To understand articulation and pronunciation well enough to improve them, an accurate way of indicating the sounds of speech is necessary. The International Phonetic Alphabet (IPA) uses one symbol for each distinctive speech sound, or phoneme (the group of slight variations of sound produced and identified as that sound). The phoneme /t/, for example, may have a strong explosion of the breath in "tone," a light puff of air in "note," and no audible escape of air in "stone." The IPA symbols (written within slanted lines) are less confusing than the diacritical marks used in some dictionaries. The sixteen symbols /p, b, t, d, k, g, f, v, s, z, m, n, l, r, h, w/ have their familiar values. Only nine other consonant symbols need to be learned. Some twenty vowel and diphthong symbols must be learned, as must the diacritical marks of other dictionaries.

It is customary dictionary practice to explain methods of indicating pronunciation and to provide a list of symbols for ready reference. The user should study the introductory material in any dictionary before looking up the pronunciation of words. The following is a list of IPA symbols, together with a common key word.

/i/ be	/d/ die
/ɪ/ bit	/k/ key
/e/ bate (often /eɪ/ bay)	/g/ gay
/ɛ/ bet	/m/ me
/æ/ bat	/n/ no
/a/ aisle[1]	/ŋ/ wing
/ʌ/ cup	/f/ foe
/ə/ above	/v/ vote
/ɜ, ɝ / her[2]	/θ/ thin
/ɚ/ herder[3]	/ð/ then
/u/ food	/s/ so
/ʊ/ good	/z/ zero
/o/ obese (often /oʊ/ know)	/ʃ/ ash
/ɔ/ awe	/ʒ/ azure
/ɒ/ hot[4]	/h/ he
/ɑ/ ah	/tʃ/ chest
/aɪ/ aisle	/dʒ/ jest
/aʊ/ how	/w/ wet
/ɔɪ/ boy	/ʍ/ whet (also /hw/)
/p/ pie	/r/ row
/b/ buy	/j/ yet
/t/ tie	/l/ lie

ˌ Indicates a syllabic sound when placed under a symbol: "cotton" /kɑtn̩/

~ Indicates nasalization when placed over a symbol: "heat" /hĩt/

: Indicates lengthening of a sound when placed after a symbol: "law" /lɔ:/

ˈ Indicates primary stress when placed before and above the beginning of a syllable: "halo /ˈhelo/

ˌ Indicates a secondary stress when placed before and below the beginning of a syllable: "oatmeal" /ˈotˌmil/

[1] Indicates the first sound in the diphthong as frequently pronounced, or the vowel of the word "ask" as pronounced by many Eastern speakers.

[2] Indicates variant pronunciations of the r-vowel in stressed syllables.

[3] Indicates the r-vowel in unstressed syllables.

[4] Indicates the vowel of the word "hot" as pronounced by many Eastern speakers.

Classification of Speech Sounds. On the basis of their function in the syllable, speech sounds are divided into syllabic and nonsyllabic sounds. These two categories correspond for the most part with the classification into vowels and consonants, both of which are further subdivided. A syllable, or unit of pronunciation and rhythm, is a single, uninterrupted impulse of breath containing one sound of definite sonority.

A syllabic sound is thus one that may be pronounced with sonority as a syllable, and is usually a vowel. However, some consonant sounds can be uttered as syllables, namely /l̩, m̩, n̩, and r̩/, as in "bottle, bottom, button, bitter." These consonants when serving as vowels are called syllabic *l,* etc. Syllabic *r,* however, is usually called the unstressed *r*-vowel /ɚ/.

A syllable may also contain less sonorous sounds that are not uttered separately as syllables; these are nonsyllabic sounds, and are usually consonants. However, in a diphthong, such as that of the word "I" /aɪ/, the second vowel is a nonsyllabic sound; otherwise the word would have two syllables.

Vowels. A vowel is a voiced, oral, frictionless, continued sound. The vocal folds are vibrating; the soft palate blocks off the nasal passages so that the sound waves pass out of the mouth; the breath does not encounter enough obstruction to cause audible friction; the breath flow is not momentarily stopped and audibly released.

Vowels are classified according to the place of articulation and height of tongue position. The front, central, and back parts of the tongue may be raised to a low, mid, or high position. In the front vowels, the front part of the tongue moves toward the hard palate. In the central vowels, the center of the tongue moves toward the roof of the mouth. In the back vowels the back part of the tongue moves toward the soft palate, or velum. Figure 4 shows the approximate height of the front, center, and back of the tongue for the corresponding vowels. The positions of the tongue and lips establish the resonance or qualities of the various vowels.

FRONT VOWELS. In forming the front vowels, from the highest to the lowest, the front of the tongue moves successively downward and backward from the hard palate, accompanied by a lowering of the jaw and a larger separation between the lips. The tip of the tongue rests behind the lower front teeth.

For the high, front, tense, unrounded vowel /i/ (as in "be"), the front of the tongue is raised toward the hard palate. The sides of the tongue contact the inner surfaces of the upper teeth. The lips are slightly open and unrounded; the tongue and lips are tense.

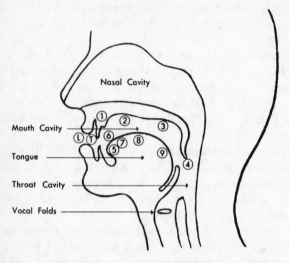

1. Upper gum ridge.   2. Hard palate.   3. Soft palate.   4. Uvula.   5. Tip of tongue.   6. Blade of tongue.   7. Front of tongue.   8. Center of tongue. 9. Back of tongue.   L. Lips.   T. Teeth.

Figure 3. Diagram of the speech organs.

For the high, front, lax, unrounded vowel /ɪ/ (as in "bit"), the tongue is slightly lower than for /i/, the mouth opening is a trifle larger, and the lips and tongue are more relaxed. The sound tends to be short.

To produce the mid, front, tense, unrounded vowel /e/ (as in "bate"), the front of the tongue is somewhat lower and farther back than for /ɪ/ and its sides contact the upper teeth. The jaw is lower, the opening between the unrounded lips larger. The musculature is tense. In stressed syllables the vowel becomes the diphthong /eɪ/: far away /fɑr ə'weɪ/.

To produce the mid, front, lax, unrounded vowel /ɛ/ (as in "bet"), the tongue is lower than for /e/, the mouth opening is larger, and the musculature more relaxed. The sound tends to be short.

For the low, front, lax, unrounded vowel /æ/ (as in "bat"), the front of the tongue is slightly raised and its sides no longer contact the inner surfaces of the upper teeth. The mouth is well-opened and the lips unrounded. The tongue and lips of many speakers are somewhat tense.

For the low, less front, lax vowel /a/ (as in the first part of the diphthong in the word "aisle"), the tongue is barely raised, the mouth is well open, and the musculature more relaxed than for /æ/. This sound is used by some speakers in words like "ask," "class," and "dance" where others use /æ/.

CENTRAL VOWELS. In forming the central vowels the center of the tongue moves from a fairly low to a mid position. The lips are moderately separated and unrounded.

For the low or mid, central, lax, unrounded vowel /ʌ/ (as in "cup"), the center of the tongue is slightly raised, the jaw somewhat open, the lips and tongue relaxed. The sound tends to be short, and appears only in stressed syllables, being replaced by /ə/ in unaccented syllables.

For the mid, central, lax vowel /ə/ (as in "above"), the tongue is usually slightly higher and more forward than for /ʌ/. The sound is extremely short and appears only in unstressed syllables. This sound is substituted for most other unaccented vowels. The word "above" shows the use of /ə and /ʌ/ in unstressed and stressed syllables /ə'bʌv/. It should be noted that in phonetic transcription the stress mark appears *before* the syllable to be stressed.

To produce the mid, central, tense, unrounded vowel /ɜ/ (as in "her"), the center of the tongue is noticeably raised toward the hard palate; the tip of the tongue rests behind the lower front teeth. This sound is used by Eastern and Southern speakers who do not "sound their r's" and lacks distinctive r-coloring. This vowel appears only in stressed syllables, being replaced by /ə/ in unaccented syllables.

For the more widely used variant /ɝ/, the tip of the tongue is raised toward the hard palate and may be slightly curled backward. The r-coloring is shown by the small mark attached to the symbol. This r-vowel sound occurs only in stressed symbols, being replaced by /ɚ/ in unaccented syllables.

The mid, central, lax, unrounded vowel /ɚ/ (as in "herder"), is very short and appears only in unstressed syllables. For this unstressed r-vowel the tongue may be slightly higher or lower than for /ɝ/. The word "herder" illustrates the use of the two r-vowels

/ɜ/ and /ɚ/ in stressed and unstressed syllables: /'hɜdɚ/. For speakers who do not sound their *r*'s, the pronunciation is /'hɜdə/.

BACK VOWELS. To produce the back vowels from high to low, the back of the tongue is progressively lowered away from the soft palate; from a slightly separated and rounded position the lips gradually unround and become wider apart as the jaw lowers. The tongue tip remains behind the lower front teeth for all back vowels.

To produce the high, back, tense, rounded vowel /u/ (as in "food"), the back of the tongue is raised to a position near the soft palate. The lips are close together and rounded; the musculature is tense.

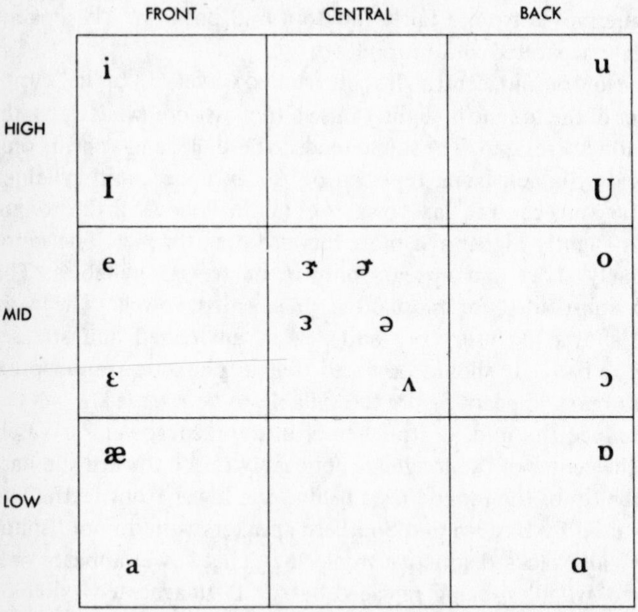

Figure 4. Schematic diagram of the representative positions of the highest part of the tongue in the mouth for the articulation of the vowels.

For the high, back, lax, rounded vowel /ʊ/ (as in "good"), the tongue is less high than for /u/, the lips slightly more separated and less rounded. The lips and tongue are more relaxed. The sound tends to be short.

To produce the mid, back, tense, rounded vowel /o/ (as in

"obese"), the arch of the tongue is lower than for /ʊ/. The lips are rounded and the musculature is tense. In accented syllables the sound becomes the diphthong /oʊ/: all alone /ɔl əˈloʊn/.

For the low-mid, back, tense, rounded vowel /ɔ/ (as in "awe"), the back of the tongue is somewhat raised, the mouth is fairly open, the lips fairly rounded. The musculature is relatively tense.

To produce the near-low, back, lax, rounded vowel /ɒ/, (as in the frequent New England pronunciation of "hot"), the tongue arch is lower than for /ɔ/, the lips are slightly rounded and may be slightly tense. The sound is not in general use in the United States, although it may appear as a phonetic variant when an /ɔ/ happens to be unrounded or an /ɑ/ is rounded. Many Eastern speakers use /ɒ/ in words spelled with "wa" and "o," such as "wash, watch, college, forest, cost."

For the low, back, lax, unrounded vowel /ɑ/ (as in "ah"), the back of the tongue is slightly raised, the lips are wide apart, the tongue and lips are relaxed.

DIPHTHONGS. A diphthong is a continuous sound made by a movement from one vowel to another in the same syllable. The first vowel of a diphthong is more stressed and longer than the second. According to one viewpoint, the mouth becomes less open and the tongue moves to a higher position for the second vowel. These movements are illustrated by the diphthong forms /eɪ/ and /oʊ/ which have already been mentioned: /ɪ/ and /ʊ/ are higher and less open vowels than /e/ and /o/.

To produce the diphthong /aɪ/ (as in "aisle"), the front of the tongue moves from a low, slightly raised position to the high front position. Many speakers start the diphthong with the back of the tongue slightly raised for /ɑ/ and move to the high front position for /ɪ/. Both /aɪ/ and ɑɪ/ are acceptable variants and are similar-sounding to many hearers.

For the diphthong /aʊ/ (as in "how"), the tongue glides from the low front position to the high back position. Many speakers start the diphthong from the low back position of /ɑ/ and move to the high back position of /ʊ/. The lips round as the opening between them becomes smaller. Both /aʊ/ and ɑʊ/ are acceptable articulations.

To form the diphthong /ɔɪ/ (as in "boy"), the arch of the tongue moves from the mid, back position of /ɔ/ to the high, front position of /ɪ/. The lips become unrounded and lose their tension.

Consonants. Consonant sounds are classified according to place of articulation and manner of articulation. In contrast to the vowel sounds, the consonants are produced by an interruption, diversion, or hindrance to the stream of breath pressure. The articulators work in pairs, the tongue being one member of the pair in two thirds of the consonant sounds; for example, for the *k*-sound, the back of the tongue meets the soft palate. Consonants may be voiced or voiceless, as /v/ or /f/. Consonants vary in sonority from the thin whisper of /h/ to the full, vowel-like quality of /l/. Figure 5 indicates the place and manner of articulation of the consonant sounds.

	Bilabial		Labiodental		Linguadental		Alveolar		Palatal		Velar		Glottal	
	vs[1]	vd[2]	vs	vd	vs	vd	vs	vd	vs	vd	vs	vd	vs	vd
Plosives	p	b					t	d			k	g		
Nasals		m						n				ŋ		
Fricatives			f	v	θ	ð	s	z	ʃ	ʒ			h	
Affricates							tʃ	dʒ						
Glides	ʍ (hw)	w						r		j				
Lateral								l						

[1] vs = voiceless   [2] vd = voiced

Figure 5. Chart of consonant sounds.

PLOSIVES. A plosive or stop consonant in its complete form requires the closing off of the nasal passage with the soft palate in addition to the closing of two articulators to cut off the flow of breath; a stop or period of compression during which the breath pressure increases; an opening of the two articulators; and an audible explosion of the breath which then passes from the mouth. A stop-plosive does not always appear in its complete form because of the influence of adjacent sounds. For example, the explosion may be omitted before another stop: in "apt" the *p*-sound is not exploded. The stop or interruption of the breath flow, however, is always present when a stop-plosive is pronounced.

To produce voiceless /p/ (as in "pie"), the lips are definitely closed for a moment, and then suddenly parted, releasing a puff of built up breath pressure. The voiced counterpart /b/ (as in "buy") is made in the same way, except that the vocal folds are made to vibrate. The /p/ has more audible plosion than /b/.

For the voiceless /t/ (as in "tie"), and its voiced counterpart /d/ (as in "die"), the tip of the tongue is pressed against the upper gum ridge, or alveolar ridge, and the sides of the tongue against the inner surfaces of the upper teeth. When the tongue is moved suddenly down, the released puff of air escapes from the mouth.

To produce the voiceless /k/ (as in "key"), and its voiced cognate /g/ (as in "gay"), the back of the tongue is pressed against the velum, and then suddenly lowered, releasing the pressurized breath through the mouth.

NASAL CONSONANTS. The nasal sounds, unlike the stops, are continuants; unlike all other consonants, the velum or soft palate is lowered and the mouth exit blocked to allow the breath stream to escape through the nose.

For /m/ (as in "me"), the lips are closed as for /b/, the vocal folds vibrate, the velum is lowered, and the sound waves pass from the throat into the nose. The position of the tongue is neutral, although it may assume the position of the following vowel.

To produce /n/ (as in "no"), the tongue tip is placed against the alveolar ridge as for /d/, the sides of the tongue contact the upper teeth, blocking the exit of breath through the mouth, the vocal folds vibrate, the velum is lowered, and the sound waves pass through the nose. The lips and teeth are normally separated as for /d/.

For /ŋ/ (as in "wing"), the back of the tongue meets the velum, blocking off the mouth cavity. Unlike for /g/, however, the velum is lowered to allow the sound waves to pass through the nose. The lips and teeth are separated as for /g/.

FRICATIVE CONSONANTS. The fricatives are produced by the breath being forced through a narrowed or restricted passageway with sufficient energy to create audible friction.

For the voiceless /f/ (as in "foe"), the lower lip is placed against the cutting edges of the upper front teeth, and the breath is forced through the obstructed opening between the teeth and lip. The voiced counterpart /v/ (as in "vote") is produced in the same way except that the vocal folds are made to vibrate.

To produce the voiceless /θ/ (as in "thin"), and its voiced counterpart /ð/ (as in "then"), the tip of the tongue rests against the cutting edges of the front teeth, or against the back surfaces of the upper front teeth. The breath is forced between the tip of the tongue and the upper front teeth. These two sounds are the only English consonants for which the tongue tip contacts the upper teeth.

For the voiceless /s/ (as in "so"), the sides of the tongue are held against the inner surfaces of the upper teeth and upper gum ridge, leaving a narrow opening between the gum ridge and the tip of the grooved tongue. The lower teeth are brought and held close to the upper teeth. Some speakers bring the blade of the tongue to the alveolar ridge, the tip being down behind the lower front teeth. Breath pressure is forced through the narrow groove between the tongue and alveolar ridge. The voiced counterpart /z/ (as in "zero") is produced in the same manner as /s/ except that the vocal folds are set into vibration.

To produce the voiceless /ʃ/ (as in "ash"), and its voiced cognate /ʒ/ (as in "azure"), the sides of the tongue are held against the inner surfaces of the upper side teeth. The blade of the tongue is raised toward the hard palate; the tongue tip may be more or less raised. The breath is forced between the restricted horizontal space between the tongue and hard palate. The teeth are close together and the lips may be slightly rounded or slightly protruded.

The voiceless glottal fricative /h/ (as in "he") is produced by forcing the breath through the partially open vocal folds. The folds, however, are not set into vibration. The /h/ resembles a whisper of the vowel that follows it.

AFFRICATES. An affricate is a combination of a plosive followed by a fricative, the sequence being uttered as a unit. For the voiceless /tʃ/ (as in "chest"), and its voiced counterpart /dʒ/ (as in "jest"), the tongue tip goes to the upper gum ridge as for /t/ and /d/, pressure is built up, and the air exploded through the opening created by the tongue immediately assuming the position of /ʃ/ or /ʒ/.

GLIDE CONSONANTS. A glide is the sound produced when the articulators pass from the position of one continuant sound to another, as in the shift from /u/ to /i/ in pronouncing "we." To produce the voiced /w/ (as in "we"), the back of the tongue is raised to the position for /u/. The lips are closely rounded, forming an extremely small mouth opening. As the vocal folds begin to vibrate, the tongue and lips glide swiftly into position for the following vowel. In the word "woo" /wu/, the tongue and lips are already in position for /u/ but are more tightly rounded and tense during the /w/. The voiceless counterpart /ʍ/ (as in "whet") is produced in the same manner except that the vocal folds do not begin to vibrate until the following vowel is reached. For instance, the *w* in the word "watt" is voiced. Since /ʍ/ is fricative, it is sometimes analyzed and symbolized as /hw/, so that "what" is then transcribed as /hwat/. Many persons do not use the voiceless sound, but pronounce both "watt" and "what" as /wɑt/.

For the voiced glide /j/ (as in "yet"), the front of the tongue is raised to the position for /i/ and then glides into place for the next vowel. This glide consonant often appears in combination with the vowels /u/ and /ʊ/, as in "you, hue, beauty" and "your, Europe, pure."

For the voiced glide /r/ (as in "row"), the center of the tongue is raised for /ɝ/; either the tip of the tongue is raised toward the hard palate or the blade is raised with the tip pointing downward. The sides of the tongue touch the inner surfaces of the upper teeth. As soon as the vocal folds begin to vibrate, the tongue moves into position for the following vowel.

LATERAL CONSONANT. English has only one lateral sound /l/ (as in "lie"). To produce it, the tip of the tongue touches the alveolar ridge and the back of the tongue is arched toward the position for /o/ or /u/. The vocal folds vibrate and the sound waves pass over the sides of the tongue and out of the mouth.

Improving Articulation.   Each person's formation of sounds is based on his past auditory and muscular habits. Forming better habits requires much careful listening and oral practice. Listening acutely to others and to one's self provides a basis for proper articulation of individual sounds, syllables, words, and phrases. In the flow of speech some words are identified by a single sound; this sound must be distinctly produced. Some phrases and sentences are interpreted by one or two words; these words must be clearly articulated.

Articulation should be smooth and distinct. Over-precise or labored articulation, or attempting to give full value to each sound, syllable, or word is artificial and interferes with the communication of ideas. Over-slurred, mumbled, or feeble articulation reduces both audibility and intelligibility. Good articulation lies somewhere between extreme care and carelessness. To be heard in public, mere loudness is not enough. The speaker needs adequate breath pressure, sufficient volume of voice, and precise and vigorous articulation of important sounds and words.

Practice should include slow, careful, and exaggeratedly distinct articulation with concentrated listening to the sounds being formed. A developed consciousness of exact, clear sounds guides the speaker when talking to others and makes him aware of errors that he may have made. Practice in rapid articulation is necessary for gaining adequate precision in the smooth flow of speech. The objective of both slow and rapid drill is to make the conversational style of speaking spontaneous and fluent, yet distinct and understandable.

Articulation Exercise

The following list of words and sentences can serve as both a test of articulation and a basis for daily drill. Read the list aloud into a tape recorder, listen carefully to the playback, and check any sounds which need more accurate articulation. Then read the list aloud to a teacher or other person interested in good speech and check his recommendations. Sounds checked by another person may be harder for you to hear and improve. Ask a good speaker to read those sounds on the list as a help to your recognition of clear articulation.

1. /i/ each, feet, tree	Feel free to leave.
2. /ɪ/ itch, fit, ninny	It's a pity he's ill.
3. /e,eɪ/ ache, bail, may	They paid low wages.
4. /ɛ/ egg, bell	Emma said to get ready.
5. /æ/ add, hand	Is the average man happy?
6. /a/* ask, class	She danced along the path.
7. /ʌ/ up, love	My brother is coming for supper.
8. /ə/ alive, talkative, idea	I was aware of the aroma of petunias.
9. /ɜ, ɝ/ urchin, heard, stir	Girls prefer furs.
10. /ɚ/ urbane, Saturday, stranger	The healthier, the better.
11. /u/ ooze, fool, grew	The moon will rise soon.
12. /ʊ/ took, full	Look it up in a good cookbook.
13. /o, oʊ/ oats, grown, flow	Obey the "Go slow" sign.
14. /ɔ/ autumn, walk, straw	He talked to an officer of the law.
15. /ɒ/* doll, god, college	The coffee was hot.
16. /ɑ/ alms, stark, Shah	The park was calm after dark.
17. /aɪ, ɑɪ/ ice, time, try	I like fried rice.
18. /au, ɑu/ owl, town, bough	The crowd sounded loud.

19. /ɔɪ/ oyster, spoil, toy — That oil burner is noisy.
20. /p/ pay, ripe, sap — Most people sleep during the trip.
21. /b/ bond, robe, rib — The robber bribed the bodyguard.
22. /t/ take, item, sit — Try not to be bitter about it.
23. /d/ down, odor, sad — I didn't drive today.
24. /k/ kitchen, acre, sick — She baked the cake quickly.
25. /g/ gone, ugly, log — The big bargain was in rugs.
26. /m/ made, ammonia, sum — The men climbed to the summit.
27. /m̩/ atom, spasm — The prism was in the bottom of the chasm.
28. /n/ night, money, ton — Turn the blinds against the sun.
29. /n̩/ hasten, cotton — The villain listened for eleven knocks.
30. /ŋ/ hanger, tongue — The ringing bells drowned out the singers.
31. /ŋg/ anger, hungry, language — He untangled it with his fingers.
32. /ŋk/ anchor, bunk — A link of her anklet broke.
33. /f/ fine, effort, strife — The film featured the after life.
34. /v/ violin, nervous, serve — The vine leaves were more vivid than ever.
35. /θ/ thick, ether, truth — I'll have to think it through.
36. /ð/ that, either, loathe — My other brother does deep breathing.
37. /s/ sun, docile, less — This will soon pass.
38. /z/ zeal, easy, tease — I was pleased to see zebras in the zoo.
39. /ʃ/ show, fashion, trash — Rash actions are foolish.
40. /ʒ/ leisure, mirage — Good vision is a treasure.
41. /h/ hero, haste — The hotel had no heat.
42. /tʃ/ chin, virtue, inch — What chance is there to get rich?
43. /dʒ/ just, urgent, edge — I was overjoyed at the judgment of the jury.
44. /w/ weather, award — Water will wear away a stone.
45. /ʍ, hw/† whether, awhile — What has white wheels?
46. /j/ yarn, canyon — The youngsters yelled and yodeled.
47. /ju/ unit, disuse, youth — A few were unusual but useless.
48. /r/ rent, daring, for — He ran far to report the wreck.
49. /l/ late, mellow, pill — The willows leaned over the pool.
50. /l̩/ bottle, camel, saddle — Ethel walked a little faster through the tunnel.

---

* Does not usually appear in General American.
† Not used by some speakers.

PRONUNCIATION

Pronunciation is the uttering of correct sounds in the sequences and with the stresses required by the language. These requirements are established by usage, for the people who speak the language are the only authority for any standards of pronunciation. Exactly what constitutes established usage is often difficult to define. The most familiar pronunciation is the one that seems best to most listeners and this familiarity depends on which dialect of the language one speaks.

Standard Dialect.   Because of many differences in vocabulary, pronunciation, and grammar, a language spoken over a broad area may be classified into dialects. In some cases, the dialect of one region becomes the accepted language of the whole area. The dialect spoken by royalty and the nobility, for example, may acquire tremendous prestige. Large numbers of people imitate the clothing, manners, and speech of the ruling classes whom they admire and wish to resemble. The dialect of Paris became the accepted and official language of France, and the dialect of London formed the basis for the accepted language in England. An accepted language is further standardized by being used in writing and adopted by authorities, dictionary makers, and educated people. It is spelled and pronounced in ways similar enough to be understood by all. Its formality is modified and vivified by the actualities of colloquial or conversational speech.

Dialect in the United States.   Earlier researchers classified American English into three major dialects: Eastern, spoken east of the Hudson River; Southern, spoken below the northern borders of Maryland, Virginia, and Kentucky, through all but the northwestern part of Missouri and down through southeastern Oklahoma and eastern Texas; and General American, spoken in the rest of the country. This traditional classification has general value, but ignores the many variations within each dialect area.

Later surveys, beginning in 1931 under the direction of Hans Kurath for the Linguistic Atlas of the United States and Canada, provided data for more accurate classifications. On the basis of pronunciation, Charles K. Thomas divided the United States into ten dialect areas: Eastern New England, New York City, Middle

Atlantic, Southern, Western Pennsylvania, Southern Mountain, Central Midland, North Central, Northwest, and Southwest. In *A Word Geography of the United States* published in 1949, Kurath, on a lexical basis, divided the eastern states from Maine to Florida into the three areas of North, Midland, and South, subdivided respectively into six, seven, and five subareas. These classifications were correlated with pronunciation data in 1961 by Kurath and Raven I. McDavid, Jr., in *The Pronunciation of English in the Atlantic States*. Within any dialect classification many variations of pronunciation exist, some of which appear in several other regions. What a classification actually indicates is that certain forms of speech are heard more often in some regions than in others.

Acceptable Pronunciation.   In the United States there is no single standard of pronunciation. The dialect of one class or region has not gained ascendancy over the others, because the majority of users have not made such a choice. The dialect of one region of the country is as acceptable as that of another.

The speakers of all dialects, however, have accepted a standardization of spelling; that is, the spelling of educated persons is the standard usage. This standard is not based on region or dialect but on literacy. The distinction between educated and uneducated persons extends beyond spelling. Educated, cultured, and professional persons have prestige; therefore, their manner of speaking has more social approval, if not social advantage, than that of poorly educated, less cultivated, and nonprofessional persons. Nevertheless the utterances of less educated and less cultivated users of language are also living acts of speech and thus have linguistic validity. Certain variant pronunciations become so common that significant numbers of educated speakers begin to use them. These new pronunciations gradually become established, even though a large number of educated speakers use and prefer the old pronunciations. For example, the established pronunciation of the word "incognito" has the accent on the second syllable "in KAHG ni toh" /ɪnˈkɑgnɪto/, but *Webster's Seventh New Collegiate Dictionary* also lists the current pronunciation "in kagh NEE to" /ˌɪnkɑgˈnito/.

In view of the equal status of dialects, and since usage is constantly changing, perhaps the best explanation of acceptable pronunciation is to say that it consists of acceptable pronunciations, and that these are the pronunciations used by great numbers of educated and cultured persons.

Dictionaries. Dictionaries collect and report the pronunciations of educated and cultured speakers; therefore it is not surprising that these pronunciations are generally considered to be a mark of education and culture. The concept "educated and cultured" applied to human beings is, however, a subjective judgment and the number of persons so designated cannot be determined. Compiling a dictionary, like preparing a linguistic atlas, is beset with sobering difficulties. All educated users of language cannot be consulted, only a presumably representative number; in the case of regional dialect, only those native to the region. Pronunciations in a given region also change because of the increasingly large number of speakers who move to different parts of the country. By the time any material on pronunciation is gathered, interpreted, and published, it has begun to be somewhat historical rather than current. Nevertheless, linguistic investigations have far-reaching results. The dictionary makers and their staff of scholars strive to record pronunciations actually in use, along with many indications of regions and levels of usage. As a result, every speaker has available a helpful and practical guide if he makes the effort to consult it.

A good dictionary only reports pronunciations but does not dictate or try to preserve them. However, dictionaries have played an important role in making known and establishing acceptable pronunciations. Innumerable persons, doubtful of their own pronunciation or dissatisfied with a local pronunciation, have been guided in their choice of usage by the dictionary. In fact, some people strongly object when a dictionary fulfills its true function and reports new current pronunciations. However, such individuals are not forced to adopt the new usage. They can use their familiar pronunciation, because old and new forms are both in current use. The dictionaries reveal that many words have several pronunciations. When faced with a choice among them, a good plan is to keep the familiar form, for that is probably the one used in the speaker's region. When in doubt about words previously unknown to him, the speaker can listen to educated people around him and adopt their pronunciation. Or, he can consult one or more recent dictionaries for more widely used forms. Where usage is divided, as it is in many words, the speaker chooses the pronunciation he happens to prefer.

The important thing is to understand the basis of accepted pronunciations and to avoid eccentric forms. In this way a person who moves to various parts of the nation will have no difficulty in communicating with others. Individual differences in usage give color and personality to speech, while basic similarities in usage give immediately clear communication.

Types of Mispronunciation. Words are mispronounced for various reasons. The speaker may not know how a word he sees in print should sound. He may know how a word sounds, but think that he is wrong when he sees it in print. For example, he may be familiar with the spoken word "breeches" (trousers) /ˈbrɪtʃɪz/, but when he sees the word in print, the two *e*'s in the spelling cause him to say /ˈbritʃɪz/. Some such spelling pronunciations have later become acceptable pronunciations. The speaker may know how a word should sound but mispronounces it without being aware of the fact. Or he may mispronounce a word because of the influence of another word, as when he says "coil oil" instead of "coal oil." There are five common types of pronunciation errors: omissions, additions, substitutions, inversions, and misplaced accent. An error does not always occur alone but may be combined with another. For example, when the number "seventy-five" is pronounced "semny-five," the /v/ and /ə/ sounds are omitted, /m/ is substituted for /n/, and /n/ is substituted for /t/ so that /sɛvəntɪ/ becomes /sɛmnɪ/.

Omissions. Either consonants or vowels may be omitted; omission of a vowel omits a syllable. In the following examples the word on the right is shown with the sounds omitted.

Consonants		Vowels	
next	nex'	geography	g'ography
help	he'p	regular	reg'lar
fifth	fif'	liable	li'ble
asked	as't	considerable	consid'able
understand	un'erstan'	medieval	med'eval

Additions. Some additions of a vowel or consonant to a word are due to the spelling, since many words, such as "debt," "talk," and "tongue," contain silent letters, or those which do not represent a sound. Other additions are made even though the sounds are not suggested by the spelling, such as "mischievious" for "mischievous."

once /wʌns/	oncet /wʌnst/	drowned	drownded
singer /sɪŋɚ/	singger /sɪŋgɚ/	umbrella	umberella
saw /sɔ/	sawr /sɔr/	somewhere	somewheres
Henry	Henary	athletic	athaletic

Substitutions. Some substitutions are caused by the inability to articulate a required sound, such as /s/, /l/, or /r/. These difficulties require special help. However, most substitutions are habitual mispronunciations which can be corrected by the desire and effort of the individual. The following are a few representative examples.

length /lɛŋθ/	len'th /lɛnθ/	facade /fəˈsɑd/	facayed /fəˈked/
similar	simular	pronunciation	pronounciation
Tuesday	Chewsday	carton	cartoon
them	dem	radish /rædɪʃ/	redish /rɛdɪʃ/

Inversions. Two sounds in a word may be uttered in reverse order rather than in their proper sequence. Inversions often include substitutions.

ask	aks	bronchial /ˈbrɑŋkɪəl/	bronichal /ˈbrɑnɪkəl/
wasp	waps	prefer	perfer
larynx	larnyx /ˈlærnɪks/	modern	modren

Misplaced Accent. Accent or stress is part of a spoken word. A word of one syllable has full stress on that syllable when uttered as a separate phrase or sentence: Whát? Óne, twó, thrée, gó! When a one-syllable word is part of a phrase, it may or may not be stressed, depending on its position in the phrase. A word of more than one syllable receives stress on one or more syllables: under /ˈʌndɚ/, understand /ˌʌndɚˈstænd/, understandability /ˌʌndɚˌstændɪˈbɪlɪtɪ/.

The following words are properly accented on the first syllable. Stress on the second syllable is occasionally heard, but such usage is not widespread enough to be reported in the dictionaries: ádmirable, cómparable, ímpotent, mémorable, órator, préferable, réputable, véhement.

The following words are properly stressed on the second syllable. Primary stress on the first or third syllable has not been sanctioned by general usage: cigár, clandéstine, distríbutive, exémplary, munícipal, políce, remónstrate, supérfluous.

WORDS USED AS NOUNS OR VERBS. Many verbs originally borrowed from French or Latin are accented on the second syllable, but the accent of related nouns has shifted to the first syllable, often with a specialized meaning. Some words used as adjectives or nouns have the same functional shift of stress.

Noun or Adjective	Verb or Adjective
áddict	addíct
cónduct	condúct
désert	desért
fréquent (adj.)	frequént
ínsult	insúlt
mínute	minúte (adj.)

COMPOUND WORDS. Certain words are used together so often that in time they come to be regarded as one word. Compounding might be considered a way to create new words out of old ones. Compound words have a distinguishing feature of stress.

• *Compound Nouns.* A compound noun has primary stress on the first word element and secondary stress on the second: 'team‚work, 'trade‚mark, 'whirl‚wind. This stress pattern differentiates a compound noun from an adjective and noun. For example, a "blue 'jacket" is any coat of that color, while a " 'blue‚jacket" is an enlisted man in the navy.

• *Compound Verbs.* Compound verbs have primary stress on the second word element. The stress differentiates them from the same forms used as nouns. For example, "over'look" is a verb, while " ‚over‚look" is a noun.

• *Other Compounds.* Among other compound words given primary stress on the second element are adverbs, prepositions, and reflexive pronouns: beyond, outside, within, indoors, underneath, myself, themselves. In some locations, the stress may shift to the first syllable for special contrast: I said *in*side, not *out*side.

Stressed and Unstressed Forms. In connected speech some words and syllables receive sentence stress and some are unstressed. The determining factor is the speaker's meaning. From the standpoint of meaning, words can be divided into two classes: content words, or those that convey considerable meaning as independent units, and function words, or those whose meaning is dependent on their grammatical function in the sentence.

Stressed Words.   The words of most importance to the meaning
are stressed by the speaker. In general, these are the content words
and are given primary or secondary sentence stress. In words of
more than one syllable, sentence stress normally coincides with word
stress. Content words include nouns, verbs (except when used as
auxiliaries), adjectives, adverbs, demonstratives (this, that, these,
those), and interrogatives. The following are representative examples.

Nouns:	The pláy was a fáilure.
Verbs:	He sáid he was góing to móve.

Verbs that include an adverb are usually stressed on the adverb:

He sáid he was góing to move óut.

Adjectives:	Hándsome mén like hómely wómen.
Adverbs:	Bríng it hére.
Demonstratives:	Thése are the bóoks I was lóoking for.
Interrogatives:	Whén can you gó?

The vowels and diphthongs of stressed syllables in connected
speech have their full value and retain their identity.

Unstressed Words.   Words of less importance to the meaning
are not stressed by the speaker. They are often function words, which
include the following classes: articles (a, an, the), prepositions, personal pronouns, relative pronouns, possessive adjectives, conjunc-
tions (the common, short ones), and auxiliary verbs (be, have, do,
will, shall, would, should, can, could, may, might, must).

Articles:	An ápple a dáy kéeps the dóctor awáy.
Prepositions:	I pút it on the táble.

Prepositions often receive stress before a pronoun:

Lét me dó it fór you.

Personal Pronouns:	I don't knów him.

Personal pronouns are sometimes stressed for emphasis:

Thís is for yóu.

Relative Pronouns:	The mán who spóke knéw what he méant.
Possessive Adjectives:	My cóat is in your cár.
Conjunctions:	I'll be thére, but I must léave éarly.
Auxiliary Verbs:	Hálf-héarted áims are forgótten.

Auxiliary verbs used as main verbs are stressed:

I'll dó áll I cán.

Auxiliary verbs are stressed when used at the ends of sentences as a question formula:

You sáid so, dídn't you?

These general principles of sentence stress are far from exhaustive. Special stress may be given to any syllable of a sentence to suit the meaning in a given situation. Stress may also be shifted for the sake of spoken rhythm. "I went to the ballét" becomes "I went to the Bállet Théater." The two adjacent stresses of "Ballét Théater" are avoided for the more flowing and easier to utter "Bállet Théater."

THE VOWELS IN UNSTRESSED SYLLABLES.. Unstressed vowels tend to lose their individual character. In some locutions, however, they may be shortened without losing their identity: "I don't know who brought it." /aɪ dont 'noʊ hu 'brɔt ɪt/.

The vowel /ɝ/ is always reduced to /ɚ/: "The senator seemed in a stupor." /ðə sɛnətɚ simd ɪn ə'stupɚ/.

In some words and utterances the vowel /e/ may or may not be replaced by /ə/: "The elite ignored the chaotic conditions." /ðɪ ə'lit ɪg'nɔrd ðə ke'atɪk kən'dɪʃənz/.

The vowel /o/ may or may not be replaced by /ə/: "He's obese, but he won't obey his doctor's orders." /hiz o'bis bət hɪ wont ə'beɪ hɪz 'dɑktɚz 'ɔrdɚz/.

In most utterances the unstressed vowels are obscured or replaced by /ə/ or /ɪ/: "I took the express to the city." /aɪ 'tʊk ðɪ ɪk'sprɛs tə ðə'sɪtɪ/. "The villagers believe in democratic regulations." /ðə 'vɪlɪdʒɚz bə'liv ɪn ˌdɛmə'krætɪk ˌrɛgjə'leʃənz/.

Unstressed vowels in the most common expressions are omitted.

do not	don't /u/ becomes /o/
did not	didn't
Ann is going	Ann's going
John is not going	John isn't going

In the case of words like *will, shall, would,* and *have,* the initial consonants are often omitted along with the vowels.

I will	I would like	I have seen
I'll	I'd like	I've seen

VOWELS IN WORDS OF ONE SYLLABLE. The most frequently used words in speaking are *the, a, and, of, to, in, it, that, is,* and *I*. These words are rarely stressed in speaking; therefore the unstressed forms of the words, in which the vowels are reduced to /ə/ or /ɪ/, should be used. Often the vowel is omitted along with a consonant.

Word	Stressed Form	Unstressed Form	Example
a	/e/	/ə/	in a word /ɪn ə wɚd/
an	/æn/	/ən/	peel an apple /pil ən ˈæpl̩/
and	/ænd/	/ənd, ən/	bread and butter /ˈbrɛd ən ˈbʌtɚ/
are	/ɑr/	/ər/	books are good /ˈbʊks ər ˈgʊd/
can	/kæn/	/kən/	I can tell /aɪ kən ˈtɛl/
had	/hæd/	həd, əd, d/	boys had gone /ˈbɔɪz həd ˈgɔn/ they had gone /ðe əd ˈgɔn/ /ðed ˈgɔn/
have	/hæv/	/həv, əv, v/	What have you /ˈʍɑt həv ju/ /ˈʍɑt əv ju/ We have been /wiv ˈbɪn/
has	/hæz/	/həz, əz/	time has flown /ˈtaɪm həz ˈfloʊn/ /ˈtaɪm əz ˈfloʊn/
of	/ɑv/	/əv/	time of night /ˈtaɪm əv ˈnaɪt/
or	/ɔr	/ər/	day or night /ˈdeɪ ər ˈnaɪt/
that	/ðæt/	/ðət/	man that I saw /ˈmæn ðət aɪˈsɔ/
the	/ði/	/ðə/ before a consonant	at the store /æt ðə ˈstɔr/
		/ðɪ/ before a vowel	on the edge /ɑn ðɪ ˈɛdʒ/
to	/tu/	/tu, tə/	so to speak /so tə ˈspik/
was	/wɑz/	/wəz/	She was pretty /ʃi wəz ˈprɪtɪ/

Some speakers favor the stressed form of these words under the unwarranted belief that they are more correct or that they lend emphasis and dignity to a public speech. The stressed forms should be used only when the words are given sentence stress. For example, "I said *a* girl, not *the* girl." "It certainly wás." "Let's see how many we háve." "We *were* late." "Ten *to* five, not ten *after*."

CONTINUED SELF-IMPROVEMENT

A speaker who wishes to improve his articulation and pronunciation needs to persist in a planned program. He should develop a keen interest in words, including both their sounds, stresses, and connotations. Interest in words includes attention to the words used by others in conversation and public speaking. Any word that the speaker hears pronounced in a different or unfamiliar way should be recorded in a small notebook carried for the purpose. Words encountered for the first time in reading should also be jotted down. The list of words can then be looked up at a convenient time in a recent dictionary. The pronunciation of each word should be entered in the notebook. The speaker should pronounce each word aloud several times, and also use it in improvised sentences. He should then try to use as many of the words as possible in conversation. Since there is no single pronunciation authority, the speaker must develop his own standards of pronunciation by continued observation and study.

11.
BODY COMMUNICATION

Listeners are impressed not only by what they hear but also by what they see. A speaker's appearance, posture, and actions can help or hinder his effectiveness. A speaker's body communication may be unconscious and therefore difficult for him to realize. Most physical actions, however, are conscious and can be controlled and made more effective.

APPEARANCE

Most persons form opinions of others by their appearance. The conclusions may be right or wrong, fair or unfair; nevertheless, each one of us is constantly being observed and judged by others. To the public speaker, the eyes of his listeners are a challenge and an opportunity.

The speaker's opinion of himself is also heightened when he knows he is neat and well groomed. Neatness demands proper attention to personal appearance and avoidance of any suggestion of sloppiness or untidiness. For instance, a man's face should be clean-shaven and a woman's makeup should be unobtrusive. Special attention should be given to the hair. A man's hair should be recently cut and well combed, while a woman should avoid extreme hairstyles.

Clothing for both male and female speakers should be appropriate for the occasion. In general, conservative clothes are best, dark colors being preferred for evening. A business suit, a white shirt, and a tie of subdued color are correct for men on most occasions. For women, clothing of simple lines and quiet colors is always suitable. Speakers should avoid sharp contrasts, clashing colors, extreme cuts or styles, excessive jewelry—anything that detracts from the message being sent. Everything worn should fit comfortably. Clothes and accessories that restrict freedom of movement, such as squeaking or high-heeled shoes, should be avoided.

POSTURE

A speaker's bearing creates a definite impression on his listeners. The way he stands, his manner of holding himself erect, the carriage of the head, shoulders, chest, and arms are part of his visual communication. A good carriage of the body gives the speaker more confidence. It also helps the voice and the delivery of the speech, since it gives a solid foundation for tones.

Elements of Good Posture.   The body is held easily erect, but not stiffly upright. The position is not tense or strained, as in rigid military attention, nor over-relaxed, hollow-chested, and slouching. Good posture consists of a proper balance between tension and relaxation. There is, of course, no single best posture. But the beginning speaker needs to know something about the relationship to posture of his feet, back, chest and shoulders, arms and hands, and head. He should also consider his posture when seated on the platform.

The Feet.   The position of the feet contributes to an appearance of ease or awkwardness. Standing with the heels together usually seems too careful or stiff; standing with feet wide apart often gives the impression of carelessness, vulgarity, or defiance.

The feet provide a comfortable foundation when they are a few inches apart. Many speakers stand with the feet on a line; others advance one foot a little. The weight, rather than being held over the heels, is usually carried over the broad part of the foot, since this practice makes it easy to step in any direction. The weight is freely adjusted during a speech and many different positions of the feet are assumed. For example, the weight might be forward on an emphatic or an intimate point, and backward on an ironic or humorous point.

Back, Chest, and Shoulders.   The torso of the body should be poised and erect for the best appearance. The back is relatively straight rather than slumped or twisted to one side. The rib cage is moderately lifted, avoiding the effect of a "collapsed chest." The shoulders are comparatively relaxed without being hunched up or thrown back; gestures can then be made with ease.

Arms and Hands.   In a natural standing position the arms and hands hang relaxed at the sides. Some individuals, because of nervousness, lose this easy position before an audience. Holding the hands in front of the body or putting them behind the back gives some speakers a feeling of security; however, these positions are not as becoming as the relaxed one. Many listeners do not object to a hand in the pocket or on the lectern. The beginning speaker must make himself as comfortable as possible on the platform; nevertheless, he should learn as quickly as he can to do nothing with his hands and arms except when he wishes to make expressive gestures. At the same time, he should not plan gestures ahead of time or attempt to imitate someone's admired gesture. It is apt to seem artificial.

Head.   The head is held erect. If the head is bowed or tilted to one side, the general effect is timid, over-humble, or insecure. If the chin is held too high, the speaker may seem haughty, dictatorial, or condescending. The head is in a natural and becoming position when the speaker looks directly at the faces of listeners seated before him.

In general, the speaker's posture should not seem apologetic or aggressive, but alert, poised, and balanced for action. To hold the same posture throughout the speech would be inflexible and unnatural. The weight, alignment, and tension of the body shifts constantly with the meaning of what is being said.

Sitting on the Platform.   On some occasions speakers sit on the platform in full view of the audience before and after giving their speeches. Each speaker is part of a unified program and his visual expression adds to the total picture. He contributes to the proper effect by listening to other speakers and refraining from actions that attract attention to himself. The best appearance results when the speaker sits erect in his chair with his feet resting on the floor. Lounging on the end of the spine or sprawling with legs outstretched may strike listeners as careless, disrespectful, or vulgar. The courtesy of the situation requires poise, alertness, and avoidance of a bored or let-down attitude. When he changes position, the speaker does so unobtrusively. He is careful not to keep swinging his foot if he sits with one leg crossed over the other.

ACTION

Gesture and movement are a natural part of everyday speech. Few human beings stand immobile while speaking with others. When a person is completely involved in what he is saying, he makes visible pictures of his thoughts, feelings, and convictions. The same person, when talking to an assembled group, may feel himself in a strange situation and become ill at ease, artificially restrained, and awkward. For that reason, many beginning public speakers need to understand the value and nature of physical action and to cultivate it for a better presentation of the speech. Three important aspects of action are facial expression, bodily motion, and gesture.

Facial Expression.   An immobile face is inexpressive, as shown by the popular terms "poker face" and "deadpan." The face should reflect the speaker's meaning. The eyes are highly important in revealing meaning and feeling. An alert, interested, and friendly face seems to have a more immediate appeal to listeners than an indifferent, morose, or hostile one. A point made with a smile is often favorably received; the same idea presented with a frown may be immediately rejected.

Bodily Motion.   A moving object attracts the eye more readily than a stationary one; thus, the speaker's movements in space give variety to the speech and help hold attention. Appropriate motions make transitions from idea to idea stand out, enabling listeners to follow the thought structure more easily.

A speaker's movements tend to reduce his muscular tensions, since the release of stored up energy enables him to forget himself and enter more completely into the expression of ideas. The speaker's motions help reveal his feelings toward his subject, his listeners, and himself, and add to the total impression of vitality, sincerity, and sharing of ideas. The speaker's physical reactions tend to arouse similar responses in his listeners. This empathy helps establish a bond of understanding. When moving during the speech, or using the speaker's stand, the body should act as a whole and give a natural impression of coordination.

Moving During the Speech.   A speaker's motions depend on the place, the occasion, and the listeners. A small platform limits the speaker's freedom to move about. A speech of praise delivered on a formal occasion requires little movement, while a pep talk to a social organization demands dynamic action. An audience of intellectual or professional men and women usually concentrates on the content of the speech; high school listeners might need lively actions to hold their interest.

Movement should be for a definite reason, such as picking up and displaying a visual aid, or going to the chalkboard to write or sketch. Many speakers move closer to their listeners to make a point, or move back before making a highly dramatic point.

A speaker's action should be energetic, alive, and complete. Timid, vague, or wooden movements will not reinforce the meaning. A nervous shift of position or obviously moving because the speaker thinks he should is less convincing than no action. A good speaker talks directly to his hearers most of the time. His back is shown only for short intervals. For instance, when using the chalkboard, he keeps turning to his audience to explain his illustration. Constant and unnecessary motion should be avoided. Pacing back and forth soon becomes distractive; listeners end up concentrating on the speaker's movements instead of on the meaning of what he is saying.

Using the Speaker's Stand. The speaker's stand is to hold the speaker's notes, not for him to lean on, and definitely not for him to hide behind. Putting the hands on the stand from time to time is a good variation to one's speaking manner, but keeping them there in a single position is monotonous to the audience. A speaker's stand may give him confidence, but the speaker should not let it restrict him to one spot. When he reads from a manuscript, or uses a microphone, naturally he must stay behind the stand, but at other times he should move around it and use it to help his speechmaking.

GESTURES

A gesture is a motion of any part of the body made to convey or reinforce meaning. Often the term gesture refers only to movement of the hands and arms. The purpose of all gesture is to give immediacy and conviction to the oral message. The main kinds of gesture are those of the head, torso, and hands and arms.

Head Gestures.   An earnest speaker does not hold his head rigidly in one position throughout the speech. The head moves almost constantly, turning as the speaker looks at different parts of the audience. The head may be tilted back or inclined forward, depending on the idea and emotion being expressed. At all times the speaker gives the impression of looking directly and communicatively at his audience.

Torso Gestures. Although the trunk may be inclined forward or the back purposefully straightened, expressive movements of the torso largely involve the shoulders and rib cage. The shoulders are at times slightly lifted, lowered, moved forward or backward. During great surprise, for example, the shoulders tend ro rise. The chest or rib cage may be raised, lowered, expanded, or contracted. The expanded chest can suggest determination, pleasure, or courage; a contracted chest often conveys fear, unhappiness, or endurance. Torso gestures usually arise automatically from the speaker's involvement in his subject. However, some individuals, because of a stoop-shouldered posture, habitual shallow breathing, or physical apathy, need to train the body to respond imaginatively to the vitality of ideas.

Hand-and-Arm Gestures. The most frequently used type of gesture is one in which the hand and arm move as a unit. Such gestures are frequently classified into emphatic, locative, descriptive, and suggestive.

Emphatic. Emphatic gestures are the most often used type. They call special attention to the meaning of a word, phrase, or sentence. Most gestures of emphasis are downward strokes, although the stroke is sometimes upward. The hand may be open, clenched, or the index finger may be pointed. Emphatic gestures should not be too strong. Pounding the lectern or desk shocks or annoys some groups of listeners. Too many emphatic gestures are monotonous and ineffective.

Locative. A locative gesture points out the position of something in space, such as objects, directions, or areas; a speaker might point out a geographical region on a wall map. In giving a speech the subjects of discussion may not be physically present. The speaker locates them imaginatively in front of himself or to each side. In doing so, he ignores himself and stays entirely out of the picture: the audience must visualize only what he is explaining. Once the locations are indicated, they should be kept in the same place. If the federal government is located in the left of the audience and local government in the right, these relative positions should be retained throughout the discussion. Moving them about will destroy the listeners' ability to visualize the illustration.

Descriptive.   Descriptive gestures are pictorial. They attempt to picture an object so the listeners can visualize it. The actual size and shape of a thing can usually be indicated. If the object is large, a gesture can suggest its size and outline. Gestures can indicate height, breadth, and thickness of an object. Manner of movement, such as fast, slow, straight, curved, or crooked can be shown. The type of action can be revealed, such as ways of holding a golf club or the on-guard stance in fencing.

Suggestive.   A suggestive gesture expresses the speaker's attitude or reaction to an object, idea, or situation. These gestures grow from the personality and imagination of the speaker and stimulate the audience to share the emotion reactions that are part of the meaning. The speaker can show distaste for an idea by a brushing aside motion, or express approval of a candidate by raising one or both arms. Through suggestive gestures he can accept, denounce, request, protest, enjoy, etc.

Requirements of Good Gestures.   A summary of the principles of good gesture may be useful to the beginning speaker who wishes to improve his visual expressiveness. (1) A gesture must be integrated with the meaning, part of the whole bodily reaction to the thought. In other words, the speaker reacts as a unit. (2) An adequate gesture expresses a definite meaning that can be grasped by the listeners. It is purposive, and opposed to random motions with notes, pencils, or charts, taking off glasses, touching or rubbing the face, etc. (3) Gestures should be varied for holding interest. The same gesture repeated over and over is dull and distracting. (4) A gesture should be coordinated. The motion should be smooth, easy, and complete. Arrested and spasmodic movements should generally be avoided. (5) Gestures should be adapted to the size and nature of the audience. For example, gestures in a large hall become wider in scope and more vigorous. Young listeners are attracted by gestures that would seem too frequent, uninhibited, or violent to an older and more conservative group of adults.

Speakers who "freeze" in front of an audience need to practice movement and gesture until the barriers to physical expression are overcome. In practicing, it is wise to overdo the motions until the individual gets the feeling of "letting himself go." However, practice should be done only at home, never before an audience. When giving a speech, the speaker's movement and gesture should come spontaneously from the expression of his ideas.

12.
AUDIOVISUAL AIDS

Audiovisual education methods and most special training programs, such as those of the armed services, recognize the fact that about one-third more is learned in a given time from instruction with audiovisual aids than from lectures alone. Specific visual and auditory materials are communicative devices external to the speaker's person. Visual aids appeal to the sense of sight; audiovisual aids are addressed to both hearing and seeing; and auditory aids present messages to the ears alone.

FUNCTIONS OF AUDIOVISUAL AIDS

Audiovisual aids are designed for various purposes. Some of them are not actual supplementary speech materials but a complete form of communication in themselves. For example, a film usually includes everything necessary to accomplish the instructional purpose of its producer. Other audiovisual aids, such as experimental apparatus or machines for demonstration, are suited to the classroom rather than to the public speaking platform. Many audiovisual aids are valuable speech materials and help the public speaker accomplish his purpose. Like verbal forms of support, they attract and hold attention, make meanings clear, emphasize ideas, and impress the memory.

Attract and Hold Attention. A visual aid offers the audience a new and different stimulus. Its appeal is stronger if it is colorful, striking in design, and large enough to be clearly seen. The visual support makes the speaker's words suddenly more real and interesting. The chart, diagram, or model, and the speaker's movements in showing and explaining it, arouse the listener's desire to know still more about the subject. Audience interest and curiosity can be sustained by a carefully planned series of drawings or diagrams, each one of which is shown at the appropriate point in the speech.

Make Meaning Clear.   An illustration can give an exact conception of something that would otherwise be obscure. Some objects or items of knowledge are difficult to describe adequately in words. For example, the techniques of fencing or judo remain vague without a demonstration. A discussion of a folk dance or a penguin's care of its eggs is made clearer by the use of film. Many complicated subjects, such as transplanting machines, annuities, or railroad mergers, need diagrams, graphs, or charts for adequate audience understanding. The explanation of extremely large or small objects, such as an Elizabethan theater or snow crystals, is made clear by pictures, models, or drawings.

Emphasize Ideas.   An idea is reinforced by presenting it again in a striking form. The appeal to the sense of sight also offers the audience a new view of the subject and allows the speaker to dwell upon and amplify it with new explanations. The variety of sense stimuli adds to the vividness of the subject and emphasizes its importance.

Prove a Point.   A speaker's ideas often remain mere statements until supported by a tangible form of evidence. The audience hesitates to believe until it sees items of proof. Photographs of injured persons and damaged automobiles, together with a chart of yearly accidents, make the arguments for new safety devices and lower speed limits convincing. The more impressive the aid is, the more receptive the audience will be to the speaker's statements.

Impress the Memory.   Pictorial material, since it is interesting in itself, is apt to be remembered; when closely tied to an idea, the idea also is usually remembered.

If the main points of a speech are illustrated as they are presented, they become more firmly established in the minds of listeners. The supplementary material for each point becomes part of the listener's grasp of that point. The visual impressions strengthen the understanding of the speech as a whole and help the audience to remember the speaker's message.

SELECTING AUDIOVISUAL AIDS

Good audiovisual aids do not in themselves produce a good speech; the determining factor is the way the speaker uses them. Like all other speech materials, they must be selected, prepared, and used with skill if they are to be forms of support rather than forms of distraction.

Method of Display. One factor in choosing aids is the way they are to be displayed to the audience. Visual material can be presented in front of the entire audience or it can be placed in the hands of each listener. Material written on a chalkboard or easel-board, large diagrams, models, projected pictures, or demonstrations are displayed in the front of the room. The speaker can speak directly to his listeners, point out the features of the display which emphasize his ideas, and, except for slide or film projections in a darkened room, observe the reactions of his audience. Small objects, pictures, diagrams, maps, detailed drawings, outlines, summaries, and pamphlets can be placed in the hands of the listeners. However, the speaker must plan such distributions so that they will not interfere with the forward movement of the speech.

Available Equipment. The choice is limited by the equipment available or that can be made available in the room. For example, material to be drawn on a chalkboard by the speaker requires a board of adequate size, chalk, and an eraser. An easel or board must be provided to display posters, charts, or maps; if these aids are to be attached to a display board or to the wall, adhesive tape or push pins are necessary. Apparatus is required for an experiment, and films require a projector, screen, and darkened room. No visual materials can be chosen until definite arrangements for equipment are made.

Appropriate to the Audience. The type of audience and the nature of the occasion condition the choice of visual aids. A visual support necessary for a young audience would be unsuited to listeners more familiar with the subject. Some charts, graphs, and diagrams are too technical for anyone but specialists to grasp. Detailed and complicated tables and charts that require considerable time to digest are not suitable for speeches to any audience. Listeners on some special occasions do not expect speakers to use visual aids. Visual supports are rarely used in graduation addresses, speeches by heads of state, eulogies, sermons, or political orations.

Appropriate to the Speaker.   Visual aids require skill for their effective presentation. To use a chalkboard the speaker must be able to write legibly and to draw well enough to produce clear and well-proportioned diagrams and sketches. Projected pictures require special skill in handling slides and films. The speaker must actually know how to use demonstration equipment, such as a foil, guitar, cutaway model, or machine; otherwise, he should not choose them.

Appropriate to the Time Limit.   The speaker should carefully check the time required to display and explain support materials to make sure that the main ideas of the speech will not be neglected; any that needs too much explanation should not be used. Many aids are not suited to short talks. For example, the demonstration part of a memory method with a volunteer from the audience would require several minutes; the explanatory part of the speech would require additional time. A visual aid should therefore be planned for suitable simplicity, clarity, and brevity.

Appropriate to the Speech.   Visual aids should be chosen not for their own interest but for the support they provide for the speech. Each illustration must be rigorously tested for its value to the speaker's ideas. Even an attractive and attention-getting aid should be omitted if it does not strongly reinforce the speaker's specific purpose. A dramatized skit, for instance, might be so absorbing that listeners would forget the point of the speech.

Many visual materials must be simplified or otherwise changed in order to clarify, emphasize, or prove the speaker's ideas. Each visual aid should also be introduced in its proper place and be so fitted into the speech that the unity and coherence of thought are not disturbed. Serious analysis, thought, and judgment are necessary for selecting and incorporating visual aids into the speaker's message.

PREPARING VISUAL AIDS

Many visual aids can be purchased, many can be borrowed, and many can be made at home. Each one should be selected or prepared in a size readily visible to all members of the audience.

Graphic material must be executed in bold, heavy lines and be well spaced on its background. Colors should be used whenever contrasts are to be shown; bright red, blue, and green are most effective. Graphic material should also be simple or schematic enough to be immediately grasped. Only salient features should be diagrammed or sketched, because details reduce the clarity of design and purpose. If a given detail is important, another large aid should be prepared to reveal it.

Each aid should illustrate a single point. The inclusion of more than one factor is confusing. Instead, a progressive series of illustrations should be made to support a sequence of points. An exception is a large cutaway model whose layers or parts can be removed as needed. Another exception is a silent film which can be accompanied by the speaker's comments. When a chalkboard or easelboard is used, the speaker should practice all printing and drawing in advance and check his results from the back of the room. A demonstration should be made with sizable objects. Items so small that they are concealed by the hands are annoying rather than informative. Enlarged models or diagrams should be prepared for that particular phase of the demonstration.

Each item should be easy to handle or operate. Giant maps are difficult and noisy to unfold; large objects may be too heavy to hold up; mechanical devices may refuse to work. It is therefore important to purchase or prepare visual materials well in advance so that their suitability and reliability can be checked and substitute aids prepared if necessary.

USING AUDIOVISUAL AIDS

Visual aids are either two-dimensional or three-dimensional. Two-dimensionals include pictorial types like pictures, photographs, and drawings, and schematic types like diagrams, graphs, and maps. Three-dimensionals include objects, models, and demonstrations by speakers. Some of the more important and interesting aids will be briefly discussed.

The Chalkboard. A chalkboard is one of the most common and convenient aids. The speaker can write unfamiliar, difficult names of persons, places, and things, terms, or important points on the board, or he can draw a simple sketch or diagram to explain an idea. The chalkboard also enables him to indicate successive steps in the progress of thought. The following suggestions will help the speaker use the chalkboard more effectively.

1. The board should be clean at the beginning of the speech.
2. The speaker should stand at one side of his work so that the audience can see the writing or drawing as it is done. For right-handed speakers the easiest position is to stand to the left side of the board. Since the speaker's back is to the audience, a diagram should be quickly drawn, and the speaker should frequently turn his head to talk to his audience. Some right-handed speakers stand to the right of their work facing three-quarters to the audience. This method maintains better eye contact with the audience but requires considerable practice for good printing and drawing.
3. Drawing and speaking should be alternated so that the audience feels a sense of constant communication.
4. Words and sketches must be drawn large enough to be easily seen from the back row of the audience.
5. The speaker should not apologize for his drawings, because the audience does not expect him to be an accomplished artist. However, he should practice everything he will put on the board in order to make it an accurate representation.
6. Schematic drawings that suggest main features are better than accurate renditions.
7. Sketches, diagrams, and words should be put in proper order from left to right.
8. All labels and terms should be kept short and written or printed legibly.
9. The board should not be crowded with material. Spacing is a form of emphasis.
10. To explain the material, the speaker turns and faces the audience, being careful to stand to one side. If he stands with the board on his right, he points to the material with his right hand with a mere glance at the board. The speaker looks and talks directly to his audience.

Flannel Board. A flannel board comes in many sizes and is covered with cotton flannel, felt, or other fuzzy material. Each picture or label to be shown has a rough type of material glued to its back. An aid will stick to the board when pressed against it, but can easily be moved or taken off. Since the visual material is prepared in advance, the speaker can maintain eye contact with his audience during his presentation. The flannel board is thus more effective than a chalkboard for the explanation of processes or subjects with several parts. Each visual illustration is quickly pressed into its proper place as each new step or point of the subject is reached.

Magnetic Board.   A magnetic board is a framed sheet of light-weight steel with a porcelain surface. Small magnets are glued on the back of each visual item to make it adhere to the metal board. The items can be displayed, moved, or removed at will. The magnetic board offers the same advantages as the flannel board and is used for the same purposes. The magnetic board can also be used as a chalkboard: the speaker can write or draw with chalk upon the porce-lainized surface and remove his work with a piece of cloth.

Pictorial Aids.   A wide range of objects can be illustrated more or less realistically by paintings, drawings, photographs, and car-toons. These may be originals or reproductions, in color or black and white. All pictures must be of adequate size. Displaying postcards and illustrations in books is distracting because the audience cannot see them. Full-page pictures in larger sized magazines may be visible, but many drawings, photographs, and cartoons cannot be used unless enlargements are made. The speaker with moderate sketching ability can prepare his own drawings and cartoons of proper size. A strip of cartoons of "stick people" often communicates an idea in an enter-taining and effective way.

Schematic Aids.   Some visual aids are more structural and math-ematical than realistic to the eye. These include charts, maps, and graphs.

Charts.   The word chart is sometimes used to designate large sheets of white paper or cardboard on which the speaker (using a wide-tipped felt marking pen) prints, writes, or draws during the speech. A chart in this sense is a substitute for a chalkboard. The drawing paper or lightweight cardboard must be fastened to the top of a sturdy easel or other surface. The use of charts avoids the necessity of erasing illustrations, for the speaker either removes the individual chart when he is done with it, or folds it back over the easel out of sight, hence the commonly used term "flip chart." The detached charts can also be taped to the wall for review, a desirable proceeding in certain discussions and conferences. Charts can be prepared in advance and displayed at the appropriate points in the speech. Prepared charts or diagrams are of various kinds and visualize time and space relationships, such as position, structure, and function.

Strip Chart. The strip chart contains a list of items or parts, each section being covered by a strip of opaque paper fastened by adhesive tape. When the speaker is ready to discuss an item, he pulls off the strip of paper covering the pertinent material.

Flow Chart. A flow chart presents a series of items in the order in which they are discussed. This type of chart is valuable in the explanation of processes. The audience can see each step in the process as well as the process as a whole.

Organization Chart. The divisions or departments of a social or business organization and their functions can be shown by labeled boxes or squares. At the top of the chart appears the chief governing body or official; grouped below and connected by lines of authority are secondary officers, divisions, and subdivisions. A similar chart is used to show hereditary lines of descent, and to indicate divisions and subdivisions of a major classification, such as that of plants into phyla, classes, orders, families, etc.

Tabular Chart. Statistical information is often presented in the form of lists or tables, such as the average weights of men and women according to height and age, or the price, earnings, dividends, and book values of a share of stock over a given period of years.

Cutaway Chart. To show the essential features of the inside of an object a cutaway chart can be used. A sketch is made of the object with part or all of one side removed. The positions of the interior parts are exposed to view and labeled to show their functional relationships. In the case of a complicated mechanism the sketch depicts only basic parts and functions so that the structure and operation of the machine as a whole can be understood.

Maps. An ordinary atlas-type map contains too much confusing detail to be used in a public speech. Most maps are prepared for special purposes; for example, road maps, railroad maps, and maps of air routes are designed for different methods of travel. A speaker also needs a map suited to his specific purpose. Such a simplified map enables the audience to see the particular feature being discussed. Many topics, such as those dealing with population shifts, natural resources, unemployment, and agricultural production, can be made clearer by the use of maps.

Most speakers use maps prepared in advance; they can then talk directly to the audience, indicating an area on the map with a pointer when necessary. Other speakers use large, blank, outline maps, drawing in needed features with colored crayons during the speech. For some political, economic, and military topics, a globe of the earth is effective, provided that it is large enough for the outlines of the continents and major islands to be clearly seen.

Graphs. Visual devices for presenting numbers or quantities in relation to time are called graphs. Since graphs present statistics in a simple, schematic manner, they are easier to understand than numerical tabulations.

Figure 6. Line graph.

Line Graph. A line graph shows by a rising and falling line the changes or fluctuations of an item, such as the inventory of a given product, over a designated period of years. The line may indicate increase and decrease either by numbers or percentages. The speaker should explain the graph and its relationship to the point being discussed.

Profile Graph. A profile graph is a line graph with shading or coloring beneath the line. The outline is thus easier to see at a distance. Like the line graph, the profile graph can be used for a visual comparison between two sets of related facts.

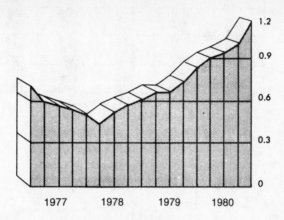

Figure 7. Profile graph.

Bar Graph. A bar graph shows changes or contrasts in a sequence
of facts by means of a series of bars or columns arranged either
vertically or horizontally. The graph can be easily understood when
the speaker explains the unit of measurement and the periods of
time.

Pie Graph. A pie graph or circular diagram shows relative sizes of
parts of an item by the sizes of the "piece of pie" wedges into
which the circle is divided. Simple statistics, such as the amounts
of city tax income from various sources, are easy to grasp when
shown in a pie graph.

Picture Graph. A picture graph or pictograph reveals the relationship
between sets of statistical facts by different-sized pictures of a pertinent object. The sketches are simplified or stylized pictures of a
human being, an animal, a mechanical object, or some other item,
about which statistics have been gathered at specified times. The
audience quickly sees the approximate relationship between the
sets of numerical data.

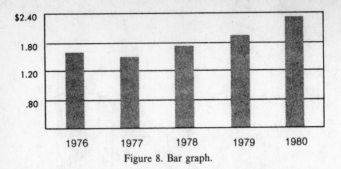

Figure 8. Bar graph.

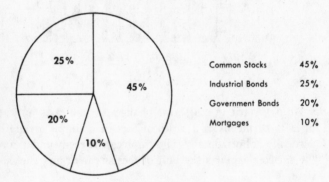

Common Stocks	45%
Industrial Bonds	25%
Government Bonds	20%
Mortgages	10%

Figure 9. Pie graph.

Figure 10. Picture graph. Shows increase of truck freight revenues; each truck represents revenues of company X.Y.Z.

Objects and Models. The most effective thing to show may be the object itself, such as a tennis racket for describing a tennis stroke, cards to explain how a card trick is done, or doll clothes to discuss the growth of a specialized clothing industry. Speakers have used an almost endless array of actual objects, including slide rules, cameras, pottery, tools, food items, skis, cosmetics, diving equipment, engines, musical instruments, animals, and babies.

Very large objects are impractical for most speaking occasions; very small objects are useless because they cannot be seen. A model scaled to proper size is therefore often used for the discussion of very large or very small items. Models of objects like boats, buildings, or rockets are sometimes built so that they can be taken apart to show inner construction and parts. Many models, such as those of cells and molecules, are schematic constructions to show the normally invisible relationship of parts.

A mock-up is an object or replica, or selected parts of an object, mounted on a display board to show essential structures and functions. Mock-ups are of special value for instructive speeches on scientific and technological subjects.

Since an object or model is in three dimensions, it has the advantage of being seen from all sides. A single visual aid thus takes the place of a series of diagrams or sketches. The disadvantages of models are that they are often expensive, not always obtainable, and usually difficult for the speaker to make.

Demonstrations. Informative speeches involving processes, such as how something works or how something is made, can be made lively and interesting by actual demonstrations. Demonstrations can be done with equipment or with human beings. Simple experiments, the operation of a gadget, the learning of a special skill, and many other subjects can profit by demonstrations. For example, the speaker can demonstrate clay modeling, or teach a volunteer to perform the first steps of the process. Demonstrations can also be in dialogue form, showing good and bad methods or results in subjects like fire prevention, courtesy, or salesmanship. Dramatized skits are most effective when they are brief, realistic, and to the point, but are unconvincing or offensive when the dialogue is over-enthusiastic, artificial, or obvious. When live models are used, rehearsal is essential.

Projections. Projected illustrations require special and expensive equipment, such as a motion-picture, filmstrip, or opaque projector, a screen of some kind, and the services of a skilled operator. Since the room must be darkened for most projections, the speaker lacks eye contact with his listeners, a fact which may lessen the communication of ideas. On the other hand, rightly chosen and rightly handled projected materials can bring the subject home to the audience.

Motion Pictures.   A silent film enables the speaker to point out and interpret important points and relate them to his topic. Travel, natural history, anthropological, and training films are familiar examples. A sound motion picture, however, being complete in itself, offers no opportunity for a running commentary and may result only in entertainment rather than in reinforcement of the subject of the speech. Great care must be taken to introduce and summarize the film and relate it to the speaker's ideas. Nevertheless, a short sound film may make unfamiliar or technical information clearer to the audience than the same time spent in verbal explanation. Brief segments, or "clips," lasting no more than a minute, may add a dramatic and stimulating element to a speech, if well chosen and well planned.

Filmstrips.   A filmstrip is a series of frames, or still pictures with titles or captions, arranged in a sequence or story. The strip is made of 35mm film from two to six feet long, containing from twenty to fifty or more individual pictures. Since filmstrips can be shown at any speed and any part can be reshown, they are excellent aids for speeches of instruction.

The speaker can project the strip from the rear of a darkened room, but an assistant to operate the projector enables the speaker to talk from the front of the room where he will be more clearly heard. The speech should be rehearsed with the operator of the projector so that cues can be arranged. The presentation will then be free from delays and unnecessary directions to the assistant.

Slides.   Verbal, graphic, and pictorial material projected on a screen offers a wide range of vivid and colorful support. Slides are often used because of their low cost, ease of procuring and storing, and their convenience. Slides available commercially are 2- by 2-inch color transparencies. A regular slide projector or an opaque projector can be used. A slide projector with a remote-control button allows the speaker to operate it from the front of the room while he is speaking. The opaque projector, which uses reflected light, projects all flat materials—such as pictures, diagrams, graphs, and pages of a book—onto a viewing screen.

Overhead Projectors. An overhead projector shows print, drawings, diagrams, and other graphic materials on a screen behind the speaker in a well-lighted room. The speaker operates the projector as he faces the audience and thus remains in direct communication with his listeners. An overhead projector offers a convenient way to display charts prepared in advance; it is also an excellent substitute for a chalkboard, especially in large rooms where a chalkboard would not be satisfactory. For example, the speaker can write, print, draw, and point out special features on the clear plastic (acetate) sheet in front of him by using a grease or ceramic marking pencil; the material appears on the screen behind him while he faces and talks to his audience. By using overlays, material can be easily added or taken away. Should the speaker want notes, they can be attached to the margin of the transparency. Also, the transparencies can be cleaned with a damp tissue after use and either used again or stored. Another advantage is that color can be used.

Handout Material. The speaker may wish his listeners to have a visual record of his ideas, such as an outline of the subject. In most cases, such material is handed out after the speech, along with an explanation of its relationship to the subject or suggestions for its use. In some discussions and speeches of instruction, the material is handed out before the speech begins in order to provide a background for the topic. It is usually unwise to distribute objects, illustrations, or printed materials during the speech, for listeners may concentrate on the handout rather than on what the speaker is saying. However, in a training or problem-solving conference, a sheet of material is often passed out as part of the presentation during a strategic pause. The sheet is read aloud, and the speaker then leads the group into a discussion of it in order to elicit ideas and suggestions from each member. For small audiences, it is often advantageous to distribute samples of unusual objects or new products, coupons, tickets, pictures, brochures, or periodicals for the listeners to use in the future. Identical material should be given to each individual in the audience, so that there is no question of equal treatment.

Auditory Aids. Sound reproducing devices—the phonograph and tape recorder—are important aids for certain speech subjects. Of the two, magnetic tape is more widely used than disk recordings, largely because tape is inexpensive and can be used both to record and play back. For example, a discussion of playwriting or acting can be illustrated by a scene from a play; the principles of good speaking can be demonstrated by a famous speaker; recent harmonic devices can be shown by selections from modern composers. Subjects like poetry, regional dialects, bird life, and dance rhythms are clarified and enhanced by auditory illustrations.

Certain topics can be made more realistic by the addition of sound effects, such as a roaring fire, an angry mob, singing birds, or ocean breakers.

Television, or videotape, while useful in training speakers by letting them see and hear their presentations and improve them, have little use in a public speaking situation. The size of the screen limits the viewing audience. However, with imagination, videotapes may sometimes be used to advantage. For instance, short segments might be used to illustrate the techniques used by selected television performers in interviewing.

GUIDING PRINCIPLES

The whole question of using audiovisual aids requires careful consideration. The speaker should be guided by basic principles applying to all audiovisuals, many of which have been mentioned in discussing individual types of material. The speaker should weigh all factors before deciding whether or not to use an aid in a given speech.

• *It should be used only when it is so relevant and important that the speech would be incomplete without it.*

• *It should save time, enabling the speaker to present information more quickly and economically than he could manage with words alone.*

• *It should make the speech more interesting. Interest depends upon new and added meaning conveyed in a novel, striking, or colorful way. Commonplace aids reduce rather than increase audience interest and understanding.*

• *It should be worth the money, effort, and time required to procure or prepare it. The test is whether it yields better results than the same time and effort spent in perfecting speech composition and delivery.*

All visual material must be clear to the eyes and to the understanding; all auditory material must be heard clearly without effort.

An aid must present accurate information gained from reliable sources, which the speaker identifies as part of his support.

Audiovisual aids should be planned to avoid hesitations and undue periods of silence during the speech. Delays while elaborate drawings are made or equipment is set up tend to kill audience interest. Aids, such as pictures, slides, and charts, should be arranged in the order of their use and numbered or labeled. The speaker should practice with each aid until he is sure that he can manage it skillfully. Even as simple an action as taping charts to the wall should be rehearsed so that they will not fall to the floor during the speech. Trial and error should occur before the speech, not before the eyes of the audience. If an assistant is being used to handle the material, the speaker should make certain that he knows exactly what to do and when to do it. The plan should be gone over with him carefully in advance and rehearsed.

The platform should be a suitable setting for the aid. There should be no other materials in view to distract attention. Each item should be placed where it can be seen to best advantage by all listeners. Lighting must be adequate for effective results, bright enough for most aids, dark enough for slides and films. Glossy material should be held so that the overhead lighting does not reflect on it and cause a glare.

Each aid must be given its proper verbal introduction and conclusion. The specific part being talked about at a given moment should be pointed out to the listeners. The visual and verbal messages must be perfectly coordinated.

The speaker should not block the audience's view of the visual material. He should stand to one side or behind it, and should perhaps use a pointer. When the speaker picks up an object for display, he should hold it high enough and still enough for all listeners to see. Diagrams, maps, and other flat illustrations should be held in front of him at chest height, face out to the audience, not turned partly toward the speaker. Each aid should be displayed for a few seconds to the left, center, and right sections of the audience. Merely flashing the aid in the air for a moment is meaningless. It should be picked up and displayed at the suitable time and then put down. The speaker only calls attention to his nervousness by continuing to handle it.

The speaker should talk to his listeners and not to his visual material. He must know each aid thoroughly so that he will not lose communication while searching for a given part. A mere glance at the aid should be sufficient. Practicing before a mirror and talking to his own image will enable the speaker to look at the listeners rather than at the material being shown.

Audiovisuals must be in working order. They should be thoroughly checked before the presentation. Facilities must be available for their use—sockets, screens, and the like. Technical failures often occur: bulbs burn out, plugs disconnect, films break, and slides are out of sequence. The speaker may prevent such breakdowns by careful planning. But if things do fail, the speaker must go on with his speech. Spending time trying to get equipment back to work does not help achieve the aim of the speech.

13.
INFORMATIVE SPEAKING

An informative speech seeks to convey knowledge, to present existing facts and ideas so that listeners will have a better understanding of them. An informative speech differs from a persuasive speech in being noncontroversial; it may state that such and such opinions exist, but does not advocate any one of them, nor does it try to shape the opinion of the audience. The informative speech is concerned only with facts and ideas as they are.

ESSENTIALS OF INFORMATIVE SPEAKING

An informative speech, if it is to be understandable and useful to listeners, has the essential qualities of accuracy, clearness, interest, and perspective.

Accuracy. All information consists of facts which are accurately observed and reported; otherwise it is misinformation. The speaker honestly evaluates his own observations and consults reliable sources to make sure that he has all the important facts comprising his topic. His information should also include the most recent data, for later developments may alter the facts and relationships shown by earlier studies. Two-year-old data, for example, would be inadequate for many financial, medical, and scientific topics. Gathering materials is discussed in Chapter 4.

Accuracy presupposes objectivity. The speaker approaches the facts of his subject with an open mind. An attitude of neutrality and suspended judgment is sometimes difficult to maintain, but it is of great practical importance. The speaker, for one thing, cannot present all the facts within the limits of a given speech, but must select the most essential data. The resulting speech should be factual, not opinionated. The speaker should not select facts that appeal to him and suppress those that do not agree with his prejudices. The facts chosen should represent the actual state of the subject; those omitted should not change the truth of the whole.

Clearness. The clear conveying of information depends on many factors already discussed in this book. The following aspects of speaking should be reviewed and applied to the informative speech: selecting the subject, determining the specific purpose, dividing the topic into parts, organizing the parts into a suitable structure, developing the parts, and showing the connections between them. A simple and definite organization of speech materials is a prerequisite for clarity. Clarity requires definitions, explanations, and illustrations expressed in familiar but accurate language. Many a speaker discovers that listeners have an astonishing aptitude for misunderstanding material that seems perfectly plain to him. Definitions therefore should be simply stated, explanations should present essential details and relationships, and illustrations should reveal the meaning of the verbal statements. The central theme of the speech and the main ideas composing and substantiating it should be impressed upon the audience by repetition and restatement so that better understanding and retention of the information can be secured. The speech when delivered should be expressed distinctly and forcefully at a rate in which the listeners can assimilate the information.

Interest. Although human beings are interested in news, gossip, and other forms of information, the speaker cannot depend solely upon natural curiosity. He must carefully plan to hold the interest of his audience. A well-knit structure for the speech not only provides clarity but also keeps the attention of listeners focused on the information being presented. Attention, being mobile and incapable of rest, tends to move around in various exploratory directions, but a progressive arrangement of speech materials keeps audience attention moving in the direction desired by the speaker.

The information can be made more lively by the use of interest elements, such as novelty, contrast and conflict, wit and humor, and human personality and experience. The information should also be adapted to the listeners' needs and motivations. The explanations, examples, and illustrations can show the importance of the subject, how it is related to daily needs, or what effect it may have upon work, leisure, finances, or other interests. The material on audience analysis, attention, interest, and motivation should be studied in this connection.

Perspective. Any fact or item of information is related to other facts and information. A fact cannot therefore be understood unless it is seen in proper perspective or relationship with its background.

The Speaker's Viewpoint. The speaker should state his approach to his subject or from what point of view he is presenting it. For example, the laws relating to the regulation of narcotics can be explained either from a medical or a moral point of view; democracy can be defined either by its principles or by its actual practices.

Proper Proportion. The relative importance of individual factors of an idea or object depend on the given situation. The speaker should not overemphasize a factor at the expense of others which may be equally or more important: to do so is to lose the proper sense of proportion in presenting the information to the audience. For example, the durability of wall-to-wall carpeting may be highly important to homeowners, but should not be developed at length for apartment house dwellers on short leases to whom reasonable price might be a more significant factor.

Standards of Judgment. When two or more items are being compared, they should be judged by the same standards and illustrated in the same manner. For instance, secretarial efficiency should not be a matter of speed, accuracy, and dependability in one case and of beauty and charm in another. Specific details should not be given about mutual funds and vague generalities about other methods of investment. A good informative speech avoids such slanting and presents the necessary parts of a subject in their proper proportion.

BARRIERS TO INFORMATION

Numerous barriers may prevent information from being understood by listeners. A knowledge of some of them should prove valuable in planning an informative speech.

Lack of Knowledge. Ignorance of a subject may cause listeners to refuse information which is unrelated to their experience and background. The speaker bridges the gap by relating new knowledge to what is known and familiar. For example, the "holes" or negative volumes in certain modern sculpture might be explained by analogy with a teacup: the empty volume inside the cup and the hole in the handle are as important to its form as the solid or positive volumes of the porcelain.

Complexity of Information.   The hearing mind can assimilate only so much complex information in a given time. Therefore the speaker reduces difficult subjects down to basic divisions supported by the simplest possible examples and explanations.

Indifference.   Apathy to knowledge may be caused by fatigue or a surfeit of facts and events. In a world of constant cataclysms and crises, nothing seems to have social importance to some listeners. The information needs to be related to the needs and interests of everyday life, which persists in spite of dangers, tragedies, and catastrophes.

Taboos.   Knowledge may be repudiated because it goes against closely held beliefs and prejudices. Facts about certain subjects, such as infanticide, mixed marriage, child prostitution, or sexual deviation may be taboo. Knowledge is often rejected because of fear: it is dangerous to know too much; man should not probe too deeply into nature's secrets or he will be destroyed. The speaker can stress the constructive and social values of the information which he is presenting, or point out that the complexities of modern life demand the taking of calculated risks for the solution of difficult problems.

Wishful Thinking.   Information may be unwelcome because it does not fit in with hopes and dreams: theories are more interesting than facts, and illusions more pleasant than actualities. The information can often be related to basic motivations and shown in new and striking applications.

KINDS OF INFORMATIVE SPEECHES

An informative speech is not only factual but also functional: it is designed for a specific situation. A great variety of occasions call for various kinds of informative talks. A few of the most important types of informative speeches will be briefly discussed.

Instructions.   A speech of instruction may be a set of directions or a detailed explanation. An instructive speech assumes that the audience has little or no previous knowledge of the subject.

Directions. A set of directions includes the explanation of processes, such as how to do something and how to make something. For speech purposes the process should be limited in scope and simple enough to be explained within the desired time limit. The following is a general plan for organizing the body of a speech about an active or constructive process.

I. Nature of the object or action.
   A. Definition in terms of basic traits and purposes.
   B. Necessary analysis for making the object or performing the action.
   C. Brief description of the product or end result.
II. Requirements for making the object or performing the action.
   A. Necessary tools and apparatus.
   B. Necessary materials and supplies.
   C. Necessary special conditions.
III. Major steps in making the object or performing the action.
   A. First main step.
      1. Tools and materials.
      2. Action to be performed.
         a. Reason for the action.
         b. Description of the action.
         c. Results of the action.
   B. Second main step, etc.

Part III of the speech presents the gist of the making or performing. The details explain why and how each step is done and what the result should be. No essential detail should be omitted. For example, in refinishing furniture, it should be stated that the first coat of varnish should be allowed to dry before it is rubbed with pumice stone or fine steel wool.

Demonstrations. A demonstration speech is the explanation of a process during the performance of the process. A demonstration speech is specially planned around audiovisual aids, but every speech using audiovisual aids is not a demonstration speech. The explanation of a process may use visual aids as illustrations, while the demonstration speech actually executes the process as it is explained. For example, the speaker can illustrate a physical exercise with drawings and diagrams, or he can demonstrate the exercise by actually performing it. The speech is usually arranged in a time or step-by-step order, or the demonstration section may be one part of a speech organized in a topical order.

Detailed Explanations. Many expository speeches are expanded definitions or systematic descriptions of objects, substances, forces, organizations, mechanisms, and so forth.

EXPANDED DEFINITION. A speech of definition shows what a given term includes and excludes. Each physical trait, function, or other attribute is described and illustrated. The main problems are to include material that makes the meaning clear and to exclude material that is too minute to be interesting along with interesting material that has no direct bearing on the term.

An informative speech on a social process may be an extended definition. For example, an explanation of the parole system includes a description of its purpose, structure, and activities. The objectives of the system are explained, its organization into divisions, departments, and units, its administration or the chain of authority and responsibility, and its methods of operation. The entire process may be shown by an anonymous but actual case study.

SYSTEMATIC DESCRIPTION. The description of a mechanical device, such as a claw-hammer, air conditioner, or diesel engine, is based on the functional parts of the implement. A functional part is any division that performs an action necessary for the operation of the device. For example, a claw-hammer is used in the hand for driving and pulling nails. Its functional parts are the handle and the ends of the head, one of which is slightly convex for driving nails and the other markedly curved with a V-shaped notch for pulling nails.

The plan of organization into definition, structure (functional parts), and operation is suitable for describing a device or explaining how something works. In a speech describing the piano accordion, for example, the instrument is divided into the following functional parts: a collapsible bellows, two keyboards with buttons or keys, valves controlled by the keys or buttons, and a set of free metal reeds in pairs. The principle of operation is to produce musical tones by causing a flow of air to vibrate the reeds. The actions of the operator are contracting and expanding the bellows with the left arm and hand and pressing the keys and buttons of one keyboard with the left fingers and pressing the keys of the other keyboard with the fingers of the right hand.

Reports. An oral report is based on specific seeing, hearing, and investigation and has two major characteristics: it presents new facts and ideas and it is presented by a speaker who has a sense of responsibility to his audience. The report tells listeners what has happened rather than what should happen. In some situations, an oral report may include a synopsis of proposals that have been considered by an investigating committee or study group and a statement of the recommended course of action. However, the report itself is informative, although it may be later used for persuasive purposes. Familiar examples of oral reports are broadcast reviews of the weather, stock market, and news events. Other important types of reports will be briefly discussed.

Report of a Speech. The report of a speech or lecture states the speaker, the title or subject, the time and place of the address, and the nature of the occasion. The main points of the address are summarized, keeping the same relative emphasis given by the speaker. The central theme of the speech should be explained. Significant audience questions and reactions can also be included.

Report of a Play. A dramatic review gives an idea of the type and construction of the play, and may compare or contrast it with other works by the author. The success of the actors and director in achieving the author's intention is discussed and also the contribution of the designer of the sets and costumes. The reporter states his own reactions to the performance and may quote the opinions of newspaper critics if these will add to the objectivity of the report.

Magazine Article Report. An article in a periodical or a newspaper feature story may be the subject of a short report. The author, title, periodical, date, and page numbers should be given. The article should be summarized or paraphrased and a brief quotation offered to illustrate the author's expression of an important point. The speaker can give his opinion of the accuracy of the writer's information, the fairness of his point of view, and the value of the knowledge he contributes to the reader.

Book Report. A book review seeks to give listeners significant information about a specific work. The author, title, type of book, and kind of subject matter are stated. In a work of fiction some idea is offered of the setting, characters, and opening action. Sketching a part of the plot usually creates more interest in the book than giving an entire synopsis. The report seeks to offer listeners information which they might not get from reading the book. Thus, material is included on the author's life, background, and previous works.

A report on a work of nonfiction gives an idea of the book's contents and often an idea of its importance. The work may be compared with others on the same subject and its contribution to knowledge can be briefly evaluated. The following questions can be considered in planning a book report: What value does the book's message have for this particular audience? Is a digest and explanation of the content sufficient or should listeners be stimulated to read the whole book? What attitude toward life does the work express? Does the book maintain an objective and balanced approach to the subject or does it present a one-sided viewpoint? Is the book written in a clear and interesting fashion or is the style extremely technical, involved, or manneristic?

Investigation Report. An investigation report is a résumé and explanation of a systematic inquiry and is of two main types: survey reports, which provide the answer to a question, and technical reports, which provide the solution to a problem. When needed information cannot be found in print, the data must be gathered firsthand.

SURVEY REPORT. A survey report is based largely on personal inspections and interviews. Its preparation comprises several steps: determining the specific questions to be asked, setting up a method of inquiry, conducting the investigation, recording the data, and organizing the report.

• *The Questions.* The background and reasons for seeking an answer should be studied to find what information is needed. The various factors involved should be listed, and questions devised and phrased in a way that will elicit pertinent answers. For example, some of the factors to be considered in buying carpeting are durability, color, texture or pile, pattern, ease of cleaning, and installation.

• *Method of Inquiry.* The method of inquiry can be by personal examination, which includes inspecting, classifying, counting, and measuring. The method of canvassing can also be used. Information about tastes, opinions, and other individual responses can be obtained by asking people questions.

• *Conducting the Inquiry.* In conducting the inquiry the investigator must see and hear what is actually before him rather than what he expects, and must seek to understand what he sees and hears. He must also have the persistence to discover enough data, which means interviewing enough persons and those representing a cross-section of a given group.

• *Recording the Data.* The results of personal examination and answers to questions are recorded immediately and accurately. After a trial inquiry, the examiner draws up a list of things to be observed and the interviewer prepares a revised list of questions whose answers can be classified and tabulated.

• *Organizing the Report.* In composing the report, the speaker tabulates the results of his investigation and prepares any necessary illustrations. He plans his speech to suit his specific audience and purpose. The report usually has four main parts:

I. An explanation of the nature and purpose of the investigation.
II. A brief summary of the findings and conclusions.
III. An explanation of the methods of inquiry which were used.
IV. A statement and explanation of the results in detail.

TECHNICAL REPORT. A technical report resembles a survey report but includes information gathered by tests or experiments. The experiments and tests are based on analyzing the problem to be solved, determining whether the problem is important enough to warrant the time, effort, and money necessary to solve it, and finding the best methods of investigation and solution.

A good technical reporter must have experience in the subject of the report, sufficient scientific knowledge for truly accurate observation, the ability to analyze what he has observed, and the judgment to reach valid conclusions. Accurate observation demands freedom from misconceptions; analysis and judgment require reason and common sense in order to stick to essentials and to interpret the actual situation. The speaker must speak accurately and at the same time make the information understandable and useful to his audience.

A few basic principles or objectives should help the speaker to plan a technical report.

• *Save the Audience Time and Effort.* The speaker spares no pains to make this possible. He uses clear arrangement of information, with transitions and necessary summaries; clear illustrations, both verbal and visual; and clear, simple statements expressed in nontechnical language.

• *Answer the Audience's Needs.* All aspects of a topic are not presented, only those of major interest and practical value to the listeners.

• *Keep the Report Objective.* The speaker presents findings and conclusions rather than personal thoughts, feelings, and experiences. The speaker, however, does feel strong interest in his subject and method of presentation.

• *Use Accurate Language.* Superlatives and exaggerations of all kinds should be avoided. Understatement may give a better picture than overstatement. Vague statements have no place in accurate reporting.

• *Interpret the Raw Facts.* Facts and statistical information alone may not lead to audience understanding. Significant items should be explained and emphasized.

Other Types of Reports.   Other forms of oral reports are used in legislative, business, professional, and social organizations.

COMMITTEE REPORT. Many organizations carry on their work by assigning questions and problems to committees. A committee report presents the results of investigation, deliberation, and tentative decision. The scope and form of the report follows the rules and procedures of the organization.

PERIODICAL REPORT. A period report usually follows a regulation form, and surveys what has occurred during a given time interval. The report often includes comparisons with similar periods in the past and makes recommendations for the future in order to help listeners decide upon the course of action.

PROGRESS REPORT. A progress report is made upon undertakings which require months or years for completion. The report is made to a board of directors or other governing body. The heads of cities, states, and nations sometimes make progress reports to the public upon aspects of their administrations. The annual report of the President of the United States is made to Congress but is also a communication to the entire nation. Although it resembles a periodic report, the progress report follows no set form, but is designed by the speaker to enlighten his audience.

Lectures.   A lecture is an informative speech based on the knowledge and experience of the speaker, who is to some extent an authority on the subject. A lecture usually assumes that the audience has some knowledge of the subject which needs enlarging. A lecture is essentially a speech of enlightenment, presenting and interpreting facts and ideas, but often has the persuasive element of impressing the listener with the importance of the subject or of stimulating his desire for further knowledge.

Explanation of Facts. A lecture does not concern itself primarily with practical knowledge but rather with interesting and stimulating knowledge. Facts are not only presented but also interpreted. The significance of the relationship among facts may be more important to the understanding than the facts themselves. However, theory alone in a lecture is not sufficient; facts should not only be interpreted, but also presented.

In planning a lecture, the specific point of view or scope of the information is set up. The facts are grouped according to some method of division and classification. The facts are interpreted according to the time, place, and manner of their occurrence. The significance of the facts to the present is also explained. A projection can be made of future relations of the audience to the subject.

Explanation of Ideas. A concept or abstract idea is more difficult to explain than most physical objects or facts. The exploration of an idea usually includes the following elements: (1) a general or overall definition; (2) the origin, sources, or history of the concept; (3) its essential aspects, qualities, or values; (4) a comparison and contrast with other ideas; and (5) examples of its influence in human affairs. The use of this basic pattern can be seen in the subject "Existentialism: What Does It Mean?"

1. Existentialism is a contemporary literary and philosophical movement of nihilism, pessimism, and individual responsibility.
2. Existentialism was formulated by Jean Paul Sartre in his book *Being and Nothingness* published in 1943. Its tenets are based upon Descartes' statement, "I think, therefore I am." Among other sources are the German philosophy of phenomenology and certain postulates of the Danish theologian Kierkegaard.
3. The main ideas of existentialism are: the universe has no meaning; reality is defined only by the mind; environment is alien, hostile, and absurd; each individual is responsible for his role in the outer world; this responsibility is the source of anguish; the individual is the result of his own choice and actions.
4. Existentialism can be compared with atheism, relativity, free will, and humanism and contrasted with theism, absolutism, determinism, and fatalism.

5. Examples of the influence of existentialism: literature, drama, ethics, and psychology (role playing, self-realization, etc.).

Some ideas can be analyzed in more than one way. The concept "realism" means different things in literature, philosophy, and business management. The definition of an idea should be from one point of view and the explanation should stick to the sense in which it is used in the given field of activity. Using an abstract term in more than one sense results in confusion rather than explanation. Many ideas are best understood when explained and illustrated in physical terms: how it affects the health, safety, income, or personal activities of the listener.

PREPARING INFORMATIVE SPEECHES

The principles of speech communication are the foundations of informative speaking. A few specific techniques of organization and development have been applied to informative speeches in this chapter. A summary of the nature of understanding may also help the speaker to adapt information to his audience. The following activities constitute understanding.

• Becoming aware of a new fact or concept which is described or defined.
• Recalling a similar known fact or idea from the memory.
• Seeing the relationship between one fact or concept and another.
• Classifying or grouping a number of facts or ideas.
• Seeing the relation of a fact or concept to the situation in which it was observed or inferred.
• Applying a fact or concept to a new situation and observing how it works or fits.
• Becoming aware of facts, other persons, and one's self in relationship to them.
• Perceiving the relationship among facts and concepts in a connected sequence or structure.
• Fixing facts, concepts, and relationships in the memory by explaining, illustrating, and repeating them.

14.
PERSUASIVE SPEAKING

Persuasion is the art of shaping conduct by using evidence, reasoning, and suggestion in connection with convictions, feelings, experiences, and motivations of audiences. In classical treatises on public speaking, *logos* was the appeal to the audience's reason, *pathos* to its emotions, and *ethos* to its esteem of the speaker. Pathos and ethos were conditioned by the sentiments, moral nature, and guiding beliefs of the listeners. The clear communication of the facts of a situation may sometimes reduce the need for persuasion. However, the facts are often imperfectly known, and known facts are not always self-evident guides to belief or action. Therefore the persuasive speaker considers not only the problem but also the people concerned with it. He is not solely concerned with shedding light; he wants his audience to think and act as he does. The persuasive speaker is not objective in purpose, although he is as objective as possible in using facts to support ideas.

Persuasion is not so much logical as psychological. The appeal to reason is relatively impersonal and suggests an element of unchangeable truth; the appeals to feelings and emotions are personal and suggest the capacity for change. Modern psychology indicates that the beliefs and activities of most individuals are largely the result of nonlogical forces.

IMPORTANCE OF PERSUASION

Persuasion exists because human beings are faced with problems and situations demanding adjustment and action. Whenever there is a difference in desire, opinion, or judgment, there is controversy; indeed, controversy creates the need for persuasion. Many noncon-

troversial subjects also demand persuasive speaking, such as appeals
for blood donations or drives for charity. Here the difference of
opinion lies in lack of desire and interest, and the speaker must
overcome apathy. Persuasion also fosters social progress: it advocates
new ideas, new programs, new forms of cooperation; it influences
others to accept responsibility; it converts indifference and disbelief
into action; and it offers desirable channels for feelings and emotions.

TYPES OF PERSUASIVE SPEECHES

There are three kinds of persuasive speeches, dependent upon the
basic purpose of the speaker toward his audience: to convince, or
to bring by argument to belief; to actuate, or to move to action;
and to stimulate, or to exert an animating influence.

Speaking to Convince.   A speech to convince seeks some kind
of mental agreement. The speaker wants the audience to accept,
approve, or recognize an idea, procedure, or solution to a problem.
A speech to convince is often given to influence public opinion or
build up a climate of thought in which action can later be advocated
and obtained.

A speech obviously cannot convince unless it is interesting. The
topic should be genuinely controversial, significant to the audience,
and capable of a probable solution. The fact that all children should
be educated is no longer controversial, but whether or not all should
be given a higher education still is controversial. Retired persons
would be unaffected by the necessity for technical education, but
this topic would be of significance to young parents in an age of
growing computerization.

Since the appeal to reason is paramount in a speech to convince,
the speaker should use adequate evidence and logical methods of
argument. At the same time he is careful to adapt his arguments
to the receptivity of his listeners. The speaker may have to offset
or counteract previous knowledge, prejudices, and desires. It is not
always enough to show listeners that a proposition is true; it is often
necessary to arouse their desire to believe the truth.

Speaking to Actuate.   A speech to actuate seeks a specific action.
Like the speech to convince, it may try to change existing beliefs
or to replace them with new ones, but it does so in order to urge

the listeners to perform a definite deed. The goal is active participation rather than passive agreement. For example: Learn to play the guitar; Buy a color TV set; Give a day's pay to the Community Fund; Grow your own mushrooms.

Speaking to Stimulate. A speech to stimulate has for its main purpose the stirring of the emotions. The speaker reminds his audience of something they value and intensifies their feelings for it; or, if it is a negative value, he arouses their emotions against it. This type of speech is often called the speech to inspire or to impress.

The speaker counts upon the tacit agreement and approval of his audience and seeks to lift it from passivity to strong, active attitudes and feelings. He seeks a general response toward his subject, rather than a specific attitude. On many occasions his aim is to create or maintain goodwill.

PERSUADING BY REASON

To be persuasive, the speaker's ideas must be acceptable as well as clear: the audience should believe that the statements he makes are true. The persuasive speaker therefore appeals by reason and bases his arguments on valid evidence.

Argumentation, or the appeal by reason, consists of methods of securing belief and of establishing the logical probability of a statement. An argument starts with known facts and travels the path of reason to a conclusion. The facts in an argument are called evidence; the reasoning based on the evidence is called inference; the process of using evidence and inference is called proof; and the result of proof is a demonstrated truth. Argument is inherently the soundest method to influence others. Essentially, argumentation is the method of showing the necessary relationship between ideas.

Every piece of valid argumentation contains the following elements: a proposition, which, when proved, becomes the conclusion; materials of proof, or evidence concerning the proposition; a process of proof, or demonstration, generally referred to as the argument; and the conclusion, which is the proposition proved or established. The study of argumentation is divided into (1) Analysis, the study of the proposition and the issues involved in it. (2) Evidence, the study of pertinent data. (3) Logic, the study of reasoning.

THE PROPOSITION

Analysis consists mainly of determining the proposition and clarifying it.

Determining the Proposition.   The word proposition implies
that there is more than one side to the problem at hand. The proposition is a single sentence; it states the side with which the speaker
wants his hearers to agree. The proposition must show exactly what
the speaker wants to prove or disprove. For example: "Advertising
should be regulated by a federal commission." The following proposition is too vague because it omits how advertising is to be judged
or controlled: "Misrepresentation in advertising should be abolished."
An unclear proposition results in futile wrangling over irrelevant
issues.

Requirements of Propositions.   A proposition should make a debatable statement. If it is obviously true or obviously false, there is
no need for argument. A proposition should not use terms that have
more than one meaning. It should not make too broad a statement
but should be limited to a specific time, place, or activity. A proposition should contain only one major idea and should put the burden
of proof on the person stating it. The status quo is already established;
therefore, the one who advocates something, or attempts to overthrow
something old, should prove the truth of his contention.

Kinds of Propositions.   A proposition may be a statement of fact—
a thing is true or false. The speaker is dealing with the truth or
falsity of an event or situation, past or present, and the emphasis
is on facts: "Chemical waste is a health hazard"; "Noise in cities
damages the hearing of the inhabitants"; "Air travel is the safest
means of transportation."

A proposition may be a statement of feeling or value—the speaker
likes or dislikes a thing. He is dealing with qualities such as the
worth of an object, an institution, or a way of life. The emphasis
is on approval or disapproval: "The new Speedmobile is the best
buy in a low-priced car"; "Good speech is a permanent letter of
recommendation."

A proposition may also be a statement of policy—a thing ought
or ought not to be done. The speaker is dealing with the future

and the emphasis is on facts and values. The word "should" usually appears in the proposition: "Public transportation should be subsidized by the federal government"; "Dogs should not be allowed in apartment houses."

Stating the Proposition. In formulating a proposition, the speaker starts with a specific question, such as "Should false advertising be forbidden by the government?" He surveys all aspects of the question to locate the issues. Is false advertising wrong because it contradicts ideal standards of truth? Is it unfair to competition? Is it harmful to consumers? Does the buyer have access to facts and statistics to come to a reliable decision? What does the federal government do at the present time to protect the consumer from false advertising? What more should the federal government do about this matter?

The speaker studies the facts, compares possible solutions, weighs probable results; then he decides on his answer to the problem. He may decide that the federal government could do a better job of protecting the average consumer than the average consumer could do on his own. He then works out a clear, single-sentence statement: "Advertising should be controlled by a federal agency." This is the proposal the speaker wants to prove.

Testing the Proposition. After he has stated a clear proposition, the speaker proceeds to prove it by testing and clarifying it. By a thorough study of the problem, the speaker should learn all the reasons for and against every part of his proposition. He may not have to prove certain points, because everyone admits them. He therefore selects the crucial issues and proves them in order to get his audience to accept his proposal. If his listeners refuse to believe the speaker's views on any one of these main issues, they will reject his proposition.

A further analysis of the problem may lead the speaker to another possible solution, or perhaps to several solutions. For example, each state may regulate advertising, or the National Association of Manufacturers might set up a strict code for the advertising of products.

By weighing all the available evidence, the speaker decides that federal advertising regulation would be the most equitable and practicable answer. He then applies his solution to individual hypothetical cases. He compares what happens now with what would happen under regulation, looking for weak points in federal regulation to make sure that these weaknesses are fewer and less important than the weaknesses of the status quo.

The final proposition should be neither too broad and complicated nor too brief and limited. It should not be vague and unqualified. It should not be too obvious for discussion or too arbitrary or capricious for serious consideration.

REASONING

Successful persuasion demands sound reasoning. The moment the speaker begins to use facts, he begins to interpret them, and interpreting facts is reasoning. When he shows that one thing is true because something else is true, he is using logical reasoning. He not only makes a judgment that something is true but also presents the proof. "The population in the state of California is increasing at a rapid rate. Census figures taken from 1930 to 1970 show this. By 1980 it will be the most populous state in the Union."

In general, reasoning has one of two objectives: to reach a conclusion about a class of things and to reach a conclusion about a member of a class. The first objective is achieved by induction, the second by deduction. Induction proceeds from particular cases to a conclusion covering the whole class; deduction proceeds from the whole class to a conclusion applying to a particular case. Causal reasoning, which involves elements of induction and deduction, depending on the situation, will be discussed separately.

Inductive Reasoning. Induction, proceeding from example to principle, is a process of generalization. A generalization is a conclusion reached about a whole group of things after examining sample members of the group. Induction can never reach absolute certainty, but it can reach a high degree of probability. There is no way of proving that summer will always be warmer than winter; however, it can be predicted satisfactorily for all practical purposes by basing the prediction on what has occurred during summers up to now.

Simple Induction. Induction in speaking is often quite simple— the speaker gives a number of examples and then draws his conclusion. The appeal to common sense is a form of induction. Here specific instances are pointed out and the obvious conclusion is drawn. Induction is a popular form of reasoning, because an audience is impressed by facts. If the speaker keeps his induction simple, clear, and practical, his audience will be convinced.

To make a generalization convincing, the speaker should first use typical examples. He examines enough of them to make sure that his examples do not lead to another conclusion, but that they lead logically to his conclusion. He shows that exceptions, if there are any, have no effect upon the generalization. The speaker should be certain that all instances mentioned are true. Finally, he makes sure that his generalization is accurately stated.

Reasoning by Analogy. A less simple form of induction is reasoning by analogy, which is drawing a conclusion about the relationship between a fact or set of data because of its similarity to another fact or set of data. Things that resemble each other are from some point of view analogous; this resemblance is noted and it is inferred that the things are alike in still another respect. For example, because of physiological likenesses among the mammals, it is inferred that a drug harmful to hamsters is harmful to human beings. An analogy may be literal; the cases compared may be of the same fundamental order. An analogy may also be figurative if the resemblance noted is between things of a basically different nature.

The strength of an analogy rests upon the vividness of the point of similarity upon which the argument turns, and the possibility of extending the resemblance to cover additional points. Valid analogy deals with logical relationships among data. The similarity, not of the objects themselves but of the logical structures of the objects forms the basis of the appeal to reason.

There is no perfectly logical analogy, because no two sets of conditions are exactly alike. Therefore, it is difficult to prove a proposition conclusively through analogy. It is best to support an analogy by other forms of argument.

Deductive Reasoning. Deduction proceeds from a general statement to a particular conclusion. Deduction assumes that what is true of the whole will be true of its parts; that what is true of a category will be true of any member of that category. Deduction can take the form of a syllogism, which contains three propositions: the major premise, the minor premise, and the conclusion.

Categorical Syllogism. The major premise in a categorical syllogism states a general law about all members of a class; the minor premise states that the specific case belongs to this class; the conclusion states that the general law applies to the specific case.

Major premise: All men are mortal.
Minor premise: Socrates is a man.
Conclusion: Therefore Socrates is mortal.

The first two propositions contain an element in common which enables the third proposition to be inferred. The element in common is called the middle term. A syllogism contains only three terms: major, middle, and minor. In the above syllogism, the major term is "mortal," the middle term is "all men" and "man," and the minor term is "Socrates." By this example of deduction, it is shown that what is true of a whole class is true of the individual member of the class.

A categorical syllogism should actually convince the audience. It may be correct in form and the conclusion may be validly drawn, but the syllogism does not establish a truth unless the main and minor premises are proved or provable statements.

Major premise: All men have immortal souls.
Minor premise: Socrates is a man.
Conclusion: Therefore Socrates has an immortal soul.

This conclusion cannot be accepted, because there is no way of proving that men have immortal souls. A syllogism can establish an acceptable truth only when the major and minor premises are true, that is, arrived at by previous valid induction. Faith may be important in many aspects of life, but it is not the basis of proof.

Disjunctive Syllogism.   When the major premise states a choice between two possibilities, the syllogism is called disjunctive. The earmarks of the disjunctive major premise are the connectives "either . . . or."

Major premise: John is either sick or pretending that he is sick.
Minor premise: John is sick.
Conclusion: Therefore John is not pretending that he is sick.

For the disjunctive syllogism to be valid, the alternatives stated in the major premise must be the only ones possible. They must also be mutually exclusive. If the minor premise affirms one of the alternatives, the conclusion must deny the other. In the foregoing syllogism, if the minor premise stated, "John is not sick," then the conclusion would be, "Therefore John is pretending that he is sick."

Hypothetical Syllogism. A great deal of the business of living depends on probability, such as predicting results from causes by saying, "If this happens, then that will happen." When the major premise states a condition, the resulting syllogism is a hypothetical one. Then it can be shown that the minor premise fulfills the condition. Consequently, the conclusion states that what is true of the generalization in the major premise is true of the particular statement in the minor premise. The "if" clause is called the antecedent, and the resulting clause the consequent.

Major premise: If the federal government reduces spending, it will balance the budget.
Minor premise: The federal government will reduce spending.
Conclusion: Therefore the federal government will balance the budget.

On the other hand, if the minor premise denies the consequent, the conclusion should deny the antecedent.

Major premise: If the federal government reduces spending, it will balance the budget.
Minor premise: The federal government will not balance the budget.
Conclusion: Therefore the federal government will not reduce spending.

The Enthymeme. In public speaking, a syllogism is rarely stated in full. At least one of the premises is so obvious that it is omitted; it is merely implied or kept in mind. A speaker may declare, "Our expanding industrial society needs more consumers." This enthymeme could be expanded into a full syllogism by supplying the missing premises.

Major premise: All expanding industrial societies need more consumers.
Minor premise: Ours is an expanding industrial society.
Conclusion: Therefore our society needs more consumers.

Convincing the Audience. In using deductive reasoning, the speaker should make sure that his audience is convinced. He can ask himself these questions: Is my major premise true, or is it a sweeping generality without foundation in fact? Is my minor premise true? Does it fall within the scope of the general statement? Even if my general statement is true, will my audience accept it as such? (If not, you will have to prove your major premise with induction before going on with your deduction.)

Causal Reasoning.   All reasoning is based on relations and many of these relations are causal. Most persons believe axiomatically that every effect has a cause. Causal reasoning is the logic of change; it is an inference, an interpretation, or a judgment about the relationship among certain facts. There are three types of reasoning from cause: cause-to-effect, effect-to-cause, and effect-to-effect.

Cause-to-Effect.   Cause-to-effect reasoning goes from a known cause to a probable effect: given a certain set of conditions, a certain effect will result. The speaker may, for example, urge the adoption of certain reforms to bring about desirable social results.

To prove the validity of a cause-to-effect argument, it should be shown that the effect occurs whenever the cause occurs. There should actually be a cause, not a coincidence. Furthermore, the cause should be adequate to produce the effect. Adequate investigation should be made to find out whether there are other causes for the effect.

Effect-to-Cause.   Effect-to-cause reasoning proceeds from a known effect to a probable cause: a given condition is the result of certain other conditions. For example, the speaker might analyze the various causes of an undesirable economic condition, such as high mortgage rates. Here he shows that the causes actually existed at the time the effect was produced and that the causes were adequate to bring about the given effect. Again, the speaker should investigate what other causes bring about the effect, and should also show that an alleged cause was not present only by chance.

Effect-to-Effect.   Effect-to-effect reasoning goes from a known effect to a probable effect. A common cause for the two effects is implied: "When roses begin to bloom, set eggplants out in the garden." The blooming of roses is not the cause of the action. Settled warm weather is the cause of setting out eggplants, just as it is the cause of the rose blossoms. Here the speaker shows that both effects always occur when the cause is present. The two effects should not be associated only by chance. Conditions should not have changed to prevent the cause from bringing about either effect.

In all three forms of causal reasoning, the truth of all facts should be carefully established. The audience should be shown that a causal relationship exists in the matter under discussion. The only connection between an assumed cause and an effect may be that one occurred after the other. Many totally unrelated events occur after other events. Assuming a causal relationship where none exists is called *post hoc, ergo propter hoc* (after this, therefore because of this). Human beings are prone to seize upon striking instances as conclusive proof.

General Errors in Reasoning.

Two general errors are all too frequently encountered in public speaking: ignoring the question and begging the question.

Ignoring the Question.   This fallacy consists of evading the point in question and diverting attention to another issue. It is often a dramatic arguing beside the point.

The *argumentum ad hominem* (argument to the man) is one of its commonest forms. If a speaker lacks proof, he may resort to personalities and judge the truth or falsity of an idea by the character, profession, or conduct of the individual advocating it. For example, he may attack public housing because socialists favor public housing. The proof of a proposition is independent of the individual, for a good man may make an untrue or foolish statement, and a scoundrel may make a true or sensible statement.

The *argumentum ad populum* (argument to the people) is the appeal to popular prejudice, to public passion, to the humor of the unthinking herd. Examples are found in most political campaigns. Condemn a thing, or laugh at it, and maybe it will go away.

The appeals to authority, tradition, and custom are other forms of ignoring the question. They concentrate on the necessity of keeping the status quo: "What was good enough for George Washington is good enough for me." "It's the law of life." "We don't do that in our society."

Ignoring the question also takes the form of shifting ground. When a speaker is trying to prove a proposition and cannot quite do it, he may be tempted to prove another point instead. A common form of shifting ground is to use a given term in more than one sense: "It is logical to vote for the Democratic candidate because we have a democratic form of government."

Begging the Question. To assume as true or false an issue that one is obliged to prove is to beg the question. A word or phrase may beg the question: "All who were in favor of this dangerous proposal signed the petition." The word "dangerous" prejudges or begs the question. Questions unfairly phrased also beg the question. "Shall we continue to tamper with our school curriculum, or shall we stick to the tried and true three R's?"

Arguing in a circle is a frequent form of this fallacy. Here the speaker states a premise as a truth, draws a conclusion from the unsupported premise, and then uses this conclusion to prove the premise: "We should have a four-hour working day so that more people will have jobs. Since more people will have jobs, it is evident that we should have a four-hour working day."

PERSUADING BY MOTIVATION

To be effective, a persuasive speech should move the listeners; it should affect them personally. The persuasive speaker therefore appeals by emotion and bases his supporting material on audience attitudes and motivations. Outstanding persuasive speeches, such as those by Daniel Webster, Abraham Lincoln, and Franklin D. Roosevelt, are distinguished by suitable emotional content. Emotions are powerful forces in human life: men believe in logic, but are usually moved to belief and action by emotion. Audience acceptance thus depends upon how well the speaker's statements fit into established patterns of belief and action. Even strong arguments may be fruitless unless they involve basic needs, desires, and aspirations.

The real sources of human actions and thoughts are probably emotional drives growing out of physiological needs. Behavior may be caused by aspects of the environment or by a person's own biological, psychological, or social needs.

The drives, or motive appeals, have been analyzed and grouped in various ways. Abraham Maslow[1] uses five categories in ascending importance: physiological needs, safety needs, belongingness and love needs, esteem needs, and self-actualization needs. Food, drink, stable temperature, and excretion are imperative physical needs. Self-preservation and security come next in the hierarchy. Love needs or belong-

---

[1] Abraham H. Maslow, *Motivation and Personality*, 2nd ed. (New York: Harper & Row, 1970), pp. 35–58.

ingness include spouse, children, relatives, and friends. Needs for esteem involve the quest for material possessions, recognition by others, desire for power and influence. The need for self-actualization drives us to grow, to achieve, to create.

Other classifications include motives like curiosity, change, conformity, loyalty, reverence, generosity, revulsion, to name only a few. One listed motive may contradict another. Another may be a combination or blend of motives. A human being is changeable, inconsistent, sometimes transformable, as he discovers himself.

At times we have certain mental sets in performing activities, and we also have certain emotional sets. A mental set is a tendency to sense, perceive, and act in a certain direction. For example, a person sitting at a typewriter is in a state of readiness to use his fingers in a manner to operate the keyboard; the same person sitting at a piano has a different mental set or readiness to use his fingers on the keyboard of that instrument.

An emotional set is a tendency to feel and react in a certain general direction. Human beings are "wired up" for various patterns of feeling when suitable stimuli are applied. Examples of powerful emotional drives are anger, sexual desire, and grief. They have led some individuals to great achievement, others to self-destruction.

What makes a person want to believe, to do, or to appreciate? No one simple answer is possible, but trial and error and experience in persuading others show that if one motivation will not do it, another might.

Safety counselors, for example, often find that self-preservation, or the desire to live and be sound of limb, will not make industrial workers use safety devices provided for the job. This fact should surprise no one who has seen pedestrians crossing busy city streets against a red light, or motorists driving at excessive speeds. A pedestrian recently killed in the middle of the street was said by her friends to be a woman who prided herself upon being "undaunted by traffic." Making a person want to act safely requires that he be shown the value of saving his own limbs: what it means to his future earning power, his future happiness in friendship, recreation, and love, or, if he is married, what it means to his wife and children.

In many subjects there are strong reasons against what the speaker recommends. He may not be able to offset them by arguments, but he may be able to overwhelm them by a deeper and more extensive combination of motivations. It is important to search for basic motives and for those which have more connections with other persistent motivations. The essential problem in any persuasive speech is to choose motives suitable to that subject for that particular audience. Then the article, idea, or value will seem desirable to the listeners.

PERSUADING BY PERSONALITY

The speaker's own personality—his character, reputation, and appearance—create a marked effect upon his auditors. The effect may be weak or powerful; it may be favorable and win the listeners over, or unfavorable and alienate them entirely. The importance of a speaker's credibility can be seen in the mixed responses of listeners during national elections.

A good man, as Plato pointed out, acquires prestige and fame for his goodness; his character has a powerful effect upon those who hear him speak. The man of honesty is believed, and the dishonest man is distrusted. The speaker who is an authority in his field has acquired prestige that bears great weight with listeners. Today's audiences respect a specialist and tend to accept what he says as probable truth.

The speaker, as Aristotle stated, should make his strongest appeal by personality while giving the speech. The speaker who presents facts and honestly discusses issues wins the respect of many listeners. The man who sincerely expresses his opinion and has the courage of his convictions may have a marked personal effect upon his audience. The influential speaker shows knowledge of his subject, experience, and seasoned judgment, and demonstrates these by the clear organization and original development of his material.

The delivery of the speech is an important part of the appeal by personality. To speak with an air of confidence and authority is proper, but the speaker must also speak with modesty and restraint. Exaggeration, extravagance, and frenzy inevitably put an audience on guard and weaken or destroy effectiveness.

SUGGESTION

Suggestion is mentioning or presenting something that arouses a thought or desire in the mind of another person. The "law" of suggestion states that every idea of an action will result in that action unless it is hindered by an opposing idea or action. Seeing a person yawn, for example, will cause us to yawn, unless we repress the impulse because we feel that it is impolite to yawn in front of others. Suggestion in persuasive speaking is closely involved with the use of language. Simple forms of suggestion are commands and requests.

The speaker can, at times, command; and some commands, when skillfully used, have a direct persuasive power. It is impossible, however, to command belief, and belief is important because it leads to constructive action.

The speaker may be able to obtain action by requests, but here too it is almost impossible to gain belief. Requests, however, have more suggestive power than commands, because they consider the feelings and self-esteem of listeners.

Suggestion is successful when it is accepted immediately by the listeners without criticism. Suggestion thus avoids criticism by avoiding controversy and gains acceptance by soliciting favorable emotional responses.

Types of Suggestion.   Suggestion may be direct or indirect. Direct suggestion makes an appeal to the listener's awareness; indirect suggestion influences listeners without their being conscious of it. Any suggestion may be positive or negative: it may encourage either favorable or unfavorable attitudes.

Factors of Suggestion.   A number of conditions make human beings open to suggestion. (1) A person is more suggestible when he is a member of a listening group. (2) A thought is accepted most quickly if it agrees with the listeners' habits, feelings, desires, and beliefs. (3) A person is more open to suggestion if his knowledge is less. Thus, children are more suggestible than adults. (4) The nature and attitude of the speaker also affect his powers of suggestion. Friendliness, for example, has great persuasive power. (5) Suggestion has the most effect if the person making it is highly regarded by the listeners. This is also true if the suggestion is part of, or connected with, an idea that has prestige. (6) Repeated suggestions have a cumulative and stronger effect, provided the repetitions are properly made without becoming irritating.

Use of Suggestion.   Sometimes a proposal will be more readily accepted if it is casually suggested rather than emphatically presented as an argumentative topic with formal proof. Listeners may act upon a suggestion without deliberation; on many occasions people respond automatically without being aware of, or feeling the need of, logical grounds for their action. For example, they may vote for a bond issue because it has been referred to as a progressive measure for a progressive community.

Indirect suggestion is usually better than direct. If a speaker says, "I'm here to persuade you to change your mind," or "I'm going to get you to agree with me," he immediately arouses resistance. Listeners accept his words as a dare and instinctively defy him to accomplish his purpose. Whenever possible, all semblance of argument or difference of opinion should be avoided. It is often wise to offer interesting supporting materials first that will suggest or lead to the point to be made.

There is a time for direct appeals, of course, but these should be made after the impulses of the audience have been stirred by indirect methods. Direct pleas for help and direct calls to duty are likely to stiffen resistance. This fact should be heeded by the persuasive speaker. He should first put his audience in the frame of mind for responding by tapping other motivations, such as the desire to be needed, love of justice, self-esteem, and admiration for human courage.

If suggestion is to be effective and is to produce the desired result, the speaker should make the idea or action irresistible to the listeners and then allow them to make up their own minds. Such tact and finesse can only be acquired by experience in living and speaking.

An outstanding example of persuasive suggestion is Martin Luther King's acceptance speech of the 1964 Nobel Peace Prize. Dr. King made no direct appeals for cooperation, but inspired belief in justice, peace, and brotherhood for all. Facts, ideas, emotions, and language were consistently used to suggest and elicit the faith, effort, and cooperation of all listeners. The speech should be read in its entirety, but the closing paragraphs may give an idea of its persuasive style.

> *You honor the ground crew without whose labor and sacrifice the jetflights to freedom could never have left the earth.*
>
> *Most of these people will never make the headlines and their names will not appear in Who's Who. Yet the years have rolled past and when the blazing light of truth is focused on this marvelous age in which we live—men and women will know and children will be taught*

that we have a finer land, a better people, a more noble civilization—because these humble children of God were willing to suffer for righteousness' sake.

I think Alfred Nobel would know what I mean when I say that I accept this award in the spirit of a curator of some precious heirloom which he holds in trust for its true owners—all those to whom beauty is truth and truth beauty—and in whose eyes the beauty of genuine brotherhood and peace is more precious than diamonds or silver or gold.[2]

Special Methods of Suggestion. Several methods of using suggestion may be singled out for special comment.

The "We" Approach. A speaker can bring his audience into the speech by frequently using the pronoun "we." He thus develops a community of interest as he thinks through a problem and reasons with his listeners. This method may enable him to lead into other aspects of the topic, to present new ideas, and to make his proposal seem inevitable.

The "Yes-Response" Approach. The "yes-response" is another indirect method of suggestion based on the avoidance of conflict. The speaker gains agreement by first presenting preliminary matters with which his listeners will readily agree. This appreciation of the speaker's viewpoints will increase their cooperation. After responding favorably to a number of primary considerations which are basic to the larger one, the listeners will be more easily motivated to accept the speaker's major proposal. They will say "yes" to what he is saying and also "yes" to what he is suggesting that they do. In other words, the oftener the speaker enables his listeners to say "yes," the easier it is for them to continue to say "yes."

The "This-or-Nothing" Approach. The speaker may convince an audience by showing them that his proposal is the only one that has value. He compares and contrasts other possible recommendations and demonstrates their inadequacies, and then proves that his solution is the sure and safe one to follow. By eliminating all other means of solving a problem, he should also show that his solution has already been accepted in some form, or that important parts of it are already approved, and that the only easy way for the audience to go is along the path of his proposal.

The Challenge.   The speaker may challenge the audience to understand and solve a problem. A challenge may succeed because it suggests that the listeners can understand and accomplish more than other people. However, anything in the wording of a challenge suggesting that listeners have been lax or unaware will turn them against the speaker and his idea.

Taking Agreement for Granted.   Sometimes the speaker can take it for granted that his audience agrees with him. This type of indirect suggestion depends on the right blend of appeals by reason, emotion, and personality, the whole being conveyed in language of the proper emotional tone.

THE USE AND ABUSE OF PERSUASION

Suggestion, which seeks immediate acceptance or rejection of persons, things, or ideas without proof or argument, depends upon the associations attached to words and symbols. Such persuasive devices can be put to fair and legitimate use for gaining cooperation toward worthy ends. Persuasion can also be put to unfair and illegitimate use for exploitation, and in the hands of the unscrupulous can be dangerous. Among the illogical techniques often used for misrepresentation are the following fallacies.

Name-Calling. An appeal is made to dislike, fears, and hostility by giving "bad" names to things, practices, and ideas which the speaker wants his audience to reject and condemn. This is sometimes called the "poison" device and consists of using such labels as appeaser, atheist, Communist, delinquent, hypocrite, reactionary, traitor, and warmonger entirely without proof.

Glittering Generalities. An attempt is made to get the audience to accept and approve something by associating it with approved ideas. "Good" names or "virtue" words are used, such as home, mother, freedom, and progress: "The defendant is a mother with three children." Sometimes the statements are so vague as to be practically meaningless: "So-and-so is a real pro."

Transference. By invoking the authority, sanction, and prestige of persons, ideas, and institutions which are respected and revered the speaker hopes that listeners will transfer their attitudes from one thing to the other: "If George Washington were alive today, he would approve this measure." "Russia has elections like any other democracy." "Furniture in the great American tradition."

The Testimonial. Another form of cashing in on the name and prestige of someone else is the testimonial, which is usually by a nonexpert in the field: "Aurora Smith prefers Drinkmore coffee." A variation is the vague testimony of alleged scientists or authorities who are not identified: "Leading financial experts approve this investment." "Recent scientific experiments prove that plant insecticides are contaminating our food supply."

Guilt by Association. When a negative attitude or rejection of a proposal is desired, the speaker associates it with persons, concepts, and institutions which are disapproved of by the audience: "This idea was once proposed by Hitler." "Communists, socialists, and radicals oppose states rights."

The "Plain Folks" Device. Persons and their ideas are praised or ridiculed by showing that they are like or different from other people. A candidate for office "has tousled hair and a boyish smile," "plays ball with the neighborhood children," or "takes his dogs along and goes fishing." "A principle as American and homely as apple pie (blueberry pie, fried chicken, ham and eggs, hot dogs, ice cream, roast turkey, steak, or in some sections baked beans, clam chowder, pecan pie, etc.)." On the other hand, "You don't have to go to college to know that." "A woman who looks after her husband and children doesn't have to run to a psychiatrist."

The "Band Wagon." Another appeal to the desire to conform is made by creating the impression that everyone believes or does something. "Don't throw your vote away—back the winner." "Everywhere you go, it's X Brand." "An idea that is sweeping the country like wildfire."

Card Stacking. An attempt is often made to establish a point by evading facts or dodging issues. The speaker chooses only favorable examples, facts, or opinions, even though they are not fair and representative. "Every housewife knows that food prices are too high." "Red-blooded, hard-working, risk-taking Americans built this great country." A new issue or "red herring" may be brought up to avoid discussing a certain point. "Our town is well run; just look at the scandals in Washington." "The record shows that we are a law abiding state when you compare it with the crime rate in New York City." "An investigation will waste the taxpayers' money."

The "Scapegoat" Device. The speaker appeals to the desire to escape responsibility for conditions by blaming them on someone else. The basis is usually racial, national, religious, or political. "The conservatives let everything go down the drain." "We didn't have this trouble before the summer people came in."

The "Black-or-White" Device. An attempt is sometimes made to justify a point by dividing people, things, or ideas into mutually exclusive "good" and "bad" groups, such as Christian and atheist, or radical and reactionary. This device ignores the fact that many items are part of a spectrum containing many divisions or "shades of gray."

The Speaker's Responsibility. The best defense against unfair persuasion is, of course, careful listening and critical evaluation. Listeners should decide whether a statement or proposal is justified by the facts. However, the whole burden of fairness should not be placed upon the audience. A good speaker does not misrepresent, but has high ethical standards of honesty, truthfulness, and justice. He realizes that he helps create the world we live in and fulfills his obligation to society by refusing to deceive, mislead, or manipulate his listeners. All his appeals, regardless of what others may do, should be guided and justified by the well-being of his fellow men.

The speaker is estimating his audience and his audience is estimating him. His ethics, his integrity, understanding, and humanity are strong forces for good and also strong components of his "ethos" or personal effect on not only his present but also his future audiences. The speaker should therefore make sure that the actual situation permits him to use a given persuasive device. Lincoln said: "If you would win a man to your cause, you must first convince him that you are his sincere friend." And, to make an adaptation of Emerson, the best way to do that is to *be* one.

15.
OCCASIONAL SPEECHES

An occasional speech is one designed for and presented at a special affair. Although every speech is suited to a given audience, the occasional speech is almost entirely conditioned by a special time, place, and event.

The occasional speech may have any of the following general purposes, singly or in combination: to inform, to persuade, to inspire, or to entertain. The last two are particularly important, because most speeches for special occasions are intended to give pleasure and to create an atmosphere of good will.

All types of occasional speeches have elements in common. Only a few of the most frequently given types will be discussed here.

GENERAL CHARACTERISTICS

The elements of public speaking previously discussed naturally apply to occasional speeches. Some considerations, however, are more important than others and deserve particular mention.

Mood. Each occasion has a special feeling or atmosphere, because the participants in the situation expect a certain tone to prevail. The speaker should heighten this mood and avoid disappointing the predisposed feeling of his audience. A formal university convocation does not lend itself to a feeling of frivolity, although the seriousness of purpose can be enlivened by suitable touches of humor. On the other hand, a speech given after cocktails and dinner is seldom solemn or impassioned, although brightness of mood can be enriched by a basically serious idea.

Material.   The content of the speech should be in keeping with what the audience expects to hear. Much of the material will come from the nature of the group or organization and its concern with this particular occasion. Besides being appropriate, the material should be accurate and just, positive rather than negative. The occasional speech is not the time to find fault, to prove a point, to bring up unpleasant matters, or to stir up controversy. Statements of constructive value are most suitable for special occasions.

Structure.   The plan of each occasional speech should be immediately perceptible and easy to follow. Ideas should flow clearly from one to the other without complications or confusion.

Language.   Since the subject matter of an occasional speech is rarely new, the language used should be fresh and vibrant. Colorful words that paint vivid and enjoyable pictures are valuable. However, flowery and superficial words and phrases should be avoided, such as "with fabulous results," "the rest is history," "this esteemed man," "this great state (country, city, company, school, etc.)."

The use of trite and hackneyed phrases is an unfortunate but common fault: "last but not least," "has become a household word," "the one and only," "a man who needs no introduction," "like the weather, everybody talks about it but nobody does anything about it." The wise speaker is careful to avoid expressions which he knows have been overused by others.

The speaker's expressions should actually reflect his emotional attitudes. Statements like the following are inadvisable unless the speaker honestly believes them: "That was the proudest moment of my life," "This is the most wonderful thing that ever happened to me."

Time.   The length of the occasional speech requires special consideration. For the most part, these speeches should be brief. Such factors as the duration of the entire ceremony, the number of other speakers on the program, and the mood of the occasion make the adherence to a time limit of the utmost importance.

Delivery.   The speaker should show confidence and poise. His tone should harmonize with the formality or the informality of the occasion, expressing the dignity or casualness that is demanded. He should seem pleasant and animated, or quiet and sincere. At times emotion plays a strong part in a ceremony, but it should be restrained. The speaker should not let emotion completely master him, so that his own individuality and self-possession disappear.

THE SPEECH OF GOODWILL

A frequent type of public speaking today is the speech of goodwill. Most business and professional organizations find them useful in winning the approval and support of the public. Organizations with extensive operations maintain speakers' bureaus and encourage officers and administrators to appear before audiences. They are thus able to fulfill the frequent requests from other groups that desire information and seasoned judgment.

Purpose. The purpose of a speech of goodwill is to inform and to get listeners to understand the topic. The information is also presented for an underlying reason; to secure the goodwill and friendship of the listeners by enabling them to appreciate the speaker's organization, project, or cause. Persuasive techniques are therefore necessary, but they must not be obtrusive. The persuasion is unexpressed: it is to promote approval rather than sales. The obvious persuasiveness of a sales talk has no place in a speech of goodwill, for it puts listeners "on guard."

Topics. The information may be about almost any aspect of an organization, its services, and how it performs them for the benefit of the community, the nation, or mankind. Other topics concern research, development of better products, methods of production and distribution, furnishing fresh solutions to new and old problems.

Occasions. Speeches of goodwill are presented at a wide variety of events. Special breakfasts, luncheons, and dinners usually have an invited speaker. Conventions, forums, meetings of business, professional, and social clubs, and other gatherings are occasions for speeches of goodwill. Speakers are also invited to churches, school and college assemblies, and special education courses and programs. The occasions have been multiplying each year.

Suggestions. When planning the speech of goodwill, make sure you offer novel or interesting facts about your topic. Present essential knowledge or "inside information." Explain newer developments and

their possibilities. Show a definite relationship between your topic
and the lives of your listeners today and in the future. Offer to
answer questions during the speech or afterward. Demonstrate that
you and your organization are at the listeners' service by offering
a specific service, such as an invitation to visit your office or plant.

A speech of goodwill is not a "bandwagon" talk. It is truthful.
It tells what your organization is, what it does, and what it can
do. Never promise that it will do what it will be unable to do. This
applies even to little things. If you say you will redeem a coupon,
redeem it. If a customer sends in a rebate form for a dollar, send
him the dollar; otherwise he may desert you and your product.

A speech of goodwill must be based on the actual conduct and
practices of your organization. We all find satisfaction in dealing
with some groups, for they have courteous, efficient people who treat
their clients as human beings. On the other hand, a speech of goodwill
is a waste of time if your organization is made up of discourteous,
inefficient beings who are interested only in their own egos. People
enjoy spending money and they also enjoy getting good value for
it.

INTRODUCTION SPEECHES

A speech of introduction presents a speaker to an audience, and
is the most frequently used occasional speech. It has a double function: to make the audience eager to hear the speaker and to make
the speaker eager to speak to the audience. The introduction speech
is a two-way bridge between speaker and listener: it arouses a favorable attitude toward the speaker and his subject, and, by so doing,
it encourages the speaker by presenting him with an interested audience.

The introduction speech should be brief but adequate. The better
known the speaker, the shorter the introduction. For example: "La-
dies and gentlemen, the President of the United States." On most
occasions the introduction speech would last a minute or two.

Preparation.   Adequate information about the guest speaker's
life, experience, and achievement should be found. If possible, the
speaker himself should be asked for important points about himself.
His topic should be considered. An overall view of its history, princi-

ples, applications, and importance is necessary. What special relationship does it have to this audience or occasion?

The audience should be analyzed. An estimate should be made of how much the listeners know about the speaker and how they regard him. If he is well known and well regarded, two or three interesting points about him in the introduction will be enough; if not, persuasive material may be needed to reveal him in a favorable light. How much the audience knows about the speaker's topic should be gauged. It may be necessary to affirm the importance of the subject or to give significant background material.

Only the outstanding points about the speaker and his qualifications should be chosen, and a minimum of essential material used about the background and importance of the subject. The task is to show as simply as possible why this topic presented by this speaker is vital to this audience at this time. If the speaker is well known, the material in the introduction speech should be about the background and importance of the subject. If the subject is well known, the material should be on the background and importance of the speaker. If neither the speaker nor the subject is well known, the importance of both must be clearly shown.

Plan.   The speech of introduction should follow a plan, such as the following, in which the essential material is arranged in a climactic order: (1) A story, incident, or anecdote based on some achievement of the speaker. This leads to the speaker's name and topic. (2) The importance of the topic in the world of today. (3) The special connection and concern of the audience with the topic. (4) The main qualifications of the speaker to deal with the topic. (5) The presentation of the speaker.

Suggestions.   The introducing speaker should not speak on the topic itself, for to do so would rob the guest speaker of his best effect. The topic is his domain. Nor should the introduction be an extended speech; that is the speaker's province. The introducer features the speaker without overpraising him or picturing him as a great speaker. It is best to let the speaker prove his ability in his own way. At the close of the introduction, the introducer announces the speaker's name, turns and yields the floor to him with a smile, and then sits down.

SPEECHES OF WELCOME

The overall purpose of a speech of welcome is to stimulate goodwill by a public greeting on certain occasions, such as introducing a new member to an organization, welcoming guests at a banquet, and greeting delegates at a convention.

The plan of the speech should make clear to whom the welcome is extended, by whom, and why. A useful arrangement is the following:

1. The name of the person or group being greeted: "Dr. John Bright"; "Members of the City Improvement League"; "Sales managers of our Chicago branch."
2. Who is offering the welcome: "As mayor of Belleville, I cordially welcome you to our city."
3. Why the welcome is being made: "All the members of the Twenty-five Year Club join me in welcoming you into our association."
4. The spirit or purpose of the occasion and what it means to those present: "Twenty years ago our Civic Orchestra was just an idea in the minds of a few amateur performers. Today it is a widely acclaimed organization of ninety professional musicians, whose concerts are an outstanding feature of our cultural life. To the founders, supporters, and members of the Orchestra the stature of our new conductor is the reward for twenty years of effort and devotion."
5. Tribute to some achievement or to the general high regard of the person being welcomed: "Miss Mary Doe is president of the State Garden Club and is author of the book *Garden Design for the Beginner*. She is perhaps best known for her column in the Daily Gazette."
6. The pleasure and benefit to be derived from mutual association now and in the future: "Mr. Blank, by locating his new plant here, proves the value of cooperation between a progressive industry and a progressive community. The enterprise will provide employment for several hundred local people, create a market for new services, and attract other industries to our township."
7. Reextension of the opening welcome: "It's a pleasure to have you here on Alumni Day and we hope you will enjoy the experience of being back on campus."

Some praise should be included in a speech of welcome; its absence will be noted and perhaps considered a slight. However, overpraise or any statement that might embarrass the guest should be avoided. Where it is suitable and comes naturally, the visitor's contact with the group and with its activities can be mentioned. A speech of welcome should be made with sincerity, cordiality, and an awareness of the importance of the occasion. The guest should not be urged to make a speech in reply. In short, everything said and done makes the visitor feel appreciated and at ease.

SPEECHES OF REPLY TO A WELCOME

On some occasions the response to a welcome is simply a warm smile and a quiet "Thank you." Such modest brevity is sufficient and appropriate when the audience is small and the atmosphere is informal. At more serious occasions and before a larger audience a formal reply to a welcome is usually needed. Listeners want to hear as well as see important visitors. When a group has been welcomed, the reply is made by a member who has been designated in advance for this task.

While the response to a welcome is short, it should be long enough to make listeners feel that the visitor appreciates the reception. The speaker is also expected to say something worth hearing; his speech therefore needs a theme. A satisfactory response to a welcome should: (1) Identify for whom and to whom the visitor is speaking. (2) Express real appreciation for being so honored. (3) Pay tribute to the person, organization, institution, or community offering the welcome. (4) Present the theme briefly. (5) Close with an anticipation of pleasant future associations.

SPEECHES OF PRESENTATION

A speech of presentation accompanies a publicly bestowed gift or honor. The purpose of such a speech is to inspire admiration for a person's character and achievement. The speech should be suited to the gift, the receiver, and the occasion. The speech is addressed to the receiver, but at the same time it should be of interest to the whole audience and phrased in such a way that each listener feels that he is included in the remarks. A typical presentation speech should: (1) Tell why the presentation is being made. (2) Identify the receiver and praise him for his accomplishments, his specific services or contributions, and for his worthy qualities. If the recipient is accepting the honor in behalf of a group, the speech of presentation identifies and commends the ideals, purposes, and services of the organization. (3) Indentify and express the speaker's own satisfaction

in presenting the gift as a symbol of continuing esteem. (4) Describe
the gift or award and present it to the receiver.

ACCEPTANCE SPEECHES

The receiver of a gift or award often gives a speech of acceptance
to show his appreciation and gratitude. The speech should be arranged to fit in naturally with the preceding speech of presentation,
and should continue in the prevailing mood. An acceptance speech
is short, certainly never longer than the speech of presentation.
Awards made to a number of persons require only a simple "Thank
you."

Whether the award is made solely to the speaker or to the organization which he represents, the speaker should keep himself out of
his acceptance remarks as much as possible as he does the following:
(1) Expresses appreciation for the gift or honor and shares his pleasure
with those present. (2) Relates himself (or the group he represents)
in some way to the giver, and praises him meaningfully without
overdoing it. (3) Gives credit for his achievement to the help of
others, to his profession, or the group to which he belongs: he does
not claim it all as a personal honor. (4) Tells what the award means
to him and how it will urge him on to greater efforts.

The speaker looks at the person who hands him the gift and then
looks directly at the gift as he shows his pleasure in it. On some
informal occasions, the listeners may wish to see a gift that is
wrapped, for many in the audience may not know what is being
presented. In that event, the speaker unwraps the gift when he receives
it and holds it up so that everyone can see it.

AFTER-DINNER SPEECHES

Any talk adapted to the social atmosphere of a group dinner is
an after-dinner speech. It may vary in subject matter and approach
but usually has congeniality and good-fellowship in common. The
mood of the occasion is relatively comfortable, relaxed, and uncritical.
The audience is interested in both light and serious topics, but may
not wish to be stirred to intellectual heights or emotional depths. A
toastmaster is usually a feature of the after-dinner speaking situation.

The general purpose of many after-dinner speeches is to entertain.
However, because dinners are given by many kinds of organizations
for a variety of reasons, the purpose of the speech may be to inform

or persuade. Although they are usually light speeches or sometimes toasts, after-dinner speeches may be serious.

Serious Speeches.   The serious after-dinner speech presents an important theme in a pleasant and graceful manner. An unusual theme is desirable or an unusual treatment of a familiar theme.

The introduction should be diverting or amusing so as to establish a comfortable feeling of rapport between the speaker and his listeners. The body of the speech should be arranged like that of other informative or persuasive speeches, but the structure should be kept as simple as possible. The ideas should be developed to suit the occasion with lively illustrations, striking analogies, or pertinent humorous examples. A story, however, should not be told just for the sake of the laugh; the laugh should be gotten for the sake of the idea. The language of the speech should stimulate the audience; a flexible, conversational style is most effective. The speaker should not read his speech unless it is absolutely necessary, because talking directly to the listeners is more intimate and persuasive.

The length of the after-dinner speech is often fifteen or twenty minutes, and a half-hour speech is sometimes expected. An experienced and gifted speaker can hold an after-dinner audience for a longer time. However, being important or famous does not automatically make a person a good speaker. Even though he may be the only speaker scheduled for the occasion, the speaker should resist the temptation to talk too long. William James once said that "nothing is worth treating in a thousand pages." At dinners, nothing is worth talking about for an hour.

Toasts.   Some after-dinner speeches include a special short tribute, or toast, usually accompanying a drink, to a person or object. It is best to fit the material to the time, place, and group. Some reference to the toastmaster or to a preceding speaker can sometimes be made. A toast usually: (1) Introduces the subject with a note of cheerfulness or even playfulness. (2) Points out and illustrates the subject's unusual or entertaining aspects, or (3) Points out and illustrates the subject's more serious and enduring aspects, or (4) Suggests some underlying value of the subject that is worth remembering.

Light Speeches.   The light speech may be an informal or narrative speech designed to be primarily humorous or entertaining.

Informal Speech. An informal after-dinner speech has a definite theme. The theme is some kind of simple central idea or viewpoint that gives purpose to the anecdotes, jokes, and other illustrations. If the material includes a worthwhile thought or serious idea, it will be more stimulating to the audience.

The material is arranged in a psychological order for variety of interest and cumulative effect. Sparkling and humorous illustrations are expressed in sprightly words. The right word at the right time is an important part of entertainment. A series of disconnected funny stories and incidents is generally less effective. A good informal speech is short, but leaves the audience wishing for more.

Narrative Speech. A narrative speech relates an interesting or humorous experience. Telling a story is an age-old way of entertaining an audience. Narratives include anecdotes from the lives of people, personal experiences, travel talks, parables, fables, episodes from history, and current events. Some humorous stories have a surprise ending and may thus resemble a long and elaborate joke. Audiences like human interest stories and tales that take them into strange and exciting situations. They enjoy sympathizing with other people and delight in living for a while in another world.

A narrative should have some sort of progression. The sequence of events may grow out of opposition or conflict and move to a climax or solution; in that case, just enough description is used to paint the characters and setting without hindering the forward movement of the plot.

A narrative speech begins with an arresting detail and gets underway at once. The sequence of actions moves ahead and gets somewhere. Events follow in their proper order, which is necessarily chronological. Jumping from place to place or from time to time in a narrative speech confuses the listeners and spoils the story. A definite, strong, and satisfying ending is a necessity.

In presenting a narrative, the speaker pictures in his mind's eye the things he is describing. He seeks to keep events happening at a fast pace, but slows down and pauses to emphasize important effects and to build up suspense. Changes of mood and emotion are often important. The speaker can sometimes use characterization: he talks as the characters would talk (if he can do it well) or suggests each character by a significant change of pitch, rate, volume, or manner of phrasing. While he is relating his story, the speaker watches his listeners and tries to adapt his manner, pacing, and wording to suit their reactions.

The Toastmaster. A common assumption is that a good toastmaster must be a funny man and tell a series of jokes throughout the dinner. This ability is helpful but is not always necessary. The toastmaster should be friendly, good-humored, alert, and able to adjust himself to the listeners and the situation in an easy, outgoing manner. Tact and good taste, of course, are necessary for directing a dinner program and keeping it running smoothly. The toastmaster's functions include the arranging of the program and the actual conducting of it.

Since the toastmaster is usually responsible for the entire dinner program, his work may start weeks before the affair. If he can get support from an effective committee in deciding and carrying out the purpose of the occasion, his workload may be lightened. Although the toastmaster may be required to plan the meal and arrange for its service, his main responsibilities are to decide the seating of the guests and to plan and conduct the program.

Seating of Guests. The guests must be seated where all can see the speaker's table, and should be placed as close together as possible in order to create an atmosphere of unity. Several seating arrangements are possible, depending on the size of the room and the number of guests. Three frequently used arrangements are in the form of a T, a U, or a square. Another common arrangement for large groups is a long table on a platform with many small tables arranged in front of it.

The toastmaster occupies the central position at the head table with the main speaker on his right. The other speakers are seated alternately to his left and right. For the benefit of arriving guests, a seating chart can be posted at the entrance to the room. This diagram will save the scramble and confusion resulting from individuals searching around the tables for their place cards.

Planning the Program. Among the toastmaster's first duties is determining the theme of the occasion and the length of the entire affair. The after-dinner program should not be too long; usually an hour is enough. The toastmaster decides the number of speakers and the time limit for each. On most occasions, preliminary speeches should last about five minutes and the main speech about twenty minutes.

The toastmaster chooses possible main and preliminary speakers and secures those available for the given date and hours. He tells all speakers exactly how long they are expected to speak and asks them not to exceed their time limit. Like the preparer of an introduction speech, the toastmaster gathers information about his scheduled speakers so as to be able to talk interestingly about them. He also makes sure he can remember their names and pronounce them correctly.

The speaking order begins with those of less importance and ends with the main speaker of the evening. However, when doubtful of protocol, the toastmaster follows the safe plan of arranging the speakers alphabetically with, of course, the main speaker still last. If possible, the program should be arranged for variety; for example, a light speech might follow a serious one, or two talks with greatly different themes could follow one another.

Conducting the Program.   Before the dinner begins, the toastmaster should arrive early enough to welcome the guest speakers. He sees that all guests are comfortable, and appoints someone to check and remedy such problems as ventilation, lighting, and serving during the entire affair.

The program should begin on time and should be kept moving along at a lively pace. The toastmaster sustains the theme of the occasion and makes sure that the program is a concerted effort of all participants. The toastmaster guides the proceedings, fills in when necessary, but carefully avoids taking over the whole show.

Some toastmasters talk too much while others say too little. A good toastmaster talks concisely and to the point, thus allowing the speakers the time they need to do their best. During the evening, the toastmaster will give a number of brief speeches, beginning the program with a warm welcome and expressing thanks to all at the program's close.

USING HUMOR

Humor, if judiciously used, is a valuable means of support, not only in speeches of entertainment but in all speeches. The use of humor demands insight, judgment, and skill; otherwise it may fail of its purpose. Successful humor is based on an understanding of its nature.

Elements of Humor. Humor is said to be composed of various psychological elements: playfulness, self-esteem, and incongruity.

Playfulness. Human beings like to have fun and enjoy themselves; they like to relieve the monotony of life with change and excitement and to escape the pressure of reality by creating an imaginary world. Language can be a form of recreation, a playing with meanings and sounds.

Self-Esteem. We laugh at peculiarities, slips of the tongue, and odd mishaps because we feel superior to them. Our point of view may be challenged for a moment, but it triumphs in the end. We laugh at the foibles and ideas of others because it gives us a sense of superiority.

Incongruity. Incongruity depends on disharmony and surprise; things are not as they usually seem. The lesser is considered greater, or the greater seems lesser for the time. The self-important are toppled down, the lowly come out on top after danger or difficulty. Exaggeration and understatement are other forms of incongruity.

Types of Humor. Humor is divided and classified in various ways; amusing stories, anecdotes, and jokes are familiar forms. A distinction is often made between wit and humor. Wit is the ability to perceive the incongruous and to reveal it in expressions which are sudden, startling, and often scornful and malicious. Humor is the ability to see and express the ludicrous and ridiculous in a kindly, sympathetic, or pathetic light. The following are a few of the forms of wit and humor that have been used in speeches.

Satire. Satire is cutting and destructive and it uses ridicule, sarcasm, and irony for moral purposes. Famous examples of satire in literature are *Aesop's Fables, Don Quixote, Gulliver's Travels,* and *Babbitt.*

Irony. Irony is the use of words humorously or sarcastically for a meaning contradictory to the literal expression.

I fear I wrong the honorable men whose daggers have stabbed Caesar.—
WILLIAM SHAKESPEARE

Epigram. An epigram is a terse, pointed, witty statement. Epigrams originally were in verse and sometimes still are. Their subject matter is practically unlimited. The following are typical examples:

LADY BRACKNELL: *I dislike arguments of all kinds. They are always vulgar, and often convincing.*—OSCAR WILDE

A pang of conscience is the cheapest way of avoiding an obligation.

Caricature. The caricature exaggerates distinguishing traits or mannerisms. Cartoons are familiar examples of emphasizing the ridiculous. Verbal caricatures are often short: His vision and ambition encompass the whole of Fort Knox. She has a weight problem: when she lies in bed she hangs down to the floor on each side.

Repartee. Repartee is the ability to make a quick, skillful retort with wit or humor. Repartee is sometimes the art of insult, an aspect that seldom suits a public speaking situation. An example of humorous repartee occurs in Sheridan's *School for Scandal:*

SIR PETER TEAZLE: *The fashion, indeed! What had you to do with fashion before you married me?*

LADY TEAZLE: *For my part, I should think you would like to have your wife thought a woman of taste.*

SIR PETER TEAZLE: *Ay, there again: taste! Zounds! madam, you had no taste when you married me!*

LADY TEAZLE: *That's very true indeed, Sir Peter; and, after having married you, I should never pretend to taste again, I allow.*

Quips. A quip is a witty or humorous expression or allusion: "She sings in five languages, and I can't even sing in English." "Look at that face: it has outlived three bodies." "She is truly like the Venus de Milo. She is unbelievably old; she has no teeth; and her body is covered with yellow spots." (Heine)

Jokes. Jokes are of a varied nature, but many of them are highly condensed stories, in which everything exists for the point. The point may be thoughtful or trivial, but it is unpredictable and arouses a surprised realization.

"Do you believe in prayer?" asked the prison chaplain.
"Sure," the convict replied. "But you have to ask for the right things."
The chaplain nodded in agreement. "What made you realize that?"
"Well, when I used to pray to be able to put money in the bank,

nothing happened. But I got real results when I began praying to be able to get money out of the bank."

Puns. A pun is a play on two or more meanings of a word or of two words with the same sound. The humorous effect of a pun depends upon its originality.

"I don't like ugly rumors."
"Neither do I. I like them young and good-looking."

Definitions. A witty or humorous definition might be called a play on ideas: *"rock-and-rollers:* long-hair singers, short-pants music." Disraeli drew the distinction between a misfortune and a calamity in this manner:

If, let us say, Mr. Gladstone were to fall into the Thames, that would be a misfortune. But if anyone were to pull him out, that would be a calamity.

Word Mergers. A word is sometimes made from elements of two other words to create a striking or humorous effect, such as "platitudinarian," and "Reno-vated." In a trial in Westchester County, Joseph Choate evolved words from Westchester and Chesterfield and from urbanity and suburb: "I hope," the opposing lawyer said, "the gentlemen of the jury will not be influenced by my opponent's Chesterfieldian urbanity." "And I hope," replied Choate, "that the gentlemen will not be misled by my opponent's Westchesterfieldian suburbanity."

Misquotations. Quotations can be distorted for humorous purposes by misquoting them or by adding extraneous material: "A thing of beauty is a joy forever if you can keep the children away from it." "Keep the home fires burning as long as the insurance company keeps paying up."

Value of Humor. Humor has several important functions in public speaking. It can illustrate and develop the theme of the speech. Humor can be used to gain, regain, and retain attention and interest. It is a good way to relieve tensions in both audience and speaker. Humor creates a friendly, comfortable atmosphere. It is apt to disarm listeners and make them less critical, and it is a perfect way to give variety and balance to a speech. Humor can be advantageous in any speech except those given in times of crisis and urgent need.

Requirements of Humor. If humor is to be helpful, it should advance the purpose of the speech. It should be fresh, friendly and good-natured and always in good taste, rather than bitter and vindictive. If in doubt about humor, the speaker should not use it, because the chances are it is not suitable.

Where to Find Humor. The best place for the speaker to find wit and humor is in himself. His own observation, experience, and imagination are all that are needed. It is useful, however, to listen to humor, to analyze it, and to understand its various forms. The following books will suggest types of material: Max Eastman's *Enjoyment of Laughter,* Louis Untermeyer's *A Treasury of Laughter,* Evan Esar's *Dictionary of Humorous Quotations,* and Bennet Cerf's *Encyclopedia of Modern American Humor.*

If an old story is used, it should be changed by giving it a new setting, some new characters, or a new slant. All borrowed humor should be adapted to fit exactly the requirements of the speech. Nothing is actually new; it is the new combination of old elements that is strikingly original.

Presenting Humor. Humor should be delivered with ease, whether in a relaxed, deadpan manner or with an air of lively enjoyment. Stiff attitudes and forced smiles are both out of key.

Whenever a speaker hears a good joke or story, he should tell it to the next few friends or acquaintances he meets. He can check the effect when he tells it with an expressionless face and also when he tells it with bodily expression, such as an expectant smile, shrug of the shoulder, or other gesture. After several tellings the speaker will find that the right words will come, the right vocal inflections and the right emphatic snap on the point.

The speaker should avoid overusing humor. Every remark should not be bright and amusing. Humor is the seasoning, not the food of the speech. The speaker must also know how to turn the audience to a serious mood again by thoughtfulness in language, tone of voice, and facial expression. The switching from humorous to serious moods can also be practiced in conversations with friends and acquaintances. The speaker should not try too hard or too persistently to be funny. If he finds he cannot use humor easily, he should avoid it.

Some humorists pause until the audience laughs, but making such a demand from listeners is unwise for most speakers. If the hearers discover the humor for themselves, they will appreciate it all the more. The speaker never laughs at his humor unless his listeners do, and even then, he joins in with their laughter with a sense of rapport.

16.
RADIO AND TELEVISION SPEAKING

The speaker who wishes to use radio and television may be more successful if he understands the nature and basic requirements of broadcast speaking. The speaker on radio or TV appeals to an invisible audience. Even though on some occasions there may be a studio audience, the main audience consists of tuned in listeners, an audience that the speaker can only imagine.

Broadcast listeners are separated in space, listening by ones, twos, or threes in their own homes. Group psychology does not work; there is no catching and sharing of common enthusiasm from other members of a large group. What may happen among studio listeners does not necessarily happen to the isolated listeners. The speaker should make his appeal to the individual listener; if he does this successfully, he may sway millions of people.

When broadcasting, the speaker cannot adjust or vary his message or presentation to his audience, because he has no way of seeing, hearing, and sensing his listeners' response. He addresses presumable listeners whom he can only hope are responding favorably.

When a studio audience is present the speaker then has the advantages of responding listeners. The microphone, however, may still hinder him, for he cannot turn away from it. A lavaliere microphone (one that hangs from the neck) gives more freedom of movement and more sense of direct communication.

The speaker must hold interest no matter what limitations are placed upon him. Home listeners can leave him at any time by turning the dial. Therefore, a climactic arrangement of material is best, with a closing that is especially strong.

AUDIENCE AND SUBJECT

The broadcast audience potentially includes everyone. A speaker on radio or TV will almost certainly have more types of listeners than with a live, present audience. Persons of all ages, occupations, beliefs, prejudices, interests, and degrees of intelligence may be listening.

Some idea of the type of audience may be realized by noting the hour of the broadcast, the day of the week, and the type of program. Nonworking women will probably predominate during the day, except on Saturday and Sunday. Late afternoon and early evening might include younger listeners, while late evening attracts an audience of adults. Certain programs draw persons with special interests. Listeners to a local station will probably be interested in regional affairs; listeners to a network, in topics of wider or national interest.

To reach a wide and mixed audience, the subject should have as broad or universal an appeal as possible and be based on human interests or motivations. The speech should be understandable to a person using common sense rather than to a person with subtle intellect. The President of the United States delivers several such speeches each year. His speech writers strive for simplicity and clarity by using nontechnical language and a logical structure. For instance, President Carter delivered such a speech to the nation on March 14, 1980, concerning the economy. After pointing out that the present high inflation was threatening the economic security of the nation, he announced and outlined five major ways to control it.

ORGANIZATION AND SUPPORT

A broadcast speech benefits by a simple and easy-to-follow arrangement, such as the topical or psychological. The best plan is usually to cover a few important points well, avoiding side issues, secondary issues, and minute details. An elaborate organization is especially hard to grasp on radio, because facial expression, gestures, and other visual clues to meaning are lacking. In his first "fireside chat" in March 1933, Franklin D. Roosevelt, in a clear, coherent sequence, explained his proclamation of a national bank holiday: the public

fear of banks leading up to their closing; the program of gradual
bank rehabilitation; the regulations permitting the banks to perform
interim necessary functions; the providing of adequate currency by
the twelve Federal Reserve Banks; the gradual reopening of banks
pending approval by the government; and the necessity for public
confidence.

Supporting material should be concrete, down-to-earth, and lively.
Developmental materials are perhaps most effective when based on
the daily experiences and activities of average people.

The first example is from a speech entitled "The Economy" by
Joseph J. Pinola, the chairman of the board of Western Bancorpora-
tion:

> *In fact, the budget has inspired a new "good news-bad news" story.
> It goes like this: The good news is that the federal government will
> be able to pay people their income tax refunds this year. The bad
> news is that it will have to use post-dated checks.*
>
> *That's because the press they use to print the money broke down.
> If that sounds like gallows humor, it's because it is gallows humor.
> But it's no laughing matter.*
>
> *To put inflation in more human terms, listen to this! The typical
> family's grocery bill has risen 60 percent in the last five years, according
> to government figures. That's an average of 12 percent a year. Has
> the "typical" family increased its income by that much? Not as far
> as I know.*[1]

The second example is from John F. Kennedy's Inaugural Address
in January, 1961:

> *To those peoples in the huts and villages of half the globe struggling
> to break the bonds of mass misery, we pledge our best efforts to help
> them help themselves, for whatever period is required—not because
> the Communists may be doing it, not because we seek their votes, but
> because it is right. If a free society cannot help the many who are
> poor, it cannot save the few who are rich.*

TIME FACTOR

The length of the speech is of prime importance. Usually, in a
fifteen minute program the speaker will speak only from twelve to
thirteen minutes. The wise speaker knows the time allotted to him

[1] *Vital Speeches,* XLIV, 14 (May 1, 1978), p. 440.

and plans, practices, and revises his speech to fill it exactly. One protection is to have both a long and short conclusion ready. Then the one that fits the time limitation best can be used. Or, before the conclusion, an example or anecdote of a certain length can be either included or omitted.

In rehearsing the speech, the manuscript should be marked at the place the speaker reaches after reading one minute, two minutes, etc. This will help him to broadcast the speech at the desired rate. When near the end, these time notations will serve as a guide in adjusting the final material to the time limit.

TAPING OF SPEECHES

In many cases the radio speech is taped in a public situation and then rebroadcast. The television studios commonly tape their programs ahead of time. The taping is usually done only once. The speaker who approaches the taping session thinking, "If I make a mistake, I can correct it," is usually wrong. Tape editing is very costly and only the major networks are in a position to edit or retape a broadcast. Even though most radio and television broadcasts are taped, the speaker should approach his presentation as though it were before a live audience.

RADIO SPEAKING

Radio speaking includes impromptu and extemporaneous speaking; speeches, however, are usually read from a manuscript. The radio speaker is guided in his preparation not only by the type of program, its purpose, and the expected kind of audience, but also by the radio situation itself.

Radio Versus Television Speaking. An important difference between giving a speech on radio and on televsion is that radio listeners cannot see the speaker. They can only imagine his character and personality from what they hear. Attention must therefore be secured at once, in the very first sentence. Attention cannot be secured and held by a smile, manner, or gestures while audience interest is gradually built up. No circular response or feedback is possible.

It is also difficult to speak extemporaneously into a cold microphone and to avoid a dead interval while one searches for words. It is better to write the speech so it can be adequately practiced and accurately timed. Since it then becomes a manuscript speech to be read aloud, the speaker will be aided by a study of Chapter 21, which deals with oral reading.

The rate for radio speaking tends to be somewhat faster than for television, because the speaker does not have the advantage of visual communication. Pauses tend to be shorter for the same reason. An over-rapid rate, however, quickly fatigues some listeners; trying to keep up with the speaker causes them to lose much of the meaning.

It is important to give careful value to essential connecting words, such as *but, since, however,* and *therefore.* Ignoring them may make the relationships of ideas unclear, because listeners cannot see how these transitions are indicated by bodily or facial gestures. Connectives are also essential to let the listeners know where they have been, where they are, and where they are going.

Using the Microphone.   When speaking into a microphone the speaker faces special technical problems. In most cases he does not have to worry in advance about these matters. The audio engineer will first get a voice level to see how the speaker's voice sounds. He will then instruct the speaker how close to the microphone he should stand or sit. This distance should be kept fairly constant. It is not necessary to speak very close to the microphone to come across. The speaker who does so may appear to place intimacy above subject matter. Swaying forward and backward or from side to side causes the volume of the voice to vary unpleasantly. Turning away from the microphone should be avoided, for words may be lost entirely. Staying in the correct position avoids distortion of tone.

Volume.   A conversational range of volume is best, as though the speaker were talking to people a few feet away. Sudden, loud, staccato stresses and blasting emphasis should not be used. Also to be avoided is a fading away into silence. Stress should be conveyed by a change in vocal color, emphasis by a gradual gain in intensity.

Pitch.   The medium or medium-low area of the speaker's pitch range allows the voice to be used with ease and flexibility. Pitch inflections for radio are generally more varied and somewhat wider than those of polite conversation.

The speaker should guard against speaking in a higher key because of nervousness. A high pitch range requires more breath, tends to make a person more nervous, and is often grating and strident. It is important to use the voice in its best range, which has the optimum pitch as its center.

Other Noises. Speech is all that should enter the microphone. The speaker should avoid clearing his throat, sniffling, or coughing directly into the microphone. If he has to perform these actions he should turn his face away, muffle the sound in a handkerchief, quietly say, "Excuse me," and resume the speech. A good radio speaker avoids smacking his lips, tapping a pencil, drumming his fingers, or scraping his feet. He does not remove a paper clip from his pages, but does that before he goes on the air. Rattling the pages of the manuscript should also be avoided. Each one should be moved aside noiselessly. Care should be taken not to touch or strike the microphone. Inhalation should be comfortable and noiseless. The microphone exaggerates gasps for breath, wheezes, and other asthmatic effects.

Manner. The speaker should use a direct, conversational tone, as if he were talking with friends. It will then be easier for him to be interested, relaxed, animated, and sincere in everything he says. Using facial expressions, gestures, and bodily movements helps to make his voice more expressive and thus conveys his personality and character to the listeners.

Watching the Time. It is necessary to be alert to the studio clock or time signals from the control room. Each time mark on the script should be noted and checked with the clock.

The speaker should say absolutely nothing, and make no sound, for at least fifteen seconds before the program begins and for fifteen seconds after it ends. The microphone might be inadvertently open.

Rehearsal. An audition or rehearsal is required by many stations. Even if it is not required, it is wise to request one. A rehearsal allows the speaker to adjust to the studio conditions. The silent atmosphere created by the special acoustics and forced restrictions on movement make the studio seem strange to many. A rehearsal also offers an opportunity to check accurately the timing of the speech.

TELEVISION SPEAKING

Television speaking includes lectures, interviews, editorials, and discussions. Much television speaking is serious of purpose and highly informative; many discussions, however, are aimed primarily at entertainment. Sometimes a mere "gab fest" takes place between members sitting in front of the cameras. While any form of discussion can be adapted to broadcasting, the panel discussion is the most frequent type. Since the television speaker can be seen by his listeners, he does not have to depend solely on vocal communication; he can also use the power of visual communication. Television appeals not so much to the listeners' creative imagination as to his full response to what he both sees and hears.

A speaker's first appearances on television may require a considerable amount of adjusting to the noise and distractions in the studio. Lights, cameras, sets, and milling people make concentrating on what is said difficult. The speaker must try to ignore all these things, think only of what he is saying, and imagine the audience in front of him: the camera with the red light. The studio crew is often the only audience present for the speech, and they usually don't listen. They are too busy with their own work.

Appearance.   Colors and materials should be worn that photograph with richness and make the speaker appear at his best. Ties, suits, and dresses should be of subtle and pleasing contrast. Bizarre patterns or stripes, checks, and plaids should be avoided. Horizontal stripes will make a speaker look heavier. White is too reflective and should not be worn, not even a white handkerchief in a man's breast pocket. For men, light blue or gray shirts are best; for women, pastel or darker dresses. Tans, grays, dark greens, and brown are good colors. Simple lines are better than elaborate designs.

No jewelry should be worn that reflects light and glitters brightly. For instance, men should not wear cuff links that will flash into the camera. A speaker who normally wears eye glasses may have to equip himself with a special pair of nonreflecting ones in order to avoid distracting reflections. It is interesting to note that President Johnson's television image was helped greatly when he changed to contact lenses.

Special television makeup (for both men and women) will often be applied by a studio makeup person before the telecast. Makeup and personal grooming matters should be checked with the director or producer to see what the broadcast situation requires. Men with heavy beards may require some makeup, and a bald pate might need some powder. It is essential that the speaker appear on the screen at his best.

Position and Movement. The speaker should find out ahead of time where he is to stand or sit and how far he can move in relation to cameras and microphone. He has to stay directly within the designated area. The floor manager is responsible for signaling the speaker to move to various positions on the studio set. All moves are rehearsed carefully before the telecast. It is most important for the speaker to acquaint himself with the floor manager's hand signals during rehearsal.

The cameras can focus on the speaker from various angles, showing him in many positions. The floor manager also signals the speaker from one camera to another and this should be rehearsed in order to avoid the jerky or "lost look" appearance of a speaker who does not know which camera to look at. All studio suggestions about movements and the handling of visual material should be followed carefully.

It is necessary to adapt immediately to the bright studio lights. Squinting, constant blinking, sighing, and mopping of the forehead should be avoided. The best way to do this is to concentrate on the message and the audience; this will help the speaker to take his attention away from what he is feeling physically. Remember that facial expression is vital.

Posture should be comfortably erect, whether standing or sitting. The speaker will look better if he does not slump, sprawl, shift weight back and forth, or sit hunched up. Fairly small and subtle gestures close to the body are best, but they should not be repeated. Nor should the speaker gesture constantly; he should give his viewer's eyes a rest. Meaningless gestures and motions are distracting. Especially avoid any nervous habits. If seated in a swivel chair one must not swivel. It will be distracting and may even evoke dizziness.

Visual Aids. Good visual aids add life and variety to a television speech. Looking steadily at a speaker soon becomes tiresome; seeing illustrations of the topic keeps the listeners interested. Simple demonstrations and display of artifacts are often effective additions to explanation. Visual aids, however, should be used only if they will help the speaker attain his specific purpose. A speaker should not include them just because he is on television. A picture says more than a thousand words only if it clearly conveys what the thousand words would express. Be sure to get permission for use of copyrighted materials.

Each illustration, diagram, chart, photograph, map, printed text, etc., should be selected carefully and discussed with the television producer well in advance of the telecast. Visual materials will need to be photographically enlarged and mounted for television purposes. When selecting visual materials, the dimensions of the television screen should be kept in mind. Illustrative materials with the same horizontal proportion as the screen are much better suited to the TV medium than long, thin, vertical ones. Sketches will have to be mounted on gray board rather than white because white overreflects the light. The use of various colors will have significance, since many viewers will be watching color television. Blue or green paper must be used for the speaker's notes, as must blue and green chalk when using a chalkboard.

It is wise to avoid hackneyed visual aids; those used should be attractive, stimulating, and illustrating. Visual aids require careful planning and thorough practice to avoid inept handling. All visual materials, however, need not be handled by the speaker. In fact, it would be more effective to have some of the visuals appear on the screen as the speaker delivers his remarks. This technique requires advance script preparation with oral cues carefully indicated so that the television director knows exactly when the illustration should appear on the camera in conjunction with specific comments.

When handling visual materials, the speaker must be certain to make decisive movements. Hesitations and extraneous movements are very distracting to the viewer. Especially to be avoided are unnecessary movements with a pointer or pencil when used with diagrams or maps. Visual aids should appear large enough on the screen to be clearly seen and understood. Arrangements must be made in advance for their proper placement and lighting. All chalkboard writing must be carefully rehearsed in the studio for correct placement and size.

The Microphone. The microphone for television differs from the radio microphone. It may be either a boom (overhead apparatus on a long pole which is controlled to swing back and forth, up and down, in accord with the speaker's movements), or a lavaliere microphone which is worn by the speaker around his neck. The latter is very sensitive to extraneous sounds, especially those like throat clearing. When using audiovisuals, a lavaliere microphone is necessary in order to have freedom of movement.

During the studio rehearsal the audio engineer will take a voice level and instruct the speaker about the proper distance from the microphone and voice projection. The floor manager in the studio will also give helpful advice.

Timing.   In television, time cues are given to the speaker by the floor manager, who is in direct communication via headset with the television director in the control room. The floor manager may give hand signals for time cues or hold up time cards. Standard cues for a 30-minute program are 15 minutes (which means the speaker has 15 minutes of *remaining* time to fill), 10 minutes, 5, 4, 3, 2, 1, 30 seconds and CUT. It is wise for the speaker to acquaint himself with the floor manager's cues during rehearsal so he is sure to understand the time cues during the broadcast.

Delivery.   Television reveals the speaker's degree of preparation. He should know his material so well that he is not at the mercy of his notes. He handles them unobtrusively, so that he does not lose direct contact with his listeners. As already stated, the television speaker must imagine that he is speaking to one person alone. He has to develop an intimate, conversational style of delivery, and must look directly at the camera lens, imagining one receptive viewer in that lens. Turning away from the camera or looking in another direction breaks this visual contact.

Using a Manuscript.   The speaker who uses a prepared manuscript should remember to speak from it, and not merely read it. The eyes should not be glued to the manuscript; the top of a bent head is not absorbing viewing interest. He should check the techniques of maintaining eye contact that were discussed in the section on "Manuscript Speaking" in Chapter 8.

Using the Teleprompter.   The teleprompter enables the speaker to read from large type displayed before him. In theory, he can read while he seems to be looking directly at the camera. In practice, however, most listeners can tell that he is reading by his eye movements. An unseeing stare at the camera is no better than an unseeing stare in the direction of a present audience. Good eye contact reveals a direct awareness of the listener.

Using Cue Cards. The use of cue cards is another technique employed by speakers with considerable experience in speaking on television. Brief notes or a concise outline with important lead phrases are hand printed in large black letters on cue cards (large white cardboard measuring approximately 30 by 20 inches). During the telecast the cue cards will be held by a stagehand or production assistant next to the camera lens. The use of cue cards requires a good deal of advance preparation, but the result will be more effective and polished than if the speaker relied on a teleprompter or a prepared manuscript. No more than six cards should be used for a thirty-minute telecast; more would become a crutch to the speaker and a barrier between him and his audience.

Speaking to the Camera. Direct contact with the audience is the greatest contribution television has to offer a speaker, but he must remember to keep his eyes on the camera as much as possible—the camera is his audience. The speaker talks to the camera with the red light, which is the one taking the picture. Actually it is possible to get "close-up" or "cover" shots without physically moving the camera. Such a camera has four lenses that rotate. The lens on top is the one looked at. When several cameras are used, the speaker should turn slowly and easily to a newly activated camera, avoiding sudden obvious shifts from one camera to another. Of course, in a discussion program, the members talk with each other and give a spontaneous effect rather than constantly looking at one camera.

Rehearsal. The TV rehearsal is not only for the speaker but also for the camera crew. Cameras must be accurately positioned to cover the speaker and his visual material at all times. It is not usually a verbatim rehearsal for the speaker, and he need not go through the entire speech. The rehearsal is mostly to rehearse his movements and positions throughout the complete presentation. Courtesy and efficiency require that the speaker arrive at the studio early—a half hour ahead of time—for both rehearsal and broadcast (or taping session).

Interviews. When interviewing or being interviewed, keep in mind the suggestions given above. Also, review the material concerning interviews in the next chapter.

17.
FACE-TO-FACE INTERACTION

The two most-used forms of face-to-face communication are conversation and interviews. In such communication, participants alternate as source and receiver. Questions and answers are essential ingredients in this interaction: the communication is always a two-way process. Two individuals, or more, take part in a give-and-take situation.

CONVERSATION

Conversation is an important element of all social relationships and is the most-used and least-studied form of speech. Much daily verbal interchange is stereotyped, inconsequential, and impersonal in that the same expressions of personal interest are used for everybody: "How's it going?" "No use complaining." "It's been nice seeing you." "Have a nice day." Of course, such token conversation has social value, because it makes casual associations easy and agreeable rather than awkward and unpleasant.

Conversation worthy of the name, however, is genuinely personal speech, or communication based on an awareness of the individuality of others. It is a meeting of minds, a form of fellowship.

Reasons for Conversations. People talk because they enjoy it. They like to share their thoughts and feelings. As David Hume said, "The free conversation of a friend is what I would prefer to any entertainment." Conversation enables a person to discover others, to understand different points of view, tastes, and ways of life. Conversation with its lively interchange of ideas and experiences enables a person to discover himself, to realize what he thinks, feels, and understands. According to Montaigne, "It is good to rub and polish our brain against that of others."

Conversation is a way of influencing others, of appealing to them, and gaining their support. Conversation is also a way of influencing ourselves through others, for we too wish to be needed, won over, and enlisted. Conversation enables one to belong, to be one with another person or group of persons. It thus encourages the bashful and reticent, comforts the unhappy, and makes the lonely feel less alien.

Qualities of Good Conversation. Good social conversation is not empty, idle chatter, but an exchange of ideas and sentiments. It is not an aimless jumping from item to item, but an exploration of a topic for as long an interval as it is of mutual interest. Good conversation is not the dull utterance of commonplaces, but a spirited exchange of thoughts, clever remarks, illustrative stories, and stimulating comments.

Since good conversation is not mere talk, it requires practice and mobilization of knowledge, background, and experience. "Conversation is the image of the mind," said Publius Syrus. "As a man is, so is his talk." A good conversationalist possesses certain well-developed traits.

A Conversationalist Is Interested. Good conversation requires an unflagging interest in the other member or members of the group and in the subject being talked about. The conversationalist never allows himself to be bored or disinclined to contribute to the success of the talk, but realizes that every person and every subject has some elements of interest.

A Conversationalist Is not Self-Centered. The conversationalist does not talk in voluminous detail about himself and his own affairs, but concentrates his attention on matters that prove of interest to others. A good conversationalist responds to questions about himself, but soon switches his attention to the other person.

A Conversationalist Is a Listener. A good conversation is not a solo performance but a group activity in which all take part. A conversationalist does not monopolize the center of attention, but exerts himself to draw others into the conversation by asking them stimulating questions. The conversationalist seldom interrupts or shows impatience for a chance to talk, but listens attentively and sympathetically to what is being said and willingly waits his turn.

A Conversationalist Is Interesting. Good conversation requires an appreciation of people and a genuine desire to interest them. A conversationalist avoids a flood of forgettable details and selects an example, incident, or thought that most aptly illustrates the topic under discussion. His remarks either illuminate a point already made or suggest a new view of the subject.

A Conversationalist Is Sincere. Good conversation requires honesty, naturalness, and integrity. A conversationalist avoids affectation, artificiality, and assumed knowledge, for false attitudes make pleasant personal associations impossible. A good conversationalist does not hesitate or hedge too much, nor does he agree with everything to the point of insincerity. Conversation is fellowship, and fellowship is based upon mutual respect between genuine persons.

A Conversationalist Is Tactful. Good conversation requires unfailing courtesy and consideration. A conversationalist does not allow himself the license of being rude and offensive. People do not agree in everything; in fact, divergent points of view and intelligent argument make conversation intensely interesting. A good conversationalist, however, does not flatly contradict anyone or make brusque statements of contrary opinions. He disagrees in a good-natured, impersonal, and diplomatic "yes, but . . ." manner, so that his companions are stimulated rather than incensed. He avoids dogmatic, "know-it-all" statements that arouse resistance, and avoids provoking others or allowing himself to be provoked. He is especially tactful when his opinion is asked about matters relating to personalities.

When argument tends toward heated dispute, the skillful speaker detours possible wrangling by introducing another aspect of the subject: "I've been wanting to ask you about____," "The thing I've often wondered about is____," "Could I ask your opinion about another possibility?"

How to Improve Conversation.
A person who converses well is so well liked and appreciated that it is worth gaining competence in the art. Skill in conversation forms an excellent basis for other forms of public speaking.

Studying People. The person who knows what others are thinking and feeling can best succeed in conversation. Since people spontaneously break up into conversational couples and groups in a wide variety of situations, the conversationalist, unlike the public speaker, cannot analyze his audience in advance. He must gain an understanding of his listeners as he goes along by listening to them. The more knowledge he has of people, the easier it is for him to do this.

In general, people are interested in themselves. The conversationalist simply accepts this fact and holds his own interest in himself in abeyance. People are also interested in their work, their home, their children, their pets, their recreations, and their health.

People like to feel important and like to impress others with their importance. The successful conversationalist restrains these feelings in himself and allows others to impress *him*. People enjoy being complimented because they have a need to be appreciated. They like to be asked for advice and thoroughly enjoy expressing their opinions. The good conversationalist does not actually give advice, but makes suggestions and lets the other person have the satisfaction of discovering the answer for himself.

In conversation, the speaker discovers as soon as possible what interests the person or persons with whom he is talking. A conventional introduction to a conversation is often practical: the weather or season, the listener's health, family, or recent activities. To move the conversation to more discussable interests, the speaker tries out one or more specific topics until the conversation is sparked into life.

Having Interesting Things to Say. A close observation of the surrounding world furnishes material for conversation. A good conversationalist maintains a lively curiosity: he keeps informed by listening to radio and television and by reading newspapers, magazines, and books. He pays special attention to subjects that interest his friends and associates so that he can discuss them intelligently. Since topics for conversation cover the whole range of human knowledge and activity, the conversationalist should know a little about everything and be willing to learn more about anything that interests a companion. A good conversationalist also knows a lot about a few subjects. He has interpreted his knowledge and experience and has formed a set of interests and a body of convictions. In other words, he has an individual point of view.

Overcoming Personal Obstacles. Certain traits or habits stand in the way of good conversation. The speaker should study himself honestly to see if he has any of them and begin to overcome them.

SHYNESS. Self-consciousness and feelings of inadequacy often render a person silent. The shy person should force himself to contribute to the conversation, because his silence may be disturbing to others. He can use "parallel talk," which shows other speakers that he is aware of what they are saying. A few possible phrases are: "I never realized that before." "I don't believe I understand." "You mean that (restating the idea in other words)?" "What happened after that?"

OBTUSENESS. Some persons are unaware of the thoughts, feelings, and reactions of others. They are wrapped up in their own concerns and utter monologues or soliloquies without wondering whether their listeners are interested. It is necessary to become aware of the other person's reaction, to give him a chance to express himself, to listen attentively, and try to understand what *he* means.

BOASTING. A good conversationalist never praises himself or brags about his accomplishments, but is modest enough to be silent about his ability, wealth, achievements, or reputation. The most attractive, charming, and gifted person is one who is seemingly unaware of the fact. Others may like to tell him that he has good looks, a vivid personality, or a brilliant mind, but they may not like to have him tell *them*.

IMPERIOUSNESS. The desire to dictate, set everybody right, or "rule the roost" makes real conversation impossible. The domineering person should learn to respect others, to appreciate their good qualities, and to give them the right of making up their own minds. This may be allowing people to make mistakes, but human beings learn valuable lessons and form their characters from their mistakes.

EXPLOITATION. Some persons view conversation only as a means of personal advantage. They want to know the right people, say the right things, and obtain the right backing. The desire to create an impression and "get ahead" is apparent and puts others on guard. Nobody converses freely with a person who wants to use him. The ambitious person should quit looking at people and conversation as tools and learn to see them as ends in themselves. He should discover the pleasure of giving pleasure to others.

Cultivating Desirable Traits. In addition to the many attributes of a good conversationalist already mentioned, a few others are worthy of consideration and cultivation.

Ease of manner puts other people at their ease and makes them enjoy being in an individual's company. A pleasant or smiling facial expression shows friendliness and interest. Patience, tolerance, and forbearance enable people to talk together with pleasure and profit, even though their ideas may not always agree. A sense of drama, a lively reaction to experience, brings color to information, suspense in telling a story, progression in presenting ideas, and conviction to the expression of reasons and arguments.

THE INTERVIEW

Unlike conversation, which is usually spontaneous and unplanned, the interview has a definite purpose, is prearranged, and usualy takes place in a somewhat formal setting. Its main purposes are to seek or give information, to solve problems, or to bring about a change. Thus, it is principally to inform or to persuade. The two main types are the fact-finding and the job-seeking interview. Before discussing these types, a few characteristics of an interview should be pointed out.

General Characteristics.   An interview is usually a conversation with a purpose between two individuals. However, an employee-selection or a therapy interview may include a group. A definite plan or pattern should be devised by the interviewer ahead of time. While careful planning is necessary, flexibility is vital during the interview. Adjustment must be made for questions already answered or for new ideas that arise. These ideas should be pursued so that the purpose of the interview can be best achieved.

Rapport must be immediately established and maintained. The informality of the situation will help, as will the attitude of each member. Good listening is essential. Both interviewer and interviewee are reacting to verbal and nonverbal cues.

Other essential characteristics of an interview will be pointed out during the discussion of the fact-finding and job-seeking types.

Fact-Finding Interview.   Gathering information from individuals is important in many fields of activity, such as journalism, banking, broadcasting, market research, politics, census-taking, and personnel work.

Planning the Interview.   A successful fact-finding interview requires careful planning and conduct of the meeting or conference.

SPECIFIC PURPOSE. The interviewer should determine the specific goal of the conference and establish the limits or area of investigation.

PERSON TO BE INTERVIEWED. The interviewer should find out all he can about the interviewee by talking with acquaintances and looking up any material in print. The person's age, family, education, achievements, hobbies, and memberships in organizations may enable the interviewer to anticipate his interest or attitude toward the matter in question.

STEPS TO BE FOLLOWED. The basic steps of an interview should be adequately planned: the approach, or establishing common ground; stating the purpose; the sequence of topics to be covered; and the close. In a fact-finding interview the list of questions to be asked and the motivating comments should be prepared in advance so that the interview may be conducted with dispatch.

The interviewer should put himself in the other person's place and anticipate questions that the latter will ask or objections that he might raise. All information, evidence, and solutions to problems should be marshalled and visual aids, papers, notebook and pencils, and other necessary materials should be made ready.

SETTING THE TIME. After he has planned the interview, the interviewer requests an appointment, allowing the other person, whenever possible, to choose the time and place of the meeting.

PERSONAL APPEARANCE. Preparation also includes personal appearance. Both grooming and dress should be appropriate and in good taste, for part of the the interviewer's communication is proper appearance.

ARRIVING ON TIME. The interviewer should be present for the interview at the appointed time. Arriving several minutes early may be inconvenient; rushing in three or four minutes late and out of breath may be annoying. It is best to arrive during the minute preceding the scheduled time.

Conducting the Interview. The interview begins as soon as the interviewer is in the presence of the other person.

THE APPROACH. The interviewer states his name unless he is announced, enters the conference room when asked, shakes hands if a hand is offered, and sits down. If he has requested the meeting, the interviewer begins the conference immediately, so that the other person is not kept in suspense.

ESTABLISHING RAPPORT. The first remarks should create an atmosphere that will encourage cooperation and understanding. These may be a few pleasantries or the expression of interest in the other person.

STATING THE PURPOSE. The reason for the interview should be stated or briefly explained so that both parties can organize pertinent questions and answers.

QUESTIONING AND ANSWERING. The mutual exchange of information constitutes the interview proper. In a good interview both parties talk in order to carry out the purpose of the meeting. Questions should deal with a sequence of specific points. Answers can then be concise, yet complete and well integrated; more information can also be gathered in a shorter period of time. Broad and general questions lead to vague or less pertinent answers which require further questions to elicit the specific information desired.

Directness and frankness of approach are usually wise. Indirect or concealed methods may appear devious, purposeless, or annoying. It is possible to get to the point pleasantly and to secure all necessary information tactfully. The interviewee should be given time to answer a question before another is thrown at him. The facts will be more accurate and valuable if the interviewer keeps an impersonal, professional point of view, forgetting his own opinions and prejudices. It is important not to pry into another's personal affairs, and it is morally necessary to reveal no information told in confidence.

NOTE-TAKING. An interviewer may legitimately take notes, but he should take a minimum number and do so as quickly, accurately, and unobtrusively as possible. It is, of course, courteous to ask the interviewee's permission before taking notes. It is especially important to ask permission when tape-recording the interview.

ENDING THE INTERVIEW. As soon as the purpose of the meeting is fulfilled, the interviewer leaves. However, if the other person wishes to chat for a few moments, a short delay is, of course, in order. Whether or not the interviewer has obtained what he wishes, he should express thanks for being granted the conference and appreciation for the consideration shown him.

Following Up. When the information obtained by an interviewer is to be interpreted, organized, and used in printed form, it is both wise and courteous to show the completed news story, magazine article, or digest of data to the person interviewed before it is published. Such thoughtfulness, desire for accuracy, and cooperation pave the way for future interviews or business dealings with the interviewee and his associates.

Job-Seeking Interview.

A vital interview to most persons is with a prospective employer. Like other interviews it uses the techniques of good conversation and discussion with added emphasis on persuasion.

Role of the Interviewee. The interviewee plays an important part in a job-seeking interview, for he is taking the initiative in applying for the position.

PREPARATION. The applicant should take stock of his assets, including his education, experience, and special abilities. He should have some idea of his goal in life and what types of work and responsibility he is capable of assuming. When asked what he would like to do, he should be prepared with a specific answer along with his reasons for wanting that type of work. To reply, "I'm interested in anything you have to offer," is equivalent to saying, "I'm not really interested in anything."

The applicant, by reading or by talking with employees and local business people, should learn as much as possible about the company—its history, kind of business, chief executives, number of employees, volume of business, and financial rating. He should be interested in some of its specific activities, understand some of its requirements, and appreciate some of its future developments and possibilities. The interviewee may then be able to answer the important question, "Why do you want to work for us?" in a way that shows not what he wants to get but what he has to contribute. Realizing that the interviewer is looking for the best person for the job, the applicant indicates not only his background but also his capacity to grow. He should be prepared to answer the interviewer's questions frankly, for he shows his ability and potential by the way he expresses himself.

CONDUCT DURING THE INTERVIEW. The applicant allows the interviewer to begin and to conduct the interview. He listens attentively to all the employer has to say without interrupting. If the interviewer says, "Tell me about yourself," the applicant, although he may have filled out an application blank, should give a concise résumé of his background.

ANSWERING QUESTIONS. The interviewee should answer all questions accurately and briefly, including those about his personal opinions and outlook on life. The interviewer will probably be checking the applicant's attentiveness, willingness to work, persistence, and practical insight as well as his emotional maturity, liking for people, cooperation, and loyalty, for the ability to communicate and get along well with others is an essential qualification.

The job applicant will make a better impression if he avoids telling a hard-luck story, apologizing for taking up the interviewer's time, giving excuses for being without a job, or criticizing a former employer. He should not have gum, candies, or cough drops in his mouth, and should not smoke unless the interviewer asks if he wishes to do so.

ASKING QUESTIONS. When given an opportunity to ask questions, the applicant should inquire about anything that he does not fully understand, such as the type of work, hours, payment, when the position starts, future possibilities, and other things which show his interest in the company and also assess the company's potential value to him. Adequate information gained in a job interview can save future disappointment and needless expense.

LEAVING. Once the question-and-answer period is concluded, the applicant should know when the interview is over. In most cases, the interviewer furnishes a clue. For example, he may shift forward in his chair, seem about to rise, glance at a folder on his desk, or simply pause significantly. Any such signal is the cue for the applicant to rise, thank the interviewer for his interest, and leave.

Role of the Interviewer. The interviewer often has advance information about an applicant by means of a letter, résumé, telephone conversation, or application blank. The interview may be considered a kind of final estimation or examination of the applicant for the job.

PHYSICAL SETTING. A place offering privacy should be chosen for the interview so that satisfactory interpersonal communication is possible. The interviewer should make the applicant comfortable and seat him where both can easily see and hear the other. In a business office, the interviewer's desk should be clear or neatly arranged. The interviewer should avoid reading correspondence, answering telephones, or allowing colleagues to interrupt him. His undivided attention should be given to the person seated before him.

CONDUCTING THE INTERVIEW. The interviewer's voice and manner should put the applicant at his ease and gain his confidence. It is wise to offer a stimulating remark or question at once so that the interviewee has something to talk about. After a brief explanation of the nature of the position, the interviewer encourages the applicant to talk by asking questions. The questions should be based on the applicant's past experience, on the requirements of the specific job, and on the needs of the department. The questions should also be organized in a logical sequence to gain essential information quickly, but without a sense of haste.

The applicant should be given a chance to ask questions, for questions are often good indicators of interest, insight, and judgment. The interviewer answers the questions put to him briefly but clearly. The interviewer listens and observes closely, sizes up the candidate, estimates how well he will fit into the company as soon as possible, guides the conversation to the desired result, and terminates the interview.

REACHING A DECISION. An interview ends in some kind of immediate or future decision. Whenever possible, the decision to hire or not hire should be made at the end of the interview. If a decision cannot be made without further information or until a certain event transpires, the interviewer should explain the circumstances.

FOLLOWING UP. If the goal of the interview is not achieved at the meeting, the decision should be made as soon as possible and the answer made known to the person interviewed. In some cases, a second interview may be necessary. In any business interview, the collected data or decided course of action should be evaluated; this may include consulting with colleagues or reporting and seeking advice from superior officers.

It is advantageous to make a later check on the results of a completed interview. For example: Is the decision working out well in practice? Is the applicant who was hired doing good work? Is the employee himself happy on the job? Since the success of an interview is measured by its results, the follow-up may be the only method by which the interviewer can discover the value of his decisions.

Summary. An interview should be carefully planned. The interviewer should formulate questions and devise a sequence that will best achieve the interviewer's purpose. The physical setting should be conducive to relaxed and uninterrupted interaction. The respondent should also learn as much about the interviewer and the situational factors as possible, as well as considering likely questions and their answers. Grooming should be suitable to the situation and promptness observed.

During the interview, both participants must listen and interact. One question should lead into another. Rather than having rigid, set questions, it is better to adapt yourself to the situation. Nonverbal cues including facial expression should be observed, and mutual rapport should be maintained by alertness to each other's ideas.

18.
DISCUSSION AND CONFERENCE

Whenever a problem exists in our society, discussion is probably used in the attempt to solve it. The United Nations, for example, allows member nations to exchange information and solve some of their common problems. The average professional person spends much time meeting with others in order to gather information, to discuss a problem, or to reach a decision.

The widespread use of the discussion method is due to several factors. First, it has been found that groups tend to make superior judgments to those made by individuals. Second, all sides of a problem are more likely to be brought to the surface and considered. Third, the members are more apt to accept new ideas and to support recommendations that they have personally discussed.

Discussion differs considerably from public speaking in that each individual exchanges ideas with the other members of a group instead of trying to get a particular group of listeners to agree with his ideas alone. While the public speaker knows exactly what he intends to accomplish by his speech, the discussion participant forms only a tentative conclusion before taking part in the discussion. Like a public speaker, every discussion group has a purpose: for example, to provide information, explore a topic, solve a problem, or decide on a course of action.

Discussion may differ in several aspects. It may be private (limited to participants), or public (including an audience). Discussion may be informal (closer to conversation), as in a round table, or formal (closer to public speaking), as in a symposium. A public discussion may or may not include audience participation.

TYPES OF PUBLIC DISCUSSION

The most common types of public discussion are the following: the dialogue, the round table, the town meeting, the panel, the colloquy, the symposium, and the forum.

The Dialogue.   A dialogue is a public discussion of a serious topic by two individuals, with or without a chairperson. In a broadcast dialogue, the participants may be in different parts of the world. The chairperson announces the subject, says something about it, and introduces the speakers. The participants face the audience and carry on a discussion, asking each other questions and stating their ideas briefly. It is wise for them to stress important issues as soon as possible and to show their final stand on the subject before closing. Doing so makes the material clearer, more interesting, and more valuable to the audience. Either the chairperson thanks the speakers, or the participants thank each other for the opportunity of talking together.

The Round Table.   A frequent form of discussion on television is the round table. As the name implies, a small group of participants, usually three to eight, talks informally on a topic of mutual concern while sitting around a table or in an open circle. The chairman opens and closes the discussion and guides it impartially. The participants, who are well informed on the subject, converse without giving set speeches. Ordinarily, the audience does not take part.

The Town Meeting.   The town meeting was a method the early American colonists used to solve their problems. The citizens would assemble in a large hall and under the leadership of one of its members would discuss a problem, following parliamentary rules. A vote was usually taken after discussion had ended. This type of discussion is still used by some localities and is popular as a method of conducting business in club meetings.

The Panel.   The panel, like the round table, is an informal type of discussion that takes place before an audience. The panel members are selected for their knowledge, experience, and opinions and are often asked to be especially concerned with some phase of the subject. Although the number of panelists is determined by the time allotted for discussion, the complexity of the problem, and the availability of experts, the ideal is perhaps about four persons.

Panel members sit facing the audience usually in an approximate half-circle, the chairperson being either in the center or to one side. Most of the time panelists talk directly to each other rather than make individual speeches. The members, by asking questions and expressing opinions, maintain a lively discussion and present a well rounded view of the subject. One of the widest uses of panel discussion is to help poorly informed audiences understand a particular problem.

The Colloquy. When one or more experts are invited to join a panel in order to furnish specific information when needed, a colloquy exists. Such a specialist can usually supply answers to puzzling questions and thus add to the contribution the panel can make to the knowledge of the audience. However, there is a strong possibility that the expert will dominate the discussion and limit the free exchange of ideas between the other panel members, either making them afraid to express their own opinions or causing them to rely upon his knowledge.

The Symposium. A symposium is a group of prepared short speeches delivered by experts on various aspects of a subject, usually in a prearranged order. The purpose is to increase audience understanding by presenting different and opposing points of view directly to listeners. Each speaker may discuss the whole question from his own viewpoint or he may talk only on a particular phase, such as the topic's history, its causes, or possible solutions. Each speaker usually stands and faces the audience. After all speeches have been heard there is a period of questions and comments followed by answers to questions from the listeners.

The chairperson, or moderator, states the purpose of the meeting, explains the nature of the topic, and introduces the speakers. He summarizes the positions taken by various speakers and moderates tempers when the discussion becomes heated. After directing questions put to the speakers from the audience, the chairperson closes the meeting by thanking the experts and the audience for their contributions.

The Forum.   Each speaker in a forum presents a brief prepared speech, but not always pro and con as in a symposium. The speakers then discuss the topic informally as in a panel, followed by questions and comments between the audience and the speakers. The success of a forum depends largely on the ability of the speakers to stimulate each other and to challenge accepted audience beliefs. The speakers should discuss controversial issues, and their remarks by their nature should elicit questions from the audience.

The word forum also describes the second part of a meeting, usually presided over by a chairperson, during which members of the audience participate in the discussion by asking questions and expressing opinions. A forum often follows a panel, symposium, or other forms of discussion. It sometimes follows a lecture or a debate.

THE CONFERENCE (INFORMAL DISCUSSION)

The most used method of discussion in the business and professional world is of an informal nature and conducted in private. The group is small, no audience is present, and usually no prepared speeches are given. The members converse spontaneously under the guidance of a leader. Conferences include meetings of boards of directors, boards of arbitration, and boards of investigation. An important form of conference is the committee meeting, for most organizations must depend upon the work of committees. The most common types of conferences are informational, training, problem-solving, and decision-making.

Informational Conference.   In an informational conference the members pool their knowledge and experience in order to improve the thinking or work of each participant. Although information may be gathered about a specific problem, the goal of the conference does not include the finding of a solution. An informational conference may have as many as fifteen members under the guidance of a skillful leader.

Training Conference.   In a training conference the leader teaches a group the method of doing something. If a problem is to be solved, the stress is on learning how to solve the problem or using the steps of problem-solving. Many training conferences are of necessity both informational and problem-solving.

Some of the toughest problems of business corporations are solved in their training conferences by role-playing. The participating individuals are told what roles they are to play and are given several minutes to plan the progress of the plot. Then they perform for about five or seven minutes. Because role-playing is spontaneous and is given without rehearsal, opportunity is given to those taking part to understand the point of view of the person they portray.

Problem-Solving Conference.   An important and frequent form of group discussion is the problem-solving conference. Most discussions follow the problem-solution pattern wholly or in part, for individuals learn by thinking together as a group and by pooling their experiences in an effort to handle mutual problems. Problem solving is based on the five steps in inquiry or reflective thinking: (1) describe problem; (2) analyze it; (3) examine possible solutions; (4) select best solution; (5) put best solution into effect.

It is not always necessary to follow each of these steps in a given discussion. When there is agreement on any step, it can be omitted. There are times, however, when the problem is so complex that an entire session must be spent on one step alone.

Among the most frequent types of problem-solving conferences are staff meetings, committee meetings, and buzz sessions.

Staff Meeting.   A group meets with its leader (supervisor, department head, director, or other chairperson) to discuss its mutual problems.

Committee Meeting.   A shortcut to the solution of many of an organization's problems is the setting up of a committee. The chairman and committee members, appointed for their special qualifications, meet together and discuss the particular problem. After adequate discussion a report of the decision is made to the organization.

Buzz Session.   When a group is unusually large, it is sometimes broken into buzz sessions. Each buzz session consists of no more than six individuals who convene and discuss a phase of the problem for a very short time. Before dividing the group into these small sections, a leader gives the entire group the background of the topic or in some way prepares them for discussion. The groups then go to various parts of the room and seat themselves in a circle with one member designated as the leader. When the allotted time has elapsed, the chairman asks each group leader to report briefly on his group's recommendations, points out similarities, differences, and other relationships, and finally invites the entire group to discuss the problem and to eventually make its decision.

Decision-Making Conference.   Individuals are continually having to make decisions, either individually or together with others. Decision-making is based on three steps: (1) state choice that must be made; (2) examine possible alternatives; (3) choose one of them which is closest to the group's goal. An effective group consists of from five to seven members.

Brainstorming Conference.   Another type of conference combining information and problem-solving is the brainstorming conference. Here the main purpose is to gather as many ideas as possible. The problem is stated and then suggestions for solving it are asked for. So as not to put a stop to a rapid flow of ideas, no criticism or discussion of stated ideas is permitted. Free-wheeling is welcomed, and a combination and improvement of ideas are sought. Reasoned judgment gives way to imagination, sometimes of the wildest sort. As an idea is expressed, it is written down or tape-recorded, so at the end of the conference a long list of ideas is often available. It is not until later that they are sorted, arranged, some discarded, and some probably found usable.

Because many people consider brainstorming an effective way of releasing creativity in a group, any discussion may employ this method at some point to generate ideas. It is often used at the beginning of a discussion.

REQUIREMENTS OF DISCUSSION

Group discussion requries a responsible and impartial leader, informed and cooperative participants, a specific subject of concern to all present, an uncomplicated plan of procedure, adequate time, and a well-conducted program. The best way to assure a successful discussion is complete preparation on the part of both the leader and each participant. Not only will the discussion be more meaningful for all present, but digressions will be avoided and progress will be made toward a solution.

Selecting the Problem.   The problem for discussion should be carefully selected, or the time spent may be a complete waste. The chief requirement is that the problem vitally concern the members of the group. It should be important enough to create a desire on the part of all to find an answer. It should also be a problem that the group is capable of discussing and for which a satisfactory solution can be anticipated in the time available. Information on the topic should be obtainable so that all members can study it prior to the discussion. However, it should not require exhaustive research.

Phrasing the Problem. Discussion depends upon the differences of opinion that exist when the solution to a problem is sought. For this reason, the problem should be phrased to elicit various points of view rather than to obtain a yes or no answer as in a debate.

The scope of a problem, however, must usually be restricted in order to make useful discussion of it possible. It may be necessary to limit the question to one aspect of the subject. Certainly, it should be only one problem and not several lumped together. The question for discussion is the counterpart of the specific-purpose sentence of a speech.

A problem in question form tends to attract greater attention than does a statement. The question should be worded briefly, clearly, and impartially. Careful editing of ambiguous and biased words may be necessary. The question must mean the same thing to all members of the group.

Studying the Problem. Members of a discussion group should know as much as possible about the problem in order to participate effectively and offer a number of sound solutions. The main problem and all related topics should be carefully reviewed by everyone. A study of the significant up-to-date facts and unbiased testimony helps each member to reach a more satisfactory tentative decision and to be prepared to offer evidence and reason soundly.

The discussion leader should also thoroughly study his group. He considers their objectives in light of the subject and of the larger unit to which the group belongs. In addition, he should consider each member of his group—his special field of knowledge, his abilities, his interests, and his influence on the other members. Thus, he can, if necessary, appoint a capable committee to investigate aspects of the problem. He is also able to call upon those individuals best equipped to discuss certain phases of the subject.

The discussion pattern to be used should be reviewed so that a plan can be drawn up for the meeting. On the basis of such a review, the agenda is prepared.

Preparing an Agenda. The leader or person calling the meeting is responsible for preparing an agenda and sending a copy of it to all those planning to attend. An agenda is a list of the items to be taken up and the approximate time to be devoted to each. Such a schedule is necessary so that the members can realize their area of responsibility, and the leader can keep the discussion from deviating from its plan. The participants can thus weigh their own thoughts on the different items and consider ahead of time the specific contributions which they can make most effectively. The agenda is often footnoted, designating an assignment for a specific individual.

The leader should expand the agenda for his own guidance. It should include all details for conducting the meeting. Each item on the agenda is broken down, questions are formulated for each point, and all materials and methods to be used are listed. Sometimes conference leaders prefer leaving a wide margin on one side of the page where they can list the time, specific aids, and methods.

Sample Agenda

Meeting of: _____ Time: _____

Purpose: _____

  3:00 _____

  3:15 _____

  3:30 _____

  4:00 _____

Suggestions: _____

(Note: Items to be considered may be numbered instead of giving the time. Also, the footnotes to be listed in the section labeled "Suggestions" may not be needed.)

Sample Leader's Guide

  I. Why should we discuss this question?
   A. How does it concern us?
   B. Does it require immediate measures?
 II. What words in the question should we define?
III. What standards should we use in judging possible solutions?
 IV. What is the problem?
   A. What are its symptoms or conditions?
   B. What are its causes?
    1. Are they weaknesses in the situation itself?
    2. Are they weaknesses in control or management?

   V. What solutions could solve the problem?
      A. Which solution would eliminate the causes?
      B. Which solution would improve conditions?
      C. Which solution would benefit the most people?
      D. Which solution would be the most feasible?
  VI. How can the solution be applied?
      A. Who will bear the cost?
      B. Who will carry it out?

Arranging for the Meeting. Those responsible for the meeting make the best possible advance arrangements. The room should be satisfactory for the group and the purpose. While a small room might be ideal for a conference, a large room would be necessary for a forum. Other factors to be considered are the lighting, acoustics, and ventilation of the room. The seating facilities should also suit the type of discussion. Necessary equipment should also be procured and on hand—visual aids, the speaker's stand, chalkboard and chalk, easel, and reference materials. In addition, each member should have a name card and a pad and pencil at his place.

Someone should be responsible for notifying the participants and for furnishing any necessary details, including the day, time, place, and purpose of the meeting. Other useful items, such as the names of members of the group or helpful sources on the subject, may be included. The notification should be sent early enough to avoid conflict with an already filled calendar. Last minute telephone calls should be avoided. As already stated, the agenda should be sent in advance, if one is available.

CONDUCTING GROUP DISCUSSION

A good discussion requires a leader, who is often chosen by members of the group. The leader's job is to make the objective of the discussion clear and to help the discussants achieve their objective. His or her major role is to focus the group on its goal.

Qualifications of the Leader. The leader's concern is to bring each member of the group into the discussion and to encourage him to do his own thinking. The leader should therefore be able to get along with others and to respect their opinions. In words and manner he should be tactful, patient and courteous, tolerant and fair. He shows that his mind is not made up about the problem.

He does not impose his own opinions on the group. He is careful not to appear superior to it and shows confidence in its members. Many times during discussion he is required to act quickly; therefore, an alert and active mind is essential.

As a speaker the leader should be able to express ideas clearly, briefly, and emphatically in the language of the group. He should appear and sound interested and avoid asking questions in a bored and funereal tone or speaking in a condescending manner. At all times he must show a willingness and desire to lead.

Starting the Discussion.   At the exact appointed hour the chairman calls the meeting to order. He usually introduces the members of the group, especially if they do not know each other. He then announces the subject. After outlining briefly what is to be done, he starts the actual discussion and attempts to stimulate interest in the problem.

The leader may do this by pointing out the importance of the problem, by briefly sketching its background, by telling a case history, by pointing out what the discussion hopes to accomplish, or by outlining the procedures to be followed. He may ask questions of the group as a whole, direct questions to individuals, present pertinent cases and statements of authorities, bring up controversial issues, or use visual aids to stimulate interest. He defines terms that are likely to be unclear or confusing. One of the quickest ways to deaden enthusiasm for discussion is to carry on an extended analysis of the problem. The leader should not only avoid this but should also make all statements brief and relevant. However, he must not be so anxious to get to the solution of the problem that he neglects to describe and examine the factors leading to the problem. The group's attitude and ability to work together toward the discussion goal can be greatly influenced by how the leader opens the discussion and sets the scene.

Guiding the Discussion.   The leader's main responsibility is to guide the oral exchange of ideas so that something is achieved as the discussion takes place. He does this by considering the participants and by keeping the discussion moving ahead.

Considering the Participants.   One of the leader's functions is to maintain orderly discussion. Since only one person at a time can speak, the leader decides who it is to be, making sure that he does not consistently ignore anyone. Usually he recognizes the first person addressing him, unless that individual has already done most of the talking. He curbs the overly talkative members and the argumentative members. For instance, the argumentative person can be asked to offer evidence in proof of his statement. However, if some members have more to contribute than others, they should not be limited as long as they are relevant and brief and provided that the others are not denied the privilege of speaking.

The leader should try to maintain pleasant relationships with the members of his group. One way to do this is to address them by name. Another is to avoid saying "I" and to say instead "us" and "you" and "our." Above all, the leader must not find fault with individuals or criticize their opinions.

The leader tries to bring out all viewpoints, clarifies areas of agreement, and keeps the discussion rational and informative.

Often one of the leader's most difficult tasks is to resolve tensions that may arise among the participants. However, it is not necessary to take sides: proponents of each side should have equal opportunity to present their case. If the discussion becomes too heated, the leader stops it and goes on to another aspect of the subject.

Keeping the Discussion Moving Ahead. In order for the discussion to move ahead the leader should prevent too much deviation from the issues. Evidence has to be revealed, important points stressed, other important issues not neglected, and a give-and-take maintained among the participants. When members attempt to go off into side issues, their statements can be questioned in a way that reveals the irrelevancy. Or they can be asked to hold such discussion until the main point under consideration has been disposed of.

USING AIDS. One of the leader's useful methods of keeping the discussion moving is the wise use of audiovisual aids. Charts, diagrams, sketches, and demonstrations may contribute greatly toward keeping the discussion clear and lively.

USING QUESTIONS. Since a question requires an answer, it is an excellent way of learning someone's thoughts, opinions, and reactions. Asking questions is therefore the leader's main method of stimulating discussion. When a member offers an opinion and then stops, the leader can ask, "Mr. Green, can you back up your statement?" When the exchange of ideas lags, a question can be asked. Questions are also important in gathering additional information and in expanding the idea under discussion. A good question can make areas of agreement stand out and allows the discussion to move along in a logical, clear order. It can also serve as a transition from point to point.

There are two basic forms of questions. The general, or overhead, question is asked of the group and may be answered by anyone, while the directed question is asked of a particular member.

Both general and directed questions may be of several types. Information may be secured by asking a factual question: *who, when, where, what, how.* An answer may be elicited by a "needling" question which is intended to provoke an answer: "Are you stating or recommending?" The controversial question invites discussion, since there are several possible answers: "Should speakers always tell the truth?" The alternative question, which asks for a yes or no answer—"Did you bring the data?"—should generally be followed by a factual question. Sometimes the leader can suggest the answer by using a leading question—"Would you favor failing him?"—although this might suggest that he is going to take sides.

The following kinds of questions should be avoided: vague and ambiguous questions; questions of a personal nature; those that the individual probably cannot answer; those putting the answerer on the spot, sarcastic questions or those exposing an individual to ridicule; those that build the leader up and knock the group down.

ASKING THE QUESTIONS. To lead off the discussion, a general question can be asked first. After a number of answers have been given, one point is singled out for further discussion by asking a specific, follow-up question concerning that one idea. Thus the discussion moves ahead by going from idea to idea. In extending the discussion on the one idea, the leader uses the provocative question, "Can you add anything to that?" The leader can present ideas to the group without making them aware of it by referring to a third person: "Quintilian said that a good public speaker is a good man. Do you agree, Bill?" A method of halting the overly talkative member or the one who rambles on about irrelevant matters is to ask, "May I have your ideas phrased in a brief statement so that I may write it on the board?"

A question asked by anyone present deserves an answer, and the answer should be intelligent and well thought out. Usually the leader does not answer the questions which are put to him, but redirects them to the group for discussion. All contributions should be accepted, not only those with which the leader agrees. The leader should also be careful in restating an answer that does not agree with his opinion.

SUMMARIZING. From time to time the leader reviews what has already been accomplished in order to bring the group to a more complete understanding of what has been said, to emphasize points of greatest importance, and to make it clear where they are heading. The leader should therefore keep a record of what has happened so that such summaries will be easy to make. It is often wise to have one of the members record these points so that the leader can give full attention to the proceedings. In this case, the recorder may be asked to read the summary when needed or when requested by the group. The main points of the discussion can also be charted on the chalkboard or on flip charts in front of the group.

WATCHING THE TIME. The leader keeps an eye on the clock and attempts to conform to the time limits set in advance for each area of the outline. If necessary, he interrupts an irrelevant or overly detailed discussion in order to avoid lingering too long in one area and thereby touching too lightly on another.

FOLLOWING THE AGENDA. In order to reach the objective of the meeting the agenda should be followed fairly closely. Since several tentative solutions may have to be considered and since the final decision should not be a hasty one at the last minute, it is important to get any deviation from the agenda back to the main objective as soon as possible. If it is evident that any part of the discussion is getting nowhere, it may be necessary to go on to the next topic.

Ending the Discussion. Before group interest diminishes or when the time set for dismissal has arrived, the leader closes the discussion. He usually does this by reviewing the main areas of the discussion and summarizing accurately and impartially what has been accomplished. If a final decision has been reached, then the action to be taken is stated. In some instances, the group at a later time may have to discuss policies to carry out this final decision. In that case, the leader indicates or designates further responsibilities.

Conducting the Forum. Audience participation is rarely permitted during a public group discussion, because it is time-consuming and may sidetrack important issues. After the discussion, the chairperson either invites questions from the floor or asks the listeners to write their questions on a piece of paper. The first method promotes the liveliest follow-up discussion, since one question tends to lead to another. However, the second method can allow a more logical order, provided there is time for the chairman to arrange the questions. This method also tends to eliminate the loquacious and contentious speakers in the audience.

Questions from listeners should be directed to individual speakers. The chairperson's function is to repeat questions that are not clear, to determine which questioner among several is to be recognized, to avoid confusion, and to stimulate questions from all parts of the audience. At the end of the question-and-answer period, the leader thanks the discussion group and the participating audience.

Reporting the Results. The leader is responsible for getting a report of the discussion to his superior officer or to the next higher administrative level. Therefore the record made either by the leader himself or by a member or observer is summarized, edited, and put in final form for submission.

PARTICIPATING IN DISCUSSION

The participant is a member of a small group of people interested in exploring a subject. His primary concern is not his individual performance, but his contribution to the thinking of the group. To carry out this responsibility and help reach a satisfactory conclusion, each member must listen as well as speak and at all times adapt himself to the others in the group

Listening. Good listening means hearing, and understanding, the questions put by the leader and the responses of the members. It also means weighing each contribution in relation to what has already been said in an effort to find areas of agreement. Unless close attention is paid, a member may make an irrelevant statement, or ask a foolish question. Too many contributors to discussion are so busy figuring out what to say next that they have no time to consider what has already been said. They should be giving the speaker support and encouragement by observing as well as listening. Consideration of others is a way of achieving the team effort that is essential to group consensus.

Contributing. Mere listening is not enough. In order to help solve the problem under consideration, the participant must also contribute something of worth. (A novice may rationalize his silence by saying that he does not know when to talk.) Naturally, if a member has been assigned an aspect of a problem he will talk on that subject and will not attempt to cover all the other aspects as well. In other areas of discussions, he contributes by adding information, by correcting an error, by helping to clarify a point, or by answering a direct question. Every single member is obligated to cooperate.

The member should make an effort to contribute to the group at an early point. All comments should be brief, as should any quotation used to back up a point.

In an informational meeting, members are often asked to prepare and give germane reports. It is recommended that they be given extemporaneously and delivered while standing. This direct communication seems to encourage better preparation and retention.

Adapting. Perhaps the most important requirement for discussion is respect for others in the group. Each participant is therefore pleasant, friendly, and patient. He uses good eye contact and looks to all members of the group. He listens with an open mind and is interested in considering the opinions of others; at the same time he is careful not to deal with personalities, but concerns himself with the point made rather than with the person who makes it. Each member should attempt to help the group understand the subject under discussion. He makes every effort to free himself from his prejudices and to weigh things objectively rather than emotionally. Although the discussion member is cooperative, he is not a "yes man," and does not give up his point of view at the first suggesting. However, he should be willing to change his position if convinced that he is wrong.

19.
DEBATE

Debate is the pro and con argument of a specific assertion, proposition, or solution to a problem. When two friends meet and argue for and against foreign aid or a state sales tax, they are debating, for each is trying to convince the other that his point of view is right. The term debate usually refers to a more formal argument taking place between two or more persons before an audience. Each speaker in a debate tries to persuade his audience to accept or reject the given proposal.

RELATION BETWEEN DISCUSSION AND DEBATE

Discussion and debate are both part of the problem-solving process and are thus neither completely opposed to nor identical with each other. Both use argument and other methods of persuasion. Discussion stresses cooperation among members of a group in order to find the solution to a problem. Debate stresses competition between certain members of a group in order to gain acceptance or rejection of a proposed solution. Discussion of necessity precedes debate; debate follows when disagreement occurs over a given solution. Discussion may consider several solutions to a problem; debate considers only one specific solution.

NATURE OF DEBATE

Debate is cooperative in that it rests upon several accepted assumptions: (1) Previous searching analysis reveals a contrast of belief. (2) The opposing beliefs compete fairly, so that their value can be judged. (3) The competition includes setting forth each belief and testing it by attacks from the opposition. (4) Decision is delayed until both views of the subject have been offered, attacked, and defended. (5) The decision is made by a nonparticipating agency (judge or audience). (6) The judges weigh and consider conflicting arguments and their application in order to reach a decision. (7) The debaters agree with the rendered decision.

Traditional debate is sometimes criticized for its narrowness and formality. Speakers may be so concerned with "correct" methods of procedure that they offer stereotyped issues and rebuttals rather than searching analysis and valid persuasion. Debate, unlike discussion, may leave no room for compromise or middle ground, for a consistent clash of opinion may lead to unresolved conflict rather than to an agreement or decision.

Debate as practiced today, however, is dynamic: it follows certain rules and restrictions in order to expedite the consideration of a proposition. One advantage of debate over discussion is its concentration. Since only one solution to a problem can be put into practice at a time, only one proposition is debated at a time. Another proposed solution, or course, can be debated at another time. Some problems, in fact, require a series of debates or a series of discussions for their solution.

IMPORTANCE OF DEBATE

Many legal, business, political, and international problems demand action, and debate is a practical way of testing arguments for and against a measure and of reaching agreement upon the action to be taken. Debate is therefore standard practice in Congress, the United Nations, and other governing bodies.

Value to Listeners.   The listener benefits by hearing opposing points of view on current problems and the reasons for their support. The individual is then better equipped to understand and decide public questions, to distinguish between truth and fraud, fairness and injustice, and to work for and achieve a better society. A democracy or republic is founded upon open discussion and debate.

Value to Debaters.   The debater benefits personally by improvement in thinking and communication. He learns: to find exact information; to analyze and distinguish between the important and unimportant; to see the relationship between ideas and to present it clearly and coherently; to prove his statements and to demand

proofs for the statements of others; to present ideas in an effective
and persuasive manner; to think clearly under pressure and to make
quick decisions in a conflict; to see both sides of a question and to
profit by opinions that differ from his own; to defend himself and
others against false propaganda methods, such as exaggeration, mini-
mizing, featuring only pleasant truths, manipulating statistics, sup-
pressing the truth, and calculated lying; to understand principles
of leadership.

TYPES OF DEBATE

Most argument in everyday life is informal, while legal cross-examination and parliamentary discussion are formalized applications of
argument. The word "debate," or debate as a specific activity, generally means the types of debate which have been developed by our
schools and colleges. A formal debate is a contest of minds, a game
of wits, a matching of insights carried on by opposing teams according
to various definite sets of rules.

Traditional Debate.   The most common type of debate occurs
between an affirmative team of two or three speakers who support
a given proposition and a negative team of an equal number of speakers who oppose the proposition. The affirmative side opens and closes
the debate; since the affirmative advocates a change in present conditions, it has the burden of proof, and is therefore given the advantage
of the last chance at rebuttal. A standard team debate usually occupies
an hour, plus a several minutes' pause after the constructive speeches
to give the debaters time to prepare their rebuttals. The following
is a typical plan.

Constructive Speeches

First affirmative	10 min
First negative	10 min
Second affirmative	10 min
Second negative	10 min

Rebuttal Speeches

First negative	5 min
First affirmative	5 min
Second negative	5 min
Second affirmative	5 min

Two-Speaker Debate.   A debate between two speakers is often called a Lincoln-Douglas debate and is still used in political campaigns. It is also suitable when a short training debate is desired or when cooperation among members of a team is impractical. The time limit is modified to suit the classroom, platform, or broadcast situation. The negative debater makes only one speech which includes both his rebuttal and constructive case. The procedure for a two-speaker training debate may be as follows:

Affirmative constructive speech	10 min
Negative rebuttal and constructive speech	15 min
Affirmative rebuttal	5 min

Split-Team Debate.   A debate team is usually made up of members representing the same school or group. This procedure is varied in split-team debating, where each team is formed of debaters from different schools. Split-team debating encourages quick thinking and immediate cooperation in exploring mutual resources and arranging strategy. One disadvantage is the lack of thorough preparation by team members working together in advance.

Cross-Examination Debate.   The traditional pattern of opposing team procedure is often modified to include cross-questioning among the speakers. This type of debate develops the ability to ask and answer significant questions effectively. Questions to be asked should be planned in advance for a definite purpose, such as establishing a point, refuting an argument, or showing up an inconsistency in the opposing evidence.

Answers to probable questions should also be prepared in advance. Replies made in cross-examination should clearly and briefly answer the questions and also maintain the speaker's fundamental position in the debate. Several different patterns of cross-examination debate are in current use.

Oregon Style.   This pattern, as developed at the University of Oregon, consists of three distinct sections: constructive speeches, questions, and summaries. Each team has two or three members. The third member of each team gives the summary; in a two-member team the first or second member does so. The time allotted to each speaker varies according to the situation.

First affirmative constructive speech
First negative constructive speech
Second negative questions the first affirmative
Second affirmative questions the first negative
Third negative summary
Third affirmative summary

Michigan Style.   In the pattern developed at the University of Michigan, the questioning occurs immediately after each constructive speech. All debaters ask and answer cross-examination questions. The plan and time limits can be adapted to teams of from one to three debaters.

First affirmative constructive speech	8 min
First affirmative questioned by first negative	4 min
First negative constructive speech	8 min
First negative questioned by second affirmative	4 min
Second affirmative constructive speech	8 min
Second affirmative questioned by second negative	4 min
Second negative constructive speech	8 min
Second negative questioned by first affirmative	4 min
Negative rejoinder	4 min
Affirmative rejoinder	4 min

A more recent Michigan pattern includes questions asked by the audience:

Affirmative constructive speech
Affirmative questioned by the negative
Affirmative questioned by the audience
Negative constructive speech
Negative questioned by the affirmative
Negative questioned by the audience
Negative rejoinder
Affirmative rejoinder

Montana Style.   The pattern developed at the University of Montana resembles the original Michigan plan; however, the speakers follow a different order in cross-examination and the debate ends with summaries.

First affirmative constructive speech
First affirmative questioned by the second negative
First negative constructive speech

First negative questioned by the first affirmative
Second affirmative constructive speech
Second affirmative questioned by the first negative
Second negative constructive speech
Second negative questioned by second affirmative
Negative summary
Affirmative summary

Heckling Debate. A heckling debate allows speakers to be questioned during their speeches rather than in a special question period. This type of debate demands a thorough knowledge of the proposition and sharpens the ability to meet questions with quick, pertinent answers. Each speaker answers heckling questions without the aid of his teammates; each heckle counts as part of the questioned speaker's allotted time.

The debate often consists of four constructive speeches of fifteen minutes in length. Each speaker may be interrupted four times during his speech, but not during the first three or last three minutes of it.

The debate sometimes includes four rebuttal speeches, during which the speaker may be interrupted twice, but not during the first minute or the last two minutes of his rebuttal. The following format is typical of this variety of heckling debate.

First affirmative constructive speech	10 min
Heckling by first negative	During min 4–7
First negative constructive speech	10 min
Heckling by second affirmative	During min 4–7
Second affirmative constructive speech	10 min
Heckling by second negative	During min 4–7
Second negative constructive speech	10 min
Heckling by first affirmative	During min 4–7
First negative rebuttal speech	5 min
Heckling by first affirmative	During min 2–3
First affirmative rebuttal speech	5 min
Heckling by second negative	During min 2–3
Second negative rebuttal speech	5 min
Heckling by second affirmative	During min 2–3
Second affirmative rebuttal speech	5 min
Heckling by first negative	During min 2–3

A heckle is a question or comment which must be relevant and brief. Since the heckling debater tries to gain knowledge which he can use to advance his own position in the debate, his questions should clarify rather than confuse. A heckler must rise and be recognized by the chairperson, who presides over the debate and rules on the length and suitability of the heckling. A timekeeper is often appointed who announces when heckling may begin and when it must stop.

Mock-Trial Debate. The mock trial, developed at Western Reserve University, adapts judicial procedure to the debating of important questions. This type of debate is interesting to audiences and has been used on radio and television. The mock trial includes a judge, two attorneys, expert witnesses, and a jury. The procedure is often as follows:

Judge presents the background of the question.	3 min
Attorney for the plaintiff (affirmative) explains the case he will seek to establish.	3 min
Attorney for the defense (negative) explains his case.	3 min
First witness for the affirmative examined by the affirmative attorney.	4 min
First witness for the affirmative cross-examined by the negative attorney.	4 min
Second witness for the affirmative, etc.	8 min
First witness for the negative examined by the negative attorney.	4 min
First witness for the negative cross-examined by affirmative attorney.	4 min
Second witness for the negative, etc.	8 min
Attorney for the negative summarizes his case.	3 min
Attorney for the affirmative summarizes his case.	3 min
Judge instructs jury to decide the case strictly on the evidence.	3 min
Jury returns its verdict.	

Direct-Clash Debate. The direct-clash pattern, which originated at North Carolina State College, consists of speeches made by two teams of debaters; the speakers, however, do not treat the proposition as a single whole, but consider or clash on each issue or sub-issue as a separate unit. Each clash is a series of speeches presented alternately by the affirmative and negative. The rules vary widely, but the affirmative usually begins the odd-numbered clashes and the negative the even-numbered ones. The debate continues until one team has won three clashes.

A. Definition and analysis
1. First affirmative defines terms, outlines the affirmative position, and states the issues it wishes to debate.
2. First negative accepts or rejects the affirmative analysis, states the negative position, and states the issues it wishes to debate.
3. Judge selects the issues to be debated.
B. First clash
1. Second affirmative presents and argues a single issue.
2. Second negative refutes the argument.
3. First affirmative reestablishes his teammate's argument.
4. First negative concludes the refutation.
5. Judge announces and records the winner of the clash.
C. Second clash
1. Second negative presents and argues a single issue.
2. Second affirmative refutes the argument.
    Etc.

Problem-Solving Debate. The problem-solving debate, originated at the University of Washington, combines features of discussion and debate. The topic for debate is phrased as a question rather than as a proposition; for example, "What should the U.S. Government do about nuclear energy?" The debate is not limited to two opposing points of view on a single proposition, but permits the presentation of several fundamental positions. This type of debate develops intellectual cooperation and honest, truth-seeking evaluation. The debate usually consists of six constructive speeches (without rebuttals, question periods, or summaries):

Analysis by speaker on A team
Analysis by speaker on B team
Solution by speaker on A team
Solution by speaker on B team
Evaluation by speaker on A team
Evaluation by speaker on B team

The first two speakers analyze the nature, scope, and causes of the problem and discuss the criteria for evaluating proposed solutions. The second two speakers can accept either of the preceding analyses, adopt elements of both, or offer new ideas. The chief task of each is to propose a solution for the problem. The last two speakers weigh the analyses and solutions of the four preceding speakers. They can accept an analysis or proposal, select the best features of each, or offer new ideas on analyzing and solving the problem.

Although the problem-solving debate involves two teams, the speakers debate independently and are judged individually. The better analysis speaker, the better solution speaker, and the better evaluation speaker are selected. The team having at least two better speakers is the winner of the debate.

THE PROPOSITION AND THE CASE

The proposition for a debate, like the proposition for a persuasive speech discussed earlier, should be searchingly analyzed, thoroughly tested, and carefully stated. The proposition indicates what the affirmative and negative teams are trying to do. A proposition when debated is supported by issues, arguments, and evidence.

The Issues. Issues are the vital points, main contentions, or basic conclusions that must be proved if the audience is to be convinced that the proposition should be accepted. For example, since the proposition recommends a change in the status quo, it is necessary to show that something is wrong in the status quo and that there is a need for change. The need for change is not self-evident, but is an issue that must be supported by arguments and evidence.

A proposition is usually analyzed by asking stock questions.

I. Does a need for a change from the status quo exist?
  A. Is the problem serious enough to warrant a change?
  B. Why does the problem exist?
II. Will the affirmative proposal solve the problem?
III. Is the solution practical and practicable?
IV. Is the proposal the best solution to the problem?
V. What will be the results of applying the solution?
  A. Will the proposal produce benefits?
  B. Does the solution have disadvantages?
  C. Will the proposal produce greater problems than it tries to solve?

The stock issues enable the debater to discover the vital points of the proposition. Further issues are found by asking more precise analytical questions, such as:

I. Does the affirmative relate the problem to inherent faults of the status quo? Can the problem be solved within the status quo?

II. Is the proposed solution consistent in itself? Is the plan of action clear or vague?

III. Is the proposed solution assumed to be practicable or is it demonstrated by evidence? Is the solution realistic?

IV. Do the facts indicate a better solution? Is the solution outside the terms of the proposition?

V. Are the alleged benefits speculative? Must the proposal be adopted to obtain the benefits?

The Arguments. An issue is not a self-standing assertion, but must be supported by arguments. An argument is an inference based upon reasoning. An argument for or against a given issue is a logical reason for accepting or refusing the issue.

The Evidence. Arguments may be self-evident, but usually require adequate evidence for their support. All assertions in a debate should therefore be established by "the raw material of proof," or evidence. The best and most acceptable evidence should be used. Any suppression or distortion of facts will only help the opposition, who will undoubtedly make the most of the avoided material. The debater's evidence should be unassailable, consisting of established facts and the opinions of recognized authorities. A debate about the existence of evidence is less interesting than a debate about the meaning of evidence. Each piece of evidence should be clearly related to the assertion it supports so that the audience understands exactly what is being proved. A well-prepared and resourceful debater has more evidence at his disposal than he plans to use: he will not allow himself or the audience to be captured by default.

PLANNING THE CASE

The meaning of a proposition often requires the definition of some of its terms. For example, in the proposition "Every person should save ten percent of his income," does "every person" mean everyone who works, or does it include those who live on interest, dividends, and annuities? Does "income" mean gross income, salary after withholding for federal and state income taxes, or take home pay after all deductions? Does "ten percent" refer to money put into savings accounts and bonds, or does it include investments in stocks and real estate and payments for social security, annuities, and endowment policies?

Interpreting the Proposition. Even a carefully worded proposition can usually be interpreted in more than one way. The affirmative side has the advantage of choosing exactly what interpretation it will support. The interpretation should be fair and reasonable, actually deal with the subject, and afford as light as possible a burden of proof. It is easier, for example, to advocate a moderate change from the status quo rather than a radical one.

The negative should interpret the proposition in a broad and general way. The negative must accept any reasonable interpretation by the affirmative and has no way of knowing what it will be until the debate begins. The negative must be prepared with arguments that apply to all probable interpretations.

Choosing the Type of Case. The choice of the type of case, or presentation, is conditioned by the side of the proposition being supported.

Affirmative Case. The affirmative has little freedom in choosing its type of case. In every debate, the affirmative must show a need for change and prove that its proposal will correct certain evils and produce certain benefits. A defensive type of argument is sometimes included, showing that the proposal will not create new evils or that no better proposal exists.

The affirmative, however, does have considerable freedom in choosing the main points to establish its case. More than one contention may be used to show the need for and the benefits of the proposal. Frequently, only one defensive main point is included in the plan of argument.

Negative Case. The negative is more fortunate in having several types of cases from which to choose. In the conventional case, the negative shows that present conditions are not disadvantageous enough to justify a change, that the affirmative proposal will not improve matters, and that new evils will probably result from the proposed change.

In the case based on agreement, the negative accepts some of the affirmative's main points and concentrates on attacking those which remain. If the negative can overthrow one of the vital contentions of need or benefits, the listeners will not logically accept the affirmative proposal. The agreement method saves the negative from arguing against a point which the listeners firmly believe, therefore gains their respect, and allows time to argue more advantageous points.

The "eggs-in-one-basket" case resembles the case based on agreement in that the negative attacks only one contention in the affirmative argument, such as the need for change. It differs, however, from the other method in that the negative does not agree with the other affirmative contentions, but simply ignores them. This type of case obliges the affirmative to prove all its points, even though the negative concentrates in attacking only one of them. Its success, however, depends on overthrowing the point which the listeners will accept as the crucial one. Otherwise, the affirmative will be able to establish more important points without opposition.

The "shotgun" case is the opposite of the concentrated approach. The attack, instead, is scattered over ten or twelve points, treating each one as a main point. Even though the arguments advanced must be brief and therefore weak, the fact that so many arguments exist may be convincing to the audience. Since the affirmative does not have time to disprove all the attacks, listeners may conclude that the others are valid. However, the listeners cannot remember all the negative attacks, and those they do remember may be too tentative to be convincing.

The Brief.   Since a case or plan consists of the major line of arguments and refutation, many debaters find it helpful to prepare a brief. A traditional brief is an inventory of all relevant arguments supported by evidence that can be used in establishing one side of a proposition. It is a full-sentence outline of the affirmative or negative approach to a proposition.

A full brief provides the debater with a more thorough preparation, because it contains both an affirmative and a negative traditional brief in parallel columns. A flexible brief is a complete brief of all possible positions which may be adopted by both sides in a debate. The flexible brief also contains refutations of all arguments which the opposition may offer.

Whether or not he prepares a written brief, or selects and organizes arguments in some other manner, the debater must be aware throughout the debate of his own arguments and those of his opponents. He must be sure of what he wants the audience to accept and be sure that the audience does not become confused over the issues (a frequent occurrence). The debater therefore speaks virtually in terms of a double outline, that of his own case and that of his opponent's case. He can thus follow the clash of issues and offer a greater amount of acceptable evidence for a contention or a refutation whenever necessary.

Constructive Speeches. The affirmative and negative cases are each arranged into constructive and rebuttal speeches. Each team decides what part of its case will be presented by each member in the constructive speeches, and usually what points each will handle in rebuttal.

Affirmative. The first affirmative constructive speaker is expected to state the proposition, define necessary terms, and present the background and importance of the question. He establishes the undesirability of present conditions and the need for change, and may state what his colleague will prove.

The second affirmative constructive speaker refutes one or more negative issues and restates the need for change. He presents the affirmative plan for action and shows its benefits.

Negative. The first negative constructive speaker accepts or rejects the affirmative definition of terms or asks for clarification. He refutes one or more of the affirmative issues and presents the negative position on the need for change. He summarizes the negative's objections to the proposal and states what his colleague will prove.

The second negative constructive speaker refutes one or more affirmative issues and recapitulates the contentions of the first negative. He concentrates on one or two weaknesses in the need issues and establishes the strongest argument against the affirmative case.

Rebuttal Speeches. Actually the first affirmative constructive speech places the burden of rebuttal on the negative. Each side then successively tries to shift the burden of rebuttal to the other side. The struggle is intensified during the rebuttal speeches. The side bearing the burden of rebuttal at the end of the debate is the loser.

Negative. The first negative rebuttal speaker refutes an affirmative issue, reestablishes arguments[1] which the affirmative tried to refute by introducing new evidence, and attacks the weakest part of the affirmative case.

---

[1] New lines of argument are not permitted in rebuttal speeches of educational debates.

The second negative rebuttal speaker refutes an affirmative issue and points out the main issues still in dispute. He establishes issues not reestablished by his colleague by introducing new evidence. He summarizes the whole debate and shows the advantages of the negative position.

Affirmative. The first affirmative rebuttal speaker refutes a negative issue and points out the main issues. He reestablishes contentions which the negative has refuted by summarizing previous affirmative arguments and by introducing further evidence to substantiate those arguments. The first affirmative attacks the negative's position on need for change and shows that proofs for its contentions are inadequate.

The second affirmative rebuttal speaker refutes a negative issue, reestablishes issues the negative attacked in rebuttal, summarizes the affirmative issues, and shows that they have been established in spite of the negative. He summarizes the answers to all negative arguments, demonstrates that the negative proof of major issues is inadequate, and shows the advantages of the affirmative position.

REFUTATION

Since debate is competition, the debater is forced to overcome objections raised by the opposition. To get the audience to accept his position he must destroy the position of his opponents. The process of overcoming evidence and reasoning by other evidence and reasoning is called refutation or rebuttal.

Nature of Refutation. Refutation can be analyzed into several component processes, some of which are direct attacks on the opponents' proof, and two of which are counter rebuttals or defenses against attacks. (1) Overcoming opposing evidence by showing that it is invalid, erroneous, or irrelevant. (2) Overcoming opposing evidence by introducing new evidence that contradicts it or weakens it. (3) Overcoming an opposing argument by showing that it is fallacious. (4) Overcoming an opposing argument by introducing another argument that contradicts it, throws doubt upon it, or weakens it. (5) Strengthening evidence by introducing new substantiating evidence. (6) Strengthening an argument by introducing a new and substantiating argument. (7) Probing the opposing position by forcing an answer to a refutation. (8) Offering a counterplan to the proposed course of action.

Knowledge of Argument.   Skillful refutation requires quick and resourceful thinking based on a thorough knowledge of argument. The debater should prepare himself by reviewing the criteria of evidence, the principles of valid reasoning, and the nature of logical fallacies.

Listening to Opposing Speakers.   The debater must listen systematically to all opposing arguments in order to be able to reply to them. Systematic listening is possible if he sees the debate as two conflicting outlines of arguments. During the debate he should make notes of each argument offered by the opposition and the appropriate reply. The debater can do this conveniently on a sheet of paper divided into two columns, listing on one side the opposition argument and on the other side the reply.

Ignoring Minor Points.   The debater should recognize and discard minor points. His time should be spent on major issues, not on nonessentials. A long quarrel over a minor point is a waste of the listeners' time. The ability to select the essentials is an important part of debating ability.

Using Refutation.   Refutation should be used in debate whenever necessary rather than saved for the rebuttal speeches. Unless a contention is countered as soon as it is offered, the audience may fully accept it and resist later attacks made upon it. The ability of the debater to weave replies to the opposition into his constructive speech makes his case more challenging, interesting, and convincing. A strong constructive case, continually maintained, is the best basis for effective refutation.

In general, refutation is followed by constructive material. For example, a rebuttal speech begins with a refutation, interweaves positive material with refuting material, and ends with constructive material that advances the speaker's position.

In making an effective refutation the speaker states the argument to be refuted; briefly declares the objections to that argument; introduces evidence and reasoning to support the objection; summarizes the new evidence and reasoning; and shows that the refutation weakens the opposing case or strengthens the speaker's case. Such specific application of a refutation is necessary to prevent listeners and debaters from becoming confused by the constant succession of charges and countercharges that characterizes sharp and lively debate.

DUTIES OF THE CHAIRPERSON

A debate is usually presided over by a chairperson who takes no part in the actual debating. The chairperson announces the subject of the debate to the audience, but does not comment on it, because he might say something that a debater might prefer to state in his speech.

The teams sit at the front of the room, the affirmative usually to the chairperson's right and the negative to his left. The chairperson introduces each debater in the proper order. For example, he stands and says, "The first speaker for the affirmative is Mr. John Smith of Blank University." The debater rises, comes to his place on the platform, addresses the chairperson and the audience, and begins his constructive speech.

The chairperson sometimes gives time signals when time limits have been set, but usually appoints a timekeeper, who sits in the front row center where his signals can clearly be seen by the speakers. The signals are given manually or in the form of small cards which are held up. When a speaker's time is exhausted, the timekeeper sometimes stands until the debater finishes, so that the judges can know whether the debaters have observed the time limits.

The chairperson knows where the judges are seated, provides them with ballots, and collects the ballots after the judges have made their decisions. He then opens each ballot, reads the decision aloud, and announces the winning team.

JUDGING DEBATE

Debates are judged in various ways. For example, a legal or legislative debate is decided by a judge, jury, or the audience. Some forms of educational debate are judged by the audience, but most are decided by one or more critical judges. An odd number of judges avoids a tie decision, the number usually used being three.

Basis of Judging. Some forms of debate, such as political debates, are decided on the merits of the proposition. Educational debates, however, exist for the purpose of developing skills in argument and are therefore judged not on the merits of the question but on the merits of the debating. The skills judged include analysis of the question, discovery of issues and their relative importance, knowledge and use of evidence, ability to reason, skill in refutation, sticking to the issues, adaptation of all arguments to the speaker's case, and

320

PUBLIC SPEAKING

public speaking ability. When competition is close, argument may be rated higher than delivery, and rebuttals higher than constructive speeches.

Requirements of a Judge. A judge should be well versed in argumentation and debate procedures. He should know the subject under discussion in order to estimate the relevance of arguments and evidence. The judge should be free from bias, judging which team did the better debating, not which team persuaded his mind. He should base his decision on the debate as it is, not on what it would be if the judge himself were debating. A judge should also be able to explain his decision and offer criticism to the debaters and coaches after the debate session is over.

The Decision. A critic judge gives his decision orally along with his reasons for making it. The usual method of rendering a decision, however, is by ballot. A judge reaches his decision by using his entire knowledge of argumentation and debate. The ballot furnished him merely records his decision by listing several important phases of debating. The ballot usually contains a rating chart for each debater, such as the one for the first affirmative in Figure 11.

1st Affirmative   Rank_____

	1	2	3	4	5
Analysis & plan of case					
Evidence					
Argument					
Refutation					
Delivery					

Speaker's total points_____

Figure 11. Sample ballot

The judge evaluates the debating skills of each speaker on a scale of 1 to 5, indicating superior, excellent, good, fair, and poor. He totals each speaker's points, and ranks the debaters from 1 to 4 according to their totals. The judge also indicates the total points for each team, and records his decision for the winning team. Many ballots are double, including copies for the affirmative and negative teams; in that case, the judge fills out the duplicate forms; he may also make special comments to each team if he desires.

20.
PARLIAMENTARY PROCEDURE

Parliamentary law is the system of rules regulating procedure and debate in deliberative bodies. It is based on the practices, rulings from the chair, and the statutes of the English Parliament, and on developments and procedures of the Congress of the United States. Parliamentary procedure has been extended and adapted to organizational meetings of all kinds. The basic purposes of parliamentary procedure are to maintain decorum, aid the orderly transaction of business, determine the will of the majority, and safeguard the rights of the minority by means of free debate.

REQUIREMENTS FOR SUCCESSFUL
PARLIAMENTARY PROCEDURE

In order for parliamentary procedure to achieve its purpose, the members of the assembly must be informed, active, and cooperative. Other requirements of a parliamentary meeting are the presence of a quorum, definite proposals for discussion, and an agenda.

Informed Members. Every member should have a working knowledge of parliamentary procedure and should know the agenda, carefully consider what has happened in past meetings, and be ready to contribute to the new agenda. If a member has something to say about what has happened or is happening, if he feels confident in his ability to contribute, he will be a vital part of the organization.

Active Members. Listening is not enough; action is necessary. Silence means consent: an apathetic assembly will not achieve an effective common goal. Each individual member should take an active interest in the proposed motions and solutions. He should intelligently contribute to the meeting, instead of complaining to friends later that nothing was accomplished. A member should promptly object if he detects an improper, unwise, or undemocratic procedure. Members who are willing to let others do all the work are to blame for the dictatorial chairperson, or the cliques, who push measures through.

Cooperative Members. A skilled parliamentarian uses procedure for strategic purposes. However, he does not deliberately attempt to confuse and slow down the pending business. Rather than attempting to exhibit his own knowledge and skills, he cooperates with the chairperson and assembly.

Able Direction. A meeting requires skilled direction. The presiding officer is responsible for maintaining an atmosphere that is conducive to discussing problems and making decisions. The chairperson preserves order and avoids procedures that waste time. He also keeps the tone of the meeting impersonal and objective.

A Quorum. Business cannot be conducted unless a quorum is present. The quorum, the minimum number of members legally required to conduct business, is usually specified in the organization's constitution or bylaws. Otherwise, a majority of all the members constitutes a quorum. Thus, one of the first considerations of a meeting is to determine whether a quorum is present.

Definite Proposals. Discussion is the heart of a meeting. In order for discussion or debate to take place, there must be a definite proposal to be acted upon. Ideas cannot be merely suggested by the members. They have to be stated as a definite proposition. It is the chairperson's duty to ask for such a statement if none exists. The chairperson and every member of the assembly must know at all times exactly what the pending proposal is.

An Agenda. The agenda, or plan of the meeting, may be decided completely by the chairperson or be worked out with the program committee or executive board. The agenda includes the regular order of business to be followed and the specific proposals to be considered at the meeting.

BASIC PRINCIPLES

Parliamentary procedure is based on certain general principles which must be followed if the method is to achieve its purpose. These concern equality, majority rule, orderliness, personalities, free debate, and privileges.

Equality.   All members of the group are equal. Each is responsible for the achievements of the meeting. Every member may offer motions and take part in debate. All have equal rights and obligations.

Majority Rule.   The vote of the majority prevails in all matters, because a special privilege would be created by minority rule. Officers of a parliamentary group are chosen by majority vote.

Orderliness.   Business is arranged and conducted in an orderly manner, following the simplest method of dispatch. An agenda should be planned for every meeting and the order of business carefully followed. Only one item of business should be considered at a time. Each item should be disposed of before entertaining a new one. The precedence of motions exists to allow the definite and logical handling of each question.

Personalities.   Every effort must be made to avoid involving the personalities of members. The ideas offered are more important than the individuals presenting them. The issue should be debated and not the person who offers it. Members are therefore addressed through the chairperson and not directly. Such terms as "the previous speaker," "my colleague," and "Mr. Blake" are used instead of the second person.

Free Debate.   Every motion and resolution that is properly presented and debatable can be freely discussed. No group may take away this right. Only through discussion can the rights of a minority be upheld and over-speedy and unfair action be avoided.

Privileges.   Each member has a right to know at all times what question is being considered and what its effects will be. A record is kept by the secretary of all transactions to provide exact information to members. The presiding officer should be impartial in answering questions, explaining motions, and exercising his other powers.

ORDER OF BUSINESS

Most organizations have an established and carefully observed order of business, which is stated in their bylaws or standing rules. If not so specified, the following order of business is customary:

Call to Order. The chairperson says, "Will the meeting please come to order."

Reading and Approving the Minutes. *Chairperson:* "Will the secretary please read the minutes of the last meeting." The secretary reads the record, which should contain the following items: kind of meeting (regular or special); name of the group; date, hour, and place of the meeting; chairperson and secretary present, or their subsitutes; whether the minutes of the preceding meeting were amended and approved; each main motion except those withdrawn; name of the member who made the motion; action taken on each motion; all points of order and appeals; total attendance; time of adjournment; and the secretary's signature.

Chairperson: "Are there any corrections to the minutes?" A member may then specify a correction. *Chairperson:* "The minutes stand approved as read," or "The minutes stand approved as corrected." The secretary writes *approved* or *approved as corrected* at the end of the minutes and signs his name.

It is a time-saving practice for the secretary to send a copy of the minutes to each member in time to be read before the next meeting. In this way it is not necessary to read them at the meeting. The chair will ask if there are any corrections to the minutes as received.

Reports. The chairperson next asks for reports: first from officers, then from standing committees (appointed to take permanent charge of certain kinds of business), and then from special committees (appointed for certain tasks until the duty is performed). Each person making a report rises and addresses the chair and, after being recognized, presents his report.

Unfinished Business. *Chairperson:* "Unfinished business is now in order." A member rises, waits for recognition, and makes a motion, such as an amendment to the bylaws, a notice of which was given at a former meeting. The chair states the question, recognizes mem-

bers for discussion, puts the question, takes the vote, and announces
the result.

New Business. *Chairperson:* "Is there any new business?" New
motions may now be made. After each motion is made, it is seconded
and discussed. It may be amended. When the discussion has ended,
the motion is brought to a vote and the chair declares the motion
passed or defeated.

Adjournment. The chairperson may ask for a motion to adjourn.
The motion is made, seconded, and voted on. If it is passed, the
chair declares the meeting adjourned.

CONDUCT OF BUSINESS

The actual business of a meeting is transacted by the means of
motions and resolutions. A motion is a proposal that the group
take a certain action, such as "I move we contribute $200 to the
Greater New York Fund." A resolution is a formal statement of
the views and opinions of the group. It is submitted in written form
and is preceded by the word "Resolved." One of the most common
resolutions is the written condolence offered to the family of a deceased member.

A main motion places a piece of business before the group and
is in order when no other business is under consideration. Most
other motions grow out of the discussion and treatment of the main
motion and must be disposed of before the main motion can be
brought to vote. The more urgent and important the motion, the
higher its precedence over other motions. Some motions deal specifically with the mechanics of parliamentary procedure, such as the
rights and privileges of members. If the meeting is to progress
smoothly, swiftly, and efficiently, all motions presented and discussed
must contain only one purpose, be clearly expressed, and be properly
presented.

Putting a Motion Before the Assembly. Before a motion is
on the floor (before the assembly) and open for discussion, the following steps must be taken: it must be introduced, it must usually be
seconded; and it must be stated.

Introducing the Motion. A member rises and addresses the chair
by his official title, preceded by Mr. or Madam, such as "Mr. Presi-

dent." The chair then recognizes the member by either announcing his name or by bowing to him. In small groups the latter method is used. The member may then use either of the following introductory phrases: "I move that _____," "I move to _____," "I move the adoption of the following resolution: _____," or "Resolved, that _____." A motion should be stated affirmatively so that a "yes" vote means a decision to act and a "no" vote means a refusal to act: "I move that we accept the Commission's budget." A negatively stated motion, "I move that we do not approve the Commission's budget," might be confusing, because a "yes" vote would mean a negative response or refusal to act.

The need for debate may be reduced and group business expedited if a new motion is made after some preliminary explanation. In some groups, a committee may offer such information in written form to members before the meeting takes place. It is also wise for a member to show the need for a motion made on the floor of the assembly (if the rules are flexible enough to permit it), for listeners may decide immediately against a new motion and not even second it, because they see no reason for considering it. A member therefore may say, "Mr. Chairman, I wish to make a motion after a few explanatory remarks." The speaker is thus able to define the problem, show the need for a solution, and win conviction before making his motion. Under strict parliamentary procedure where no debate is permitted until the chair states the question, the member cannot do this. In that case, he should be sure to exercise his right to speak first on behalf of his motion before other members can gain the floor and speak against it.

During the debate, the chair may ask the introducer of the motion to clarify it and to answer attacks upon it; however, he may have to grant many members their right to be heard once before allowing the author of the motion to speak twice. As a result, the majority may have decided against the motion before its author has a real chance to defend it.

Seconding the Motion. It is not necessary to obtain the floor in seconding a motion. Any member of the group, without rising, may say, "I second the motion." If no member immediately seconds the motion, the chairperson repeats the motion and asks, "Is the motion seconded?" The motion does not have to be repeated in small groups where it was obviously heard by all. The chairperson may say, "You have heard the motion; is it seconded?" If there is no second, he says, "There being no second, the motion is not before the assembly." If, however, the motion is seconded, the chair is ready to state the question.

Stating the Question. No member can be granted the floor for actual debate until the motion is stated by the chairperson. After the motion is seconded, the chairperson says: "It is moved and seconded that _____." Unless someone immediately claims the floor, he asks, "Are you ready for the question, or is there any discussion?" If the members choose to discuss the motion, he does not put the question until the discussion has ended. It should be noted that a *motion* is referred to as the *question* once it has been restated by the chair and is thus before the assembly.

Treating the Motion.

When a motion is before the assembly, it can be debated, altered, delayed, disposed of, and voted upon.

Debating the Motion. All ordinary or main motions that introduce proposals for consideration are debatable. There are, however, certain motions that concern the parliamentary procedure used or which are intended to bring the discussion to an end: these are not debatable. It is important to remember that only one principal motion can be before the assembly at any one time.

REQUIREMENTS FOR DISCUSSION. An orderly and profitable debate depends upon certain requirements. Every motion must be clearly phrased by the chair so that each member immediately understands its intent. Except for the chairperson (unless he relinquishes the chair), any member of the group may speak either for or against the motion on the floor. His main objective is to influence the members' vote. One of the most effective methods is to focus attention on one main idea, so that members will remember it. The idea should be stated, supported with proof, and then restated.

Discussion must be confined to the issue being considered. All irrelevant and unessential matters should be eliminated. The chairperson and all the members must therefore know what the issue is. The chair must carefully follow the order of motions and keep the members clearly informed about what is before them.

LIMITING DEBATE. Sometimes a few people dominate the meeting and talk both too much and too often. In such a case, a more democratic debate can be assured by limiting discussion. The group may determine ahead of time the length and number of times each member can speak. For instance, no one can speak in debate (except by permission of the assembly) more than twice on the same question on the same day, nor longer than ten minutes at a time.

If any member who has not spoken desires to speak, a member should refrain from speaking a second time on a given question. The member making the motion has the right to speak first (if he claims it with a reasonable promptness) even though other members have addressed the chair first. If several members claim the floor at the same time, and the chairperson knows on which side they will speak, he should assign the floor to one opposed to the preceding speaker.

Debate can also be limited or extended by offering a specific motion. A member says, "I move to limit (extend) debate on the question to _____" (a specific number of minutes), or "I move to limit (extend) the time of each speaker on this question to _____ minutes." This motion is not debatable, is amendable, and requires a two-thirds vote to pass.

CLOSING DEBATE. When discussion seems to be at an end, a member may call out, "Question." If no member requests the floor, the chairperson may ask, "Are you ready for the question?" If he receives no response or hears a call of "Question," he then takes a vote on the motion. Debate can be definitely brought to an end by a motion. A member is recognized by the chair and says, for example, "Mr. Chairman, I move the previous question," or "Mr. Chairman, I move that we close debate." Time is often saved by such a motion when it is evident that most members want to vote although a few talkative ones are still repeating themselves.

The motion to close debate requires a second, is not debatable, and requires a two-thirds majority vote in order to be carried. If the motion carries, the chair announces the decision and then takes a vote on the motion that is being debated. It is possible to close debate on *all* motions on the floor by stating, "I move the previous question on all pending business." If this motion carries, it is then necessary for the chair to take a vote on the amendments or subsidiary motions and then on the main motion.

Altering Motions. Motions may be changed by amending them and by dividing the question.

AMENDING THE MOTION. When a change in the wording of the motion is desirable, it may be amended. This is done in one of three ways: by adding words, by omitting words, or by substituting words.

For example, "I move to amend by deleting the word *required*." Like the main motion it amends, an amendment must be seconded and requires a majority vote.

No main motion can have more than two amendments; a primary amendment (modification of the main motion), and a secondary amendment (modification of the primary amendment). The addition of a third amendment would only cause confusion. A secondary amendment (amendment to an amendment), has precedence over a primary amendment, which itself has precedence over the main motion. For example, a main motion is moved, seconded, and stated. A primary amendment is moved, seconded, and stated. During discussion a secondary amendment is moved, seconded, and stated. The secondary amendment must first be considered and acted upon. Then the primary amendment, as amended, is adopted. Finally, the main motion, as amended, is pending and must be debated or voted upon. Once back to the main motion, it is possible to have further primary and secondary amendments emanating from it. In all cases, the particular amendment must be pertinent.

DIVIDING OF THE QUESTION. The division of a complex question is demanded so that each part may be discussed and voted on separately. Not only does this motion help promote clarity, it also allows those members who favor the main motion to vote against those parts they disagree with and thus get rid of them. The chair usually decides on the motion to divide the question, and no vote is necessary. If approved, the assembly votes separately on each of the parts of the question.

Delaying Action on Motions.   It is often desirable to postpone action on a motion. Perhaps there is a need to prevent a hasty decision by the group, or perhaps a member thinks the motion is completely undesirable. The following motions may be offered: to lay on the table, to postpone definitely, or to refer it to a committee for study and recommendations.

LAY ON THE TABLE. The object of this motion is to postpone the matter under discussion until a later, unspecified time, when a motion "to take from the table" would be in order. However, unless the latter motion is offered at the same meeting or at the next one, in most organizations the motion laid on the table is considered dead and must be presented as a new main motion at a subsequent meeting. The motion to lay on the table cannot be qualified or made definite by moving to lay the question on the table until a specified time. The motion to lay on the table takes precedence over main motions and their amendments. It is not debatable or amendable and requires a majority vote.

POSTPONE DEFINITELY. This motion proposes to postpone consideration of a motion until a definite and specified time. The form would be: "I move to postpone a discussion of this matter until _____ (stating when)." The motion is both debatable and amendable.

REFER TO A COMMITTEE. When the subject requires more investigation or discussion than can be given in the assembly, the proper course is to move thus: "I move that the question be referred to a committee of _____ (specifying the number), to be appointed by the chair." If the motion does not specify how the committee is to be appointed, after it is adopted the chair asks, "How shall the committee be appointed?" Any member, without rising, may mention one of the following three methods: by nominations from the floor, by nominations by the chair, or by appointment by the chair. It can be seen that much time is saved by the member making a complete motion rather than merely moving to refer the question to a committee.

The committee considers and reports on the resolution and recommends an action to be taken by the organization. The report is given orally at the specified time by the chair of the committee. After the reading of the committee report, the chair states the question on adopting the resolution. The resolution is then open to debate and amendment exactly as if it had been offered by a member, the committee chair having the right to speak first. When the committee reports merely facts and opinions and makes no recommendations, no motion is made, nor is a vote taken for the adoption of the report. The chair announces that the next business is in order as soon as the report is read.

Disposing of Motions.   When a motion seems undesirable, an assembly may refuse to discuss it. A motion may be killed in three ways: by objecting to its consideration, by postponing it indefinitely, or by withdrawing it.

OBJECT TO CONSIDERATION. Any member may object to a consideration of a matter as long as he does so before the first speaker has ceased talking. The chair may say: "Objection has been raised to this motion. I call for a vote. Shall the question be considered?

All in favor of further consideration say *aye*, all opposed to any further consideration say *no*." Unless the no votes have a two-thirds majority, the matter is again up for discussion.

POSTPONE INDEFINITELY. Instead of voting down a motion, it may be disposed of by adopting the motion to postpone it indefinitely. If the motion to postpone indefinitely is lost, a consideration of the main question is resumed. If the motion carries, the main motion is lost.

WITHDRAW A MOTION. A motion may be withdrawn by consent of the assembly. When a member says, "I wish to withdraw my motion," the chair responds (without waiting for a second) with, "Mr. Blake asks permission to withdraw his motion. Is there any objection?" If an objection exists, a vote must be taken. If there is no objection, the chairperson states, "There being no objection, the motion is withdrawn."

Resuming Consideration. A motion to take from the table may be made at any time when no question is pending, and when new or unfinished business is in order. It is not debatable or amendable and must be put to vote immediately upon being seconded. The form of the motion is: "I move to take from the table the motion relating to _____."

Modifying Previous Actions. Sometimes second thoughts cause a different reaction to a proposal. Although definite action has already been taken, a decision may be corrected by one of the following methods: the action may be reconsidered or rescinded.

RECONSIDER. A member may move to reconsider an adopted motion and to have it entered in the minutes for consideration at the next meeting. Similarly, a motion that has been defeated may also be reconsidered. However, the motion must be made on the same day or the next calendar day of the adopted or lost motion. It is not possible to reconsider the same question twice. Two votes are required: first, on the motion to reconsider; second, on the original motion after reconsideration.

RESCIND. The member says, "I move that the action of the organization on _____ be rescinded," or "I move that the motion be rescinded, and that it be expunged from the minutes." In addition, an action that has carried may also be renewed and amended by offering a new motion in its place.

Voting on the Motions. When the chair asks, "Are you ready for the question?" and there is no response, he rises and puts the question: "The question is _____. As many as are in favor say, *Aye*." (The members respond.) "Those opposed, *No*." (Members respond.) It should be noted that a negative vote is taken even though the affirmative seems to have carried. The chair should always identify the exact motion that is to be voted on. To merely say, "Those in favor of the previous question," would be incorrect. Instead, he should say, "Those in favor of _____ (stating the specific question)."

METHODS OF VOTING. The chair should specify a definite method of response. He does not say, "Those in favor of the motion to _____ will signify in the usual manner (or by the usual sign)." Any one of the following methods of voting may be used.

Acclamation (vocal). This is the most used method. The form is: "As many as are in favor of _____ say, *Aye*. Those opposed, *No.*"

Show of Hands. This method is used when a more accurate count is desired.

Standing. Recommended when there is doubt and a division of the vote is desired.

General Consent. A method of silent voting when the business is not deemed sufficiently important to take time to go through the routine procedure. However, if anyone objects to this method, another method must be used.

Ballot (when secrecy is desired). The chairperson may write his ballot and cast it with the rest.

Roll Call. This method is used when it is desired that a record of the vote be kept. The chairperson says, "Those in favor of the motion to _____ will say, *aye*; those opposed will say, *no*. The secretary will call the roll."

KINDS OF VOTES. All main motions are decided by majority votes, or more than half the votes cast. A two-thirds vote is required on the motions to close debate, to suspend rules, to object to consideration, and to make a special order. This vote is used less often than the majority vote because such a proportion often results in a deadlock.

TABLE OF MOTIONS

Order of precedence	Applies to what?
PRIVILEGED MOTIONS	
1. Fix time to which to adjourn	No other motion
2. Adjourn	No other motion
3. Recess	No other motion
4. Question of privilege	No other motion
5. Orders of the day	Any special or general order
SUBSIDIARY MOTIONS	
6. Lay on the table	Main, amend, appeal
7. Previous question (close debate)	Debatable motions
8. Limit or extend debate	Debatable motions
9. Postpone definitely	Main motion
10. Refer to committee (commit)	Main, amend
11. Amend	Variable
12. Postpone indefinitely	Main motion
MAIN MOTIONS*	
13. a. General main motion	No motion
b. Other main motions	
Rescind	Main motion
Make a special order	Main motion
UNCLASSIFIED MOTIONS*	
Reconsider	Main, amend, appeal
Take from the table	Main, amend, appeal
INCIDENTAL MOTIONS*	
Appeal	Decision of chair
Point of order	Any error
Parliamentary inquiry	No motion
Suspend rules	No motion
Object to consideration	Main motion
Division of the question	Main, amend
Division of the assembly	Voice votes
Withdraw a motion	All motions

1. Not debatable if another motion is pending.
2. Only length of recess is amendable.
3. Only propriety of postponement is debatable.
4. Amendable only as to time.

Interrupts speaker?	Requires a second?	Can be debated?	Can be amended?	Vote required?
No	Yes	Yes[1]	Yes	Majority
No	Yes	No	No	Majority
No	Yes	No	Yes[2]	Majority
Yes	No	No	No	No vote
Yes	No	No	No	No vote
No	Yes	No	No	Majority
No	Yes	No	No	Two-thirds
No	Yes	No	Yes	Two-thirds
No	Yes	Yes[3]	Yes[4]	Majority
No	Yes	Yes[5]	Yes	Majority
No	Yes	Yes	Yes	Majority
No	Yes	Yes	No	Majority
No	Yes	Yes	Yes	Majority
No	Yes	Yes	Yes	Majority
No	Yes	Yes	Yes	Two-thirds
Yes	Yes	Yes	No	Majority
No	Yes	No	No	Majority
Yes	Yes	Yes	No	Tie or majority
Yes	No	No	No	No vote
Yes	No	No	No	No vote
No	Yes	No	No	Two-thirds
Yes	No	No	No	Two-thirds negative
No	No	No	Yes	No vote[6]
Yes	No	No	No	No vote[6]
No	No	No	No	No vote[6]

5. Only propriety of referral is debatable.
6. If an objection is raised, a majority vote is required.
* No order of precedence among themselves. Incidental motions rank above subsidiary motions and take precedence over the motions from which they arise.

Announcing the Vote. The chairperson must state clearly whether the motion has been carried or lost. For example, "The ayes have it, and the motion (or resolution) is adopted (or carried)" or "The negative have it, and the motion is lost." He should not say, "Those opposed have it." If the vote is a tie, the chairperson may say, "There are _____ in the affirmative and _____ in the negative. There being a tie, the motion is lost." In such cases the chair usually decides the vote, unless he has already voted.

The chair, if a member of the assembly, may vote whenever his vote will affect the result, or when the vote is by ballot or by roll call. After announcing the vote, the chair then explains what question, if any, is pending.

Enforcing Correct Parliamentary Procedure. There are several motions that grow from the business being treated and which are largely concerned with the rights of the members. Their enforcement aids in the judicious use of the parliamentary method. Since these motions concern matters requiring immediate decision, they are called points of privilege and may be raised even though someone has the floor. Thus, pending business can be interrupted. No second is required, except on the appeal from the decision of the chair. As soon as such a matter is introduced, it must be disposed of immediately.

Question of Privilege. A question of privilege enables a member to get immediate action on such items as heating, lighting, ventilation, and other matters concerning himself and others. He may rise to a "question of privilege" while another speaker has the floor, and if sufficiently urgent may even interrupt his speech. The chairperson directs him to state his question of privilege and, if he considers it such a question, takes immediate action. The interrupted business is then resumed.

Point of Order. When a member wishes to focus attention upon an error in procedure, a violation of a rule, or a digression from the question he says, for example, "Mr Chairman, I rise to a point of order." The chair says, "Please state your point of order." After the member has stated his objection the chair answers: "Your point of order is (or is not) well taken."

If a point of order reveals that a proposed motion is out of order, the chair states, "The motion is out of order." He may inform the member who introduced it when his motion will be in order, if it will be so later. The chair should not say "The gentleman is out of order," unless the member is disorderly in his conduct.

Appeal of the Decision of the Chair. If any member is not satisfied with the chairman's decision and wants the group to decide the justice of it, he appeals. The chairperson asks the assembly, "Shall the decision of the chair be sustained?" This motion is debatable. In order to reverse the decision of the chair, a majority of "no" votes is required.

Parliamentary Inquiry. When a member is not sure of parliamentary procedure or is not certain of the meaning of a motion, he may request information: "Mr. Chairman, is it in order to _____?"

Point of Information. This motion, which is a request for information, does not require recognition by the chair. The member desiring such information may interrupt the member speaking. He may say, "I rise to a request for information. I should like the speaker to make clear _____." The member, however, who tries to *give* information rather than *ask* for it should be ruled out or order by the chairperson. For example, the member who says, "Is it not true _____?" is attempting to debate.

Division of Assembly. A division of the assembly secures an accurate tally of votes. When a member, without obtaining recognition, calls out "Division," the chair retakes the vote. A voice vote may thus be verified by asking each group of voters to rise and be counted.

Orders of the Day. The purpose of this motion is to demand that the order of business adopted by the assembly be followed. It may be called for if an issue definitely scheduled has been skipped over or if the time scheduled for its discussion has passed. The motion may be made while another member has the floor or after a motion has been made but not stated by the chair. After the motion for the orders of the day has been made, the chair announces the business that properly comes before the assembly at that time.

Motions Affecting the Meeting Itself.
Other motions having top priority deal with the meeting itself. These are the motions to take a recess, to fix the time to which to adjourn, and to adjourn.

Recess. A motion to recess must state how long it is to be or when the meeting will resume. "I move that we take a recess" and "I move that we recess until _____" are correct. A speaker may not be interrupted, a second is required, and the motion is amendable.

Fix the Time to which to Adjourn. A motion to fix the time to which to adjourn is made to ensure another meeting. This motion is necessary when a regular meeting has not been scheduled, for in that case a motion to adjourn would dissolve the organization. A member says, "I move that when we adjourn, we adjourn until _____ (specified hour, day, and date)."

Adjourn. Whenever the assembly desires, the meeting can be terminated. The motion to adjourn is always in order except when the assembly is occupied with important business, when a speaker has the floor, when a vote is being taken, or when a motion to adjourn has just been voted down. The motion to adjourn must be seconded, is not debatable or amendable. The motion to adjourn may be qualified as to time, thus being treated like any other main motion. The form of an unqualified motion to adjourn is: "I move that we adjourn." The form of a qualified motion to adjourn is: "I move that we adjourn at five o'clock."

21.
ORAL READING

Oral reading is the communication of the written word to listeners. The reader interprets a manuscript or printed page to make its meaning clear, interesting, and convincing to an audience. The oral reader is essentially a public speaker who reads his message.

IMPORTANCE OF READING ALOUD

Oral reading is a valuable and widely used form of speech. Much that is called public speaking and public discussion is actually public reading. A communication is read to save time or to insure content accuracy. Reports and directives are read at staff meetings and before boards of directors. Even at public speaking conferences, papers are read. Sermons are read regularly in churches throughout the land and most public and educational lectures are what their name implies, readings. Many teachers use oral reading as an approach to literature, for they have found that pupils, even those in "difficult" schools, enjoy listening to imaginative works.

Oral reading trains the speech mechanism in different contexts and makes it more responsive for the communication of any message. Reading aloud thus greatly helps public speaking. It also improves one's daily talking.

REQUIREMENTS OF ORAL READING

There are two main requirements for reading to others: First, the public reader has the same moral and social responsibilities as the public speaker: he must offer something of true worth to his audience; his opinions and interpretations must be honest and well-founded; and his sense of values must be based on the well-being of his listeners. Second, reading aloud, if it is to be effective, must sound like person-to-person talk, like genuine, living communication.

Oral reading, however, is a special skill, different from both speaking and writing. Many writers and speakers are indifferent readers of their own compositions. Good reading aloud requires insight, effort, and disciplined imagination.

The present chapter presupposes familiarity with the preceding chapters on public speaking, voice, and language. It is, concerned mostly with the oral reading of more artistic material, such as essays, stories, poems, scenes from plays, and other literary works. The reading of public speeches written by oneself is discussed in Chapter 8.

PREPARING TO READ ALOUD

Since his task is to interest, enlighten, and move his listeners, the reader must prepare his material as thoroughly as a speaker prepares his speech.

Selecting Material.   The text to be read, whether prose or poetry, must appeal to the interpreter. His appreciation should be so strong that he wishes to share it with others; the material is too valuable to be kept to himself.

Considering the Audience.   The reader, however, must temper his enthusiasm with a consideration of his audience. Readings should suit the age, background, and taste of the listeners. In general, material that is simple in construction, clearly written, and definite in character is easier to understand when heard than material of elaborate design, complicated style, or hidden significance. For example, the parable of the Prodigal Son or a passage from Thoreau can be more easily grasped by most listeners than a passage by Sir Thomas Browne or James Joyce.

Familiar selections should not be overlooked, nor should they be overworked. Listeners to readings, like audiences at a concert, ballet, opera, or performance of Shakespeare, enjoy familiar works whose meanings become richer with repeated hearings. Like most theatergoers, listeners also like new and different works. The oral reader should explore later-day literature for fresh material of good quality; this includes known works which the audience has never had the opportunity to hear. The real test of a reading selection is not whether it is new or old, but whether it presents a view of experience that has significance for listeners today.

Considering the Reader.   The reader must also consider his own ability. As Angna Enters said of dance-mime, "The only law to obey is your own limitations." Some readers cannot do justice to selections containing humor, dialect, lyricism, or characterization. The reader should practice various types of selections to find out where his talents lie. From the vast wealth of printed material he should then choose whatever pieces he can do best. This does not mean that he should not enlarge his scope as his ability grows. He might start, for instance, with the Twenty-third Psalm and later on master the difficulties of Shelley's "Ode to the West Wind."

Understanding the Selection.   The meaning of a selection to
be read aloud is often called the author's meaning. However, readers cannot always be sure what the author intended. Some passages in William Blake, Hart Crane, and T. S. Eliot, for example, are obscure; passages in many authors can be construed in more than one way. There is frequently an unconscious element in creative work: the author may have expressed more meaning than he was aware of. In addition, different generations have different backgrounds, viewpoints, and problems; thus, they interpret and evaluate a given literary work in different ways. The reader can but *try* to find the author's meaning; what he actually does find is his own understanding of the author's creation. When a reader presents an oral selection, he is offering *his own* version of what the work means. To do this well, he must thoroughly investigate the potentialities of the composition, such as the author's ideas, forms of support, organization of material, language, and style. Most of these have been considered under choosing, organizing, and developing a speech; oral reading, however, involves special problems in finding and interpreting the works of others.

Author's Approach.   The first step in preparation is to read the selection carefully to decide the author's intention, his manner of presentation, and his attitude toward his topic. Does the material give facts or direct information, does it tell a story, does it reveal character, offer a personal viewpoint, give reasons for a belief, or express a mood or atmosphere? Is the approach and treatment romantic in tone, realistic, spiritual, scientific, satirical, nostalgic, humorous, cynical, or some other type? To answer these questions it may be necessary to know something about the author's life and times, the conditions upon which the work is based, and his general outlook on life.

Central Theme. The theme or central idea of the composition should be clearly understood. If the reading is a selection from a longer work, the theme of the excerpt is the same as or part of the theme of the whole work. The reader should grasp the central theme clearly enough to state it in a subject sentence. He is then ready to discover how all elements in the piece contribute to the central theme.

Structure. The author's plan of organizing his material must be determined. Usually there is some form of introduction to the theme, an unfolding or development, a culmination or climax, and a resolution or ending. The structure may consist of main ideas supported by subsidiary ideas, a sequence of observations leading to a conclusion, or an escape from or solution of a difficulty. A narrative is largely an arrangement of incidents. A drama charts changing relationships between characters in a sequence of acts and scenes; each scene and each act has a climax and the drama itself has a major climax. Other poetic and prose works are designed in various patterns, such as cause and effect, discovery of a secret, growth of an emotion, or loss of an illusion.

Situation. The situation or status of events in the selection must also be thoroughly understood. What caused it, what is the result? Is there any conflict in the material, any opposition of idea or desire, any contrast of mood or feeling? Pointing up any opposing or contrasting elements in the piece will bring it to more vivid life.

Setting. It is highly important to know where and when the action in the piece takes place. A story or poem set in Arabia would be read differently from one set in Scotland: the background of time and place is part of the meaning.

Persons. The reader must also know what sort of person is thinking the thoughts or feeling the emotions, and to whom he is speaking or about whom he is thinking. A monologue, lyric poem, or first-person narrative may be entirely conditioned by the character or personality factor. Many other works, such as Katherine Mansfield's *Bliss* or Edwin Arlington Robinson's "Miniver Cheevy," could not be read well without a searching analysis and insight into the characters involved.

Meaning of Words. The reader must know the exact shade of meaning of all words; otherwise he cannot clearly express the thought and feeling of a selection. The reader, like his listeners, sometimes has a general idea of what a word means, but no specific or real meaning. All doubtful words should be looked up in the dictionary. The meaning of a word must also be realized in the context, together with its complete connotation. This knowledge avoids merely pronouncing words and ignoring the subtlety of meaning intended by the author. The "feeling" of a word is especially important in poetry and poetic prose. Poetic authors use words to arouse emotion. The created images must be vividly real in the imagination of the reader. Before they can be vivid to the imagination they must be clear to the understanding. Keats uses unusual words and images in the following stanza from "The Eve of St. Agnes":

> *That ancient Beadsman heard the prelude soft;*
> *And so it chanced, for many a door was wide,*
> *The silver, snarling trumpets 'gan to chide:*
> *The level chambers, ready with their pride,*
> *Were glowing to receive a thousand guests:*
> *The carved angels, ever eager-eyed,*
> *Stared, where upon their heads the cornice rests,*
> *With hair blown back, and wings put crosswise on their breasts.*

The reader should get a specific knowledge of the meaning of Beadsman (one who prays for a benefactor in return for subsistence), prelude (introductory music to a social ceremony or event), wide (wide open), level (lower level in contrast with aloft), pride (magnificence, splendid display), glowing (illuminated, probably with tapers and torches), cornice (horizontal molding projecting along the top of a wall).

The following phrases should bring significant pictures to his mind: *ancient Beadsman, carved angels,* and *wings put crosswise on their breasts,* which indicate the religious background of the occasion and legend; *silver, snarling trumpets* which suggest the feud between two noble houses; *ever eager-eyed, stared* and *with hair blown back,* which symbolize the presence, protection, and perhaps admiration of the heavenly messengers who have hurried down from heaven in answer to the Beadsman's prayers.

Grouping of Words.   Since words are not used singly but are put together in thought groups, another key to meaning is grammar or syntax. The arrangement of subject and predicate in a sentence shows the structure of a given thought. Main clauses convey important parts of the meaning, subordinate clauses, supporting parts. Parenthetical and appositional material is usually less important. Each subject and predicate has main or key words around which the other words are grouped according to various grammatical or syntactical rules.

Selections for Words and Images

"Magnificent Autumn! He comes not like a pilgrim, clad in russet weeds. He comes not like a hermit, clad in grey. But he comes like a warrior, with the stain of blood upon his brazen mail. His crimson scarf is rent. His scarlet banner drips with gore. His step is like a flail upon the threshing floor."—HENRY WADSWORTH LONGFELLOW, *The Blank Book of a Country Schoolmaster.*

"Mr. Heathcliff was there—laid on his back. His eyes met mine so keen and fierce, I started; and then he seemed to smile. I could not think him dead: but his face and throat were washed with rain; the bedclothes dripped, and he was perfectly still. The lattice, flapping to and fro, had grazed one hand that rested on the sill; no blood trickled from the broken skin, and when I put my fingers to it, I could doubt no more: he was dead and stark!

"I hasped the window; I combed his long, black hair from his forehead; I tried to close his eyes: to extinguish, if possible, that frightful, life-like gaze of exultation before anyone else beheld it. They would not shut: they seemed to sneer at my attempts, and his parted lips and sharp white teeth sneered too!"—EMILY, BRONTË, *Wuthering Heights*

EXPRESSING MEANING

The audible expression of meaning is through time, loudness, pitch, and quality of the voice. The vocal attributes cannot be used in isolation but only in conjunction with one another. To handle them separately is arbitrary and artificial, but necessary and valuable for learning purposes.

Meaning and Loudness. Many persons, in private life, prefer speech that is quiet, reserved, and "well-modulated." However, in reading to an audience, speech must have enough loudness and volume to carry to the ears of the listeners. A soft-spoken person is annoying when appearing before the public, because he cannot be heard. Public reading and speaking are expanded or strengthened forms of conversation: an *absolute duty* of any performer is to make himself clearly heard.

On the other hand, half-shouting or talking too loudly soon becomes tiresome. Making oneself heard does not mean yelling or punishing the listeners' ear drums. A medium range of dynamics should be used, avoiding both the extremely loud and the extremely soft. Within this middle range of force lie the quiet style, the animated conversational style, and the emphatic or dynamic style. In each of these styles, effective contrasts of loudness and emphasis can be successfully attained.

Emphasizing Key Words. Picking out the key words of the subject and predicate of a sentence or clauses of a sentence yields the essence of the thought. If these key words are stressed, the thought can be readily grasped by listeners. Other words in the sentence are naturally subordinated, especially articles, prepositions, and auxiliary verbs which indicate the grammatical structure.

New Elements of Thought. In a stream of discourse each idea is related to the one which precedes it as well as to the one which follows. Each new phase of the unfoldment of the meaning should be emphasized. The words conveying a new idea or new aspect of thought are stressed. Ideas and elements already stated and understood are subordinated; however, an old element may be reintroduced and stressed for emphasis. The train of thought cannot move forward unless the new phase of meaning is consistently featured.

Emphasizing Ideas. All sentences in a given paragraph or passage do not have the same dynamic value. The more important sentences receive more force. In a selection as a whole, emphasis includes a climax of intensity. The emphatic pattern reaches minor climaxes and at some point builds to a major climax. Every selection read aloud should have some sort of suspense and climax, some peak of meaning toward which development travels.

The climactic peak of a selection does not always have to be the loudest. There are times when a sudden dropping of volume affords an effective climax through contrast. Such subdued understatements must be clearly articulated and be at a high enough pitch if they are to be successful; they are ruined by mumbling.

Special Loudness Effects. Important ideas can be emphasized by repeating them at an appropriate place. The purpose of the repetition may be to emphasize mood, atmosphere, emotion, or dramatic effect. The loudness can be gradually increased, as in this stanza from Omar Khayyam's *Rubáiyát*:

> *The Ball no question makes of Ayes and Noes,*
> *But Here or There as strikes the Player goes;*
> *And He that tossed you down into the Field*
> *He knows about it all—HE knows—HE knows!*

The loudness can gradually fade, as indicated in various repetitions in Tennyson's "Bugle Song":

> *O, hark, O, hear! how thin and clear,*
> *   And thinner, clearer, farther going!*
> *O, sweet and far from cliff and scar,*
> *   The horns of Elfland faintly blowing!*
> *Blow, let us hear the purple glens replying:*
> *Blow, bugle; answer, echoes, dying, dying, dying.*

Controlling Loudness. One of the most difficult things for a reader to learn is to make important parts of the meaning stand out. The beginning of a selection should not be so loud and vigorous that a later climax cannot be reached. The strongest and most forceful part of a selection should not be near the beginning, but near the ending. If it is near the opening, all that follows is an anticlimax; if it is near the close, it is the goal toward which the selection moves.

If the reader should not "give his all" when he starts, should he do so later? No. Actually, he should never in any part of the selection "give it all he's got." To do so is to scream and shout. Volume should never get out of control, leaving a sense of depletion and exhaustion in its wake. The reader should *always hold something back*. No matter what force he uses in a climax, he should still be able to use more. It is this reserve force that gives genuine and thrilling power to the peaks of expression.

Mastery of dynamic changes are important to speech as they are to music. Changes of force help to get and regain attention. The change can be either to more or less loudness. A right use of force also shows that the reader is in earnest and means what he says. The relative changes of loudness spring from the significant relationships among the elements of the material. The good reader does not manipulate volume or force for its own sake or just for the sake of external variety: he uses it to make the internal meaning live.

Selections for Loudness

1. Read the following passage aloud. Do you agree to all indicated stress markings? Decide which ones are best eliminated.

> "Cást your bréad upón the wáters, for yóu will fínd it áfter mány dáys.
> Gíve a pórtion to séven, or éven to éight, for yóu know nót what évil may háppen on éarth.
> If the clóuds are fúll of ráin, they émpty themsélves upón the éarth; and if a trée fálls to the sóuth or tó the nórth in the pláce where the trée fálls, thére it will líe.
> Hé who obsérves the wínd will nót sów; and hé who regárds the clóuds will nót réap."—Ecclesiastes

2. Experiment with loudness control as you read this passage aloud.

> "We sometimes forget that there can be no electronic computers for setting standards of human probity or for differentiating between good and evil. We sometimes overlook the fact that there can be no automated substitutes for conscience or character.
> "Only when something like the vegetable oil case comes up do we take time to reflect on these matters—and then it is often too late. For the money market, more than any other segment of the business community, lives by the saying that 'a man's word is as good as his bond.' Nobody expressed this better than the elder J. P. Morgan in his testimony before a Congressional Committee. Asked whether commercial credit was not based primarily upon money or property, he replied emphatically: 'No, sir, the first thing is character'."—DAVID ROCKEFELLER[1]

Meaning and Timing.   Material read aloud must be presented at an understandable rate. All symbols must not only be heard but the meaning they convey must be intelligible. This achievement requires continual shadings of tempo. A constant use of the same rate of utterance creates monotony and interferes with the proper phrasing and interpretation of the thought.

Variation in Rate.   Since an emphasized syllable receives more time than an unstressed one, the breaking up of material into short

---

[1] *Vital Speeches*, XXX, 9 (Feb. 15, 1964), pp. 267–8.

phrases and emphasizing more words slow down the presentation. In fact, the elongation of important words adds more to the intelligibility than the slowing down of the overall rate. Short phrases and more frequent word emphasis, however, should be used mostly for more important or main ideas. Conversely, emphasizing fewer words and using longer phrases speeds up the presentation and is used on less important thoughts, such as illustrative, parenthetical, and other supporting material. Nevertheless, to use either of these methods throughout a selection is to reduce both meaning and interest.

The reader should never construe the general rate to mean a regular rate. A more rapid tempo is suitable for light comments, cheerful moods, scenes of activity, or material easy to understand. A moderate rate is adaptable for the thoughts, feelings, and experiences of everyday life or other ordinary information. A slow general rate is needed for difficult or hard-to-understand material, serious ideas, and solemn, nostalgic, or sorrowful moods.

Selections for Rate

1. Establish a slow general rate for the following selection.

> "I sleep—a long—time—two or three hours perhaps—then a dream—no—a nightmare lays hold on me. I feel that I am in bed and asleep . . . I feel it and I know it . . . and I feel that somebody is coming close to me, is looking at me, touching, is getting on my bed, is kneeling on my chest, is taking my neck between his hands and squeezing it . . . squeezing it with all his might in order to strangle me."—GUY DE MAUPASSANT, *The Horla*

2. Establish different general rates for Lady Teazle and Joseph Surface in this bit of conversation from Sheridan's *School for Scandal.*

> LADY TEAZLE: "But isn't it provoking, to have the most ill-natured things said of one? And there's my friend, Lady Sneerwell, has circulated I don't know how many scandalous tales of me, and all without any foundation too; that's what vexes me."
> JOSEPH SURFACE: "Ay, madam, to be sure, that is the provoking circumstance—without foundation. Yes, yes, there's the mortification, indeed; for when a scandalous story is believed against one, there certainly is no comfort like the consciousness of having deserved it."

Pausing. Good reading cannot exist without pauses. They show the phrasing, the sentences or units of thought, and the end of a paragraph or idea. Pauses show the beginning and ending of a quotation; they mark off the dialogue in a story. If all pauses are short, the elements of meaning are run together and are not clearly enough differentiated. If all pauses are long, the meaning gets lost in the delay. Using more pauses slows down the rate of presentation; using fewer pauses speeds it up. In general, more pauses should be used in important passages, fewer in less important passages.

Meaning and Pitch. The reader's voice should move freely through a range of at least an octave. Many fine readers have a usable range of nearly two octaves. A range of only half an octave means that the voice will not be sufficiently interesting or expressive.

Use of Range. A narrow pitch pattern can suggest monotony, boredom, repression, and concealment. In certain selections, a narrow range is used momentarily for special effect. However, in painting monotony in a longer passage, such as the beginning of Poe's *"Fall of the House of Usher,"* variety must be used to make the monotony interesting to the listener. To suggest monotony, the reader should not become monotonous himself.

An extremely wide pitch pattern can suggest things like pleasure, excitement, enthusiasm, delirium, mania. A free use of such wide variations is usually unwise in reading aloud, since emotional abandon repels most listeners. Very wide pitch changes should be reserved for humorous effects or for slowly built up climaxes, such as Queen Margaret's cursing of Gloucester in Shakespeare's *King Richard III*.

> GLOUCESTER: *Have done thy charm, thou hateful wither'd hag.*
> QUEEN MARGARET: *And leave out thee? stay, dog, for thou shalt hear me.*
>
> > *If heaven have any grievous plague in store,*
> > *Exceeding those that I can wish upon thee,*
> > *O, let them keep it, till thy sins be ripe,*
> > *And then hurl down their indignation*
> > *On thee, the troubler of the poor world's peace!*
> > *The worm of conscience still begnaw thy soul!*
> > *Thy friends suspect for traitors while thou liv'st,*
> > *And take deep traitors for thy dearest friends!*
> > *No sleep close up that deadly eye of thine,*
> > *Unless it be while some tormenting dream*
> > *Affrights thee with a hell of ugly devils!*
> > *Thou elvish-marked, abortive, rooting hog!*
> > *Thou that was seal'd in thy nativity*

> *The slave of nature, and the son of hell!*
> *Thou loathed issue of thy father's loins!*
> *Thou rag of honor!*

Use of Key. A use of higher levels or keys of the voice can suggest immaturity, shallowness, nervousness, complaining, or grief. The lower part of keys of the voice can suggest threat, determination, awe, and sorrow.

There is, however, no one way of conveying any of the above meanings. The middle range of the voice can suggest all of the above as well as all other meanings. To bring out the variety of the meaning a shift of key up or down, like a widening or narrowing of the range, is often desirable. The chief thing is that it be part of the meaning and not a mere mechanical manipulation of vocal pitch.

An example of upward shift in key occurs in the speech of Cassius against Julius Caesar, as indicated by the scathing phrase, "as a sick girl."

> *Aye, and that tongue of his that bade the Romans*
> *Mark him and write his speeches in their books,*
> *Alas, it cried, "Give me some drink, Titinius,"*
> *As a sick girl. Ye Gods! it doth amaze me,*
> *A man of such feeble temper should*
> *So get the start of the majestic world,*
> *And bear the palm alone.*
>
> —WILLIAM SHAKESPEARE, *Julius Caesar*

Use of Pitch Inflections. Pitch inflections and combinations of pitch change and timing can be used to convey and suggest an almost infinite world of meanings. There are no definite rules governing the expressive use of inflections, since their validity depends on the insight, sensitivity, and judgment of the reader. Sometimes, when an inflection seems false, the "right" one can be found by applying the traditional device of asking the question "What?" at that point, and answering definitely with the word or phrase in question. For example, if you speak "Is this the face that launched a thousand ships?" as a straight question, the rising inflection seems put out of place, because Faust is not asking directly for information. By asking oneself "that launched what?" and answering with emphasis "a thousand ships!" it will be found that the rising-falling tone of the answer is a natural one to use in the reading, since it suggests Faust's exclamation of surprise and pleasure at what he sees.

The overuse of any one pitch inflection should be avoided. A steady succession of falling inflections is dull and depressing; a constant series of rising ones, empty and artificial. A less marked or higher-falling inflection can show incompleteness as does the rising inflection; it is the strong falling inflection that shows completeness. A rising-falling or falling-rising inflection can often be substituted for the rising and falling ones.

At the ends of sentences, the reader's voice should not fall at exactly the same pitch level. Final inflections, like all others, should be discriminatingly varied in range: some higher, some lower. It is also poor expression of meaning to start each sentence on a high pitch level and then let it run downhill. Instead, the pitch should be brought up just before the end and the sentence finished with a slightly higher falling inflection. The higher fall is more audible and thus more meaningful than the low fall. Stressing the last word or two in the sentence makes a variety of falling inflections easier to execute. Such a "lift" to the sentence embosses it and makes the meaning stand out in relief.

Meaning and Quality. The expression of meaning through vocal tones is subtle and complex, because it is the expression of feelings and emotions with their related bodily attitudes.

Types of Quality. Although vocal qualities cannot be intellectually classified and mechanically used, considering a few of those often recognized may help the reader to realize the almost limitless subjective possibilities of tone qualities.

BREATHY QUALITY. An aspirate or whispered quality of voice can be effective in an aside, or material conveyed to the audience which is not heard by the person presumably addressed by the reader. Aspirate tones are often suitable for confidences or other intimacies, and might be sparingly used in the last stanza of Shelley's "The Indian Serenade":

> *Oh! lift me from the grass!*
> *I die! I faint! I fail!*
> *Let thy love in kisses rain*
> *On my lips and eyelids pale.*

The shock of sudden surprise, fear, or horror can be communicated by a sudden breathy quality, as perhaps in the second line and the last two words in this passage from Marlowe's *Doctor Faustus:*

> *My God, my God, look not so fierce on me!*
> *Adders and serpents, let me breathe a while!*
> *Ugly hell, gape not! come not, Lucifer!*
> *I'll burn my books!—Ah, Mephistophilis!*

THROATY OR HARSH QUALITY. A throaty, rasping, or growling quality can be made to reveal anger, resentment, aggression, hatred, and other intense emotional attitudes. Robert Browning suggests this quality in his "Soliloquy of the Spanish Cloister":

> *Gr-r-r—there go, my heart's abhorrence!*
> *Water your damned flower-pots, do!*
> *If hate killed men, Brother Lawrence,*
> *God's blood, would not mine kill you!*

Shakespeare's Caliban, Dickens' Bill Sykes, O'Neill's Hairy Ape, and other uncouth, belligerent, or brutal characters from modern literature could be suggested by this quality. Curses, such as King Lear's or Queen Margaret's (quoted above), might be more convincing and real if re-created with a suitable use of harsh voice.

NASAL QUALITY. A nasal quality is sometimes used for a plaintive or pathetic effect or for humorous characterization. A nasal twang can suggest provincial matter-of-factness or "adenoidal" stupidity. A whining, nasal tone is suitable for wheedling, a pressing nasal tone for nagging. Nasal quality is most effective when used sparingly for contrast.

HOLLOW QUALITY. A hollow or "deep down" quality can express awe, depression, or heavy anguish. Since the hollow quality seems remote or even disembodied, it is often used to characterize apparitions, such as the ghost in Hamlet.

IMITATIVE QUALITIES. The nonhuman sounds of the surrounding world often appear in an author's work. Imitative qualities include onomatopoeia, where the sounds of the words, such as *ripple, lisp, boom, shriek,* suggest the meaning. The reader transfers these suggestions by means of subtle vocal qualities.

Some works contain specific imitations of animal sounds, such as the screech owl in the Thoreau selection below. For best effect, such colorful, sometimes amusing, but always meaningful sounds, should be skillfully imitated in their appropriate rhythmic pattern.

> *They give me a new sense of the variety and capacity of that nature which is our common dwelling.* Oh-o-o-o-o *that I never had been bor-r-r-r-n!* sighs one on this side of the pond, and circles with the restlessness

of despair to some new perch on the gray oaks. Then—that I never
had been bor-r-r-r-n! *echoes another on the farther side with tremulous
sincerity, and*—bor-r-r-r-n! *comes faintly from far in the Lincoln woods.*
—HENRY DAVID THOREAU, *Walden*

Using Voice Quality. Convincing vocal qualities cannot be merely
assumed, but must result from the reader's physical, intellectual,
emotional, and imaginative awareness. The direct attempt to manipulate voice qualities leads to artificial reading. An effective reader
allows his voice to reflect the full meaning indirectly.

Reading Prose. Most oral readings consist of some form of
prose. Forms of prose include the oration, lecture, sermon, essay,
story, novel, biography, editorial, article, and many other types of
composition. Poetic or imaginative prose lies near the boundary of
verse, and dialogue in fiction resembles prose drama.

The purpose of prose is to inform, persuade, or entertain an audience. Informative prose is the easiest for most beginning readers.
It seems a natural form of expression, because it is nearer to everyday
speaking and habits of thought. Informative prose deals mostly with
ideas; therefore, a limited use is made of feeling and emotion. Entertaining prose involves emotions, especially those of a lighter or less
disturbing nature. Persuasive prose includes a wide variety of feelings,
emotions, and attitudes. All prose includes images based on the
senses. The reader must visualize all the author's descriptions and
illustrations. Persuasive and entertaining prose also contains figures
of speech, whose meaning must be sharply realized and expressed.

Prose has a rhythm based on the writer's use of the figures of
arrangement, the alternation of speech and silence found in phrases,
clauses, and sentences, and the recurrence of stressed syllables at
more or less regular intervals. The reader must experience and convey
the rhythm of a selection for it is an integral part of the author's
style and message.

Narrative prose, like narrative poetry and drama, usually contains
dialogue. The reader faces the necessity of understanding and indicating more than one character. A thorough realization of the individual
nature of all personages and their differences from one another is
the answer to the problem. Characters can be differentiated in the
minds of the audience by proper use of the voice attributes. A man's
speech, for example, can be in a slightly lower key than a woman's,

or it can have a narrower pitch range, be slower, louder, or richer in quality. A child can speak more rapidly, excitedly, and with a higher and wider range than an adult. One person can speak more slowly than another of the same sex, use more pauses, more volume, wider inflections, or a distinguishing vocal quality.

The actual combination of vocal elements used by the reader depends on his grasp of the ideas, feelings, attitudes, and background of each character. An author reveals the nature of a character by the speech he puts into his mouth. In addition, he gives directions or clues for their manner of speaking; for example, he snarled, answered with considerable hesitation, said impetuously, dryly, with curling lip, from far away, through his teeth, with a grin, etc. The way a thing was said can often be inferred from the reaction of the character to whom it was spoken. Later on in a selection, the author may indicate how a thing was uttered; for instance, "She could still hear those words being hissed in her ear." Careful reading, analysis, insight, and practice are necessary for successful delineation of character in an oral reading.

Reading Poetry.   The meaning of a poem should be found like the significance of any other selection in accordance with the methods suggested above. The thoughts, the feelings, the images should be clearly apprehended.

Rhythm.   Rhythm is the stumbling block in the oral reading of poetry. Most persons can read the surface stresses, but miss the rhythm that underlies such simple counting. They lose the rhythm of speech (which is the rhythm of thought and feeling) in an artificial metronomic beat. The real rhythm of a poem is not merely a matter of metrics: scanning feet is not the rhythm of a Keats ode any more than beating time is the rhythm of a Debussy tone poem. The metrical pattern should be suggested, not thumped out; it should be varied, or forgotten entirely to suit the beauty of the meaning. When the meaning of a poem is completely realized, there will be enough of the external rhythmical pattern to serve as a sustaining background or accompaniment to the true, inner rhythm. Many poems, such as nursery rhymes and poems of action, have a basic, regular rhythm. But these, too, need variety of tempo, proper phrasing, and dynamic shading to bring out their real vitality. Everything else in a poem should not be sacrificed to its "lilt" or "swing." Individuals vary in their tolerance of regularity, but true or absolute regularity is always deadly monotony.

Rhyme. The reader should not clump down heavily on every rhyme. The rhyme will be heard without vocal emphasis; the fact that it is a rhyme has already emphasized it. Some poems, like Tennyson's "Lotus Eaters" and Coleridge's "Kubla Khan," use rhymes to help weave a spell. To stress these rhymes unduly in reading is to destroy the very effect the poets have built up. There are times, of course, when sing-song, strong beats, or bringing out the rhyme is needed. But these things are for pointed effects in certain places and lose their charm if continued all through a poem.

The reader should remember that a poem is a genuine communication of meaning. The meaning can be a mood, feeling, experience, image, realization, struggle, or a moment of gain or loss. A poem is a human awareness of the universe around us, the reaction of the human heart to life and experience. The reader should try to convey the full variety of such human reactions honestly, sincerely, and unaffectedly.

STYLES OF READING

Style as used in written expression is a more or less vague and subjective term. The style of one author differs from another; the style of one work is not the same as that of another. Each selection can be said to have a style peculiarly its own; therefore it will have a spoken style of its own. This style, which the reader must determine, will also be colored by his style or manner of presentation. From a more objective standpoint, three general styles or manners of reading aloud can be distinguished.

The Straight Style. The straight style is the direct relaying of the meaning through the reader's own self. This is the manner of the public speaker, the essayist, the tale-teller, the lyric poet. The reader steps into the author's position and presents the material in a person-to-person communication.

The Style with Suggested Characterization. This is the manner of the story, sketch, or essay colored by a definite temperament. The reader shows the listener that a highly individual personality is behind the material, but does not step completely into that character's shoes. This style is often combined with the straight style: conversation or dialogue in a story or poem is colored to suggest the character who is talking, while the straight method is used for the rest of the material.

The Characterized Style. The reader steps inside the character's skin and completely embodies his thoughts, feelings, and reactions. This is the method of the actor or monologuist who lives the thing as if it were actually happening. This involves some degree of mime: the reader stands, looks, gestures, moves, and reacts totally in character.

These classifications are, of course, more or less arbitrary. They are not separate categories, but shade one into another. There is no law that compels the reader to remain absolutely in any one of these or any other possible styles. Some selections require considerable freedom or plasticity of approach. For example, in Eliot's *Murder in the Cathedral* the murderers address the audience directly to plead their case, although in the rest of the play the characters address only one another. The meaning of the selection, the taste of the reader, the nature of the audience, and the occasion determine the treatment of the material.

THE ROLE OF EMOTION

Merely pronouncing words is not good oral reading. Neither is communicating only the factual content. Some persons are so inhibited, so afraid of feeling and emotion, that they believe in reading the "thought content" or ideas alone. Emotion is ridiculous and unreliable, they say, so read without it. Their plodding, matter-of-fact, or intellectualized presentation is pedantic, monotonous, and boring to most listeners: it leaves them cold.

The things and events in Coleridge's "Christabel" or Faulkner's *A Rose for Emily,* for example, are not the real meaning of the works: they are only the stimuli to evoke the meaning, which is a set of emotional reactions in the listener. Part of the stimuli is the atmosphere or mood which envelops the action. The intellectual content of these selections would scarcely compel interest. Their strange power to fascinate depends upon the feelings and emotions suggested and aroused. The reader must feel these atmospheres and adequately convey them as part of the meaning.

Faults of Emotion. Too much emotion, of course, is embarrassing to listen to. There should be subtlety and restraint in the expression of feeling. The reader's voice should not tremble, whine, and cry with grief, nor prance, ripple, or gurgle with gaiety. Emotional exaggeration, "hamming it up," is one reason why some "interpretation" is laughed at. DeQuincey made some interesting remarks about reading aloud: "Actors are the worst readers of all . . . Our feelings, as not free to take any natural expression, can be of no value . . . People in general read poetry without any passion at all, or else overstep the modesty of nature."

Another emotional fault is monotony, or using only one prevailing emotion, such as religious fervor or despair. Emotion, like thought, constantly changes, although it changes much more slowly. Even in a lament there are elements of joy or exaltation in remembering how wonderful the dead person was. If he were not a pleasure to be with when alive, he would not be deeply mourned when dead. Likewise, there is often a vein of sadness in a humorous piece. Many poems are composites of contrasted and varied feelings and realizations. Some images evoke rapture, others evoke bitterness. The purpose or reaction *behind* a poetic image should be realized.

Control of Emotion. The reader should feel all the moods, feelings, and emotions within himself, but he should not attempt to put emotion directly into the voice. Exaggerating the externals leads to lack of conviction. Emotions are felt inside: the voice should be a mirror, merely reflecting the inward feelings. Rule emotion, or it will ruin the interpretation. For modern listeners, it is usually better to keep the lid down on strong emotion: repressing the emotion is what reveals it. Such underplaying can have a more intense effect than much ranting, raving, or wild abandon.

There are times when the meaning requires that the reader give vent to a strong or violent outburst. Such an emotional climax must be *reached,* not jumped into. First comes the physical reaction, then a growing realization, and then a rising wave of feeling. The emotions, like a motor, do not work well until they are warmed up. A new or different emotion in turn must have a period of growth before it is strongly felt. Lightning changes of emotion, favored by some writers and actors, do violence to physiological and psychological reality. In fact, such swift and incongruous changes are the stock

in trade of satirists and comedians. The reader must actually feel
an emotion, understand it, and direct it.

PREPARING COPY

The copy for a public reading should be in suitable form. The
manuscript should not be too large or heavy to hold; the pages
should be easy to manage without wrinkling, crackling, or falling
to the floor; the type should be easy to read. A medium-sized book
is suitable: it looks well and its pages are simple to turn. The part
or parts of the book to be read should be marked with slips so
that they can be found without embarrassing delay. The starting
and ending points on a page should also be clearly marked.

A newspaper or large magazine is unwieldly and looks it, and
the pages cannot be turned without distracting motion and noise.
Copy from newspapers, magazines, and unsuitable books should be
typed. Typewriter paper should be of good weight to reduce the
chance of wrinkling or blowing away. The ordinary 8½" x 11" typewriter sheet is too large for efficient handling; about 6" x 8½" is
more satisfactory.

The material should be typed in double or triple spacing with
good margins. The pages should be numbered at the top to prevent
mixups. The copy should be clean, free from corrections, crossed
out passages, and insertions. The reader, if he so desires, can use a
few markings to help his reading.

When holding typed copy, each sheet must be removed after it
is read and shifted to the bottom of the sheaf. To avoid this necessity,
many readers paste or otherwise attach their copy to the pages of
a suitable book. Other readers type their copy on the pages of a
medium-sized loose-leaf notebook. The copy should facilitate and
not hinder the presentation.

PRESENTING THE READING

The reader conveys meaning by both visual and auditory symbols.

Using a Reading Stand. A reading stand is liked by some
readers and disapproved of by others. A lectern leaves the hands
free to gesture, but sometimes encourages leaning on it for support.
A reading stand also tends to limit expressive actions and obscure
them from the audience.

Standing Alone. Standing in full view of the audience with the manuscript in the hands enables the reader to move more freely, but tends to restrict gestures to those of one hand.

The book or manuscript is part of the presentation and should be in attractive condition rather than battered and torn. Pages should be turned or changed silently and unobtrusively. The book should not be held down opposite the waist line. This makes the head bob up and down as the reader looks from the page to the audience or causes the reader to keep his head bowed. The manuscript should be held opposite the chest, high enough to be legible by merely dropping the glance, and low enough so that all members of the audience can see the reader's full face.

Eye Contact. The oral reader must look at his audience much of the time and give the illusion of eye contact the rest of the time. This means that he must feel his communication to his listeners all the time. Keeping his nose buried in the book does not produce the best reading. The person who glues his eyes to the page does not seem to know his material and does not adequately communicate it. How can he convey something that is not part of himself? Even an excellent selection will lose value and interest if it is not communicated directly to the listener.

The straight style of presentation requires direct eye contact with the entire audience, front, back, sides, and center. The style with suggested characterization needs eye contact except for dialogue, during which the reader turns slightly to address someone apparently at his side. The completely characterized style would seem to require no eye contact, since the person is presumably not addressing the audience. The reader, however, cannot turn his back to the audience or always be talking to the side. Imaginary characters should be located a bit forward to the side, so that the reader is facing his audience most of the time. When the reader is not addressing an imaginary character but is thinking out loud or talking to himself, he should look toward some part of the audience rather than keep his eyes elsewhere. A reader does not pretend to ignore his audience as completely as does an actor behind footlights. The reader does not actually look at individual listeners at such times, but allows them to focus their eyes on him. Beside dramatic characterizations, lyric poetry and emotional prose are often most moving when listeners

360

PUBLIC SPEAKING

are allowed to look on in this manner and react at a proper and unembarrassing aesthetic distance.

Bodily Expression.   The reader's bearing, posture, facial expressions, changes of position, and gestures are visual methods of conveying meaning. The reader's activity is restrained compared to that of an actor, and is usually more limited in scope than that of the public speaker. The reader uses concentration and the power of suggestion: a slight change of position signifies action, a step represents walking on the platform, or a slight beginning of a gesture indicates the complete gesture. A story with action and dialogue, of course, may need more motion and gesture than an essay or lyric poem.

Indicating Locations.   Some gestures and motions, including the turn of the head, direction of the gaze, and change of stance, are to indicate the object or person being mentioned or addressed. Objects and characters should be definitely located in space. In dialogue, for example, one character should be located either to the right or left of the reader. If the character is on the right, the reader looks slightly to the right when addressing him, and when the character is speaking to him, the reader looks to the left.

If the reader must represent three characters, he locates one on either side. When speaking, the character on the left looks right, the one in the middle looks straight front, and the one on the right looks left. These spatial signals, discreetly used, enable the audience to know immediately which character is speaking. In the opening lines of Browning's "My Last Duchess," for example, the emissary is located to the Duke's right and the portrait of the Duchess to his left, or vice versa. In the closing lines, the statue of Neptune can be effectively located directly in front toward the audience.

> That's my last Duchess painted on the wall,
> Looking as if she were alive. I call
> That piece a wonder, now: Frà Pandolf's hands
> Worked busily a day, and there she stands.
>   . . . Nay, we'll go
> Together down, sir! Notice Neptune, though,
> Taming a sea-horse, thought a rarity,
> Which Claus of Innsbruck cast in bronze for me!

Beginning the Reading. The oral reader goes to his place on the platform in a direct, poised, and natural manner. He acknowledges his audience by waiting a moment, and then begins his introductory remarks. These may be a simple announcement of the author and title of his selection, an account of the reader's discovery of and interest in the piece, or a brief explanation of the social, historical, or artistic background of the selection. If the reading is an excerpt, a synopsis of what leads up to it may be suitable.

If the selection consists of widely separated parts of a longer work, it may be necessary to bridge the gap between them with a brief paraphrase of the omitted material. Such information should be done in the spirit of the piece, so that the mood and continuity of style is unbroken. In some types of informative material, the reader may interpolate his own observations, explanations, and summaries in order to make the author's meaning clearer to the audience.

Ending the Reading. A good reader indicates when he is ending. The best way is perhaps to be guided by a strong feeling for form, a sense of structure, an acute awareness of the beginning, growth, and completion of the meaning, which the reader establishes in the minds of the audience. This sense of form and structure can be developed through the study and understanding of literature and other works of art.

More specifically, the reader might borrow a device from Bach's music and slow down and emphasize the last thought.

> *A political victory, a rise of rents, the recovery of your sick, or the return of your absent friend, or some other favorable event, raises your spirit, and you think good days are preparing for you. Do not believe it. Nothing can bring you peace but yourself. Nothing can bring you peace, but the TRIUMPH OF* PRINCIPLES.
>
> —RALPH WALDO EMERSON, *Self-Reliance*

Or, like Chopin in certain of his compositions, the reader can slow down and subdue the final phrase.

> NOTHING BESIDE REMAINS. ROUND THE DECAY
> *OF THAT COLOSSAL WRECK,* boundless and bare
> The lone and level sands *stretch far away.*
>
> —PERCY SHELLEY, "Ozymandias"

Final words can also be separated by pauses rather than by a marked increase or decrease in loudness.

> *He hailed the bird in Spanish speech.*
> *The bird in Spanish speech replied,*
> *Flapped round the cage with joyous screech,*
> *Dropt down and died.*
> —THOMAS CAMPBELL, "The Parrott"

After the final word of the selection has been spoken, the reader pauses a few moments to allow the audience to preserve its impressions, silently closes his book, turns slowly, and walks away.

Freshness of Communication. One secret of good oral reading is intelligent preparation and rehearsal of a selection. In a thoroughly prepared selection, where the meaning becomes part of one's self, it is not difficult to maintain good communication. However, another problem arises: routine or false reading. The selection is no longer fresh and new to the reader and is apt to show flatness or artificiality. The great secret of oral reading is fresh, spontaneous sharing of material. The reader must learn to give the illusion of saying it for the first time, of actually experiencing the meaning. The imagination and feelings must be trained until they respond easily and fully. The entire process is aided by reading all kinds of material aloud. The eye becomes accustomed to seeing more text at a glance; familiarity with many types of expression makes it easier to utter what the eye sees. Long-continued practice in thinking the thought, feeling the emotion, experiencing the reaction, and sustaining the mood enables the interpreter, when he reads to an audience, to see everything in his mind's eye, to recreate it in his imagination, and to live it as if it were real.

INDEX